Peter Herrmann

Diary from a Journey into another World

Diaries against nationalism, inspired by trying to overcome personal resentments

EHV)

Herrmann, Peter

Diary from a Journey into another World
Diaries against nationalism, inspired by trying to overcome personal resentments

Illustrations by Kerstin Walsh

ISBN/EAN: 978-3-86741-775-4
First published in 2012 by Europaeischer Hochschulverlag GmbH & Co KG, Bremen, Germany.

Peter Herrmann

Diary from a Journey into another World

Diaries against nationalism, inspired by trying to overcome personal resentments.

Written against the little poodles, demarcating the empire by pissing at every tree, and feeling so proud in the little pink dress and wearing the bow knot it got delivered with the Marshall's Plan.[1]

Written for the people who really settled

– by overcoming their dependence on roots and definitions.

In love and admiration for Stephanie and Zsuzsa

---

[1] *Disclaimer*
What is true, what is saga? Basically, everything is written as it happened though the dialogues are of course not quotes but something as my interpretation, what I understood. Some aspects had been 'dramatised', sometimes just by changing sequences or by emphasising certain aspects of the frame. And in any case, it is – despite having an objective and pedagogical dimension – a personal account. If anybody who plays a role in this little story, who had been mentioned, feels not appropriately reflected I can only do one thing: ask for apologies. Though the texts and reflections are spanning over a longer time and more locations, they had been compiled mainly during those three month end of 2006.
I cannot take any responsibility for consequences arising from making reference to what is said though every possible caution had been taken.

Diary from a Journey into another World

Budapest, Brussels, Chişinău, Cork, Firenze, Lille, Munich – September to December 2006

Titus went on, 'Every picture has an optimum place from which it should be seen. At a shorter or greater distance, there is a blurred perception. The parts mingle and become confused.'

'That's just what we will do, then,' the Prince said.

'But even if one looks at a painting from the proper distance,' I blurted out, 'the eyes tend to stray and single out some aspect or another. And if one looks at a picture from other points of view, at various angles or distances, while it may appear changed, there is no difference in reality.'

Titus laughed. 'Speak with my father about that...'

(Miano, Sarah Emily: Van Rijn. A Novel; London: Macmillan, 2006; 18)

I.   **23–24/10/2006**

Clash of Cultures as Clash of Histories

The aircraft touches smoothly the Moldovan ground. Though I had not been afraid that this 'tiny tin' might crash I am glad to be able to leave the plane – more a sport-jet than a real airliner, too small and close for a flight of 1 ½ hours after already travelling 3 hours from Cork to Budapest. But why should they use a larger one for the couple of people who travelled from Budapest to the destination which will be my home for about a week. Dimitri, the driver, already on the runway, collects me directly from the plane. Still, it does not save me the procedure at the border control. Although I have a visa, commissioned by the EU-administration, I have to fill in the form and answer some more or less weird questions. Is it despite having the visa or is it because I have it? Several years ago – during those times when the country was part of the Soviet Union – I would have felt more comfortable; but now? Who are these lads at the desk? Representatives of their country – real representatives? Or marionettes of foreign powers – can't help, being a child of *US-McCarthyism* and the German *Berufsverbote*, the CIA comes to mind. – A question from the preparatory administrative work comes to my mind: in one of the forms a question was: 'whom to inform in case of urgency'. And perhaps my answer 'None' was not only a personal matter but also a matter of the old conspiracy against the western-German BND.[2]

Still, a little later, driving along the broad though bumpy boulevard I am really getting caught in the contradiction that will probably be a decisive feature of the next weeks and months – perhaps not as decisive as in this second but still decisive. Moldova – as well as Hungary – is one of the countries that belonged to the former 'Soviet Bloc', the *Council for Mutual Economic Assistance* and the *Warsaw Pact* – alliances established as counter powers against the Western world. It was Mikhail Gorbachev who said in the middle of the 1980s that those who come too late would be castigated by history – and although the situation was much more complicated, it was Gorbachev who opened the doors to the West, to imperialism. I remember at the time I read in a journal from the government of the USSR, an article

---

[2]   Bundesnachrichtendienst, the German Intelligence which evidently opened my post, recorded phone calls – the 'group photos' during rallies are not worth to be mentioned. As Joan Baez sings in one song, on Sacco and Vanzetti, it is the 'Royal Treatment'

celebrating the opening of the first McDonald's franchise in Russia, on the Red Square. I felt a shock; I perceived this as a sad development – and as betrayal of all the hopes and efforts from before. The efforts of not only the Russian people who fought back Fascism; the sufferings of people who had to pay high prices for their resistance against war and persecution, many losing their life or at least health; my own efforts, striving for a democratic Germany – and the price many of us paid: *Berufsverbot* – not being allowed to work as teachers, as postmen and women, as workers in any public enterprise. And the shock was also due to the fact that those of us who had been punished now had to face the situation that those who punished us had been welcomed into the new world.

History does not follow a straight path – and so we could anticipate in the middle of the 1980s the paradox of history: The first German chancellor after WW II *(Konrad Adenauer)* refused the offer of a common government when he was asked to collaborate with the government in the east in order to develop a democratic country – in Adenauer's words: I prefer to be able to have complete control over half of Germany rather than having half of the control over the complete Germany. And it was this stance which finally led to a situation in which his successors have complete control over the complete Germany, and beyond.

We are driving, leaving the airport behind – soon the tall houses become visible: 'socialist estates' behind which the idea of some kind of communal living was at least at the heart of the ideology and planning. These houses are still here – and something else is still left: the width of the boulevard, the munificence. At first I can ignore the huge advertisements along the road and it is only when I see the first supermarket a little bit later – the huge yellow letters against the blue background of the walls let me know: METRO; just a little bit further I see the huge yellow M on the red background. Well, never lost. Especially, when one is a traveller as I am. We all know the large M; and though we do not all know the METRO I know that it is one of the supermarket chains that are present in the west. Last year already, travelling to Slovakia, the Czech Republic, Poland, Latvia and other countries I could see what Lenin wrote about in his piece on 'Imperialism, the Highest Stage of Capitalism': The division of the world amongst the economic magnates. The borders from the "new EU member states" were not thought to be the end – there is no limit to subordination. Not in quantitative terms nor in qualitative terms.

The exciting aspect of this one week mission is embittered by these impressions. But it is actually much more – not only the multinationals but as well the experience of being myself one of the intruders. Seeing METRO,

VODAPHONE and others, I see as well the 'car fleet of the missionaries': United Nations, World Bank, OSCE, European Commission...

First I am brought to my apartment, and after getting the instructions of security codes etc I am brought to the office. *Tatjana* welcomes me, *Victor* asks me if I have any need regarding information technology, *Ludmila*, the team leader introduces *Wojciech* with whom I will have a long conversation later in the day after I get a welcome pack in a more or less celebratory manner from *Olga*. All nice people, though the language situation is somewhat difficult. Most of them speak English but for me it is difficult to understand – the hard pronunciation gives the language a difficult slant. Sometimes my interpreter has to translate even the English I hear from the others.

We manage – all is going well – and I am actually somewhat satisfied that all these people know too well what is going on. A mission that should not be completely executed: Training of Trainers in a corrupt system. All agree that there is no point in training people in corruption – be it corruption in terms of bribery or be it political corruption of Mafiosi-like social steering. The talks go well – as well as they can work under these conditions. Part of it is the preparation of next day's talks with the Minister for Health, the representative of the Delegation of the European Commission to Moldova and the project team. What is striking and deserves at least a side remark: the entire project – suggesting the strengthening of civil society – at the end is not driven by the European bodies although they administer it and are responsible for the implementation. I am informed that the power in the background is the Soros-Foundation and the *World Bank* – not the information I need to arrive at 'mental wellness'. The other tiny piece deserving attention: I ask the colleague from the EUC-Delegation if the status of the Delegation in *Moldova* (and other countries) is the same as the one of the *European Commission's* representations as we have it for instance in *Dublin*. 'Nope [of course, the English is rather Americanised], I have the status of an ambassador' – of course, those who are already 'in' do not deserve so much attention anymore as those who are yet to be caught. And, although I am not explicitly informed, I can put the pieces from the jigsaw – the matters the local crowd talks about – together: the future position will be strengthened by more personnel and the main office being in *Chişinău* rather than in *Кúев (Kiev)*.

– Earlier on I mentioned the hard pronunciation of the *English* language – dyed by *Ukrainian* or *Romanian (Moldavian)* language. What a contrast to the soft *Russian* language which I hear later while walking through the *Puškin*

Park which neighbours the street that hosts my apartment; what a contrast to the silkiness of the language I hear later in the restaurant.

Is it not better to leave it with this softness – the harshness of life in this definitely poor, not to say deprived area of the world cannot take it away. Walking through the streets and parks provokes the immediate wish to join the people – they are chatting – not many people are there on their own, they're exchanging something: joys and sorrows, experiences and plans, hopes and disenchantments... – they are playing cards, maybe some of them magic cards, hiding something that others cannot see, cannot see by just looking at them and their game. A warm, spring-like evening – the park invites the many loving couples, sitting on the banks, kissing and babbling. – The opera house on the one side, nearly opposite – across the wide boulevard – the huge building of the Prime Minister, supposedly closer to a tyrant than to a *prior inter pares.* Still – or again – the floating between the fine arts and sensitivity of writers as *Aleksandr Sergeevič Puškin* and Czarism's harshness. It is a floating which does not take concrete form – somewhat lacking determination like the floating of the people I see. They are walking along the 'shopping mall without shops' – chatting; debating; standing, reading the publicly displayed newspapers; playing chess and card games; eating popcorn (one could think it is the main national dish) and buying lottery tickets. Some are begging, some trying to get by with any weird business: offering digital photos for sale, letting electronic cars that can be driven by children and the like. The only people that are obviously working in the ordinary understanding are the bus drivers; the only shops that are aggressively popping up are those for money exchange and those for mobile phones – the others are kind of hidden in houses, more converted apartments. Posters are promising 'careers in the West' – inviting people to go to Europe, the US or Canada.

Before I take up my real job, before being able to understand more of the country and the people, I have these extremely mixed feelings – if the price for overcoming poverty is a society in which not all are poor but some are extremely rich and others remain extremely poor; if the price for overcoming 'democratic centralism' of the Bolshevist system is a new Czar, playing the game hand in hand with the international Czars of politics and economic power – perhaps in the form of the Moldovan M welted together with the yellow M on the red background; if the price of progress is replacing these beautiful old buildings with new shopping centres with all the fancy names; *Boss, Aigner, BMW, LG electronics...* it may well be one day we will say

Those who leave too early are reprimanded by future

II.   25–29/10/2006

The chaos was consecutively replaced by something which was much worse: order.

(Gyoergi Dalos: Hungary in a Nutshell; Munich: Beck, 2005: 78)

Beginner's Jolt

The first teaching day – I stay a little longer after my own teaching as there is a second session. Some additional education for me as this deals with the national and local situation and some additional knowledge in law cannot do any harm, especially as I can easily link into it: the national law has strong roots in the Roman tradition. Furthermore, the presenter works in a very traditional way with overheads and a projector. And as little as I understand people when they are talking I can manage quite well to read various texts – the language, actually Moldavian is more or less the same as Romanian, is closely linked to Italian. In addition Aha, my interpreter, stays on and is a help I could not afford to miss.

Thus, being in the privileged situation of having a driver at my disposal I can decide the time I want to leave – there is always an easy way back from the school, which is located in a suburban area in the middle of a forest. It is a beautiful drive, the colourful leaves shining in the sunlight of these nice and warm late October days. Although it is a forest area, the road is wide and I am wondering if there is an Irish-English influence in Moldovan law: Dimitri drives on the left side of the road. After looking around, I soon find the reason: the right side of the road is simply so bad that it could easily cause the end of the car's existence – God, never say Irish roads are for horse carts.

Now, the problem is that such a system works perfectly well within its own terms of reference: the chaos – difficulties only arise when it mixes with an imposed order. And there is such a difficulty arising as being serious when transport systems change from a mainly public system with more or less rare individual cars – a system that requires limited space – to an individual transport system that tends toward permanent congestion.

Now, let's start more from the beginning – not from leaving the school, but from arriving there and doing the job.

When I opened my bag for the first seminar session, taking my notes I was a little bit puzzled (to say the least as this is just a kind way of saying: the blood began to freeze in my veins, although I felt a wave of feverish discomposure). Instead of finding my own notes I look on a sheet of paper, saying *Европейская социальная политика. Вступление – Несоциальная политика или новая интерпретация термина «социальный»... Hmm?* I see that it is my paper as it bears the same format as my usual texts and my name is on top of it. A slight hope. There is another document. I grab for it: *Politica social Europeană. S...* - well it sounds familiar.... I continue 'reading': *Introducere – inexistenţa politicii sau reinterpretarea politicii.* And then *De obicei se spune că politica socială ca afacere europeană nu există dat fiind faptul că depăşeşte responsabilităţile şi competenţele instituţiilor UE. Cei care ţin să afirme că există măcar ceva tendinţe de dezvoltare a unor activităţi în domeniu li se va spune că astfel de competenţe nu existau cu câţiva ani în urmă.* I admit I do not feel too comfortable, although the language is quite familiar when looking at it (different to its sound which in my ears is more like Russian). And finally, why should the students here in Chişinău suffer more than other students do? Teaching can barely be based on reading any text – even if it is your own one. And I made some new notes the evening before which are much more comprehensive: four or five questions along which we work together, the entire class: a colleague from Poland, mainly people from Moldova and some from... – well, I don't even know the name of the place. I only know that they speak Russian and another local language (not dialect: language). It is worth remarking that the lads from this minority from the very south of the country are the ones who speak a little bit of English.

Uncovering Meaning

– What a way of learning? – For all of us. Aha has frequently difficulties: Yep, I know the term. The young Moldovan woman looks at me, somewhat anxious, helpless. But the Moldovan language has no equivalent, she continues .

What are social services, what is society, what is social policy – during the meeting such simple questions come up and we realise very soon that we're starting from entirely different understandings. Thatcher's phrase gets an entirely different meaning from what the iron lady had in mind – and here it is a true meaning: There is no such thing as society. There are only societies – different societies, following their own orders, shaped by the concrete action of concrete beings under concrete circumstances.

I am pleased with the teaching – as the group allowed me to work with them: they listened, and yet they intervened. No, we do not accept that! – Where is that? In Germany? In Ireland? Well, I am really proud as I can say that we in Moldova are far ahead. – And of course as well: Where is that? Belgium? We really have to go there. Can you give us any address of such a service provider? We have to see that with our own eyes.

It was not scepticism behind the latter remark but simply the difficulty of understanding what a *woonwinkel* is. We are looking for terms to translate *woonwinkel* – hopeless. *Community care? – Yeah, ah – not really though there is something of community care in it. – A one-stop-shop? – No, definitely not that. One-stop-shops are more of an administrative tool – and a tool for information? – An advice office? – Well, something like it. But it is not an office as long as you understand an office as a bureaucratic instance.* Hopeless. And still the debate of the different terms clarifies it – examples from other countries come into play and here I really appreciate that I do not have real in-depth knowledge of any one of the systems (don't ask me for the budget and don't ask me if they would have to be organised under article 80 or 85 of the Moldovan Law on Local Public Administration [123/18.03.2003]) but on the other hand at least a reasonable insight into the functioning of some systems across the EU.

Approaching Economy

However, understanding what is behind the specific meaning takes time – something we do not have. After talking the day before more or less extensively with Wojciech, after reading the report from the World Bank (signed by the Moldovan government and obviously mocked-up), after – well, not least after walking through the city of Chişinău I have at least some idea.

I mentioned already the 'lack of visible business' and others. – What springs to the eyes to us Westerners is something that we can name as hidden market economy, the emphasis on all elements of the terms and the various possible combinations. It is a hidden economy – shops do not have the large displays as we know them. After a while I found one of the huge stores – the 'Moldovan Roches' or so. In a way comparable as there were various 'departments'. However, here departments means different individual 'stands' – shopping seems to be just an economic activity – something to supply certain needed goods (an exception is the buying of flowers – a common matter of the heart – and of books – no less a matter of love. Besides the tryst of the brand names, there is no rush on all this glamour – Poverty? Other values? Other aims? – So many different reasons play a role in this market economy: a market economy in which little stands seem to play a more important role than shops. Here and there somebody has a little table, just a cloth or the bare ground, selling something which seems less than the breath it costs to get it there. It is a hidden economy not only because it lacks the belligerence of developed capitalist marketing; it is also hidden in terms of the shadow economy although everybody knows about it.

Chişinău's economy, seen in more analytical terms, is characterised historically by its trade-strategic location on the oriental-occidental border – on the other hand this had been the foundation for orienting the city's activities on trade and – though much later – administration. Besides the role played by the location (with the subsequent negative effect of being destroyed several times throughout) another factor is the economic base of the *Republica Moldova* – climate and good farmland are favourable conditions for agriculture, however lagging behind in any other terms. The previously important export of vine ceased due to Putin's politics. What cannot be easily understood, however, is what I see in the supermarket: Turkish grapes – and the wrapping paper states in German without the slightest mistake *garantiert kernlose Trauben.*[3]

Other areas are only slowly gaining ground – and in any case it has to be asked if the (invited) invasion of foreign capital can be used to develop a sustainable economy. The same is true for service industries – a huge state administration may be needed for administering and distributing wealth, but it cannot produce it. Consequently it is no surprise that many people are working outside of the Republic, Italy being one of the favourite places to go to. However, this means not only loss of people – the consequences reach much further. It is the young, active generation that leaves – and it leaves behind the older generation and the children. Sure, money is sent back: Western Union offices all over the city are witnesses. However, the Western Union is not a witness that can be used in terms of calculating national balance sheets – the money never shows up in the budget of the state – another black whole in the economy.

The lack of taxable people, the low tax paying moral and the low (or one could say virtually non-existent) moral of prosecuting breaches are the basis for a vicious circle: growing poverty, increasing social problems and decreasing means for answering the challenges.

Social Policy Issues

Well, social policy issues were mentioned just before. The lack of a group in the middle of life's age span can be seen as well as one of the factors behind the lack of a middle class. The 'over-aged' population and the children and young people are somewhat determining the picture, a large poor populace or at least one that lives at most at the borderline. On the other hand a group

---

[3]   Grapes guaranteed without seed

of people which is quite well-off – as nationals the senior officials and a new group of some rich shop owners. And as foreigners the settled 'real senior officials' from EU and US administrations, and from international companies. As little money as many of the expatriates return into the country, as much money is not 'nationalised' by these foreigners. Foreign investment is tricky and poverty – although to some extent invisible[4] – is the major problem, reflecting a population that is not of working age. And even if people were, there would not be sufficient employment opportunities. Table-shops – an answer which is not really a solution.

However, to some extent the guiding, though not outspoken principle seems to be *Investing in the – likely capitalist – future by maintaining the – socialist – past.* While social benefits – split into a huge number of different payments, not in any way linked – are hugely inefficient, social policy focuses on children: necessarily as they are neglected by the parents who are working abroad. And the health service is apparently excellent – Lucy mentioned it and she smiled, said that she could enjoy it, only after having used the term enjoying, recognising the faux-pas: even a good health system is nothing one enjoys as its use is a must and having used it reminds at the pain that brought one there. Misuse at least is unlikely.

Another kind of social policy can probably be seen as part of social quality policy. At least it is a – though tiny – part of the life regime: despite the normal huge buses[5] there is a frequent bus transport – taxi-like. Small buses, though having certain lines being designated by the various numbers, stop like taxis – no reliability what time they come, but the frequency doesn't require anything like this. And there is always a space left – they work along the line: If we managed to get 10 people into the vehicle we will manage 11, if we managed 11, the same will work with 12, and if we managed with n we will manage with n+1.

Coming more to the mode of life then, the amount of public libraries is remarkable and so is the opportunity of public places where one can meet: for a chat, to play chess or card games, for reading different newspapers which are provided in display cabinets in the parks – sure, besides mildness or warm clothes it is necessary that it is dry.

---

[4] another interesting detail which has to be researched: some wealth seems to be hidden as well – not the real wealth but the wealth of ordinary people. Looking at many houses from the outside one would not believe that any person is living in them. However, entering them it looks quite different.

[5] Although even they are not entirely normal as they are trolley buses, using electric power.

Family policies – a topic which I have to give a miss. However, I can say that the couples from the park, mentioned earlier, do not stop with kissing and babbling on the park banks. Fridays and Saturdays are wedding days – I see many couples. Perhaps they made their first step in this park where they now meet again. And what makes it remarkable for me is that all of them – after the obligatory 'photography in white' under the golden-leafed trees or in front of the shrubs that shine in the October sun – leave flowers at the foot of the monument at the park's entrance, dedicated to Stefan cel Mare.[6] Tying the knot, respecting the history, respecting life's character as chain of chains.

At least at first glance an interesting contradiction: the hidden economy and a very public life. And as public as it is and as much as it is obviously a multinational society, it is also a somewhat closed society – I feel observed, again and again I can see in eyes looking at me the exclamation: *You are a foreigner – and what else are you? What brought you here?* I cannot deny feeling somewhat guilty: Yes, my father entered the country with a tank (though didn't get so far) – and I enter it with the logo of the successors, with the logo of the fortress EU. I want to stop them: I was fighting against him – and I am not fighting with them today even if I am walking on the blue carpet with the yellow stars. – Fortunately I can always remember the situation in the classroom where we worked and walked together, taking the direction we wanted to take.

Aodhán's tea kettle

For the foreigner here, for somebody who does not have sufficient time to settle and probably for those who have the time as well, many patterns remain hidden in other ways as it is so difficult – different values, different understandings, different behavioural patterns. All the consequences of a different accumulation regime – consequences for the life regimes; consequences of different modes of regulation with their repercussions on the mode of life. – Orders that remain somewhat chaotic as long as we do not fully adapt the rules. Of course, such adaptation does not necessarily mean that we accept them – still we have to appropriate them to find appropriate answers to circumvent them. A little play on words – and after reading the paper on Methodology and after the lectures all this should make sense. I can turn it, however, into a little story – a true story about Aodhán, a priest from Cork whom I once met in a small village near Stuttgart in the South of Germany where we both 'represented Ireland' during a celebration. – Ok, may be that I should not represent Ireland. But why should

---

6   Stefan the Great

he do it then – a Catholic Irish priest who spent most of his life in missionary services? Be it as it is – the little true story is on change and stability and how people cope with it. Down in the South of Germany, Aodhán and I met during the celebrations – a school celebrating five years of its existence and success. After the official part there was a small group left. Together we went for a nice meal. Another birthday, we had to celebrate: Aodhán's birthday although he didn't know for some time that we knew. A nice old guy, in a way so unlike a priest – or very much like a priest in the sense of a nice man, looking openly on life and on the joy of it. Probably his slogan of life was *God gave us our life to enjoy it whenever we have the opportunity.* So this was what we did. The good old Irish songs, the German's competing, mixing the voices, the melodies – forgetting even the slightest notion of possible problems and sorrows. Aodhán celebrated his birthday with us – perhaps it was his 65th or his 70th birthday. A happy man, without sorrows although he had definitely faced enough of them during his lifetime: 'standing his man far away from home'.

Next time we met was the morning of the following day for breakfast. The old priest was the last to turn up – after being the one who did most of the singing he had the right to do so. And he turned up with a tiny teakettle, protected by a knitted coat, unique in its colours. The old man kept it close to his body, went to the buffet, got the tea into his little companion and joined us – smiling, sitting down and celebrating a cup of tea as they did in so many places around the world before they came to the little village in the South of Germany. – The safety he needed. Just enough to stand the differences he wanted and had to face in his job. And what is remarkable is the fact that this little bit of admitted stability and even rigidity on which he insisted allowed him to be one of the most open creatures I ever came across – much more so than many who claim that they do not have any roots and that the world is just one huge village. It may well be so, but still it has different houses and the houses have different rooms.

Losses and findings

Now, personally I definitely lost my tea kettle again – the misunderstandings, the non-understanding, the search for meanings. But all this meant as well that the teaching was a learning process. I did not want to sell them anything – although the programme of my 'mission' wanted me to 'sell Europe', to present it as the best of all worlds. I am afraid in this regard they put the fox in charge of the hen house. Probably, after the course, after my teaching, most of the participants are more Eurosceptic than even the French and Dutch showed with their votes on the EU-Draft-Constitution.

That this was possible was simply a consequence of the fact that at least for the trainees in the classroom the last ten years or so brought one important experience: the new world was not what had been promised to them. From outside, what was brought to them through the various channels was a gloomy system – gloomy in terms of a rich world of choice goods, individualism of an advanced market society and of course in political terms – a gloomy world of wealth and democracy for all. However, what they did not expect was the increasing gap between rich and poor, the regulation of life by a huge bureaucratic machinery and the invention of a new idol: Goods as God; and Politics as Good – a matter of popularity rather than debate and negotiation. Of course, democracy, political systems in general are rather complex systems – and I mention it by dropping a brick. Lucy, the project leader, Wojciech, the long-term expert trainer and I are sitting together in the car that makes the way home. For me it is already the last day and we are talking about the entire project – it is as such EU project. Wojciech says the difference with these projects, if compared to US Aid, would be that they are actually determined by the states themselves – during annual meetings between the EU bodies and the national government they would draw up a plan, largely determined by what Moldovan's say and demand. US Aid would work in a different way: The US agency draws up a plan: They determine what the problem is, they determine the means and tools and they determine how the tools have to be used. I scoff: *And when EU programmes are negotiated, the Moldovan government sits at the table, repeats what the US told them to say and they get the money!?* – Wojciech smiles resentfully: *Yes, you can say so.* Lucy intervenes: *I worked for several years for US Aid. That is not true. You find there as well ways of influencing policies. What definitely is true is that the bureaucracy is much higher there.* – A little quarrel arises – I can only listen, not knowing enough about these concrete programmes. And on the other hand knowing too much about how the systems work: the US did not allow people like me into the country, just by applying a bureaucratic rule: If you are member of a certain party, you are not allowed to enter the States. And the EU bodies, claiming democratic RULES, the openness and calculability of formal processes that promise in the defined framework the right of the individual, can be so suppressing simply applying rules that do not exist – you do not sit in the strong beam of a lamp, shining into your face to feel like being in a situation of interrogation as we know it from James Bond films or the like – there is supposedly a soft way of 'convincing' people of what they are expected to do and to say without formal rules and coercion – and it needs a strong personality to refuse.

Be it as it is, I leave this discussion to them. Dimitri stops the black limousine in front of the office. We walk over the carpet of yellow and brown leaves that shine in the sunlight of another beautiful autumn day – a brief discussion in the office, deciding about the work which still has to be done.

I leave relatively early, wanting to go for a stroll through town as I can do some work in the evening – the latter being dead time for me as it is not so much fun to sit with an interpreter in a pub. I walk along the broad boulevard – the *Bd. Stefan Cel Mare*. I know the area in the meantime reasonably well, not least from each morning's jog. Still, *Τα παντα ρει*[7] – and this means as well changing impressions, again and again a different look at everything, discovering new perspectives. Coming to the end of this short and intense stay in Chişinău, I pass once more the President's building – from where I approach it, it is on the left side of the street – the tall building, the tower-like building excelling the Parliament building on the other side of the street. It is the first time that I do not see the individual buildings but the two buildings in relation – perhaps it is because I have learned in the meantime a little bit more about the political system and the ruling of a party which seems to be a contradiction in terms: as *Partidul Comuniştilor din Republica Moldova* (Party of Communists of the Republic of Moldova) strongly orientated towards western capitalism, it has to raise scepticism. I do not bother too much however, not having sufficient time to study in depth the party's program with four pillars, namely

1. A new quality of life,

2. Economic modernisation,

3. European integration,

4. Consolidation of society.

I know at least enough to see contradictions – the orientation on Creation of a society in which the freedom of the individual and the freedom of choice will be ensured by welfare and prosperity clashing with the wish of Moldova's transformation into a state of European standards and efficient investments in the country's economy, opening new western markets for Moldovan goods; the demand of Free circulation, without visas, of Moldovan citizens in European countries, reliable legal and social protection of our compatriots being abroad on the one hand, being at least in a tensional relationship with the resources that are actually available and with the reality of international relations and power imbalances.

---

[7]   *Ta panta rei*/Everything is in flux (Heraclitus [535–475 BC])

But how could there be a relationship without tensions if the Moldovan President, PCRM leader Vladimir Voronin starts from an assumption of general interest, expressed in the words

> *Moldova's Party of Communists (PCRM) is the only party which aspires to express the whole society's long-term interests. The teacher, the worker, the peasant and the businessman are equally dear to us. We do not have favourites, as well as discriminated people under the social aspect.*
>
> *(Moldovan Party of Communists Marks Five Years of Government; 23 March 2006)*

As I said, I do not have sufficient time to obtain the knowledge for further deliberations. I walk on – hesitate, should I just walk through the park or should I walk further along the road. I decide to walk straight on, seeing one more time the government building – on the right hand side, the 'parliament side'. Across the street, on the left, the same side where the President's building is, and a little bit back from the street, there is the somewhat monumental orthodox cathedral – although the tower does not excel the government building, there is a 'moral emanation', the charisma that gives the impression of the cathedral being more monumental than the actually larger government building.

The reason for this? The reason is that even the heathen that I am gets the impression. Perhaps it is the knowledge of the cathedral's inner sight. – Light plays at least a role in all Western religions.[8] Remember the star of Bethlehem – the light aiming to guide the three kings who were looking for the newborn child. At least to my knowledge this was more or less the general meaning of light in the future: in one way or another the representation of lambency. Entering orthodox churches in several places, I always got the impression that the lambency, which can be found here, is refusing any kind of enlightenment. Sure, I am the last who would impute to the Catholic Church or any church actually a truly enlightening role. However, entering the cathedral cannot even claim to give light to find any way. Rather, at least a person such as me can only see the luminance and glossiness as being a false front – the individual can only make a bow and subordinate him or herself, asking for mercy and guidance in the form of a 'leading hand', being dazzled by the glow. – The Quadrant of the President's tower, the parliament and government building and the charismatic monumental cathedral are an arrangement that can make one think. Especially when one sees it against the background of a special room in the *Muzeul National de Arta al Moldovei*, dedicated to 15 years of independence:

---

[8]   And this Orthodox Church has at least strong Western roots.

It is an exhibition on the recuperation of the Orthodox Church. – The National Palace, located in the back of the government building is an additional feature giving some additional spice to the thoughts.

Farewell – I am looking forward to see you again

Sunday morning – the last day in Chişinău. I should be at home in the appartment, as there is plenty of work which remains to be done – and there is even more work which I should do today in preparation for tomorrow's meeting on another project with the European Commission in Brussels, the last stop before moving on Wednesday into my new home in Budapest. Ah, who knows if I will ever have the opportunity again… - So I walk one of the as yet unknown tracks. I arrive soon at the entrance of the *Parcul Valea Morilor*, quite a large park area, more correct: just a natural resort with a beautiful lake. On the way there a familiar smell of burning timber reaches me – and being early enough I can take the time to sit down for a while – the smell, the sun rising over the valley, shining through the trees, the golden leaves on the ground and the birds – waking and making their first excursion in the cold of the early morning. Putrid smell coming from the water – and nevertheless it is pleasant fresh air.

Finally I feel kind of home; no guard, no interpreter, no driver – just the universal language of nature and people enjoying themselves. My hand looks for something – and it sinks back into the relaxed position on my lap. No, here Aodhán would do as well without his tea kettle – and so there is no reason for me to look for one. After a while I awake from this daydream. I have to go home, get my things organised before the driver arrives.

Punctually, the doorbell rings. I open it and Dimitri makes a step forward. He nods in the direction of the small suitcase, then in my direction. *Da da* – my little bit of active, spoken language allows me already to let him know that he can take it and so he does.

– I have to smile. *Da* is the Moldovan word for *yes.* And one can say it without problem a couple of times – *da da* seems to be a common way, a diffuse expression of affirmation and resignation and perhaps as well of a defiant *I will show you who will succeed.* – *Dada,* also the name of a new style of art in the 1900s (peaking 1916-1920), gets a new meaning – the tendering tension of affirmation and rejection, the dialectic of *Aufhebung* as sublation and supersession that DADAism was, indeed.

I follow Dimitri. – Fortunately Irina sits in the car. I do not have to face an endless silence on the way to the airport. We talk about the project – but soon we talk about other things. Her plans: doing such project work, studying and teaching at the same time. And despite all this, she looks relaxed. She shows that she is calculating her steps exactly; but she shows as well that she is not calculating for herself. She is one of those people who stayed home, who did not leave her parents nor her child.

– The car parks in front of the terminal building. Dimitri grabs for the suitcase and the three of us go to the small SAAB aircraft after passing the necessary formalities. – La revedere. Multumesc.[9] Especially, thank you for not just following the program and for allowing me to do the same.

I force myself into the seat of the plane – and still, I feel a certain freedom despite the closeness and the five hour flight ahead of me. Not being under the indirect scrutiny of big brother's development program. After having this experience I know once more why the contract used the term *mission*. I am used to represent somebody or something – and I do not have problems even if the represented is something I cannot fully stand for; usually even in those cases I am actually still representing more myself than others – and I am officially allowed to do so. To be *on mission* is somewhat different in this regard – although doing very much my own thing, while teaching what I think is worthwhile and important for the people here, I have this permanent impression of being on the wrong side, fighting on the wrong section of development. I know that many of the people with whom I worked together in Chişinău have the same attitude. But still knowing is one thing; the feeling of being on a mission, the impression of being sent by somebody, the sentiment that the director's book is written by somebody else, is like a chain, heavily laying on my shoulders.

I feel free in this close 'tiny tin'– and I know I want to come back one day.

The engine starts – looking out of the window, waving for a last time at Dimitri and Irina I would like to say to give the words back to Irina. Once when we talked and she mentioned: *A friend of mine lives in Ireland. She always says I should come there – life would be much easier. But I don't want – I think there is hope for my country. – Yes, Irina, there is still hope. There is hope, as long as we take things in our own hands.*

My hands are looking for something – a little tea kettle or something like it. I am not allowed to use it – but I cannot resist and switch on the MP3-player.

Imagine there's no Heaven
It's easy if you try
No Hell below us
Above us only sky.

---

9   Good bye. Thank you for everything.

...

You, you may say I am a dreamer
But I'm not the only one
I hope someday you'll join us
And the world will be as one.

III. 29/10–1/11/2006

> *Three passions, simple but overwhelmingly strong, have*
> *governed my life: the longing for love, the search for*
> *knowledge, and unbearable pity for the suffering of*
> *mankind. These passions, like the great winds, have*
> *blown me hither and thither, in a wayward course, over a*
> *deep ocean of anguish, reaching to the very verge of*
> *despair.*
>
> *(Bertrand Russell. Autobiography; London/New York:*
> *Routledge, [1967] 2000: 9)*

Corridors – Run(a)ways

Sunday evening, arriving in Cork – the situation is quite normal – but what does that mean? As I do not have a vehicle at my disposal, I have to take a taxi to get to Cork city for the night. After waiting quite a while for the luggage, I have to wait now for a taxi. Jazz Festival I guess – and I say to the driver – after a taxi is eventually available: *Busy evening, is it? – Not really, there are so many flights diverted to Shannon.* And he begins to lament Cork airport: the new terminal, the huge amount of money spent and the continuation of an unbearable situation: an airport located in a fog-spot – the money that changed hands, some of it likely changing owners in brown envelopes.

Sometime that evening I return to Cork where I stay over night rather than going out to Aghabullogue – it will be a short night anyway as some work still has to be done before I finally leave Cork for the rest of the year. God, what a relief that Steph is there, helping me with so many things – my desk is full of papers, well prepared stuff, I just have to sign, write some comments… and unfortunately I have to leave a couple of new things for her on the desk. Such a great help and still I don't like to give her such work – a waste of talent. Together we wrote an article and she showed that this is something she should do – rather than administrative work. Actually, she wrote the article whereas I made some changes and added tiny things at the end, I played a rather limited role. And then I have to think that many of those tasks I consider being admin stuff, is actually not really that; there is always more substance to it than one tends to recognise after things are established as routines – sometimes you might see the term routine-ised, expressing that one does something without thinking about it, although one has to think if one does it for the first time.– Well, as great as the Internet and all the technology is (devices I actually hate worse than the Black Death), it's better and definitely indispensable to have somebody who can deal with things because of being a human being and being there as person and personality – not being part of any long chain which lies like a fetter around the neck. – Strange that it seems to be necessary to say it, as we are living in a world where some people don't get this – and even more strange that some people get such an opportunity and behave like machines themselves. However, a human being is better than any machine; but if a human being tries to be a better machine this will definitely result in one of the worse humans and defective machines.

Values of Social Services and Values in Social Science

A short night, as said – the alarm clock rings, calls me back to the airport (after my jogging, of course): *Brussels* via *Budapest* where *István*, my colleague in Budapest, kindly collects my main luggage in order to take it to my apartment on the *Pest*-side of the city. The taxi driver in *Cork*, though another, again talks about the airport, the new terminal building – *Michael O'Leary would be the man – if he would have been allowed he would have built the new terminal for half the amount.* I only think without speaking out loud: yes, probably he would have done it! In any case, he is allowed to develop an economy which rebuilds feudal structures – an economy which does not speak of exploitation anymore because there is no time left for thinking – from the idealist *Cartesian cogito ergo sum* to the pseudo-materialist *consumo ergo sum*. – And still..., well, who does not know the *Shakespearean* questions, though today's answer is different.

The woman: Does she come regularly? Has she got a claim on you?
Shen Teh: No claim, but she's hungry: and that's more important.

(Bertolt Brecht: The Good Person of Szechwan. Translated by John Willet; edited and introduced by John Willet and Ralph Manheim; London: Methuen, 2000: 15)

Appropriate thoughts, getting me into the mood I need for the meeting in Brussels – a meeting which is part of a research project on *social and health services as services of general interest*. A project which is important for me as I try to continue the work which I have undertaken over the last couple of years: The rejection of the strategy of liberalisation policies – already in general terms more than problematic, it is the death of anything humane as a guiding principle of the delivery of services, not only relevant for people who cannot afford to pay for services but a matter for all, the undermining of even a notion of general interest. Of course, latest since for instance *Karl*

Marx's Contribution to the Critique of Hegel's Philosophy of Law (Marx, Karl: Contribution to the Critique of Hegel's Philosophy of Law; 1843; in: Karl Marx. Frederick Engels. Collected Works. Volume 3: Marx and Engels 1843-1844; London: Lawrence&Wishart, 1975: 3-129) it is clear that there is no general interest anyway. But the declared denial of such interest, the definition of general interest in terms of market economy – though disguised as a matter of increasing the choice of consumers – makes it even worse. Finally social services, including social services of general interest – are entirely commodified, thus perverted to be individual services.[10]

The project, supposedly the major 'fact finding exercise' of the Commission's Directorate General of Employment, Social Affairs and Gender Equality (not sure, old-fashioned as I am I still use the overcome nomenclature: DGV), is concerned with the evaluation of service provision, the different providers and how they actually provide them, the mechanisms of financing them and the question if – and if so in which way EUorpean legislation effects the development. My role is the dubious role of what is called 'lead researcher on stakeholder issues'. Once more the fox in charge of the hen house, guaranteeing a little bit of the feeling-good temper while getting upset about the naïve proposals of some members of the research group. Without any doubt, most are highly qualified and all are good-willed. And I admire many of them for their knowledge, consideration and not least as good friends. Still, the problem is one which is not outspoken, standing like a spectre in all the rooms where scientific work is undertaken: the spectre of value freedom of research. All the considerations, all the work done on this most fundamental are permanently present although nobody mentions or probably even thinks of one of them: Dilthey, Weber, Lenin, Adorno... Of course, there is the issue of passion of

the search for knowledge,

and knowledge is about facts – objective, existing without any input, without our doing or the doing of others. However, there is as well

---

[10] Worth a side remark, Esping-Andersen, praised for his approach of decommodification which he presented in his book on *Three Worlds of Welfare Capitalism (Esping-Andersen, G. (1990), The three worlds of welfare capitalism; Cambridge: Polity Press)* shows for another time and from another angle limitations, remaining caught in thinking about how to increase justice of capitalism rather than thinking about replacing an unjust system, a system that cannot be justified. In the given case we have see the necessity of what? That area which is supposedly the one of decommodifcation is being itself increasingly commodified – something like the Cunning of Reason as Hegel called it *(Hegel, G. W.F. (1991), The philosophy of history, Prometheus Buffalo: New York)*, but in a perverted form.

the longing for love,…, and unbearable pity for the suffering
of mankind.

As true as it is that we, working in social science, are also dealing with objective facts, it is not less true that two decisive points have to raised: 1) On whose behalf, in the interest of whom do we ask questions? And 2) What do we do with the results of the investigation? – This is about objectivity, though it is strongly as well a matter of interests. And there is actually a third question, usually forgotten. The interests themselves are part of a bundle having an objective dimension, actually interests themselves are objective – and this is a matter of the historical process and of social and societal existence. – Sure, Michael O'Leary may have built Cork airport cheaper, and he is even creating new employment, to some extent new 'wealth' for those who otherwise did not get another job. However, at the end it is the Leary's being responsible for the processes of 'rationalisation' – the rationality of putting people severely under stress by overwork, by density of work processes, by competition, by fear of losing their job – justified fear as on the other hand there are the many who do not have any work, who are working under precarious conditions…

The good
Cannot remain good for a long time in our country
Where cupboards are bare, house wives start to
squabble.
Oh, the divine commandments
Are not much use against hunger.
So why can't the gods share out what they've created.

(Bertolt Brecht: The Good Person of Szechwan. Translated
by John Willet; edited and introduced by John Willet and
Ralph Manheim; London: Methuen, 2000: 48)

Special Kind of Services in the Private Interest and the Interest of Privacy

Another social service – flying from Cork to Budapest two girls – nice kids – entertain us, making the flight lively and by their obvious bliss it is somewhat enjoyable for me. Only when the mother of the one admonishes: *Don't run! Come here now and sit down.* the lovely 'quietness of discomposure' is replaced by a nasty skirmish and whining between mother and child.

The next flight – Budapest to Brussels – I nearly feel sorry for a guy who sits in the business class. He is the only one, nobody there to talk to, nothing to do after reading *Le Soir,* a rather unexciting Belgium newspaper – the third glass of Champagne has to serve as (at least from my point of view, but what do the words of an abstinent person count for in this case) meagre comfort.

Cats and Mice or: Policy Research and Research Politics

*The women: What a cheek, begging for tobacco. 'Tisn't as if
it had been bread.
The unemployed man: Bread's expensive. A few puffs at
a fag and I'm a new man. I'm so done in.
Shen Teh gives him cigarettes: That's very important,
being a new man.*

*(Bertolt Brecht: The Good Person of Szechwan. Translated
by John Willet; edited and introduced by John Willet and
Ralph Manheim; London: Methuen, 2000: 14)*

I finally arrive in Brussels, taking the train from the airport to the hotel – this time I cannot go to the apartment where I usually stay. In the lounge of the hotel I am welcomed by two colleagues, they grant just enough time to go to my room, have a quick shower, grab the documents I need – the invitation for dinner turns out to be an invitation to a little workshop where some food is served. It takes place in the rooms of an Italian restaurant – *Fa caldo si può aprire il finestrino, per favore??* The waiter opens the window. *Hai ragione – you are right, it is a nice and mild evening and there would be nicer things to do, isn't that right?* It is right but the decision is not my decision and not even the decision of the others who are here with me.

It is not only the time of this pre-meeting which seems to be out of the control of those who actually do the work. Commissioned research – called 'commissioned' not because it is work the European Commission asked for, though it is actually the Commission of the European Communities who asked for it. It is not necessarily a problem – but here it is a problem as in this case there is quite a lot of interference, a permanent battle about the questions that have to be asked, that are 'suggested' to be relevant. This evening we prepare for the meeting which is taking place the next day – a meeting at the Rue Joseph II, the building of the European Commission's DGV. The usual: passport control, R.M. from the Commission welcomes us and we go to the meeting room. B.S., the legal expert, M.H., the expert on services for disabilities, B.M., the boss of the partner from Vienna... – all this, especially this reception procedure, is a little bit like cats and mice, playing with and against each other. Of course it is a nice atmosphere, as nobody actually knows if s/he is mouse, cat or the adjudicator. The real equality emerges later the day, when we face a power cut, the equality increases when the G.F., another colleague from the EUC, enters the room: *We do not know what the problem is but the light should be back latest in half an hour.* – His broad Vienna-English is always nice to listen to. Before he leaves he, knuckling down briefly to me, says *Hallo* and asks me if I could provide some documents from the Foundation I am working for. After I promise to ask the office in Amsterdam to send them, he leaves – but only to return a couple of minutes later: *You have to leave, the building has to be evacuated.* – The second he stops speaking, a loud voice can be heard – the tone from the bullhorn, asking us to remain patient, not to panic but to leave immediately the building – while we leave the men from fire brigade enter. All without panic, well ordered – only G.'s mordant voice can be heard. *It is the oldest building of the Commission, what can you expect for social affairs.* – It may be a kind of paranoia to see any link between what happens and the fact that it occurs just while focus is on service modernisation. We move into another building, soon the projector is connected – the crutch for many who are afraid to speak without it, afraid of not having sufficient stuff they can talk about. We move on in the agenda. Social services, provision and providers, financing, legal issues – there is no general interest, it proves to be true during this debate. The political debate is faded out – it is much easier to fasten a bundle which does not show any contradictions, and tensions; it is less captious when one talks about issues that do not require political or any other decisions.

> *The bureaucracy takes itself to be the ultimate purpose of the state. Because the bureaucracy turns its 'formal' objectives into its content, it comes into conflict everywhere with 'real' objectives.*
>
> *(Marx, Karl: Contribution to the Critique of Hegel's Philosophy of Law; 1843; in: Karl Marx. Frederick Engels. Collected Works. Volume 3: Marx and Engels 1843-1844; London: Lawrence&Wishart, 1975: 3-129; here: 46)*

And the same is also true with the issues mentioned, the truly political character of services – but who wants conflicts. So the easiest is not to talk about real objectives; why look at reality if we can avoid complicated and complicating conflicts. – Passions?

> *The player: What is your answer? Nothing's been arranged.*
> *Should men be better? Should the world be changed?*
> *Or just the gods? Or ought there be none?*
> *We for our part feel well and truly done.*
> *There is only one solution that we know: That you should*
> *now consider as you go*
> *What sort of measures you would recommend*
> *To help good people to a happy end.*
> *Ladies and gentlemen, in you we trust:*
> *there must be happy endings, must, must, must!*
>
> *(Bertolt Brecht: The Good Person of Szechwan. Translated by John Willet; edited and introduced by John Willet and Ralph Manheim; London: Methuen, 2000: 109)*

Finally, I feel morally supported in my decision to take a twofold approach: working within the project, trying to ask the correct questions there and at the same time working on a publication on the topic which looks at these real objectives, the complex reality which is faded out – and I am glad that some of the colleagues from the project will contribute to that publication as well. Actually, it is even more than that. If plans turn out as they are made, early/middle of next year will see the launch of three publications – and politically rather sensitive documents on social services of general interest

- the official study from the European Commission

- the book in which providers and users of theses services have a say and

- a book that I wrote on the topic – a theoretical study, looking at European values and philosophical and legal questions around this subject (at least I just got the conformation from my publisher on this).

Passions, yes, though they sometimes may require a kind of schizophrenic split. And there is the danger, of course, that I am building the gallows which will be used to hang me after I finished building it. – I would not be the first one hanging; and it would not be the first time for me being hung.

Home, Sweet Home

Wednesday, I finally move to Budapest – still in Brussels I am going jogging in the early hours of the morning. As mild as the evening before was, it is now a bitterly cold and damp morning.

At the airport I am confronted with long queues – extremely long queues, standing at the check-in desks. I go to the check-in desk as well – one of five machines standing aside. Some form of identification and the entire procedure takes about 1 ½ minutes, not enough time for the device to smile at me, to have a nice word, not enough time for me to be angry or happy – I listen to the cogwheels in my brain, to the nerve and muscular cords that move my legs; the eyes that receive light waves... – Just walk on, walk on..., in my inner mind I hear the words of Bert Brecht's and Kurt Weill's song:

Trabt schneller!
Herr Dschinn hat einen Wald
Der muß vor Nacht gerodet sein
Und Nacht ist jetzt schon bald!

I walk through the passport control – the queue at the desk for EU-PASSPORTS ONLY is much longer than the other queue: NON-EU PASSENGERS – but it moves much faster. – Still it is not the fault of the guards sitting there – after he returns my passport, the usual game of being in a multilanguage country, respecting diversity: *Merci, Bedankt, Danke, Thanks.*[11] – Security check – again I resist asking if I should go on with taking off my clothes, after putting my two jackets, the belt and my shoes into the plastic box. After all this I sit down, open the laptop to do some work – urgent mails have to be written and sent, I still have to go on finalising an article which has been overdue for a long time – the rain against the thick windows distracts me a little bit – or is it the distraction of what I did in recent days? Of course, the usual happens. Last minute panic: where is the passport, my flight ticket. Why didn't I get organised in time, why did I have to sit there, writing until the last call – one never should leave me alone as I am simply not capable of looking after myself.

---

[11] At least in Brussels two languages are more or less obligatory (Flemish and French); the German language is an official language in Belgium as well (though rarely spoken in Brussels when you move around the city – actually I only heard it once used by non-migrants), and English is common: at the airport anyway and in the city as well, as due to EU, NATO and others plus the global market players who all have their workforce, customers, clients, etc here – a huge economic force, as important as the glass cleaners who have to take care of the palaces of the many EU-buildings.

Many other languages are spoken as well – Brussels is probably one of the most fascinating cities with a very unusual pattern of integration and segmentation. For instance, one interesting issue is that even many of the highly 'integrated' migrants – people working in the Commission, the Parliament or any other inter- and supranational organisations stick together. Another issue is that, although the same is true for people coming from African and Islamic countries etc. and – due to the large numbers – they have even their own 'quarters', many of the these quarters seem to be 'in the middle of the cities'. Although this is, of course, not least an expression of the fact that the 'Belgian aborigines' live outside, actually often in very nice peripheral city areas or suburbs, it gives two options for the visitor: you can get the impression that they are deluging the city or you can see them as being highly integrated. Only time, talking to people from the various groups and familiarising with their lives, dreams and hopes and as well disappointments and defeats, shows the truth, visible only under the surface. A truth which is in many cases linked to dramas – in many cases as well linked to dramas though one does not see anything other than harmony, the 'real multiculty', the real cosmopolitan. – It is not least against this background that I would like to make a thorough study on the 'newly emerging travelling communities', a project for after retirement.

– At the gate, I arrive just when the speaker announces the very last call and get a text message – Welcome to Proximus[12] and I can only think the answer – Good Bye, too late now anyway, about two hours left and I will arrive home, teaching a course for PhD students... – from Europe.

– Didn't I say home?

---

[12]   One of the Belgium mobile phone providers.

Finding Home

In a way having been in Budapest a long time now – sure, it was shortened by another trip to Brussels last week, three days not around for half an hour of a speech and having the occasion to get hold of a little tea kettle, but shortened especially by all the new impressions, requirements and demands. And seen in retrospective it was – at least for people like me – long enough to settle in a new home. Something that has, of course, several dimensions to it.

The first one is quite simple – and actually means for people like me: they definitely have only one home, and perhaps not even that. Well, if there is one home it is the place where all the routines are well established, where things do not have to be questioned – there is a German saying: People who are well organised are just too lazy to search for things. Now, I won't say that I am well organised but at least my life is – despite all other impressions I might occasionally give – very much caught in routines; and this is just another expression of the fact that I am actually unable to live.

Did you ever read texts from the great novelist Aleksandr Sergeyevich Pushkin? I do not remember in which piece, but once he wrote about two ladies and their conversation during a private evening reception. The two are talking about a singer who performs a beautiful song with his stunning voice. And the lady's talk goes somewhat like this: *Look at him. Listen to this voice – beyond words. He can do everything with it.* – The other lady, laconically, retorts *Well, Love, you are right – the voice is startling. However, if he really can do everything with it I am wondering why he doesn't buy proper trousers with it.* This little scene comes back to me when I am told I would pack my suitcase with fantasy. At least the result of the preparation is not really a positive expression of fantasy: t-shirts, light shoes… – why didn't I trust more in the calendar which would have told me: it is going to be winter.

Things are sorted in the meantime – I regain certain routines: know the route for my jogging, know where the public pool is and its opening hours, know when and where to do the shopping – and this prepares me for the many other things, unforeseen and unforeseeable; the things for which one needs fantasy, some strength and a kind of imperturbability.

After having been here, I finally moved three days or so later into my office – just about 25 minutes walk from my flat. I am lucky to meet *István* in front of the building of the university. He brings me there after being briefly in his office. As on so many occasions I feel somewhat awkward: He shares an office with three other people, and he shares his computer with one other person. On the other hand, I have my own office; and although I do use my own laptop, I have another computer there. I am in the office for only a short time when somebody comes along – well, actually two people come along. Gábor is the first, he wants to arrange a meeting for a kind of inaugural lecture to the staff of the department – 'EU enlargement and the meaning for social work in the old and the new EU member states', a vast field and though it is one of the presentations I will have to work on quite a lot in preparation, it is an exciting topic. It will be an opportunity and challenge: *Zsuzsa Ferge*, an old colleague and in the meantime friend, has asked to arrange the meeting in a way that she can join and 'co-present'. I am really flattered. While *Gábor Juhász* and I are talking, a second person knocks at the door: *I was asked to connect the computer to the Internet. –* I am near to crying as I know another place where such little things do not happen at all or at least it takes a very, very long time.

So, besides routines there is something else: privileges may be one term to grasp it, another term is appropriation. At the end it is simply the control over a situation. I am becoming aware of it just this moment – and in this position – in positive terms as I am at least to some extent in control of what is happening. Though the new tasks are not easy, there is something with it that allows me to deal with the situation rather than giving me the feeling that I am the object of the situation. It is the feeling and knowing of being part of something and having at last some influence and control.

How different were these first days – nice in a way. The exercise was to get acquainted with the place which would be for some time now my home. But I was simply thrown into the water, left alone paddling – *Just take your time, enjoy life and get around. If you need anything, if I can do anything for you, just give me a buzz. –* Well, the first task I faced was to find out where to buy a knife, as despite having everything else, the flat lacked one. It took me about two to three hours to find one. Souvenirs, clothes, coffee shops, restaurants – everything. Even a most beautiful market – the English market in Cork would blush. It is a market where local residents and tourists meet. And it is probably good advice to watch out: where do the locals do their shopping? The others might be just tourist-vampires, attracting the sightseers with the local colours, the tourists indeed behaving like mosquitoes when they see the folklore – and pay every price for the 'romanticisms' of the goulash, the pepper, the salami... and the 'real gypsy culture'. Here is not the place to think about members of the travelling community, the Sinti and Roma. I see all these shops, stands and markets – but for a long time I do not see a shop to buy something very simple: a knife for the kitchen. And as nice as all this is, as little I lack: nevertheless, in some regard I feel somewhat lost.

Sure, I had been in Bruges – the worst of all nice places: a 'life museum', difficult to imagine that people are actually living there; I know Vienna with which Budapest is usually compared, a place where the tourists are dominant but where ordinary people from Vienna can also be found. But it is not really a place one lives – usually they live at least not directly in the centre, at least just a little bit aside. It is different in Budapest. To be more precise: I am living in Pest whereas I am working on the Buda-side of the city, rarely going there for any other reason than work or swimming (the pool is just the other side of the bridge, seven minutes walk perhaps from my flat). These first days are somewhat meaningless for me – I see things, I enjoy things but there is one burning question: I have to live here now... and what? Is it living with the tourists? Just with the colleagues?

One evening as I am maundering back to the flat, the phone rings. Peter – Yes, speaking. Who is it? – Alice here. I was just thinking... –Alice, good to hear from you. Are you back from hospital? Didn't dare to contact you as I knew that your broken rib... –Ah, that is OK, well, at least so far. Any plans for the evening? I have had plans for the evening – just having a bite to eat, then writing some stuff which I have to get ready for the publisher. No, not really. We could meet if you are free. Alice, whom I know from a European project and who is working here for the Red Cross, is free. I'll be there in about 15 minutes, OK? We can meet in front of the house. We go for dinner – a really nice place, in the style of one of those nice Vienna-style coffee houses. Packed with tourists, and packed with locals. Sitting there I am wondering if this is a film or if films are real life? – Maybe I am just schizophrenic, which would not make a major difference to the answers of the questions asked. It is simply a nice spot, with its mundane cosmopolitan character. – It is the beginning of settling, as even here in this extraordinary place, something which is ordinary: people's lives, people who are there not to look at something from outside, but who are involved, engaged.

How many melodies...?

As so often, while being in unknown terrain my jogging is not just different in terms of the route – it is different as well with respect to the parallel entertainment. Usually I listen to any audio book – there is a good range available and it is nice to fill the time with readings on Aristotle (or from Aristotle, such as his *The Nicomachean Ethics,* though of course, not read by him,), or some more light reading such as Giovanni Boccaccio's *Decameron,* Ernest Hemingway's *For Whom the Bell Tolls* or Dan Brown's *Illuminati* etc. However, as even the lightest reading requires some attention, I prefer to switch to music – easy listening is the best so it is not clearly defined – while entering a new field with all the attractions and distractions. Everything is getting so simple, easy going – even a song, like the one on *The Bare Necessities* from the *Jungle Book, is* not really about reducing activities on what is essential but is about enhancing essentials to activities – again, and in another form: appropriation. Actually, although I do it virtually everyday, I don't really like jogging – it is sometimes dangerous (I have stumbled over the root of a tree more than once), sometimes dirty (just running like mad across the dirty country roads on a nasty and wet morning), it is quite dull (as the audio books are not really an intrinsic part of it) – and it is demanding: moving the body of which the engine apparently has to work like the engine of a tractor while ploughing a wet field. Why I do it nevertheless? I like to have it done – just to feel better. But an amazing experience again and again is that jogging with music, rather than with more or less demanding listening and thinking, gives the feeling that everything goes quite easy – the heavy engine of the tractor develops into a light and flexible mechanism, gives the feeling of gliding like a sailing yacht through smooth water – the rhythm of the music fosters the running, the sprint seems to give even more beat to the songs. Any resistance fades away – and allows one to develop more strength, more resistance and *pouvoir.*

Sure, this works in a very complex interaction – individual, rhythm, conditions – all and more go hand in hand to mutually enrich and stimulate each other. And depending on the exact interplay, the results are quite different. As much as we find examples where music is being used as means of subordination – the slave galleys the most expressive example and also illustrated by the Blues and Jazz-culture which emerged as a 'means to cope'. We also find music as a means of protest and resistance – expressive and fostering action. Military marches – fostering, if not forcing cadence and at the very same time focusing on a common goal, giving strength by giving the impression of having something in common: one goal and one step. But also the more or less chaotic culture of the sympathy of the devil[13] – the music and wider cultural scene of the subculture of the 1960s – the merging of a culture of Uncle Tom in his hut[14] – caught in subordination and the search for ways to muddle through the subordination, coping with the blues – with the partisan outcry of a protest culture, ridiculing the ruler by imitation and infestation. Jimmy Hendrix, The Star-Spangled Banner, performed in Woodstock, is a pronounced example in this respect, having earlier expressions in the dodecaphonism ('twelve-tone technique') composed and set in scene by people as Arnold Franz Walter Schoenberg,

---

[13]   Alluding to a song by the Rolling Stones.
[14]   Of course, alluding to Harriet Beecher Stowe's novel Uncle Tom's Cabin or A Life Among the Lowly

Alban Berg and Anton Webern; however, all this is only a culmination of the earlier forms of outbreaks. For instance the rock and roll culture preceding Jimi Hendrix – all started with a more rhythmic stress of resistance which is dormant in the reclusiveness of the blues, creeping into a mainstream protest of the pop culture, culminating in the brisk refutation of the establishment – and finally ending again in the living rooms of the new establishment – the hits of the once protesting Beatles as evergreens played by the Big Bands of the times.

Well, all this is not just a brief – and truncated – history of music and protest. It is also dealing with a fundamental question, namely asking *How many melodies can a society sing at the same time – and how many melodies, how many songs are actually necessary for a society to be one?* A society with only one song will be as limited in its powers to sustain integrity as a society in which too many songs are acted[15] at the same time. And as much as music is a perfect example, expressing this dialectical tension between the two poles of *Aufhebung,* the same tension can be seen everyday – again and again, dealing with 'social' issues as much as it is part of individual life. As much as the rhythm of the music possibly eases the double quick by establishing harmony, it helps as well to build up tensions, makes us think – and find our own rhythms within the orchestra.

– The first morning for me to go to College – everything looks a little bit different now, though I walk the first mile or so the very same way from my flat at the Duna Ucta, as I did the days before. People going to work, the bus, stopping more or less in front of my house spits out a large number of people – that there is no huge gate of an industrial site shows: Budapest, at least Budapest city is not an industrial place though it is without any doubt industrious.

Just after having walked some hundred yards, I see somebody sweeping the pavement – against the wind. Well, there are often many reasons to act against the stream, not going the same way as the many. But it has to be appropriate. In some cases it can and should be done, in some cases it can and should be done though the price may be high, and at the first sight too high. In some cases it is simply impossible – the stream is too strong, only knowing exactly the rules – the undertow and craggedness – can help finding the rules of overcoming the hindrances, of dealing with the obstacles. Good-Will may help, but it cannot move mountains. Freedom is not about living without laws – natural laws, laws of social behaviour, political systems and economic frameworks. Freedom is to know all about the laws and rules, thus

---

[15] Yes, this kind of songs is acted – nobody can simply sing them or perform them on any instrument.

being enabled to deal with them. Freedom of will might suggest different interpretations but freedom suggests different actions, actions aiming for change – and of course, Marx' definition of freedom springs to mind and so do the *Theses on Feuerbach*.

There is a poetic version on the topic – a song by *Bettina Wegener* (thanks, Steph!)

Sind so kleine Hände, winzige Finger dran. Darf man nie drauf schlagen, sie zerbrechen dann.

Sind so kleine Füße mit so kleinen Zeh'n, darf man nie drauf treten, könn' sie sonst nicht geh'n.

Sind so kleine Ohren, scharf, und ihr erlaubt: Darf man nie zerbrüllen, werden davon taub.

Sind so kleine Münder, sprechen alles aus. Darf man nie verbieten, kommt sonst nichts mehr raus. 16

(uncorrected; taken from http://www.c-schulz.de/geburt.htm)

Of course, any society, being built on some kind of homogeneity or cohesion, has to balance carefully the relationship of independence, interdependence and dependence. In this sense it has to look at how many melodies can be played within this one orchestra and how it still remains an overall chorus. Walking further, again passing the large market hall, I have to think again about gipsy music and discrimination of the travelling people. More than once I fell over it – the 'marketisation' of the romantic culture of your travelling people versus the harsh discrimination and defiance of the 'tinkers'; the celebration of our gipsy music and culture versus the betrayal of any rights of the Roma and Sinti living here in my country – the only right being that the neglect is now geared to a people who have a politically more correct denotation; the holocaust that happened in the 'new Germany' where homes of asylum seekers and 'dirty niggers' were burned down by neo-fascists – fathers, mothers and children were killed under the applause

---

16   Free translation – PH:
So small the hands with tiny fingers added. Never beat them as they then will break
So small the feet with tiny, tiny toes. Never ever step on them as then they'll never run.
So small are the ears, sharp – and please accept: Never shout as they'll be deaf from that
So small is their jaws, they'll tell you everything. But never forbid as that might close them forever.

of the national residents – and in the city centres people kindly applauded, listening to the vivid music by black people – and these black children are so sweet, aren't they?

Surprises

Now, thinking about all these contradictions, I finally arrive at *Eötvös Loránd University* – my department – *Szociális Munka és Szociálpolitika Tanszék* – is accommodated in an impressive new building, co-financed by the EU. As said, I meet *István*, otherwise I would not have found the place. And as I ask for apologies when he shows me the office that I do not have to share, he has a kind reassurance for me: *That is the advantage of getting old. – Thanks, István* – He does not see my smirk and I am really grateful, perhaps not especially with regard to the last remark but for the general friendly and warm welcome.

This is my first teaching day as well – I will meet the students early in the afternoon. Of course, after the first introductory remarks (more chitchat than anything else), it is time to ask the students to present themselves – I only had been told that they are 'working somewhere as social workers' and that they sometimes travel long distances from their places of residence and work to attend this course, which they need for their PhD. At this stage they just talk a little bit about their background – from where they come from and where they go to? (you may remember this question?). If I remember it right, just one out of the group is actually working as a social worker. The others are in different positions, mainly with the central or the regional government. *Right* – I am slightly sighing, however in a way that nobody is becoming aware of it. In a way it is the game I had been told I would join. However, the players are poles apart from what had been said – experience matters; the rules are slightly different – the students are not writing and get some additional information, but the lectures should also be some seminary *études;* and the table is altered – despite having a policy background already the experiences are quite different, depending on their nationality (students from Hungary, Italy, Norway) and on the stage they are at (first to third year students of the course). Briefly I close the eyes – a matter of seconds only, just long enough to think: *You didn't know it, but you know it.* The second part of the thought meaning: I know now what it is all about. And it means: I probably know enough to tell them something which is worthwhile and new for them.

These are interesting hours – after struggling for a couple of minutes with appropriateness. After laying some general foundations and talking about methodology, after facing the usual difficulties – we do not need methodology, we have the 'terms', followed by my answer: what you have are flowery phrases, set phrases. But if you want to govern rather than to work for the government, if you want to be in control of a situation rather than rule, if you want to interact rather than act, you need the readiness to question all these lapidary concepts – we enter a debate. Well, at least after I talked for the usual lengthy 1 ½ to 2 hours.

Part of the presentation is concerned with what we may call a historical shift. As said, before we come to that, we talk about methodological questions. I introduce the social quality approach, highlighting that it allows to go beyond social policy as a normative setting of 'being good' and working on 'problems'. Social policy has to be defined rather than taken as matter of the given institutional system. Social policy is not social policy because somebody said this and that is social policy. Social policy is policy that is dealing with the social – thus we have to define what the social is about. A slight disorientation amongst the students; but what harm – roughing up government cadres is not something new for me.

And in a way this leads on to the next surprise – after I had been surprised by what kind of students I would be teaching, and they had been surprised by the outlook that something cannot be taken for granted even if the rich uncle from America or Europe came at the end of the last century, supposedly bringing them all the wisdom. The third surprise is that we are going on to look at differences within the seemingly equal. One of the many terminological traps in which we fall several times a day while talking about social policy is the mixing of terms such as poverty, exclusion and inclusion. Of course, first (at least after the word as such which supposedly was the very first as it is said in the bible) was poverty, simply being concerned with the harshness of not having sufficient resources to maintain oneself. Although this seems to be very simple and a longstanding question we have already several questions arising from here: What are the real needs? What is the appropriate answer of supporting people without creating dependency? What is the responsibility of society and what is the responsibility of the individual? Is society the state? Is it the people or part thereof? Is there anything that civil society has to take responsibility for and if so, which kind of responsibility? What is the role of the Church? Names such as Thomas of Aquinas, Juan Louis Vives and others spring to mind – in terms of time we go back to the medieval ages. And a closer study is interesting as it shows many parallels with the discussions we have today – and discussions as well which we avoid, ousting theses issues on grounds of ideological blindness. Questions of poverty dominated for a long time – Peter Townsend being one of the outstanding colleagues, who showed that, though it is about the lack of resources, it is in combination with this more: deprivation. As such, it is a matter of lack of appropriate control. As much as we found already in the early phases of the discussion – with Aquinas, Vives etc. – despite all the differences and disregarding all the different national policy conclusions, a kind of European debate, we find this as well in the middle/second half of the last century: Peter Townswend's work was complemented for instance in Germany by the *Lebenslage*-concept as promoted by Gerhard Weisser and particularly in France there was a wide debate on this – finally concluding in the rejection of the term poverty. There, not poverty, but social exclusion is at stake. It cannot elaborated how this links into the system of Jacobinist understanding of the state. In any case, it was an important shift, also overcoming ideological differences to some extent – for instance Pierre Bourdieu worked extensively on a new concept, linking poverty, exclusion and inclusion to the availability of different kinds of capital. However, now the European debate was a different one. Whereas in medieval times the debate had been led in the widest sense by representatives of humanist enlightenment, the new European debate was, though originally a somewhat politico-academic debate,[17] now overshadowed and instrumentalised by policy makers. To them, the shift to exclusion was welcome not in terms of a more differentiated approach on the way of combating poverty. Rather, talking about exclusion was kind of 'overcoming poverty'. Looking at the major players in the EU-political debate of the time in question – France, Germany and the UK – the picture has to be drawn with respecting fine lines. In France, the concept of social exclusion followed very much the academic endeavours: poverty – and this is what we are still dealing with. It can only be overcome when it is understood as a matter of disadvantage and exclusion – as a multifaceted occurrence for which the individual cannot be made responsible, but for which society has to be made answerable. Although it had been in France that the term exclusion had been born, it was still understood as a matter of poverty. And as government at the time did not fundamentally question its own responsibility, it was in one way or another a confession of feebleness.[18] Germany found another way out of it – not

---

[17]   One actually could say it had been lead by a kind of 'social reformist academic international', comparable with the national *Katheder-Socialisten* and the *Centralverein für Socialreform* in Germany end of the 1800s/early 1900s.

[18]   Actually it is in state philosophical terms a quite difficult question. As said, the link to Jacobinism plays an important role. This means, however, that there are two readings. The one says, government, state, society etc. neglected the people in question, not giving them sufficient support. The other reading is that the government, state, society etc. had not been able to sufficiently control the individuals, forcing them to integrate (may be that I write something on this in the article which I published together with Frances Zielinski: The Systems of Guaranteeing Sufficient Resources in the Republic of France and the United Kingdom

admitting such weakness. The German government at the time (Kohl) simply declared that poverty cannot exist: Everybody in need has the right to claim benefits and consequently poverty could not be possible – the new slogan was 'overcome poverty'.

Eating with Closed Eyes

How was it possible?

– I remember sitting once with a chap from the German government for lunch – it must have been in the early/middle 1990s. It had been the time when the German government began to move from Bonn to Berlin – still, at the time only few people had been there, including this senior official from the ministry for housing, urban and regional planning etc. His personal portfolio in the ministry was to deal with questions around housing and poverty. We talked about our jobs – kind of general mutual nosing, just as dogs do in general. I won't forget what he said: *Just last weekend I went out for a walk – the usual Sunday family business. I was quite surprised as we walked a different way, not the one we usually take. It had been the first time that I saw there are actually people sleeping rough. We came along a kind of shanty town...* – No, I did not begin to cry, no, I did not shout at him nor did I say something as *Sorry, didn't know. And you actually never told me that you are nearly blind.* As said, at that time he lived there for about three months. It had been in Berlin, actually it had been October. But this October nothing happened – everything remained quiet. The machinery of the government moved on to overcome poverty which did not exist because they did not want to see it. The machinery went on to settle ever deeper in all parts of Germany, promising blossoming landscapes – places which hold today the highest rates of unemployment. As blind as people from governments sometimes are and as visionary they are on other days, I can well imagine that my then partner for lunch would see the blooming field in that part of Germany that looks to others like ghost towns, nicely furbished for a gloomy film.

Progress !?

As much as the German government was keen to see poverty as being overcome, the UK found it easier to accept social exclusion as a new formula – at the end it meant that poverty was not at all a matter in question.

---

of Great Britain and Northern Ireland; in: Herrmann [Ed.]: Between Politics and Sociology: Mapping Applied Social Studies; New York: Nova Science, 2003: 31 – 76). In any case mind, much changed over the last years.

Everybody could be excluded – sure, everybody has the right to sleep under the bridges across the Seine and even the very rich are not excluded there – and sure that the same is true for the Thames. But there are always processes of exclusion – even the very rich person who is bound to the wheelchair is excluded from climbing up the stairs. And of course there are serious issues around this. However, to use exclusion in this way and replacing the debate on poverty by it, means in a way to trim the problem of severe material deprivation as it can be found in the so-called well developed economies.

In a way, for some time exclusion was taken as a compromise, as a formula under which everybody could discuss what was seen as worthwhile to be discussed. All thinkable policy measures could be dealt with under this generalist – and watered-down – formula. It meant as well that another three or four years of programs to combat poverty, sorry to fight exclusion, had been secured. And this meant that progress was made – and was planned as well. The idea was to develop another European programme as a follow-up.[19] This time, however, it was not to do even with exclusion but... – no way to go back to poverty – a notion which actually was now more on the agenda in France then before, after they mentioned the misuse of the exclusion formula. No, the new idea was to focus on integration – the short title of the program was in actual fact PROGRESS. With this, progress was bound to inclusion; and inclusion meant integration – and this meant integration into the labour market.

Progress ?!

It was a long way to develop this – I am standing in front of the class, looking into the faces of the future senior government officials. Being thrown into a world – after the systems changed and occupation by Tesco, M&S, C&A, Auchan, Pennies, BMW, Rover, Nike and all the others – of which they didn't now anything before. How much progress is actually possible for a people who are in time forced to accept a history that is not their own – well, is it not their own?

How many melodies can a people bear as well in terms of different conductors? Though it had been a long time ago – too long to be in any direct way tangible – it is something that affects me. The current situation can only be understood by looking at the recent history – the exhibition of black and white photographs in the Citadel hotel reminds in a frightening

---

[19]   It failed in the middle of the 1990s, but was revived in a modified form just short time ago.

way what happened during fascism – and the massively destroyed city still carries some of the abrasion. The bunker on the top of the hill, three floors, huge, massive and not just in terms of the mere aspect of building, but stating the contrast to what is exhibited in the rooms: the intellectual weakness of a system of which the only means of appropriation was the brisk use of carnage, the suppression of a people which was only kept together by external force anyway.

Supposedly Chişinău, which I visited before, is a city bridging orient and occident. What I never experienced as a strong feature there, is so visible here in Budapest – a walk across the market gives just one expression. And this is just one of the splits which had been so typical for the country: aspects of multiculturalism and multi-nationalism, moments of different religions (the Jews have been a strong group here for many decades) and of different traditions. The various occupations – and with this a kind of disruption between east and west, an inner conflict in terms of belonging. And there was always somebody who openly claimed the role of the conductor – positioning himself in front of an orchestra that did not really want to play the tune.

Of course I am not reminded of fascism as the only occupier. Another 'German' intrusion goes further back. One recent day in Budapest I saw a book on Sissy – this is the nickname for the Austrian Empress.[20] And it is not only this that brings another role of the former Germany back to mind – the 'Vienna coffee houses', the glamorous Opera house which can compete with all other music pavilions of the Austrian monarchy, the literature I see – simply the vast amount of volumes in German language in the antiquarian bookshops and as well in the shops of the LIRBI trade chain. Much of this is linked to one name: von Habsburg. Despite all that I see around, there is 'another something' which tells me how near history is – or should I ask how close history is, then taking the meaning of bone-crushing of the term close? – I am still not sure if it is just one of the dreams – though nightmarish – I apparently have when sitting in one of the old coffee-houses.

Traveller's Rest

– I know that travelling makes it somewhat difficult to maintain a certain stability, to enter into regular relationships – be they in private life or be they a matter of overall identity. But I know as well that travelling, with open eyes establishes relationships – establishes friendships across various borders:

---

[20] Elisabeth Amalie Eugenie, Duchess in Bavaria and Princess of Bavaria (December 24, 1837 – September 10, 1898), of the House of Wittelsbach.

spatial, political, professional... . And it establishes a new relationship to oneself: acknowledging the own smallness, and allowing to see yourself still as being part and parcel of a larger system: executing a role in society and contributing to its development in one or the other direction; being part of the entire history, its largeness, its precincts and its eccentricity.

It is only from here that inclusion, societal integrity – be it sustainable or temporary – can actually be understood – from the new relationship we gain from travelling and which may force us to leave some of the old kith and kin behind.[21]

> *Sind so kleine Augen, die noch alles seh'n. Darf man nie verbinden, könn' sie nichts versteh'n.*
>
> *Sind so kleine Seelen, offen und ganz frei. Darf man niemals quälen, geh'n kaputt dabei.*
>
> *Ist so'n kleines Rückgrad, sieht man fast noch nicht. Darf man niemals beugen, weil es sonst zerbricht.*
>
> *Gerade klare Menschen wär'n ein schönes Ziel, Leute ohne Rückgrad hab', wir schon zuviel.[22]*
>
> *(uncorrected; taken from http://www.c-schulz.de/geburt.htm)*

Sitting again in my room in Brussels I am asking myself – as so often – such questions: integration, history, being part of something. And how much backbone is needed and possible on the one hand. And in which way and to which extent is integration and inclusion possible and necessary – integration and inclusion by way of identity building. Questions usually hidden in every day's work. I remember the students on Monday in Budapest – amazing how easy it is for them to listen, listening attentively as soon as I am talking about something they already know, and how difficult it seems to

---

[21] Though I am talking about travelling in terms of physically moving from one place to another it is not really this – what is more important is the 'life's journey'. The development of personality, the establishing the own character and with this as well the changes of it can well be seen as journey as well – and here the same applies – gaining new friends, establishing new insights can and will mean in many cases to say farewell to others.

[22] Free translation – PH:
So small are the eyes and still they see it all. But never blind them as they will stop them to understand
So small their souls, open, absolutely free. Never shall you torment them, as that will smash the will.
So small the spine, it nearly can't be seen. Never try to bend it as this will break it soon
Clear, straightforward beings – that would be a goal to strive for; people without backbone? We already have enough of them.

be open for something that is entirely new. – It is here in the room on the 3rd floor in the house in the *Rue de Pascale* where the connection of seemingly remote things is coming to my mind: experiences and impressions of living in Budapest, things we talked about in class – in Budapest, Chişinău and Cork – and matters that had been subject of the talks with the representatives of the EUC that afternoon. The question being, can we build a new, now European society although the old society still is a manifest challenge?

It is late – my thoughts mix with memories of the recent cultural event – *The Gala Concert* at the Budapest Opera with one remarkable interlude.

Painters, Conductors and Directors

I am a little bit drowsy, hearing a voice, directed to me: Ti senti bene? Tutto a posto? – Si, ~~Beh~~ beh, soltanto un po' stanco di camminare sempre. Avevo solo bisogno di una pennichella.[23]

Didn't she speak Italian? Am I not in Budapest? My eyes get caught by the letters and logo on my linen bag – right, from there she could assume from where I might come. It is only after some seconds that I find where I am: *a szépmüvészeti museum*[24] in Budapest where I sat down and slept my daily 10-minute-nap (well, daily, if I get the 10 minutes which usually happens four times per year – not much to make good for the nights-sleep – I manage nearly every night to miss that). Looking up again, my eyes get caught by huge posters: *Vincent Van Gogh* and *Rembrandt van Rijn.* Right, the museum, indeed. A truly European place, gathering all the traditions and bringing them together in one place at one time. Or is it the other way round: they had been together – a large Europe which is now more and more dispersed – globalisation, rather than creating one world, evoking a split of competing nations, bound together by 'capital flowing through broadband connections' but only to underline the competition of these states – a competition which is seemingly at least for some time calmed down by what Lenin called something like a temporary equilibrium after the world powers distributed the countries amongst themselves.

Sitting here for a little rest, I remember as well the evening with the Gala Concert in the *Magyar Állami Operaház* (State Opera). Another gathering of Europe, actually of the world. Sure, most of the pieces performed had been European – arias from *Giuseppe Fortunino Francesco Verdi's Nabucco*, from *Amilcare Ponchielli's Gioconda* and *Giacomo Puccini's Turandot*. But taking for instance Wolfgang Amadeus *Mozart*, who could well be in this row and his *Magic Flute* – wasn't it here where he clearly showed the simultaneity of being caught in specific traditions and then again, leaving them, broadening the view by adapting to some extent to and from another world – thus showing his Masonic-enlightened view? What was really remarkable that evening, however, was a symphonic interlude, conducted by a Japanese artist. I cannot remember that I ever heard *Zoltán Kodály's Galántai Táncok* played with such verve. Sitting there in one of the first rows, I could even see

---

[23]   Are you feeling well? Is everything OK with you? – Yes, I am just a little bit exhausted
       from walking all the time. Just needed a little nap.
[24]   Museum of fine arts

the vigour, with which *Ken-Ichiro Kobayashi*, the conductor, lived the pieces – I could even hear him humming the different instruments when they entered the scene. As remarkable as this was – and of course, the music was the most significant when going to a concert – there was something else. When *Ken-Ichiro Kobayashi* entered, the conductor's desk was obviously dislocated, not having the right position, the right height. He kneeled down, a few grips and turns and everything was sorted. This was already an exceptional preparation, or lets say start. Then, the music ended – the usual applause, the usual... . No, the conductor himself walked to the back of the full symphony orchestra. Instead of allowing the audience to celebrate him he celebrated the orchestra – without leader, or with a leader in the background the orchestra did not at all disintegrate, the members did not compete for the now free place in the front and what emerged was the feeling of gratefulness – without knowing whom to thank for what. A new experience – two or more cultures evolving and emerging to something new.

At the End: Who's Head?

Will Europe ever be able to truly and honestly go that way? Or will it be just a new form of capitalism, finding a new temporary equilibrium of distributing power between the rich and excluding the poor and even more: excluding the majority by keeping them in iron cages and keeping them under control of different fetters: some getting golden chains, some silver and bronze, and more and more getting just the pure and rusty iron. And if the latter trend of development is such a strong power is there any sense in still trying to fight for something that can be called just, good, responsible, sustainable society?

There had been another poster – and exhibition in the *szépmüvészeti museum*, not mentioned yet: *Michelangelo Merisi da Caravaggio* and around that name the exhibition of pictures, all dealing with one topic: David with the Head of Goliath. No danger, I am not concerted and I won't enter a biblical exegesis.

I am sitting there, thinking about recent experiences: meetings in Brussels, quarrelling, dealing with tiny things and knowing that any success – if there is any success – will not change the world; the work at the Elte-University, an institution that had been founded in the best spirit of liberalism, standing at the cradle of enlightenment, now being n the 'modern neighbourhood' of T-COM, HP and other multinationals, my Department – *Szociális Munka és Szociálpolitika Tanszék* – a small island in the ocean of biotechnology, IT and others, well funded by the EU; the involvement in a EU-monitoring project – high level project meaning high level of political intervention, undermining any kind of freedom of research (if something like this exists – and I know very well, not least from *Vladimir Ilyich Ulyanov's (= Lenin's) Materialism and Empiriocriticism* and the so-called *Werturteilsfreiheits-Streit* in the German *Staatswissenschaft* [science of the state - see text on the *Developing a Methodology Based on the History of Ideas for Social Professions – The Meaning of the Founding of the State*] – that it cannot exist at all). Sitting there with these reviews of the recent past I am hesitating again: is there any point in going through such trouble and frequent disappointment. Can I really take the responsibility for offering somebody support in going such a way? A more or less precarious career in science, in possibly engaging in political activities – not immediately helping people with their day-to-day concerns but to work for something larger?

Perhaps it is the illusion, searching for a justification of the own failure; perhaps it is the misinterpretation of a hopeless situation in the light of a story from the Holy Scripture which is apt to comfort the weak – a story which I do not really know sufficiently. Or it might be something like a foreordination?

Especially while working on social service research for the European Commission, I feel at least very much in the situation of little David – a feeling simply due to my smallness, facing a huge political machinery on the one hand and on the other hand a largely affirmative research team – affirmative in the strict sense of at least in terms of opportunist behaviour.

I am getting aware of the smallness but as well of the fact that somebody tried – and succeeded. And as much as David's fight against Goliath springs to mind, I could name others: *Don Quijote de la Mancha, Miguel de Cervantes Saavedra's* hero who at least tried – and at the end it was not really getting clear who was the lampooned. *Jonathan Swift's* book on *Gulliver's Travels*. And at the end all much more successful than those who accepted their exclusion as *Daniel Defoe's Robinson Crusoe*.

It is actually interesting to see that all these 'fighting heroes' were actually fighting battles which had been very much fighting their personal battles as battles concerned with societal developments.

Not Getting Lost in a World that is Easily Growing Too Large

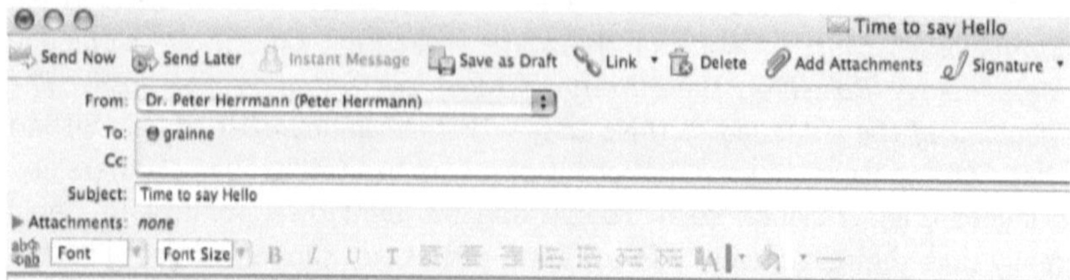

Hi Grainne, how are things. Was sitting yesterday evening in the Central café, listening to some piano music, and was dreaming of an entire world as peaceful as that little place. Actually, it had been the second visit that day - the afternoon I had been meeting with Balazs in the most famous place of town, the Gellert Hotel: nice atmosphere, beautiful chestnut stuff (don't know the name but I do know: it really tasted lovely). He is conservative advisor to the government, part of "my large family", the academic social workers and social policy people of the country. A nice crowed as far I can see as they are extremely diverse, conservatives, technicians ... - and still sticking to their "mother", Zsuzsa, who probably brought me here (though it may actually well be as well that somebody else is behind it - ex post I am wondering how many people I know here).Back to Zsuzsa, a lovely old lady, still active though emeritus - and it seems that she holds the family together. I had been visiting her recently and we had been joined by Katus who is head of the Department. What is the nice thing with this "family": despite all the differences it seems to be possible that people talk to and with each other - rather than talking about each other behind the back of those concerned. And although she was directing the much younger colleague (Katus is probably my age), she did it in a 'non-directive way' (sure, such a term can only be used by somebody who worked for a long time in social work settings). But really, it was a nice and respecting relationship. Sure, I am not full member of the family - language is a real problem here, much worse as my first stumbling after I put my feet on Irish

soil). But it is nice to be in this position for a while – demanding as they are organising so many things, presentations, discussions and debates, just 'relaxed dialogues' on certain topics, but as well some sightseeing. Demanding as well as there are several thing I have to do and I want to do. And without doubt, some of these things are somewhat strange: Why should one go to a Rembrandt exhibition or a Greek music/dance performance in Hungary? Why to a German/Austrian opera or Russian ballet? Well, after having done so I know at least two reasons. The one is simply to experience how "European" and cosmopolitan people had been a long time before EUrope had been invented. The other is that all these exhibitions and performances are different – here, for example they work extensively with light - as Rembrandt van Rijn did himself. Actually, both the Rembrandt engravings and the Caravaggio-exhibition had been more than worthwhile. Teaching here and there are going fine - and so this kind of unsettle live – Moldova, Budapest, Brussels, Lille – is somewhat demanding you know me well enough: though occasionally complaining... – well, as Kremer Balaz said today: at the end we are in a more than privileged situation, a sphere of freedom, of intellectual freedom – strangely enough he, the conservative advisor of today, confirmed what I always say: as well under communist conditions there had been this spirit: a real dispute, a real debate – and looking at today's situation in life, my jobs and jobs as you have in the Health Board up there I am still convinced from my own experiences from the time: probably this freedom was more pronounced then; and not only for people like me.

So far. I hope you are well. I am afraid now that we won't see anymore for a while – at least not before I will return from Florence early next year; will meet my jet-setting daughter there as this poor girl cannot meet her father at any fixed adobe. But she likes it - and Florence is not the worse places to meet. It will give me some, 'excuses' as well to step back from my obligations there.

Drop a line or two if you feel like - and best regards to the yours there and in Kerry, slán go foill,

Peter

Highlights

Sometime ago, when I had been in Paris at 'my headquarters' at the *2 place du Colonel Fabien,* and going to *la fete,* Alain mentioned *Ken Loach's* film *The wind that shakes the Barley;* some weeks before, a colleague in Amsterdam mentioned it – Stephanie, being now the "Irish chick" (I remember too well hearing these words, when people talked about me as the "young Irish man" some ten years ago), might be interested I thought – learning this way something about her new, though temporary home country. And with this, I was getting interested as well. Still, she managed to watch it (though I didn't know) and finally, after trying in Cork, in Dublin, in Amsterdam I managed in Brussels to see it. This is what we Irish are – here and there – our culture, our history – not bad as it is a realist, though gruesome story, causing me to cry as I had to cry when watching *Roman Polanski's The Pianist.* Not bad as well as it stands aside – or goes hand in hand in hand – with the great story tellers: *James Joyce, George Bernard Shaw* – and not least the many story tellers: members of the travelling community, settled farmers passing traditions, knowledge, learning on from generation to generation.

Sure, it is of Greek origin; but not only that I saw *Μίκης Θεοδωράκης'* (*Mikis Theodorakis')* Zorba, the Greek (going back to a novel by *Nikos Kazantzakis)* here in the *Erkel Színház* made it for me a Hungarian experience. There is one scene: the insider of the village not allowed to leave, the outsider not allowed to enter, to join – a tension which reflects very much not just the Greek culture but as well the culture of the place where I live. It is not the encapsulation of *James Augustine Aloysius Joyce's Ulysses*, the story of somebody who is lost in their own country. Zorba is lost between the countries – like a country which is somewhat lost between two more or less fundamentally different worlds: orient and occident.

Another country, being of some relevance in my daily life – preparing the trip with the course, preparing my own trip earlier next year and some other links in the framework of a new cooperation. Summer sun, skiing during the winter – despite these nice memories my thoughts go to *Giovanni Boccaccio's Decameron*, to *Michelangelo di Lodovico Buonarroti Simoni* and the Florentine Arts, as well to Giordano Bruno, and *Galileo Galilei* – and of course, the Catholic church, here not being state church but – in a way it is justified to say so – being the state itself.

Three countries – three cultures – three ways of expressing and dealing with life in arts. Three different societies and understandings of what holds them together. Sure, it is a daring theses – still, perhaps worthwhile to think about it – a basis on which an understanding of who and what we are can be developed – depending on where we are (from), constructing our own, personal borders, our own personal identity not least on the basis of the identity of the countries – liked or disliked, but being the subject matter of our permanent objective practical reasoning.

And in this sense we are still dealing at home with the frontier going through the country, subtle and not in any way visible in every day's life – but still there, perhaps even in the reminder by the chime being heard from so many churches – translating *Ernest Hemingway's For Whom The Bell Tolls* into an Irish version *From Where Does The Bell Get The Chime*. And looking at the economy, there is still much influence from this – the permanent reproduction of the colonialist and peripheral situation, the godfather perhaps replaced by the Big Brother. And of course, all this shapes life – of society and in the living rooms. Not least, in a society with this kind of 'inner border' another inner border could never develop as fundamentally determinant: the border of classes. And this border is actually only today gaining virulence – paradoxically at a time when some speak not just from the meaninglessness of classes but want to convince us of *The End Of History*.

Here, we do not have such an inner border – our border is going through the country as well but it is a border of which one can say that we are 'sitting on it'. Hungary is obviously a country which is living on the border between orient and occident. Supposedly, looking at the annals of the city of Chişinău, this had been much more the case there. Still, here it is something visible – walking through the huge market hall at the end of the *Vací Ucta* one can see, feel, smell the cultures – not clashing, not fully merging; not peacefully at each one's side and not quarrelling, *fluctuat nec mergitur*[25] – in any case colourful and enigmatic in the same way as it is when one enters one of the most beautiful Turkish Baths, the *Rudas fürdö*. And it is beautiful – though to fully enjoy it, one has to repressing that it is only since April of this year women are allowed to enter the Turkish bath – and only on grounds of a threatening lawsuit: feminists claimed their right to enjoy the bath which had been renovated with huge amounts of Forint. Is it just the colourful strangeness which gives me the impression? Or is it my 'personal involvement' in the history of this country: The German, who is in one way or another linked to the conquest by the *Habsburg* monarchs, subduing the county under the patronage – the strange mix of subordination and mercy? Or is it the awareness that there is a strange tradition continuing: the Turks conquering Hungary, being defeated; the Habsburgs taking over – *Otto von Habsburg*, claiming to be European and being European in the sense that he is one of those for whom Europe means the subordination under *Habsburgian* rule and under the rule of Western capital.

– The diversity of colour, the exciting variety of a life on the border, as well the tensions and contradictions eclipses: In the shop – the Penny-supermarket, which I know too well from my German past – standing in the queue, I am looking at the goods, the guy in front of me bought: amongst it *Greek table vine* as I can see from the label – it is good to know languages, isn't it – making it possible to survive while on the move. And the label clearly states it: *Griechischer Tafelwein*. The old *Habsburgian* spirit though wrapped in different paper. – And, again, it seems that everybody is perfectly served: *Aldi, Tesco, Auchan...* – of course, nearly all working, with PC, the *Intels* and *Microsofts...*

So it may well be that this is as well the end of living on the border. And by what will such pattern be replaced? Perhaps by living on another border: the border between an actively lived past and a contemporary situation that is "lived by others", degrading subjects to objects – leaving the question open what the difference is between being *Subject to Her Majesty, the Queen* and being *Object in the Iron cage of Bureaucracy and Commodities of Super-Brands*, including of course the *Pennys, Lidles , Dunnes* for the less well-off.

In a nutshell,

---

[25] 'tossed by the waves, she does not sink'

- nation building in Ireland can be seen as beginning from the 'separation', after being excluded within a nation

- nation building in Hungary can be thought as homogenising processes of a nomadic people and a people that is 'integrated' from different sides and regimes – between *Aga Khan* and the *Habsburgs;* finally

- nation building in Italy as bringing and keeping together the different and independent under a wide umbrella – loosely coupled and coupled by vagueness – the inner borders made possible and qualified by the one common border: the empire of God, represented on earth by the Roman Empire. And perhaps it was actually its fall which made possible to maintain itself: though wrong in strict terms of nationality, it was Italy which paved large part of the way to European modernity.

Sure, there are shortcomings, open questions: Hungary is actually quite nationalist, seemingly contradicting a pattern of living on the border; Italy is strongly coined by class structure – and the open dealing with it; and despite the unification by looseness of the bonds is strongly hit as well by separatist notions – South Tyrol, the Mezzogiorno with the *Mongibello (Mount Etna)* which may have a metaphorical meaning as well in political terms; the Pagan Catholicism of a movement that claims to be not only anti-imperialist but as well socialist.

Bertolt Brecht once wrote a poem titled Questions of a Reading Worker,[26] the last lines reading

---

[26]   Wer baute das siebentorige Theben?
In den Büchern stehen die Namen von Königen.
Haben die Könige die Felsbrocken herbeigeschleppt?
Und das mehrmals zerstörte Babylon -
Wer baute es so viele Male auf? In welchen Häusern
Des goldstrahlenden Lima wohnten die Bauleute?
Wohin gingen an dem Abend, wo die Chinesische Mauer fertig war
die Maurer? Das große Rom
Ist voll von Triumphbögen. Wer errichtete sie? Über wen
triumphierten die Cäsaren? Hatte das vielbesungene Byzanz
nur Paläste für seine Bewohner? Selbst in dem sagenhaften Atlantis
brüllten in der Nacht, wo das Meer es verschlang
die Ersaufenden nach ihren Sklaven.

Der junge Alexander eroberte Indien.
Er allein?
Cäsar schlug die Gallier.
Hatte er nicht wenigstens einen Koch, bei sich?
Philipp von Spanien weinte, als seine Flotte
Untergegangen war. Weinte sonst niemand?

Exclusion, then, has not least something to do with exclusiveness – the uniqueness of finding ways of inclusion, of founding and maintaining identity.

Living (in) History

Saturday, after the conference on minimum standards, part of an international project, I meet *Zsuzsa* and *John Veit-Wilson*. A little excursion to *Szentendre*, a little old village near Budapest. We park the car near the little stream and walk across the small market – again, the fresh smell of vegetables and fruit; and of course, for me as vegetarian less pleasant, the smell of the various animals: dead and (nearly) ready to eat. It is the start of a very touristy enterprise through this rather small village – a place where many artists settled; John is especially interested if it is comparable with the *German Worpswede,* near *Bremen* – as well a village which has been flooded by artists. It was in the same period of the time, a similar setting as both are small places, though near to larger agglomerations. Later it turns out that John, actually coming from *Newcastle* has a German and so he is quite familiar not only with German language but as well with German culture – and colleagues I know from the time I worked in *Bremen* and *Bielefeld: Stephan Leibfried, Lutz Leisering, Franz-Xaver Kaufmann.* – Another form of European encounter. Another form, as it shows that these movements, crossing borders take place since a long time already. This is something one tends to forget, always thinking about the new character, although one might even be one of the moved and moving people); it is something we forget as easily as forget the small movements and developments: coming

---

Friedrich der Zweite siegte im Siebenjährigen Krieg. Wer
Siegte außer ihm?
Jede Seite ein Sieg.
Wer kochte den Siegesschmaus?
Alle zehn Jahre ein großer Mann.
Wer bezahlte die Spesen?
So viele Berichte.
So viele Fragen.

to any place that is new for us we tend to think it had been this way for ever, including thinking of the people we meet there as being always the same: seeing our neighbours as already being there and the same for ages.

This Saturday, we visit churches, gazing at the icons and talk about the different influences: *Greek orthodoxy, Serbs, Turkish, Russian orthodoxy, socialism* but as well the old *feudalism;* secular and religious. We go as well to the little museum, the exhibition of the sculptures of *Margit Kovács.* Finally, we end up in a restaurant, having a late lunch – or an early dinner. At this stage *Zsorka Tóth* joined us. Sitting there in a very traditional place, eating trout, geese (finally it is "goose time", around St Martins) and roasted vegetables, drinking vine – well, celebrating the drinking of vine in a manner that makes even me as somebody who does not drink it felling part of it the history comes back. Still, it is a paradox: The history is our own history – as different as we are and our histories are; it is diverse and linked. Three generations, not feeling as being apart though we have different and even contradicting views, we have entirely different styles of life; however, acknowledging the differences and being able to argue, we feel the strong bounds – being part of a jigsaw, integrating to a picture in its own right.

It is like so many things which impressed me during the day: All the variety which came together in this tiny place: different religions, different ethnic groups... – at the time people had been perhaps equally worried and complaining about the same: civilising as standardising. Finally even baroque is baroque even if it is a Hungarian one; and even the *Jugendstil* is nothing so special, even if the English language uses the term art nouveau to have at least a name for what was part of the culture as well on the island in the late 19th and early 20th centuries – something which flooded Europe at the times, perhaps in a similar way as today the supermarket chains.

– It is already late, dark outside, the smell of the wood in the fireplace drowning the smell of the tobacco. The music gets more 'aggressive', more demanding. A quarrel of the landlord with a drunken guy is irritating; still it has some strange effect. After he was, well, let say guided to the door, asked to leave, the others are getting up as well – from the neighbouring tables, and we get up as well. Leaving because of the unpleasant interruption? On the contrary: time was flying in a relaxed atmosphere – debating, singing, making plans for future projects or discussing existing plans of the others and singing again. It is only late that evening, that we return to Budapest – not drunken from the vine, but from being together with all these different people, from different ways of life, different age, different national backgrounds.

Being already in bed I remember a question I asked earlier: Can I really take the responsibility for offering somebody support in going such a way? A more or less precarious career in science, in possibly engaging in political activities – not immediately helping people with their day-to-day concerns but to work for something larger? I think I can take the responsibility. Actually I think I have to take the responsibility – it is a way some people have to go, and if they are well able to do it they should go it, not disregarding private concerns but reinterpreting them.

– fluctuat nec mergitur

Feudalism – Capitalism — Modern Times

It is somewhat strange that in a village as *Szentendre* we get easily the impression that historical borders, the borders of epochs get blurred, that we need historical monuments to get aware of presence. And in such comparative perspective we are getting aware of presence as 'lived topicality', but as well as presence as part of history – a step which is following predecessors; and a step which has successors if we do not follow a suggestion of the end of history.

However, just living this presence, concentrating on this timeliness we are rarely getting aware of historicity. Perhaps in the odd moments, meeting people whom we get to know as contemporary witness of something that is something of the past. And occasionally we might get aware of it as well in situations where we have a kind of personal intuition: This had been different when... – Is it a kind of 'natural protection', shielding us against an overwhelming complexity? Protecting us against the insight or impression that we are in historical terms even smaller than the tiniest grain of sand in relation to the desert? Or is it an ideology keeping us intentionally small, prevent that we claim changes? Or is it just a kind of blindness – again guard, here in the sense of better not knowing too much about things we cannot change or we can at most change very little?

It had been Friday that Alice called me – I mentioned her before. *Do you have time on Monday morning? For a meeting here at the Red Cross?* I agreed although I didn't really want to go to this meeting, not really seeing the point of it. On the other hand I had to accept – I didn't want to let Alice down, I didn't want to act against one of the principles of ESOSC, my institute – the principle being: *We are not working, we are networking.* And there was an additional – perhaps even the most exciting, tempting point: some kind of childishness, of mischievous inquisitiveness. Ever thought about the devil that hates god as the holy water and nevertheless is tempted to peep around the corner to see HIM (may be to detect that HE is a SHE)? Ever thought about god for whom the devil does not exist and for whom the encounter with his counterpart is an irresistible temptation? – Sure, there is a serious dimension to it: poles of any contradiction do get their own identity from their counterpart by which they are defined as one side of the contradiction. As much as the devil is not simply defined as the evil as such, and god not as the good as such but they are defined as opposites as much they are defined by each other – and depend on each other. The same as with the worker – as wage-worker – who cannot exist without the owner of capital and the owner of capital who cannot exist without the worker as wage-worker though their relationship is of antagonistic nature. The difference with the two entities of contradictions – devil and god; wage-worker and capital owner – is that we seriously do not know about the power of god and devil whereas we know about the power of proletarian/proletariat and bourgeois/bourgeoisie.

Stories – Hi-Stories

Not sure, which role to take – or which role I am given in history – most likely nearer to the devil than to god; no harm – as said, the power question is not yet solved anyway.

I meet Alice at *Ferenciek Tere* Metro station. As I could assume from our previous meeting, she arrived late, a little bit hectic and calm at the same time. The usual welcome rite; she buys the tickets and does not accept that I pay – again: as I could assume from meeting her previously; we went down the 'high-speed moving stairs', definitely nothing for people who are not even frail but just a little bit insecure, even tired.

After two stations we leave the train, and walk – after managing another high-speed-escalator – we reach the exit, walk across the *Arany János Utca*, and enter the large building of the *Red Cross*. It looks a little bit tatty – not only from outside. Alice introduces me kindly – and informally – to the colleagues with whom she shares the office. I accept the offered coffee – although Alice and the colleagues in her office say something as *Well, you might wait as well as you will get a coffee later, a much better one.* After sitting down, looking through some documents – *Red Cross* stuff from 1908, 1930 and 1938 – Alice turns towards me: *I'll be back in a second, just going there first on my own.* And it is not much more than a second – she returns and we walk along the long corridor, open one of the large, padded doors: a nice, well furnished office, I am introduced again: *Dr Peter Herrmann, visiting professor at the Elte University, he is lecturing at Cork and founder and director of an independent European research institute – he was scientific advisor to the project on Quality and Accessibility of Social Services for Social Inclusion.* Well, she just uses the acronym QUASI. The general secretary kindly answers with some more or less empty flowery phrase – however, I positively mention her strong handclasp: apparently a determined women. We stand already in a little corridor behind the office; the general secretary opens another door – I can only glimpse into the next room, see somebody walking, shaking friendly but dissenting the head. But only a minute later or so the door is opened from inside. A more or less young (well, probably my age), dynamic man comes towards me: *Entschuldigen Sie, ich hatte gerade noch einen Telefonanruf bekommen. Nun, manchmal... Aber seien Sie nun ganz Herzlich*

Willkommen.[27] I do not feel insecure, hearing the voice speaking pure German –without the slightest accent or dialect. But I feel uncomfortable knowing Alice at my side who – as far as I am aware – does not speak German. Can we simply exclude her? We enter the large office: a large wall unit at the one end, a desk with most beautiful inlay work, the bright timber shines in the light which comes through the wide windows. The beautiful large carpet still allows to see at the sides that underneath is a not less beautiful wooden floor. *Setzen Sie sich bitte.* I follow and take the seat and while the host briefly goes to the door, to exchange some words with the General Secretary, Alice tells me *It is fine, I understand German – sufficiently. I cannot speak it though.*

Still, I feel uncomfortable – there is another reason. It is not that I fear the president of the *Red Cross* as it is he who is my host for the next hour or so. It is not fear – but it is the feeling or even knowledge that I entered a reality that does not exist anymore or at least that should not exist further, a reality to which I nevertheless have to grin and bear it. Finally, he sits down as well: *Georg von Habsburg* (well, the sign at the door says György), one of the sons of *Otto von Habsburg.* Of course, I know sufficiently from my own studies in history about the *Habsburgs.* Still, in preparation of this visit I looked for some information, more 'personal stuff' – and there are some 'details' that I did not know, better: I had not been aware of, even better: one cannot grasp while using just common sense and so one pushes them aside. At the end of 2006, at times when social science contemplate about democracy, governance and complex mechanisms of political steering, at times when the *European Union* talks about an *Open Method of Coordination* as means of political planning and approaching a 'higher form of democracy', at a time when the same *Union* considers a new Treaty, now as *Constitutional Treaty* at such time we have to admit on the other hand that we did not even arrive at the basic, crude parliamentary democracy. We are still far away from the basic principles of what had been written on the *drapeau tricolore* of the French revolution, supposedly standing at the cradle of the modern Europe. Europe, instead of being truly based on this 'unity of trinity', the parole of *liberté, égalité, fraternité* is still dealing with the old ruling class, the unity of the power in one hand, supposedly given by god:

---

[27] *Sorry, I just got another phone call. Well, sometimes …; But now, be warmly welcome*

House of Habsburg-Lothringen		
Born: 20 November 1912; Died:		
Titles in pretence		
Preceded by: **Karl I**	* NOT REIGNING * *Emperor of Austria* (1922-) * **Reason for Succession Failure:** * Empire abolished in 1918	**Incumbent** *Designated heir:* *Archduke Karl*
Preceded by: **Charles IV**	* NOT REIGNING * *King of Hungary* (1922-) * **Reason for Succession Failure:** * Kingdom abolished in 1918	**Incumbent** *Designated heir:* *Archduke Karl*
Preceded by: **Charles III**	* NOT REIGNING * *King of Bohemia* (1922-) * **Reason for Succession Failure:** * Kingdom abolished in 1918	**Incumbent** *Designated heir:* *Archduke Karl*

(from: http://en.wikipedia.org/wiki/Otto_von_Habsburg - 13/12/2006)

The reason mentioned for 'succession failure' has to be qualified. Though it is correct that he 'did not get the job', it is exactly this *Otto von Habsburg*, the father of my vis-à-vis, who allows that on the 'authorised honorary site' (http://otto.twschwarzer.de/ - 13/12/2006) we read under his portrait: Christ, Kaiser, Europäer – Christian, Emperor, European. It is this individual who represented an extreme conservatism in the European Parliament. And though I do not know the material situation of this family, I know that many28 of his aristocratic colleagues still own tremendous reservoirs of land, estates, well translated into power. As such they are even in the early 21st century ruling as the old gentry. – Don't say that the emperor is out of office – though he is in formal terms, he found his new premises. Although much of this is Kafkaesque, my further browsing comes to the point where incensement, rancour, disdain – helplessness just stop me to go any further. He, the European, he who actually was living during fascism in exile because his nationalism rejected that German nationalism reigned in Austria rather than his own chauvinism.... – just one mouse click away from being near to cry or heave: http://www.pro-monarchie.de/ – a rational answer is not possible.

– Perhaps it is personal sensibility, the overreaction by somebody who has close friends who hardly survived fascism, the sentiment of somebody who fought together with them against a resurrection of a system of which the conditions had been still alive and are still not overcome in a fundamental

---

[28] Sure, there is as well the impoverished aristocracy. And there are even rich aristocratic individuals, rich on grounds of work ...

way; a system not much else than an aristocratic system built on a different foundations.

Still, can I blame *György*, the son, for all this? – Despite my general anger and bitter feeling I try to be as open, as impartial as possible. He should have the same right as I claim to have – my father is a 'historical contingency' and although I cannot deny the connection to him, I do not want to be too closely linked to him. Not by myself and not by others. Even more, there are aspects which are... – well, another opportunity to talk about god, the devil and contradictions.

My readiness to maintain openness is limited however – and I am not sure if it is very limited or if he is fast in reaching them. Of course, we talk about the situation in the different countries, here meaning Hungary and Ireland. And it is of course especially Hungary, that is standing in the centre – finally it is here where we are, and my only idea of making some use of this meeting is getting at least some information, some views of what is going on in the country that I cannot learn from books and the people I am usually working with. And another idea is, to try to possibly succeed in some kind of lobbing. Actually, Alice asked me to try to go this way. The socio-economic situation in the country is – in many regards – seemingly very similar to what I know from other countries, in general: reduced resources and at the same time increasing demands, as well increasing need for changing the existing structures.

Many patterns are actually quite similar to the situation in Ireland. A bulk of different benefits and legislations, instead of providing a strategic approach to social policy there is a bulk of different 'gap filling mechanisms', jumping from one to the other, looking for short term 'solutions' rather than providing any holistic approach. And of course, the system dos not look for a systematic approach of tackling the fundamental ways of how society integrates; instead, it looks at how individuals can be integrated. Such approach has another fundamental advantage with regard to social rights interpreted form a capitalist perspective. The citizen degrades, being only a participant in exchange processes; the social power of people degrades, making them responsible individuals, responsible for their own social situation and the polis degrades to the market – finally...

New Feudalism

... finally we are looking again for the deserving poor and the undeserving poor, blaming the victims – the victims whom I will see the other day, crouching in a corner of the train station of *Debrecen:* forced to live a life without power, perhaps even without will, just vegetating and driven by the last tiny sparkle to follow needs of a body which is not ready to give up –

men and women being condemned to be objects rather than given the right to be subject.

There is a frequent debate on poor people, 'clients' and 'users of services' being actors themselves – being despite their 'needs' and 'disadvantages' subject and able and willing to act. Here I see a situation where I am in doubt. It seems to me that these people have been pushed aside to such an degree that they lost such capability, that they are just struggling to survive, using the term from Italian history: not being *popolo minuto*, but popolo magro. In other words, being less than small people, being lean. With reference to Marx we can say as well, whereas the proletariat does not have anything to loose than the chains of capitalist servitude, the people I see here do not have even these chains.

As abysmal as these living standards are, there is one thing that strikes me. We are usually – and rightly – talking about the relative character of poverty and again and again. Though questionable, we hear that even the poorest in the 'developed world' are actually better off than the moderately poor in the so called 'developing countries'. Instead of entering a dispute about this, comparing quantitative figures there is another point we frequently forget. What we are actually talking about is not only and perhaps not primarily the right to access sufficient means; rather it is about the right to be human being and this means to be a social being – the participation as being part of, taking a part of and taking part in something. This is as well about mutual support, about solidarity and cohesion. Or in other words: it is about socio-economic security, inclusion, cohesion and empowerment. Thus arriving at Social Quality as

> the extent to which people are able to participate in the socio-economic, cultural, juridical and political life of their communities under conditions which enhance their well-being and individual potentials for contributing to societal development as well.

Seen in this light we can see that any comparative perspective has to be understood as well and primarily from a historical perspective. And as much as this means to look at individual actors it is more to look at how the various historical actors act within the given structures. It is a complex network of national and international relations, of individuals and groups. And it is about power relationships. As much as it is possible to understand actions and developments, as little is the possible to actually change and consciously change the system according to purely rational rules. And still, the understanding is so important for any kind of progress, of executing influence.

Let it be!

By now the scene changed. After the meeting with the president of the *Hungarian Red Cross,* I had to rush to be in time back at the University for lecturing. This time it had been an interesting debate, engaging in a dispute about the value – and the standards, the measurement tools of comparative research. Still, as interesting as it is I have to conclude at four o'clock sharp, still having a long day ahead – the driver, bringing me to the airport is waiting already. I do not have much time: check in, going to the gate, boarding to Munich, going on from there to Brussels where I will arrive only after midnight, walking through the drizzle to the hotel. Two conference days ahead, some interviews for a project – some are arranged, some are just possible by getting hold of people who are passing by: members of NGOs who attend the same conference. Stephanie joined me, arriving earlier than I did from Cork, takes some notes, helps to prepare the workshop in which we are involved, discussing *The political role of social services providers in defining and negotiating social values.*

When we left the last meeting, it is already Thursday of the week and it was a political meeting of a steering body of a large organisation, Richard asked if we would be exhausted – though I do not really know if he is serious about it and how others feel, I personally do not really agree: Ok, three days: one conference, one meeting of a political body and a couple of interviews for a research project; commenting on some essays, little bit writing at night and some other things. Still, one nice evening in delightful company, another evening ahead and looking forward to the nice company – these are actually days which are more or less on the 'holiday side of life'. (It is strange, by the way, that such company is remarkable as amongst people working in the social field we find a relatively low rate of socialising amongst each other: a rather strict division of 'work' and 'life', probably the reason that they speak more about 'work-life-balance' than people in other jobs do.) Anyway, despite the nice things I can enjoy, there is probably another reason for not feeling exhausted – it is concerned with something that makes these meetings exhausting for others: I know what it is about and I do not play this game which is frequently called politics. Or lets express it another way: For me politics is about taking position – a position I am convinced of; for others it may be more about getting into a position – a position that is estimated, has reputation, is perhaps even well paid.

In the evening we go through the illuminated city – some distraction, and some 'food for thought': enlightenment is about thinking, isn't it? So really not physically nor in terms of huge intellectual requirements there is something which is exhausting these days from Monday to Friday: The farewell. Is it just the usual end-of-the-year melancholy? Like a child standing in front of a window, full of Teddy bears, the nose pressed against the cold glass – the excitement of not knowing if they will be once jumping out of the window. Is it the fear they come out one day and loose their sparkle? It is probably this – and it is something else too. The feeling linked to all this is – in politics, policies, solidarity, friendships – that there seems to be more and more something which is out of control. On the first day, during the conference titled *Social Values and Democracy: Renewing the guiding principles of the European Union* it seemed quite clear: there are others – people and structures – that give us terms, that provide definitions and we simply are asked to accept them. *Agenda setting power* – is the term in political science. And this may be, then, that we are talking about democratic processes – and a colleagues from Bulgaria and Ireland jointly said last week, during a conference I attended in Budapest: *Well, we are allowed to sit around the table. But we have to agree in advance.*

In politics it is quite easy – at least as long as one has skin like an elephant: not easy to be hurt as far as it can be seen. That it is a permanent struggle of staying and leaving does not interest anybody – and seems to be fine. What is unbearable however is the illusions we get: illumination without light. Illumination as illusion. Being involved and gaining power – and seeing at the end of the day: nothing is changed. *Niklas Luhmann*, who was one of my teachers, once said: *we know more and more – and as more as we know, as more the possibility to change something shrinks.* Perhaps I can add from my perspective: *We are more and more involved into political processes, we get increasingly involved in processes of political debates and as more as this is the case and as more political processes are defined in technical terms as less we can impact.* Perhaps the long chains of interdependence are beginning to wear out. Everything and anything, all and everybody have to be confronted with the question *Will we see again?* And it seems that the answer *Perhaps never* is the most appropriate – still allowing us once during the year, at its end to see again in a festive mood. In such a mood we do not need real understanding – the sociology of *Max Weber,* the *interpretative sociology* in every day's life.

– I am walking across the *Grote Markt.* A little bit more than twelve hours ago it showed all the glimmer of the lights – a special Christmas decoration which actually made me the first day aware of the beauty of so many gable of the old patrician houses which I passed so many times before. Was it the Christmas illumination or something else? Now, when there are no lights, while I am walking to the train station, I try just to walk – the drizzling rain was apt, reflecting and underlining a quite miserable mood. During the last couple of days I frequently had to think about something I read near the exit of the *Anne Frank House* in *Amsterdam: Why we are so worried about the fate of this one child, admittedly hard; however just being one amongst thousands and thousand of people who had been tortured and killed during the tyranny of German fascism? It is because we could not cope with all of them – it simply would drive us crazy.* Such an important hint – the individual – not forgetting the masses, and in a way standing as their representative. But still, another question is: how much can we cope alone with all this – be it such extremes, but as well the small things of daily life? – Farewell, welcome to the new; trying to be wise.

Will we see again? Definitely not as young as we are now... – but perhaps in a world that we can still lead to wisdom?

And when the broken hearted people
Living in the world agree,
There will be an answer, let it be.
For though they may be parted there is
Still a chance that they will see
There will be an answer, let it be.
Let it be, let it be. Yeah
There will be an answer, let it be.
Let it be, let it be,
Whisper words of wisdom, let it be.

Let it be, let it be,
Whisper words of wisdom, let it be.

Such wisdom requires probably a lot of the seemingly unwise – something which cannot put into any toolbox of life. – And as usual I am struggling: Is it worthwhile to go this way? Are the tiny changes which might be possible worthwhile all these permanent struggles?

Let It Be?

I am at *Brussels' gare de midi,* waiting for the *Eurostar* which will bring me to *Lille* in *France,* a quick trip, spending a day and a half with friends, discussing the latest developments of politics in France – one of the more or less rare opportunities to get directly involved in 'our matters' – being German, living in Ireland, working in Hungary and being member of a party in France... Globalisation is not only a capitalist matter – the difference: for capital it definitely makes sense as capital is interested in short term profit. Maintaining a long-term perspective is less simple. – After sipping my coffee, I move on, passing the border control – nearly as strict as on airports. The arrogance of the police; and my powerlessness. Guards are leading a small group of people through a back transit – handcuffs, well: strings with which the hands are bound together show what it is about: deportation – in the middle of our open and democratic Europe – cynicism creeps over sadness and disorientation. I won't to cry, to shout – and I feel paralysed, alone. Was it two weeks ago? I talked to *Jerome Vignon*. It had been on the previous trip to *Brussels*. Jerome mentioned a book from a colleague from Munich: *I came across it by luck – really interesting. The title is 'The Enabling Social Europe'. I will send you the author's name.* Only briefly later, just back in Budapest then, I received his mail with the details of the book. Indeed: *The Enabling Social Europe.* Being now in the middle of what happens at the *gare de midi,* I would like to know the author of the book which is relevant here, the title perhaps being *Undividable Human Rights – But Who Defines Who is Human Being.* It may be another *Aristotelian* dimension to current politics. The old Greek philosopher was fighting for democratic and social rights for the citizens – and he was supportive as well of treating slaves well and sociable. But still, he denied their rights as they had not been citizens. The same old story? Today we – perhaps too many of us – are looking as well for rights for the citizen and for 'treating others well'. Too few of us, however, are fighting for rights – for rights for all. For rights of the past, the present and future – as the meetings over the last couple of days showed again: it is so difficult to talk at the same time about structure and actor and process.

As I wrote elsewhere, talking about social professional activity (SPA):

Developing the before presented methodological framework further, is a self-referential and self-reflexive process. This simply means that detailing and weighing criteria can only emerge from already applying the historical analysis, by this enabling us to develop the foundation further theoretical and then more detailed historical analysis. Thus, SPA can be localised dialectically as part of the process of socialisation.

To conceptualise socialisation and the models of socialisation – and aiming by this on developing a framework for the analysis of SPA – has to start, however, by analysing the reality on which the theoretical thinking is grounded, which it mirrors. To truly understand the different contractualist ideas we first have to understand the conditions and their development from where and as part of which they emerge and into which they provide an input, actively influencing contemporary developments.

Focusing on SPA then means to approach such activities from three sides, namely

- *from their self-understanding, however developing this*
- *from the general framework of soci(et)al development and*

- *developing an understanding of how this general soci(et)al development is concretised.*

*(Herrmann, Peter: Developing a Methodology Based on the History of Ideas
for Social Professions – The Meaning of the Founding of the State. Meta-
Theoretical Perspectives for Developing a Methodology for an International
Approach; 2006 – unpublished: 113)*

I feel a little bit lost, alone; looking for the author of the book I just titled imaginatively *Undividable Human Rights – But Who Defines Who is Human Being?* The author of the book in which human beings are deported and only few act against those who are responsible. And even less do it publicly – I am angry with myself for not getting up, standing against the police force.

Rationales and Rationalities

The exhausting part of examining who the author is, is actually not the search itself but the fact that we frequently look for it by going the wrong way. As hopeless it is to buy milk in the basket and carry a huge pile of firewood in a paper bag, it is not more promising to search for an explanation of irrational systems by looking for their rational structure. Sure, there is a rationale behind and within them; but that does not mean that such rationale is rational. – Ever tried to connect in the following graph all dots with not more than four lines in one go?

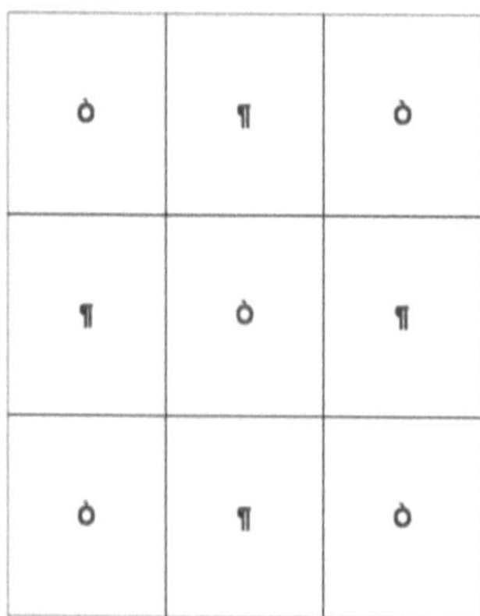

The solution is quite simple: Never get caught in cages – don't get caught in traps you define yourself or in those that are defined by others. I could say as well: if others argue with rationales do not try to counter their arguments with rational advice. All the scientific games are finally about power – power rather than correctness is truth.

Finally, not only the last days on the political stage reconfirmed this. Being back home for one day now, I had been reassured another time, well, to be precise: twice that we are talking about interests rather than pure reason. The morning I had to give a public lecture – a good preparation for next days exercise in the east of the country. Title – I had been stupid enough to propose this complex topic myself: *Ireland as Enlargement Country of the 70s. A showcase for member states of the last round of enlargement?* Of course, most of it had been concerned with Irish issues – and the interest in the question if and what can be done for the country that only recently joint the Union. I talked about the history – the situation at home before 1973 and the development afterwards. Policies and politics. The early development, just after joining; and the later experiences and the showcase: the tiger. And I mentioned the claws, leaving behind terrible injuries to the entire system, to what is called social fabric and with it to so many individuals: crisis and stagnation, boom and new stagnation though now on a higher level. The audience was quite curious – mostly colleagues from the department; interested in the reality behind the glossy stories that are used by politicians to fuel competition and free market ideology. But then, some said as well: *Good to know; but do not tell it to anybody; we are using so many of the 'good examples' for influencing our politicians.* Well, fair enough. But can we establish progress on this basis? Can we force systems to behave by using such approaches, systematically denying reality, or at least part of the reality?

I talk about similar aspects later in class with my PhD students – and I conclude, after listening to their 'summary views' on what the EU means: To make any changes we are probably most successful, entering the system, fighting for small internal changes and acting along the lines of the given agenda. However, with this we may be able to improve the given situation. To change it, will be more complicated and we have to go a somewhat thorny way: leaving the agenda aside. I make a link between this and something we frequently talked about in class: the discussion about welfare regimes and the deficiencies of these debates. It is of crucial importance to improve these systems: change the 'breadwinner models'. However, we have to question as well the breadwinner model in more fundamental terms: What is the role of employment, what is work and what is the entire economic system about. Can we sufficiently deal with the contractualist models as I proposed elsewhere? Or do we have to go further? Can the elaboration of the regulationist approach do suffice – or at least help in developing an understanding? In any case: Never get caught in cages. Still, I tell the students as well – frankly and with some kind of multiple bitterness: *If you want that somebody to listen, fight for changes by following the agenda; if you want to really change something, don't expect people to listen – they hopefully will get it after a while, you need a long breath and you will permanently learn; not least learn to understand.*

After lecturing I return to the office. The usual tiny business; a lengthy phone call with *Stephanie* – the last of this kind, as *'ESOSC moves to Germany'* and she continues working from there for a while. It is about six o'clock that we end – time for me to go home, doing some shopping for dinner, getting organised for the trip tomorrow to *Debrecen*. I get up from the chair, take my jacket – the phone rings: *Köszön?* – I could have said *Hallo?* in *German* as a colleague from *Frankfurt* rings, asks if it is OK to talk about a report I produced in the framework of a research project for the *EU* – the one for which I did the interviews the days in *Brussels*. Sometimes I think that in a way this project largely contributes to 2006 being my *annus horribilis*. Well, it is not so bad and actually some of the work and some of the cooperation were most delightful and satisfying. However, I never ever had been involved in work which was so tightly reviewed and controlled by political scrutiny – a more friendly way to talk about a kind of censorship. What is frightening with such things – and this was the difference to previous 'censoring experiences' where I could answer direct intervention with rejecting to work under those conditions – is the following what are inner scissors. The use of terms that do not follow a rational interpretation or even the commonly agreed definition and understanding. Terms as quality, modernisation and the like are interpreted by political forces; social services – as consequence of using certain terms as 'stakeholders', 'effective', 'open to consumer decisions' and even 'provider of a service' etc. – are redefined and understood as commodities on a market place. Vocations are downgraded to prostitution. – Well, a wide field to talk about. What satisfies me after this lengthy phone call: My report is basically accepted though several items had been seen as much too critical. The way out for the project managers was quite simple. The report will be annexed as research in the framework of the project, reflecting the 'personal opinion/work' of the individual research concerned with this field. I interpreted this in plain words – knowing what was behind it: We always wanted to say something like this; however, we do not dare frank criticism of official political bodies; but now we found somebody who does this 'dirty work' for us. – *Keep your own head up; the heads of others can role.* Still, when we started the project, when we have had the first preparatory meeting in January 2006, everything I said and which is now in the report was rejected so that I see this kind of acceptance actually as of success. – Enforcement of rationality? Of Rationales? Does it really matter?

Two days later I am getting aware of it, leaving *Debrecen* after giving the day before a lecture. Walking to the train station, being confronted with life in poverty by the people I see – sleeping rough, searching the bins for something to eat, not having any real rights, i.e. rights that are not just a matter of paper. – What am I doing here? What did *Calvin*, what did *Zwingli* so many years ago when they lectured at the university here? Did we get any further since then? Can we get any further form the point at which we are now?

Waiting for the train my thoughts are getting blurred. All these rationales and rationalities, all these dark developments – continuing after enlightenment and some actually starting from there – remind me at something which I once experienced a few years before as part of working for the *OSCE (Organization for Security and Co-operation in Europe)*. In the early 1970s, still living in *Germany*, I actively pushed for supporting the then *Conference for Security and Co-operation*, an initiative by the then existing alliance of socialist countries. It was considered as a means of the policies of *détente*; a means against war. It was not just a legal system; it was part of a wider social and political system and development. To some extent, the global project went the once intended way: a neutral organisation securing peace as we envisaged it. And we, my political group supported this, despite the warnings of some amongst us: This system may well develop into a new power, being controlled by the US. Acknowledging this danger, we still wanted to go the difficult way, taking the risk. We knew: Not going this way is not less risky as there is no other way. But what developed was exactly what we feared and what did not take sufficiently serious. Policies changed, the *Conference* developed to be an *Organisation (1995)* – and the only thing I know is that this Treaty for peace that I once supported, finally emerged to be an instrument which once pushed me in the middle of war. A short time only that worked in this war zone, for a project in the crisis area of Macedonia, trying to develop what is called civil society. The time there was still long enough to get brutally aware of the fact that many of these actions – actions of war, social activities, involvement into policy making and probably even personal behaviour are part of 'wars', of power games, of following rationales rather than rationalities. – And many of the rationales, rejections of rationalities in all this are consequences of misunderstandings, lambencies, improvidence due to... ? – We are back to *Max Weber* for every day's life, providing understanding, forcing us to look at and consider contexts. Our own personal understanding of something always depends on the situation in which we are and act. And this is the same for others. So, to understand the other, we have to take the context in which the other acts into account. As said elsewhere: any comparative perspective has to be understood as well and primarily from a historical perspective. Forgetting this, forgetting global and personal histories and contexts is probably the reason for many of the tensions we face. – It is another question how far it helps us to act, to change our own and the action of others.

And the lesson of all this – the lesson for analysis, for scientific work? It is strange that actually by applying *Weber's* rules with regard to interpretative sociology we arrive at a result that contradicts his own approach, the claim that research has to be without referring to values. The lesson is: There is nothing like a neutral research, research that is impartial.

Jesters only

– Do you know the answer on the questions all this poses? Perhaps only jesters are able to know it, to find it. It is the same answer as to the task from above: connect in the following graph all dots with not more than four lines in one go. As said: Never get caught in cages – you might find possibilities and opportunities that do not exist at the first glance:

3	11	10	9
4	2	8	
5	7	1	
6			

And some times it means: If you want somebody to listen, fight for changes by following the agenda; if you want to change something more fundamentally, don't expect people to listen – hope that they will get it after a while. Fight for it although you will need a long breath.

And be prepared that you will have to fight alone, though occasionally finding out that you are actually not the only one.

– Sitting in the train from *Debrecen,* feeling a little bit lost. I am apparently the only person who sits in the one first class wagon of the train, an awkward feeling after leaving the train station which proved to be a bivouac for stranded people. Sitting a somewhat nauseated remembrance is getting hold of me: the Four Seasons Hotel in *Budapest.*

Thinking about poverty, means as well to think about wealth. And although political justice is not about equalising in a downgrading way, rejecting any kind of comfort it is definitely about rejecting this excessive and despising lavishness – the website announcing room rates of...? – Well have a guess. If you are still looking for a Christmas present, here is your choice

Formula One Grand Prix Package

Experience the excitement of the Formula One Hungarian Grand Prix and explore Budapest's treasures of the past and present. While you take advantage of the city's attractions, indulge in the comfort, luxury and fine cuisine of your home base – Four Seasons Hotel Gresham Palace Budapest, an Art Nouveau palace.

This rate includes:
- Luxurious accommodations
- Full American breakfast for two daily in Gresham Kávéház or through In-Room Dining

Minimum Stay:
4 Nights

Offered:
August 02, 2007 - August 06, 2007

Nightly rates per room per night (EUR)
Subject to availability

View rates for: 2 adults

Valid days: Monday, Tuesday, Wednesday, Thursday, Friday, and Sunday

Guest Rooms	Aug 2, 2007 - Aug 6, 2007
Royal Suite	4,870.00
Presidential Suite	4,470.00
Crown Suite	2,970.00
Palace Suite	2,170.00
Tower Suite	2,065.00
Park Suite	1,120.00
Danube Premier Room	930.00
Danube Deluxe Room	660.00
Danube Superior Room	590.00
Gresham Room	520.00

I look out of the window – the view across the rolling countryside helps to overcome the disrelish. The music in my head comes from *Joan Baez,* proposing to *Imagine;* though the words I am thinking about are different – trying to find the potential actors in this world of madness:

Kinder und Narren

Kinder und Narren brauchen die Freiheit,
lieben die Wahrheit, die Sonne, das Licht.

Kinder und Narren verlachen das Gold,
verachten die Macht, die Mensch ihnen verspricht.

Nur Kinder und Narren spielen mit Träumen,
sprechen mit Bäumen, wissen, daß Mensch das kann.

Nur Kinder und Narren leben im Märchen,
in Zauberwelten und glauben daran.[29]

---

[29] (more or less free translation of a poem Stephanie once provided)
Children and jesters
Children and jesters need freedom
They love truth, sun an light
Children and jesters ridicule the gold
Despise the power that men promises to give
Only children and jesters are playing with dreams
They talk with trees and know; it is possible for men
It is only children and jesters who live in fairy tales
They live in magic worlds – and they believe in them to make them true.

A Fairy Tale

Every fairy tale has a happy end – and isn't life at the end nothing else than such a story? Isn't the story of life about such battle that is usually the content of such narratives? The dictionary on my computer defines as follows

fair·y tale n

1. a story for children about fairies or other imaginary beings and events, often containing a moral message

2. an improbable invented account of something, often a false excuse[30]

It does not say that it is usually about some kind of love, but love that does not play a role in the common sense but as a kind of... – I am not sure, it the expression of goodness and hope: peace, harmony... Nor does the definition say anything that is in a way behind such love, imaginations, moral messages and inventions: the battle between good and bad. Further, such definition does not say anything about what the underlying morale of such yarn is about – from where it comes. Is it given by something as god? By emotional 'sympathies' we feel for things, developments, decisions, groups or individuals? Or is it derived from something else – situations, activities and actions, being founded in the situation and the action. Expression of soci(et)al practice, appropriation as termed elsewhere?

Strange enough that in many cases the dreamers of romanticism – for instance *E.T.A. Hoffmann, Novalis* and *Giuseppe Gioacchino Belli* in writing; *Jean-Jacques Rousseau* in philosophy; musicians as *Franz Schubert, Ralph Vaughan Williams* and *Hector Berlioz* or painters as *Egide Charles Gustave Wappers, Visconde de Taunay* and *Francisco Goya* – lived very much such fairy tales, gained influence with their ideas and – well: as every fairy tale has a good end, it has some bitterness: in many cases these writers, philosophers, musicians and painters had been expelled or expelled themselves. Times had not been ready for such dreams as reality – let alone that times allowed to actually live these dreams in reality.[31] And is little way there had been even

---

[30]   *Encarta® World English Dictionary © 1999 Microsoft Corporation. All rights reserved. Developed for Microsoft by Bloomsbury Publishing Plc.*

[31]   It is remarkable and worth more intense studies that actually many of the romanticists did not just leave it with dreaming but (pro-)actively engaged in politics and showing huge interest in natural science – including 'real politics' as for instance *Johann Wolfgang (von) Goethe.*

for these dreamers there had been even less prospect for revolutionaries who had not been satisfied with dreaming but who started from scientific analysis, demanding change not least by questioning powers.

Now, not back to the sad stories – what I wrote so far might still find its happy end. And if this is the happy end of a fairy tale or of actual action – real appropriation, real change of striving for real change – does it really matter?

Finally Arriving in Hungary

> *In short, I reckon the studies to be the seed, and the more one sows, the more one may hope to reap.*
>
> *(Letter from Vincent van Gogh to his brother Theo, 18.9.1882)*

Some time ago, *Marcello* worked for my institute, coming from abroad – an Italian student. Young, dynamic, full of life – vivid is the more appropriate expression. One Sunday, after he worked already a couple of weeks in the country, I invited him to my place, to be more accurate: to the cross-country event organised by my neighbour. We had been sitting in the Jeep, watching the horses jumping over the fences – I had to mark in the list if they failed or not. When driving down to the entry of the glen, Marcello was sitting quietly on the seat besides me – perhaps he was a little bit scared when I drove down the steep way across the field? A few minutes later I knew it was not fear but apparently excitement as he exclaimed *Finalmente arrivato in Irlanda.* – Yes, it seems that there are places and events causing such a feeling.

– Saturday of my last weekend in *Hungary*. *Zsuzsa* collected me very early at my apartment – we arranged already some time ago to go out to the *Balaton*, visiting the countryside.

A short and friendly *Hello*, I sit down – being strangely ignored by *Kobak* who is sitting in the boot of the car.

We leave *Budapest* to the south-west, first going the motor highway through the city, going a little bit further the same route beyond the city borders and leaving then, travelling further on a back road. Apparently many of the topics we are talking about are going in parallel with the areas we are passing with the car – as they are all in one or the other way informed by our professional background of sociology, history, economics, philosophy and some kind of social professions – one might say it is a kind of 'road sociology', 'road history'… – all the topics can be found on the road.

The large shopping centres and superstores needed space, pushing the small shops out of the market, Of course, there is an advantage – you can get everything and the prices are lower. However, the shop is just a shop and lost the social function. For those who are not mobile, who are living in the centres it is difficult to get by. – I add supporting the argument And those living on their own. There is no point in going for the little bit one needs, the fresh stuff, such a distance, moving the car and at the end paying more than at the corner shop. – She adds: Well, there is no point but you have to. All the small shops are closing. And the bus? Yes there is a bus, but being old... Besides the fact that – at least for many – everything is getting more expensive by the 'cheap shops' there is another paradox: Supposedly, capitalist markets now enhanced the choice – everybody can buy everything. Actually, there may be even some truth in this. However, that chain shops have a paradox effect is that certain groups cannot buy anything – not having the means to satisfy even their crudest needs. Another point of paradox is had been indirectly mentioned frequently before: The same shops, the same goods – not even price tags are changed as they have already the one-fits-all format: one Euro-price, Canadian and US-Dollar, GBP... – Still, we talk about those developments – coining now Hungary, after they moved during the last odd ten years like a tornado across the island of Ireland. Zsuzsa moves the car safely from the motor highway, approaching a junction and stops at the traffic light. Will history, will these developments come as well to a stop – whenever somebody says: It is enough now – we cannot move in this way! Will politicians or merchants or industrialists or scientists one-day stop the tank which is on the verge of crunching all of us? Is that actually necessary? – As much as I complain with all others, as much the lady at my side speaks deridingly of progress, we talk as well about the Medici-family, the Italian family that emerged in the middle of the last century as superpower of international standards: banking was their core business, but trading and manufacturing brought them for instance as far as Antwerp. Talking about this, and both knowing Antwerp, we independently praise the beauty, still characteristic for the old Flemish town. And today we adore the patriarchal town villas, the arts, for instance produced by van Rijn for the patrician traders – for the moneybags. Travelling around the country side in some parts of Belgium, even some parts of France and definitely in the Netherlands, we admiring the windmills, giving a lovely romantic flair to being their.

– I briefly talk to *Zsuzsa* about my experience from the summer – working in *Amsterdam*, working in most exciting library of the old *Universiteit van Amsterdam* and profiting: well, profiting from what had been propagated by the *Calvinist* system – a system which, together with the *Fuggers*, the *Medici*,

Christopher Columbus, Francisco Pizarro, Walter Raleigh, Niccolò Machiavelli and so many others from economics, politics, fine arts and navigation of the Renaissance laid the foundation stones for the system we criticise today as spawn of capitalism.

It is – amongst others – here where the words of *Karl Marx* are so manifestly true: At the time, the new class was an up-and-coming class, later becoming fetters of the systems which they founded. But at that time they had been developing a system, enhancing possibilities and opportunities. They developed businesses, and as well politics, manufacturing, arts... – and of course, poverty, suppression, exclusion, bribery and all the other impediments of real progress. However, there is some good reason to that today's superpowers – the *Tescos, Marks&Spencers, Shells, Ryanairs* and *Microsofts* – develop primarily poverty, suppression, exclusion, bribery and all the other impediments of real progress and only little businesses, and as well little real politics, manufacturing, arts... and instead rushing on to short term 'successes' being satisfied by Pyrrhic victories – taking for instance arts, it is quite obvious that really good artworks moved more and more away from capitals, being produced in rear buildings, by forces in many cases opposing the mainstream, defending themselves against being overtaken by big business and dominant politics.

In the 32nd Chapter of Part VIII of the 1st volume of The Capital, Karl Marx writes:

> *As soon as this process of transformation has sufficiently decomposed the old society from top to bottom, as soon as the laborers are turned into proletarians, their means of labor into capital, as soon as the capitalist mode of production stands on its own feet, then the further socialization of labor and further transformation of the land and other means of production into socially exploited and, therefore, common means of production, as well as the further expropriation of private proprietors, takes a new form. That which is now to be expropriated is no longer the laborer working for himself, but the capitalist exploiting many laborers. This expropriation is accomplished by the action of the immanent laws of capitalistic production itself, by the centralization of capital. One capitalist always kills many. Hand in hand with this centralization, or this expropriation of many capitalists by few, develop, on an ever-extending scale, the co-operative form of the labor-process, the conscious technical application of science, the methodical cultivation of the soil, the transformation of the instruments of labor into instruments of labor only usable in common, the economizing of all means of production by their use as means of production of combined, socialized labor, the entanglement of all peoples in the net of the world-market, and with this, the international character of the capitalistic regime. Along with the constantly diminishing number of the magnates of capital, who usurp and monopolize all advantages of this process of transformation, grows the mass*

of misery, oppression, slavery, degradation, exploitation; but with this too grows the revolt of the working-class, a class always increasing in numbers, and disciplined, united, organized by the very mechanism of the process of capitalist production itself. The monopoly of capital becomes a fetter upon the mode of production, which has sprung up and flourished along with, and under it. Centralization of the means of production and socialization of labor at last reach a point where they become incompatible with their capitalist integument. Thus integument is burst asunder. The knell of capitalist private property sounds. The expropriators are expropriated.

The capitalist mode of appropriation, the result of the capitalist mode of production, produces capitalist private property. This is the first negation of individual private property, as founded on the labor of the proprietor. But capitalist production begets, with the inexorability of a law of Nature, its own negation. It is the negation of negation. This does not re-establish private property for the producer, but gives him individual property based on the acquisition of the capitalist era: i.e., on co-operation and the possession in common of the land and of the means of production.

Looking at the surface level, it is difficult, not to fall into historical relativism but – as *Bill Bryson* underlines in his *Short History of Nearly Everything* in relation to the theory of relativity – *It is all to do, you see, with your position relative to the moving object.*

We are still on a kind of motor highway, already outside of the densely populated area of *Budapest.* However, the road is more work in progress – and so are the buildings, the plants at the roadside. *Progress, here as well.* I ask her my neighbour what kind of industries are the main foundation of the *Hungarian* industry. But I have to wait for answer, instead she says: *Every time I am driving here I tend to get lost. There is always something new, a new road outlay. And the sign posting is really bad.*

After having managed the needle eye, I get the answer on my question – a kind of answer, at least. Difficult to say. I think it is more or less everything. Since the mining and heavy industries closed down all others compete to compensate for it. Well, actually they compete to find a market here – to be close to the new markets and to exploit the social conditions: extremely low social standards after the turn; a highly vulnerable social structure and low labour costs. Still, probably the most important are electronics/IT and pharmaceutical industry. I dare to ask if this might develop to a new tiger economy, instead of the Celtic tiger now a Magyar tiger. The Irish model at least is close to the East Asian Tiger, roaring between the 1960 to 1990s – before the beast collapsed and left a disaster behind. Is this the future for Hungary now?

What is definitely different here is – already mentioned – what I see in one of the next towns along the way. We are standing in the little traffic jam, due to road works and I learn *An old mining town with an extremely high rate of unemployment. – People are still living here? From what do they make a living now* I ask, not least as I have been in the beginning of the year in *Austria*, visiting an entirely deserted mining town there. There, a handful of old people still could be seen, for me a scene as I imagine from *Marienthal: The Sociography of an Unemployed Community* – the excellently written and frightening research by *Marie Jahoda, Paul F. Lazarsfeld, Hans Zeisel.*

– Yes, people are still living here. Where else should they go. There is no alternative for them. – Perhaps, I think for myself, there is some kind of alternative, or even hope for the people: building the new roads, developing infrastructure… I don't know, if this can be sustainable, *durable* as we say in *French.* It is not only the matter of lasting in time, it is as well the question of providing a perspective that allows people to really appropriate their environment, their lives…

Before, during the times of socialism, there had been at least several questions answered: there had been work, there had been housing provided, education was secured… – driving along I remember what *Steph* said the other day, after I asked her for some comments on what I wrote before in this little *Diary from a Journey into Another World.* She said *All this sounds a little bit negative. Negative in the sense of some discontent with what you are doing – coming from the EU, working there and… – well… All this is your impression, of course; but do you think that it reflects as well the feeling of the people there – in Chişinău, in Budapest, in all these places you mention.* I hesitate, knowing that the young women points on a crucial issue, being an equally pleasant dialogue partner as the lady with whom I am approaching the countryside. *Yes, I know, Steph; I know as well that before they didn't have everything – you know where I am politically standing and still I do not have any problems of criticising our old system. I know as well, when I studied in Berlin in the 70s that I had been in a somewhat privileged position. But I am not talking about the past and perhaps I am not even talking about the present. I am negotiating about the future and the presence of a special future. What did they promise us and what do they pledge – the Gates, O'Learys and Habsburgs? Instead…* She interrupts me: *I know it is the same as they did in my place – the blossoming landscapes of Mister Kohl. But is that the final word? – This is the reason why I am writing further, why I didn't want to stop with what I wrote up to the 13th in this diary. I did not want to leave just with this… I know that very much what I am doing is part of what is still best described as imperialist strategy – now not coming from nation states but from the fortress Europe. Still, I wanted to come to an end with a more positive picture. And I am still struggling... –* I hesitate, recognising that *Stephanie* wants to say something: *Positive? It is not about positive, I guess. It is more about optimist, about hope.*

She is right. I looked in so many eyes during my lifetime – marked by hopelessness... But I looked in many eyes as well that had been full of hope, full of curiosity and cuteness, I heard so many songs, taking in one or another way forward the refrain from *Ferdinand Freiligrath's* poem, saying

Und wenn der Reichstag sich blamiert,
Professorhaft trotz alledem!
Und wenn der Teufel reagiert,
Mit Huf und Horn und alledem!
Trotz alledem und alledem -
Es kommt dazu trotz alledem,
Daß rings der Mensch die Bruderhand
Dem Menschen reicht trotz alledem![32][33]

---

[32] *Translation of the quoted stave:*
And if the Parliament stultifies
Professorial for all that
And if Old Nick reacts
With hoof and horn and all of that
for all that and all this -
it will come the day in spite of everything,
that men around reaches out
the brotherly hand to other men – in spite of everything.

[33] *The complete text of the poem from http://de.wikipedia.org/wiki/Trotz_alledem*
1.
Das war 'ne heiße Märzenzeit,
Trotz Regen, Schnee und alledem!
Nun aber, da es Blüten schneit,
Nun ist es kalt, trotz alledem!
Trotz alledem und alledem-
Trotz Wien, Berlin und alledem,
Ein schnöder scharfer Winterwind
Durchfröstelt uns trotz alledem!
2.
Die Waffen, die der Sieg uns gab,
Der Sieg des Rechts trotz alledem,
Die nimmt man uns sacht wieder ab,
Samt Pulver, Blei und alledem!
Trotz alledem und alledem-
Trotz Parlament und alledem,
Wir werden unsre Büchsen los,
Soldatenwild, trotz alledem!

There must be a way forward – and there must be another way forward, acknowledging, respecting the human being in his and her own right.

At least with the car, we moved forward, arriving at a small village of which I forgot the name. We stop for a while, visiting a quite remarkable Jewish graveyard. I know about the killing of the Jews – the direct killing and the silent, 'soft' killing by persecuting them and suppressing them by prejudices and scapegoating. *German* fascism was not alone – a fact that does not make anything more bearable for me. I am remembered at old friends: *Christian, Liesschen, Michel...* – are they still alive. And can I, being *German*, just follow the former prime-minister *Helmut Josef Michael Kohl,* who claimed the 'right of being born late', claiming that he was convinced that by the fact that he was born too late to be actively involved in the historical outrage he was exculpated? The then *German* chancellor apparently thought this to be an exculpation for the future and got heavily involved in bribery – feeling another time being exculpated by a short sentence: *Oh, ich kann mich nicht erinnern* – believe me, the *German* does not sound better than what we hear from *Irish* politicians: *Oh, I have forgotten about this.* And not having been involved I still feel a responsibility – the responsibility of seeing political science as matter of not interpreting the world in a different way but of being

the seed, and the more one sows, the more one may hope to reap.–

in spite of everything.

3.
Heißt gnädiger Herr, das Bürschlein dort,
Man sieht's am Stolz und alledem!
Und lenkt auch Hunderte sein Wort,
Es bleibt ein Tropf, trotz alledem!
Trotz alledem und alledem-
Trotz Band und Stern und alledem,
Ein Mann von unabhäng'm Sinn,
Schaut zu und lacht trotz alledem!
4.
Und wenn der Reichstag sich blamiert,
Professorhaft trotz alledem!
Und wenn der Teufel reagiert,
Mit Huf und Horn und alledem!
Trotz alledem und alledem-
Es kommt dazu trotz alledem,
Daß rings der Mensch die Bruderhand
Dem Menschen reicht trotz alledem!

Being back in the car I turn to *Zsuzsa*, switching to another topic, not to look for distraction but – well, actually we switch together to the other topic – and it is a topic we briefly talked about before. *Zsuzsa* says, when we move back into the car after visiting the *Jewish* cemetery, *Actually there are no similar places of the Roma.* I ask how they are actually burying their relatives – but I add another question which is for me not less interesting – and as much as I am interested in the historical questions and questions around their life and customs, the enquiry I have is a more contemporary one, actually not really concerned with 'the other' but looking for 'us'. *Now you said Roma. Didn't you say cigány (gypsies) when we talked about them before. I heard a couple of times... – Political correctness...* I am a little bit stammering, not being sufficiently informed and knowing that I am the stranger, keeping myself in a kind of 'polite demureness'. Still, I always have had some headache – when talking about gypsies and as well when using the supposedly political correct terminology: Roma, Sinti and Members of the Travelling Community.

Well, they usually talk amongst themselves as cigány, gipsy. I have an ambivalent feeling. Sure, we have to look for politically correct terminology. But I know that many actually do not fit under Roma or Sinti. In many cases this political correctness is very much a matter of middle class elitism. – Thank you, Zsuzsa. I am glad that you say this. I feel this ambivalence myself. And for me, there is in many cases not least the question of identity and its enforced loss by smart-alec intellectual interference – or should I even say: discursive colonisation. Isn't it in many cases a question of destroying the identity of people by being politically correct? This is debate that keeps us busy for some time – actually a delicate topic. And it is a topic that lives from its inner contradiction, striving for a solution but possibly finding such a solution only when we respect the necessity of a dialectical approach. The question of Aufhebung as sublation and supersession in every day's life. And discussing about cigány, gypsies, Roma, Sinti and Members of the Travelling Community, talking about the contradicting character, we are indirectly talking about the incapability of the current political systems: They are built on fundamental contradictions – the contradiction between classes, between urban and rural areas, between the sexes but today's politics are too shy to accept these contradictions in their discourses – here any contradictions have to be all spruced up.

– Whereas we both vehemently reject the glossy shimmer which politicians use to calm us down, we both love the glossy shine of the hoarfrost covering the trees and shrubs along the road. We cannot see far but what we see is a most beautiful wintry landscape. Forest, wide fields (well, *Zsuzsa* says they are wide and of course, I believe her – the mist around prohibits to look far) and the vineyards are pretty to look at. – Is this kind of debate, sitting there in the car, driving through *Hungary*, intellectual work? Is it pleasure? Is it leisure time activity? Does it matter? – It is definitely pleasant to be together with this experienced, circumspect and intelligent women; and it is a special honour. It is a special honour as well because I am as much looking up to her as much as I feel respected by her – may I say that I feel as child, lacking all the knowledge and experience and at the same time as colleague and friend?

Is it mainly wine growing people are engaged in? – Yes and now. These are mostly very small areas, too small to really make a living from it – there is only one large vineyard left, probably still owned by the state. They do some experimental work there – looking for new crops...

A major problem seems to be that large areas, run collectively under socialism, had been split into small, well: tiny allotments. And there is a problematic lack of re-collectivising. Instead of looking for a perspective by building cooperatives, they are individually struggling, most of them not having any real future.

– In historical terms, this is different as well. Here in the country we find two particularly interesting patterns, the one I get to know the next day, visiting *Zorka – Szikra Dorottya –* in *Gyöngyössolymos*. When she collects me and we drive through *Gyöngyös*, she shows me the tiny houses in one area of the town, remarkable not because they are so small but because each of them – as tiny as it is – has an own garden, or better even: some farmland. *It is from the tradition of farm workers,* the young colleague explains. *All of them worked on farms – nobody could afford to have an own farm. But still, it was a kind of right, a rule that they have had their own land, just enough to grow some vegetables, some potatoes and perhaps even to keep some livestock.* It is interesting to look at this and at what at another stage in history of the country was called productive social policy – a system of integrating socially disadvantaged people and beginning of a national welfare state. Actually, this is *Zorka's* current main field of research. And she mentions an article on the latter in which she wrote

> *By the mid 30's the "social state" – as it was called by the time - created the so called "active social policy". The idea came from Lajos Esztergál from the South of Hungary where there had been a dramatic drop in birth rates because of financial reasons and having only one child became very common ("egykék"- "little ones"). The essence of productive social policy was to make people able "to stand on their own feet". Instead of free lunch or money it provided seeds to plant vegetables and loans to start up own ventures. The peak of this experience was the creation of a state-fund in 1940 called "Fund for the Protection of the Nation and the Families" (ONCSA). They provided small lands and houses and loans plus benefits in nature for Christian families with children–- about 12 thousand small houses altogether, mainly*

I heard about the other pattern the week before, in *Debrecen,* walking with *Judit Csoba* a little bit through the town – early starts allow to include even some sightseeing. *This is a feature you will find nowhere else – the farmer-citizen,* she said. Though being farmers, they had been apparently at the same time citizens – here referring to having the full rights and being – in a way – part of the *citoyenneté* – definitely an interesting matter to look after. What raises my special interest in all this, is the fact that behind the cured class structure, still valid, there had always been a differentiated structure not least in the farming strata and the lower classes. As much as I see it here, I feel another time reminded at the early *Italian* times of the Renaissance with the differentiation between *popolo minuto* and *popolo magro* though they are there actually to be found within the cities.

– I have to think as well about Ireland – an agricultural society, making the step to the so-called service society without really developing industrial structures at any time – a topic I had been working on during the last week or two. Despite agriculture, a real productive basis of any wealth could never develop. Here, however, in *Hungary,* we have had for a long time parallel foundation – agriculture (actually quite varied) and industry though this was mainly heavy industry. And – although not without problems and especially facing the challenge of lack of sustainability[35] – this industry based system allowed at least for considerable time even in this country which lacked natural advantages having a basic social security net in place: homelessness, unemployment and severe poverty, characterising our society today, did basically not exist.

After stopping at a filling station, we go on for a few miles, looking for a car park in *Veszprém.* The fresh, cold air is nice, it is nice as well to be able to stretch the legs. It is only now, after opening the boot, that I can really see *Kobak.* She is immediately confided and accepts that I put a leash on her. First we walk through the old town centre – later, in *Tihany,* I will hear again a similar remark on the church. *I cannot understand it but the state gave all*

---

[34]   Footnotes from text ignored; P.H.

[35]   History will show what this actually meant – what the reasons behind some of the flaws of real socialism had been. One does not have to follow any kind of conspiracy theory to see that CIA and crude imperialist strategies had been a permanent and heavily supported companion of efforts to establish socialism.

the property, nearly all at least, back to the church. The Hungarians are cowards. – The Hungarians? I ask. *You do think it would have happened under any other government as well. – The socialist party is even worse.* The power of the church is amazing, indeed. I saw it frequently in the city – and here I see it by looking at the monumental buildings. Not only as museum-like buildings but also used as schools, hospitals and the like. The monuments of *István* and *Gisela,* the country's most important saints, topping the viewing platform which opens a stunning view over the old roofs and the ledge, again the wider view blocked by the dense fog. Still, fog and revived power of the church cannot question the fact that it is a most beautiful town.

Our next stop is the old abbey in *Tihany* – it is time for lunch. After I have a brief look into the church – *Zsuzsa* knows it and I get a 'special entry offer', slipping for free through the door, pretending that I am one of the tourist group that just went into the church – we go for a short walk along some old cottages – *Kobak* found another dog to play with and I learn how to distinguish a fisherman's cottage from other cottages.

And I learn as well about the somewhat unusual friendship between a dog and a rabbit. It is a little story about *Kobak's* relationship to a rabbit – the pet of one of *Zsuzsa's* neighbours. And it obviously gives evidence that there is no definite 'racist gene' in dogs. Acting together, enjoyment, play and work are – in some ways at least – more important than DNA and RNA-codes.

As said, it is time for lunch – and later we know that it had been good luck that *Gulyas Udvar Keszeg Vendéglöje* had been the only place we could find open. A beautiful old pub-like restaurant – old pictures, old farming utensils and a cosy nice place to sit – the warmth is welcome after walking through one of the first really cold days this year. A modest, but most pleasant lunch is crowned by *Tùrò gombòc*[36] which we share. – Yummy. Now it is pleasant to get back – the fresh air, before perceived as cold and uncomfortable, is now nice and refreshing, inviting for a brisk walk across the fields.

But first we have to get to the fields. *Kobak* jumps into the boot – after I arrived slightly delayed at the car, and we make the last few miles to the small village – a hamlet with 200 people during summer, 130 during winter. It is already since some time that the smell of burning timber gives me the feeling of familiarity – not only because I know it from my own place in *Aghabullogue* in *Ireland.* It is as well the acquaintance of directness of thinking and acting, the familiarity of an immediate relatedness with the surrounding.

---

[36] *White Cheese dumplings – you may try http://www.cheflaszlo.com/recipesturogomboc.html though I doubt that they will be as good as the ones we enjoyed; they had been made as they really should be made.*

Juri awaits us – well, he awaits *Zsuzsa* who has to do some business with him as he is looking after the house. They sit down, I take some reading and sit down as well – only *Kobak* is getting a little bit uneasy. Time for me: *Shall I take her for a walk? – That would be great. You would take some burden from me – and it gives you the opportunity to get known to the Hungarian countryside.* I get my jacket and wrap myself up. *Just turn left and going straight on will bring you for a nice walk.* That is what I do and it is beautiful, indeed. Still, the frost is determining the picture unfolding in front of me. The icicled shrubs and trees show in a bizarre way – the water, while freezing had been distracted by the wind so that the white icicles are now in a horizontal position; occasionally the fruit of the *rose canina (rosehip)* loosens the view on the clear freezing white.

I delve into the countryside – being twice remembered that it is not just me and *Kobak* who are on this world. *Jana*, a friend from the *Czech Republic* just sends *Hello* via text message – and another SMS confirms what I just feel myself so deeply. *Welcome to Hungary on T-mobile network.* Yes, indeed, I finally arrived though it took nearly two month.

Being back home in the cottage, I sit down in front of the fireplace. I take my reading, intend to work at least a little bit. The buzzing of the burning timer, the pleasant warmth and the quietness decide else – from dozing I fall in a soft dormancy, though not being able if my dream is not actually the reflection on the world, about the experiences over the recent weeks.

With this I am getting aware that the frequently upcoming disaffection is not least expression of deeply sensing that much of the work, of negotiations, of efforts are actually very much more a matter of looking for new interpretations of the world, of profiling something on a very superficial level, looking at most for solutions on the surface. It is so difficult to get through to real change – even in science we are barely coming to terms, and instead, we seemingly prefer to reproduce what others already said before. With aiming on selling our 'products', the products of scientific work we actually sell our soul.

And this is the pleasure here – the open discussion, the interest not in mourning how bad the world is but in analysing the world, in looking for solutions, for ways to change. Again and again this day we talk about it – about the 'large family' of which we are part and the standing of social science. We speak about others who had been doing this kind of work and teaching. Colleagues as *Abram de Swan, Göran Therborn, Georg Vobruba, Stefan Hradil, John,* whom I mentioned before and others who have shown that it is possible to go a straight line in honesty and success. Is it by accident that we are shifting to social policy rather than remaining in social work areas? That people like them are part of this 'family' is something which is a sign for the fact that it is not just important to stick to what one is saying, developing it systematically further in terms of in-depth research. Beyond this it is important to take all the opportunities of exchange, of honest debate. And this is, how I know colleagues of this kind: Though we do not agree in everything, we can enter fundamental debates – discourses, to use the term, as it is en vogue now. Yes, there is some bitterness in saying it. Research, teaching, scientific work is more and more about grades, standards in the meaning of equalisation and business success. *How many places can we sell for which amount of money?* is more and more the question that guides educational policies. Students are not touted by scientific work and independent thinking but by promising them grades and success in their later standing in the job. *Professional criteria? Are we actually still professionals? Are universities still engaged in teaching universalism?* As much as I talk with *Zsuzsa* about it, I talked frequently over the last days with *Balázs* about it – the *Bologna* process, the need to open third level education and the need to keep academic, professional standards. – From my experience – not of being here in Hungary although the trend is of course visible here as well – I sometimes think universities might just as well offer courses by advertising a nice and touristy environment. But beyond this bitterness there is this optimism of getting aware of the still existing part of the larger family, committed to other things than sales figures.

Talking about it means as well to talk about questions as what actually justifies talking of scientists, researchers and academics – basic questions of methodology which are for many times forgotten as we start immediately talking about methods. Reproducing knowledge? Pooling information? Fettling contradictions? Managing projects? Translating matters into technical and administrable questions which can be dealt with as solution for short-term tasks? Managing social progress that is defined by the economically powerful? Or is it about developing understanding? The tightrope walk, having soberness on the one hand and empathy on the other? Is there a tension between personality and an imaginative 'research machine'? What is with handicraft and intuition? Sure, difficult questions, balances are required – the words of *Lev Nikolayevich Tolstoy* come to my mind

> *He never chooses an opinion; he just wears whatever*
> *happens to be in style.*

Compromises are needed as well not only in terms of dealing with requirements of the system we are living in (or under?) but as well in terms of equity, social justice. Equity and social justice are not matters of preaching them but as well about allowing people to developing the skills and performance that is required for research and scholarly work. How can we deal with language? Having difficulties to express oneself is, of course, a problem especially in social science. Having difficulties of understanding complexity is another problem, of course. However, difficulties of expressing oneself due to a 'restricted code'[37] have to be overcome as well as the temptation of ironing out contradictions by mounting quotes.

In the meantime going home – it is already dark, I am now driving the car – and we are now speaking about these issues and agree: Power in a point, not to say power points are something we should meet with suspicion. *Well, I am really very much in favour of holistic approaches* – says *Zsuzsa*, bringing it in a powerful way to the point.

Another farewell – though I hate parting, my kind of feeling homesick: I am always homesick before I leave any home, not being in a new home and thinking of previous places of life to which I might return or not. Still, these farewells will be something characterising the next days. And despite my general dislike, it is in this case in some way easy as I know that we will go on the same route – perhaps meeting on one or the other occasion, but in any case being welded together by something strong: a commitment of honesty and values of social justice and as well something that may be seen as old-fashioned: social commitment. This includes much dispute – but dispute on a common ground.

---

[37] There is a huge amount of studies on language and social class as linked to names as for instance *Chomsky, Bernstein* but as well, though indirectly much earlier thinkers as *Bernfeld.*

Looking forward into the past

Holistic approaches – well, another dimension of the large family. I remember, once, while still working in Germany, I felt harassed by a colleague from the social work side. I cannot recall what I said but I remember well that he flared up: *Sociologists. How can you actually permanently dare to be so arrogant? Sociologists always want to tell us what we should do, how we should approach things. We have our own scientific approaches. We have instruments and we are well able to decide what is correct and what is not, what we need and what we do not need.*

I felt harassed not least as I had been absolutely not aware of any 'wrong doing', of any attempt from my side to question the independence of any social work science – and the same is still true today. And I admit, though working in the field of what I usually call social professions, social professional activities or the like, I feel that I am not entirely part of it – I have a different approach, I have many questions – and I respect the 'independence'. And I nevertheless think that it may be just fruitful to say something as one coming from outside. This coming from outside is for me more and more not just a disciplinary question but as well a question of having at least some savour, perhaps only a notion of different national perspective.

It is one of the recent days that I talk with *István Sziklai* about the understanding of social work – beginning with the usual more individualised and victimising approach versus an approach that is more looking at the social causes of certain behaviour – trying there to overcome 'misconduct'. I am not entirely happy with what *István* proposes and suggest an alternative, looking at three options

- Individualised victimisation – a line suggesting that the individual 'has problems' or even 'is a problem' – and that it actually is the individual's own responsibility

- Individualised matching – an approach portentous in – though looking at the individual – pointing on a mismatch of social and societal conditions, not really asking who is responsible but searching for a functional 'solution of the conflict'

- Socialisational changing and appropriating – a strategy that actually starts from the individual and social groups and classes.

Still, it would leave us with the open question of how to deal with the trinity of social work/social pedagogy, community work/youth work and social policy. Even more difficult to solve: any of these typologies does not have the slightest notion on the differences and tensions within the different fields – allowing 'conservative' and 'progressive', 'liberal' and 'coercive', 'supportive' and 'dictating' provisions. And not least there is a paradox, namely that the latter approach – centring on the social dimension – starts very much from the individual as class or at least social being, taking his/her needs as point of departure whereas the line which had been named individualised victimisation is largely and fundamentally neglecting the individual. In any case, it does not give any answers to methods, but it may well be helpful with regard to methodological questions.

After talking with *István* about the different approaches and discussing the different approaches, the limitations, after delving in the satisfying talks with *Zsuzsa* the other day, and after discussing frequently with *Zorka* some aspects of the history of social professional activities, I feel actually rather optimistic – knowing that students are waiting in *Ireland*, working on similar issues as I did during the last weeks

- Marge, looking at asylum seekers and refugees

- Tracy, investigating special needs education

- Tim, being interested in youth homelessness and housing

- Joe, intending to work on homelessness (rough sleepers) and housing

- Gerrie, working on disability and the deaf community

- Clare, showing interest in questions around travellers

- Lee, focusing on lone parents

- Sinead, looking at children leaving the care system at 18

- Niamh, unveiling interest in social policy questions around the elderly

- Edel, working on schizophrenia

- Shirine, intending to work on mental health and homelessness (supported housing)

What is the optimism about? One aspect is that all these issues are not concerned with anything which promises to be profitable. So, in a profit-oriented society it is obviously possible to work against the stream. Part of this optimism is as well the readiness to accept an approach that is today not usual, which actually faces some difficulties in the administrative order – and I am always thankful that *Joe* supports this effort: group work and to work under a common heading, namely *Does social policy make social inclusion a reality for vulnerable groups?* In a competitive framework this is a somewhat brave step, especially as it is more or less a matter of jumping not only into somewhat cold water, but at the same time to do so at the very deep end. Finally, all showed a certain readiness to go a somewhat thorny way, accepting some difficulties by having a lecturer who was for a large part of the time not present, and who left them somewhat struggling – which he would have done anyway. A lecturer who encouraged them to start with looking for a question rather than beginning with finding the answer to which nobody knows the question. Sure, *Steph* was there and – a little bit supported by my 'supervision over distance' – she was definitely a great help in this more or less unconventional undertaking. But it was important – and receptively courageous – that students showed that they are not entirely dependent, addicted to power point, that they are ready to take up the challenge of being asked to develop powerful points. – What the result will look like? Who knows at this stage. There is still a long way to go. If it is only the learning of being ready to develop own questions, the willingness to dispute, it will be a lot!

A Concert

Katus – Katalin Tausz, Head of my Department – called me during the day at the *Balaton* – well, she called *Zsuzsa* though she was looking for me. *Are you free the evening? I've got tickets for the Művészetek Palotája.*[38] Sure, I am free – and if I would not be I probably would have tried to make it possible to meet her. We met frequently, once – when I went one evening to visit *Zuszsa* at her apartment – having even more or less some more time to talk. But usually, when we met in the University one or the other was rushing – apparently business as usual and as everywhere. And actually, it had been enough time to enjoy the day out to the *Balaton* and to go the evening to the concert.

It promised to be a special evening not only because *Katus* found and took the time, but as well as it had been a performance by a former student of our Department. Being gypsy and an excellent student – and not being ready to compromise, *Jenö Zsigó* decided to turn his back to what he sensed as being a hopeless fight, and to work instead as musician. Together with the performance of the *Ando Drom,* three artists from *France* performed the second half of the evening the evening: the *Titi Robin Trio.* It was really an exciting evening, both groups excelling in their performance. Actually, one can ask if this was a performance or allowing us to have a glimpse into their life. They did not really play 'for' the audience – every single note, every single beat and melody, every drive on the stage was lived music, expression of the deepest feelings. Still, it was a life and the stage, in the limelight.

---

[38]   The gigantic modern concert hall.

Seen from another perspective, then, the concert, despite the musical escapade showed something else – a weird division of life. – Actually, the best dances can be found on the backstage. It had been here where some helpers of the groups, some friends and relatives apparently lived the music even more intensive – an open climate of support, celebration and as well critique. Proposals for improvement although the artists had been on the stage. And usually it is just the stage at which we can have look – we see the product but not the seed and the sowing. – Those on the backstage rarely come to the fore – and actually in many cases they are even consciously kept there, excluded from what is visible.

And the harvest? The harvest is usually another thing – it is the applause from the audience, the appreciation of the spectator and the price paid by the customer. Stage-hands, technicians and choreographers, artists and audience are divided as producer, merchants and customers, and they are divided as sower, farmer and eater. – Well, *Vincent* had not been entirely correct, then:

> *In short, I reckon the studies to be the seed, and the more*
> *one sows, the more one may hope to reap.*

But there seems to be a force than can reunite them. It had been the *French* artists who showed such power. One piece began as exchange of 'words' of the guitar and the accordion, beginning with one repeating the 'words' of the other, the other going on, being repeated by the other – one can say an 'instrumental scat singing', then merging and while coming together developing independence, each playing an own theme, with the underlay of a common premise. The beginning a way of finding common ground, the further elaboration as matter of disputing what one found. The music, the rhythm – it is impossible to describe it with words. And it was as well impossible to remain quite, sitting in the chair. Soon, the huge hall was moved by a common rhythmic movement – and if happened what is so rare in concerts of this kind. The different standpoints blurred, merged and one common standpoint developed. Not much later, the stage was a dancing place for people who joined from the audience, others dancing in the hall itself – all performing in very different styles and all coming together.

Farewell

An extremely interesting time, packed with new experiences, full of studying new things, learning about new ways of looking at people's activities and actions and the results of their doing – individually, socially and on the societal level. Full of confirmations of approaches and visions. An enjoyable time; not being minted by repetition; allowing – by neglecting some needs and habits – having sufficient time for the so-called joys of life as visiting museums and concerts; enjoying the beautiful city of *Budapest* and lovely areas of *Balaton*, the east of the country and the *Mátra mountains*; going out though not in bars and pubs, allowing to get pleasure from the witty atmosphere of coffee houses – sitting in the *Gellért* some hour the afternoons or the *Centrál Kávéház* which – being near my apartment at the *Duna Ucta* – develops over time to a favourite for the evenings. A place for reading, writing and enjoying the music of the piano player – for getting known of new people and making friendships. – Time to say *Good-Bye*. Though it seems to be half of the life of a traveller, it allows looking forward to say *Hello* – the other part of the same life. *Hello* not only to things to come but as well to the new friendships, some of them likely – and hopefully – lasting.

It is the last evening that I am sitting in the *Centrál Kávéház*, I declined an invitation for the evening of a friend after spending already the afternoon in nice company. I felt urged to lean back for a while in this old, now familiar new environment, just looking back. A fairy tale? Coming to a good end?

The cup of nice smelling coffee and the *vargabèles*[39] in front of me, I actually manage to lean back, to 'relax in tension'. The smell of the strong beverage is nice, the piano music in the background, the humming of people around me, talking is somewhat calming down.

This part, the finale of this little report is introduced by the words of *Vincent van Gogh*, saying

> *In short, I reckon the studies to be the seed, and the more*
> *one sows, the more one may hope to reap.*

And surely, these words are true. However, seeds – in natural and social science – are of a paradox character. As much as they increase the harvest, as much the gatherings grow to new questions – seeds for new sketches. It is the remaining melancholy of fare-wells of this kind; the feeling of being helpless, only being able to wish that people do well but not being able to help them in doing so. The impression of sailing on the same sea, having the same course but everybody sailing alone. The poverty which I saw, the biased bribery and mendaciousness, the political ignorance, the disdain of work and personality of people, the restraints forcing all of us to live a kind of part-time life, dedicating another part to the requirements of others, as well

---

[39]   You may try http://www.elook.org/recipes/european/28835.html

improvidences and humiliations others caused and I might have caused –
individually and 'systematically', forces by individuals and from 'structures'.

– in spite of everything.

Still, perhaps another painter is able to teach in this situation, to allow as
seeing the light – not the one at the end of the tunnel, but the light within
the darkness itself.

Once my senses learnt to be patient, and grew accustomed
to my surroundings, I began to see a glare filtering
through the seemingly endless layers of greyish-green, a
world beyond. Then I gently embraced whatever was
there, however amorphous, and whatever I suspected to
be there. Like a painter, I moulded these forms and
images, coloured and recoloured them, reversed and
forwarded them until they seemed recognizable to
the eye.

(Miano, Sarah Emily: Van Rijn. A Novel; London: Macmillan,
2006: 1)

I do not know – and I will never really know, there will be sorrows and still –
there is some excitement beggaring description in being able to see the new
colours and to gain new standpoints – *Every picture has an optimum place
from which it should be seen* and every standpoint has some justification as
long as it does not look for new interpretations but for changes on grounds
of justice and solidarity; a matter of arts and of theory of relativity and of
dialectics – three worlds, three sciences brought together.

– Yes, at the end it had been a great time and I hope already now to come
back one day – still saying *I do not know* but then perhaps knowing a little bit
more about facts and questions.

I lock the door of my apartment, step down the stairs and go to the taxi that
is waiting in front of the door. – *Sorry, I just have to return – won't take a
second.* I nearly missed one thing. People have to find their right position,
locate themselves in social spaces – and *cum grano salis* the same is true for
chairs. So I return into the apartment in order to put the chairs back into
those positions from which I removed them to suit my own comfort. –
Adaptation, change, and acceptance of a very special kind.

Epilogue

It had been what one can call quite Christmas – arriving home on the 21st, finding my place in *Aghabullogue* as a place that can be called home: some decoration, a Christmas cake... . Coming home the evening, relatively late, the place irritated me. Being used to it for so many years now, I was irritated as I actually did not find what I left. Instead, it was the place that I occupied for some years, just the first years living in *Aghabullogue* and before taking up a slightly hectic life style, moving in and out, travelling here and there – loosing one place and gaining so many others. This day I arrived in place that showed signs of somebody living there and as such I have had the impression of looking into a mirror. Was this the feeling *Alice* went through with the looking glasses and reflecting on the dreams? – As said, I was irritated, literally looked around if somebody was still there, though knowing nobody would be. A riddle? Well, let us leave it be one then, a riddle. Let us accept the solution being a kind of mystery – it is inside, anyway. Finally we should know that

> *Mr. Weekley's dictionary told us that mirror came from the Latin mirari, 'to wonder at', and that miracle came from the Latin mirus, 'wonderful.'*
>
> *(Fynn: Mister God, This Is Anna; New York Ballantine Books; 1976: 100)*

A few days, sorting out things, saying Hello to the neighbours – and Good-Bye.

It is already the 28th, very early the morning when I open the door to my apartment at the *Via Ardiglione* in *Florence*. Walking there from the train station gave me the feeling of walking through the extinct city, gave me another time the feeling of estrangement. Even at this time I got the feeling of entering a place being full of life. It reminded me at the times when I lived and worked in this country many, many years go. All was a little bit unreal – streets having more the character of alley; the old plaster rather than new-stylish tarmacadam; passing *Cappella dei Medici*, the *Duomo*, crossing the *Piazza della Repubblica*, getting at the other side of the *Arno* by walking across the *Ponte Vecchio*, following the *Borgo S. Jacopo*, continuing the *Via S. Spirito*, turning into the *Via Maffia*. Only a few minutes left now to get home. The old buildings, then after walking altogether for about twenty minutes, I open the door to my apartment. I had been afraid the loud jar of the door in the hinges might wake up the other people living in the building. Everything in the house remained quite. It was nice to enter the warm rooms, to see that there had been life here as well — the fruit on the kitchen table, the newspaper in the living room…, and it was nice to lay down, to fall asleep.

I have to admit this morning I skipped the jogging. Going to the post office to send a letter which I couldn't do the day before in *Cork*, resting in the *Caffè le Torri* for a quick espresso, after walking a little bit around, I have the feeling of the city which has still some of the character of its high time of the Renaissance (before the crowds of tourists run around). It was early enough to get a glimpse of every day's life — every picture book, full of prejudices, came to life: the street cleaners are taking away what people left carelessly behind the other day, market stands are being set up, people walk to work, the humming of the *VESPAS* may remind those who are still in their beds that it is time to get up. The old buildings at the *Palazzo di Pitti*, just around the apartment or the little shops on *Ponte Vecchio* are still quite — even the owners are not yet around. Although the place is still awaking, people are getting ready for work, it is already very vivid and at the same time somewhat quite, in a well shaped 'order' — a kind of natural order, showing some kind of appropriateness. The fruit shops already displaying the colourful goods… — the music, the talks of the people, buying the newspapers, sitting for their cappuccini, the *tabacchi*.

— Is it my recent work, the recent research I did, looking a little bit more into history? I begin to think if what I find and feel here is what life actually is about: living in history, living history. I really do not mean the outside of it — walking through places that are of historical meaning, which played a role during history and that had been housing historically meaningful people. It is the inside, I mean. It is the history which 'brought us here' and of which we are active part — a nightmare, as *Karl Marx* once rightly said; but as well a stepping stone of hope.

These days I received some lines I got fond of. They can be an end of thinking and writing and they can be as well a new beginning.

> *I want to know how God created this world. I am not interested in this and that phenomenon or this or that element; I want to know his thoughts. The rest are details.*
>
> *Einstein*

Taiwanese Chronicle – Thoughts of Love from a Journey to Taiwan

*Wenn Du wach liegst, in der Nacht, dann stell dir vor, dass
ich vielleicht auch nicht schlafe und grad an dich denke.
Dann treffen sich unsere Gedanken auf dem halben Weg
und gehen zusammen auf dem Lakavitos spazieren, im
Mondschein.*[40]

Arrival and questions

Gosh, and we in Ireland say that we know what rain is. – Finally I arrived yesterday in *Taipei*, learning something new about the dimensions of pouring rainfalls.

But it is of course not really this, what is employing my thoughts, indeed. The kindness and discreet extravagance which I faced as I had been collected from the airport by *Viola Lin* and *Ai-ling Liu*, the warm-hearted welcome by the people here in the *Institute of Advanced Studies in Humanities and Social Sciences* and the *Policy Centre* at the *National Taiwan University*, the excellent and mindful preparation of my stay – *Chien Fu Jeff Lin* took even care of a bicycle being ready for me right from the beginning – and he cannot be sure of only my gratefulness but as well of the praise of the *Taiwanese* colleagues. And the attention by *Shu-Chun Chang, Emily* and *Jaclyn Guo...,* showing me *en lieu* what I already experienced during the preparation especially by *Ben Wang:* mindfulness and friendliness and kindness – already now I could go on with a long list of names and..., no, persons who gave me the feeling of friendliness and respect and by this evoking me to be friendly and respectful though the expression of it may well be quite different.

Now, already a day or so *Taiwanese* citizen by choice, I am sitting in my office – a very modern place, equipped with everything from a brand-new computer over an inviting leather lounge and the table with the glass resting on the deep-brown timber frame, over a cup on a coaster to tiny post-it stickers, allowing me a convenient way of marking while I will be reading books on a rather new topic. I arrive here in my office just after lunch with my new colleagues – we all, the *Taiwanese* colleagues and myself, had been invited by *Tzong-Ho Bau*, the Dean of the *Institute for Advanced Studies in Humanities and Social Sciences.* And after a short tour across the Campus, which gave me the opportunity to talk with *Lih-Rong Wang (Lillian).*

Lillian – it is especially her merit that made it possible for me to enter this for me new world. We met the first time – as well here in *Taipei* – end of

---

[40] Erasmus Schoefer: Sonnenflucht. Die Kinder des Sisyfos; Berlin: Dittrich Verlag, 2005: 109

February. She was the major organiser of a large conference, bringing together scholars especially from the *Asian countries.* I really felt honoured by being invited to this event, and actually being allowed to contribute in a substantial way to an exciting project of developing a sustainable welfare society for *Asian countries.* February's stay in *Taipei* had been very short – arriving here rather late the evening of the conference and leaving very early the morning after the two-day event. After my presentation which was nearly at the end of the gathering, just followed by some closing remarks, the speakers went out for dinner – and some time during the evening, I think it was actually when we walked back to the hotel, *Lillian* talked to me about the presentation I made – and she asked if I wouldn't like to come to visit the *National Taiwan University: "We need some inspiration, we would like to take advantage of your experience...."* It was, of course, an honour to hear such acknowledgement from the mindful, energetic, pleasant and friendly women though I had to reject humbly this praise – but not the invitation. Yes, it would be definitely interesting to come for a longer stay, but not in the sense of "talking to you as the external expert"; rather I would see myself as a colleague with different experiences. And together, with the different knowledge and experiences, we could try to develop something meaningful for the social policy debate in *Asia* and in *Europe* alike. To do the easy thing and change the world, as my friend *Laurent* would say. And accepting the invitation was quite easy as it had been only a tentative projection. Let us see...

Some e-mails – still concerned with the conference, but now as well regarding my possible stay in *Taiwan.* So it was true: The invitation was a firm plan. And still, it was apparently a tough procedure when it came its realisation, i.e. to get the money from the *IHS* that finally allowed getting me to *Taipei.* The criteria for such fellowship had been quite strict and despite me failing to fulfil any of the formal criteria, I had been accepted – *Lillian* frequently mentioned in our conversation my productivity which had been seen in my CV and list of publications.

Criteria and their interpretation – a question about which I thought frequently during my career of failures and successes, not least during recent struggles to obtain my habilitation: a matter where the assessment takes apparently longer than the writing of the actual work and its publication with NOVA.

However, sitting now in my office, I have a different question – it is about five pm. and nearly dark. The clouds are covering the sunlight, locking it away, the *cicadas* stopped their whirling communication and the only thing one can see and hear is the extreme thunder and the patter of heavy rain. Nobody even dares to walk along, though it is not the tornado of which *Lillian* heralded as possibility. One does not even think about the colourfulness of some members of the larger cicada-family.

Now the question. Why am I here? What is the actual matter of my visit in *Taiwan* – a country of which I know so little? On the surface it is clear and quite simple: Supporting the *Policy Centre* at the *National Taiwan University* in *Taipei* to develop an integrated framework for the future social policy in theory and practice, discussing this with colleagues from academia and thus developing a reference for future collaboration and organising a conference or better: workshop for discussing this framework with representatives of the government. And all this against the background of the broad framework of the *Social Quality Approach.* At the end, this is meant to be a core contribution for the development of a *Social Quality Approach* for *Asia.* So far the "simple" matter of being hear – simple as it is clearly defined. The more difficult one is the learning of...? Well, this is not clear for me. Another culture? My own culture? The differences and commonalities? Not least the perspectives on private and public as well as on individual and social? – And as much as all this seems to be a matter of work, in any case: work for a sociologist and philosopher, it is even more a matter just of life. I admit, though not being tourist I want to know something just of the country, just

<hr>

[41]   http://en.wikipedia.org/wiki/Image:Graphocephala_coccinea_6.jpg - *16/07/07; 7:51*

see something of the environment in which I will live now for a while. And a country and region that might be even for the future, when being back in *Europe*, a certain point of reference for my work. All this is only vaguely passing my mind, with multitudinous facets; a jigsaw of which I have a template and where, at the same time, I refuse to accept this template as guidance. – The notion of a question of which I have the feeling that it may be interesting and important but which I cannot formulate yet.

Templates and Guidance

Hi love,

Being here now, actually already thinking of going here I had to think frequently of you. Only some time ago you did something similar: travelling to another country, far away from home – and still it was entirely different (and even the two of us, with our *unique* travels are only two of many, many people who do something similar every year for short or for long time spans). You moved to an entirely different world of excitement in the *Caribbean Sea*, eager to learn and eager to explore the new – for you – unexplored. However, I moved in a similar new and different world, as well eager to learn and eager to explore the new – for me – unexplored; but the difference is: you are a realist full of dreams whereas I am a dreamer full of realism. Maybe that the difference of our age suggests the opposite, but this is another question.

If I remember it right, it had been just the day before I left that we had been speaking briefly on the phone. You asked if I would be already excited – honestly: I wasn't. My major concern was the work I would be facing. And I only knew that this would be a huge task – and I knew: I have to try to give my best, some weeks or even months of tough work. Excitement? Well, sure, some kind of looking forward to a new challenge ahead, a work much more interesting than the routine of editing books, discussing European policy papers and writing articles on at least very similar topics. But as well... – do you remember? I frequently said: at the end all this excitement of a new, another world is just about 'difference' (yep, I am scholar of *Niklas Luhmann*, know him from *Bielefeld* and from the time when he lived later in *Italy*). And having been in many surroundings during my life I experienced many differences but even more similarities.

When travelling, I am usually exposed to every day's life – and the what is the beautiful white snow for the tourist when going for skiing holidays is the perpetual grimy sludge for the local person in the *Alpine mountains*; and what is the beautiful sun for the holiday maker at the seaside, is the burning

heat that destroys the harvest for the farmer near the shores; and what is –
for the occasional reader – the experience of the exciting library in the old
colonial city of *Amsterdam*, who can enjoy literature in the various languages
of the world, is the oubliette for the person who is doing the daily work
there.

– And at the same time, however, I am usually very much in a privileged
position: on a mission, as it had been defined when I stayed last year in
Moldova. This adds to a position as tourist in matters of every day's life.

Now, I do not want to preach relativism, only realism – you remember the
quote I once showed you from *Herbert Marcuse?*

> ***You should sleep nine hours without dreams.***
> ***Then you have the day for dreams.***

Billy, one of my neighbours, once said that I would be an eternal tourist – and
he said this long before I actually started my frequent travels. He probably
was right. And there is one question that I have in my luggage – a permanent
companion in the same was as *Aodhán* has his little kettle or I have a little
memory, reminding me of 'home'. The question is *What actually matters?*
The permanent difference and newness? The position from which we approach
the situation or the general position, the actual power we have in life? Or is it
just the beauty and pleasure of occasional experiences – people with whom we
enjoy nice experiences (the sharing of something *as it is more a typical US*
American expression), just personal adventures a place gets identified with?

I know, it sounds as much academic as much as the *Caribbean* and the
Taiwanese shores and forests are actually exotic – and as much as academic
and exotic notions are real they are as well…, now, matter of dreams and
reality (I know you are aware of the shift of the 'expected' sequence).

Leaving on Monday, rather early from *Cork,* I arrived – travelling via *London*
Heathrow – on Tuesday in *Taipei.* Gosh, so tired – just getting about three
hours sleep the night before I left, not getting any sleep during the flight is
exhausting, without doubt. Strange enough, I sleep during every flight – for
about five minutes. Rarely that I experienced a take-off in the state of
alertness. The engine starts, I fall asleep – and a couple of minutes later,
even before the fasten-seat-belts-sign is switched off, my computer is
turned on. The length of this flight to *Taipei* didn't really make a difference –
and the man loudly snoring in a seat somewhere nearby didn't really help.
Well, the contentment of the one, causing grieve for the other. The
difference to other flights: I didn't work so much on the laptop but kept
myself entertained with reading. As I am a slow reader, I didn't carry many

books with me – but at times I am faster than I expect and so I don't have much of my own reading left now. I read three books during the flight, amongst them one on *"East Asian Welfare Regimes in Transition"*. Why do we have to state again that we do not agree with *Esping-Andersen* – and continue working on ground of premises? Frequently I have the impression that much of today's writing is very much simplified – going hand in hand with what may be called the *empirical shift of social science.* Actually, what had been, in the fifties perhaps, a truly empirical shift *(think of the stunning studies by Gabriel Abraham Almond and Sidney Verba, Rene Koenig, Seymour Martin Lipset – though you could start, of course, much earlier, looking at the work undertaken by Marie Jahoda, Paul Felix Lazarsfeld and Hans Zeisel or even Frederick Engels' study on the English Working Class)* experienced a further drift: a crude positivist shift, which took place probably in the 1960s/1970s with a kind of fierce *Americanisation* of sociology. Since then, we are not dealing with exploring social reality; instead, we are looking for results. Do you remember sending me the exciting quote from *Albert Einstein*, where he says that he is not looking for details but for the explanation of the universe? Sadly, today it is the other way round: people look for details, not showing much interest in the wider context. That makes writing – and reading – some books so easy: First, there is an answer; then we look for the question and reformulate the answer from this perspective: ontological and even more epistemological humbug. Sadly we are more and more asked to teach this way.

– Leaving the aircraft, having my passport and visa checked, getting the luggage, I walk through the glass-door, looking around for *Viola Lin* and *Ai-ling Liu,* the two who wanted to collect me. Is it tiredness? I don't see them – I just spot a man nodding at me, turning around and walking to the exit of the foyer. I follow, he turns around and answers my hesitating look with another, confirming nod. Leaving the building, I bounce against a wall of heat. *Keep on going* I say to myself. The man... – yes, there he is, nearly out of sight – and then..., yes he is out of sight. Briefly dithering, I return into the hall, walk back as if would come again from the entrance door – and now I see the large sign with my name and the words *National Taiwan University. Viola Lin* and *Ai-ling Liu* are waiting for me, we walk in front of the building where the black limousine is waiting. I sit down in the comfortable and air-conditioned car; I don't dare to take the water, which is in the back of the driver's seat. I am brought to the apartment, only briefly being there. It is just time enough to set down my luggage and refresh myself. Back in the limousine, we drive to the University, where I am brought to the office of the Institute. A short welcome in the main office – between warm-hearted friendliness and some kind of confusion caused by meeting the stranger – little bit like going back to school, meeting the new classmates for the first time. And mind, we are all strangers, on both sides.

Lunch – a "casual lunch" with *Chien Fu Jeff Lin;* going shopping with *Jaclyn* and *Viola* who show me the way to the convenient store on the campus. After getting the bike adapted to my convenience and walking through the shop, my nose begins bleeding – *the heat,* the girls diagnose. If this is the reason or something else, I appreciate their offer to sit down and relax a little bit – I don't want to get sick now. At least a short while we sit down before moving on: some other brief meetings,...; so many, though tiny events before I go home, do some more shopping (the urgent stuff I need in the apartment and before... – no, it is not bedtime yet. We, i.e. *Lillian* and I arranged to meet the evening for dinner. Just back in the apartment, I switch on the laptop, checking for e-mails. Despite the many others, there is one as well from my escort for the evening – a mail for which there was in a way no need, it had been just a very brief confirmation, reading as follows:

------ Forwarded Message

From:...
Date: Wed, 11 July 2007 06:14:54 +0800
To:...
Subject:...

Dear Peter:
Welcome to Taipei...
Yes, I will come to pick you up.
Please just wait for me until 6:45pm
Sorry for late coming...
Looking forward to seeing you.
L...

------ End of Forwarded Message

I am reminded of this mail when I receive the next day a mail from somebody else, from another place on this world – as well "a mail for which there was in a way no need, it had been just a very brief confirmation". This one reads different:

No assessment nor judgement – just the alertness of a tiny conspicuity.

Anyway, perhaps 15 minutes after reading the mail, the phone rings: *I am waiting downstairs for you. Lillian* arrived for the arranged dinner. Such a pleasure to see her again – and after the short personal *salut* we cycle to the restaurant where we meet *Max,* a colleague I know as well from my first visit here. It is nice to know they are caring; and so is the waitress. Together they look for the best option – more precise: the best four options, as the menu consists of a salad, the main dish, a *dolce* and a drink. And all this brings me in the very modern, but nice surrounding nearer to the pleasant pre-state of the *dolce far niente* before starting the next day.

Arriving the next day in the office, everything is sorted – well nearly everything. Something is left to be done in terms of logistics. A setting on my laptop has to be changed to allow access to the LAN of the University – a matter of less than five minutes. And I do not have to go to the computer people; instead, somebody comes to my office – and he really comes without further ado. Actually, I do not mind that it is not me who does the move. Though it is early reasonably early in the morning, the heat is already suffocating and it is the first time in my life that I really appreciate the well working air-condition.

Though being here, having arrived *en lieu,* I am not really here yet. Despite some work, chasing me from the old world, there is something else – I just quote from a mail – actually I wrote it even one or two days later:

> *Dear..., thank you for your mail.*
>
> *I arrived, all right but am struggling with the jet lag. Actually, it is probably the fact that this coincides with a heat stroke (not in the strict and medical sense but at least in the sense of the need to cope with tremendous heat and humidity) – possibly this is as well somewhat explaining that people did well with the water clocks (I liked the reminder of this little story about the water clocks, thank you). Under these conditions, life cannot be lead mechanically*

but only by adapting to some natural "guidance". And taking this heat, what could be more appropriate than being guided by water. Though I usually forget doing so, I tend to drink plenty of water here (though not reaching the recommended 4 litre minimum per day [and I miss the coffee very much]).

Well, it is definitely a quite interesting experience – though I hesitate making any conclusions yet: being a "natural", Buddhist-rooted, collectivist-egalitarian (see the mass activities in practice) society on the one hand, there is apparently still much of the elitist spirit alive which Ricci looked at in his Journals – coincidently I am reading these right now. He stated:

> *"Only such as have earned a doctor's degree or that of licentiate are admitted to take part in the government of the kingdom, and due to the interest of the magistrates and of the King him self there is no lack of such candidates. Every public office is therefore fortified with and dependent on the attested science, prudence, and diplomacy of the person assigned to it whether he be taking office for the first time or is already experienced in the conduct of civil life."*

So in a way: lucky me, that I am considered being in a "distinguished and senior position". Though the expectations are very high, the treatment is stunning. Furniture and equipment in the office and apartment are of high standard and, if perhaps not new, so at least especially cleaned and marked as being so; the access to the library and use of anything from the computer laboratory, the car park (ops, the place for leaving my bike); the respect of asking me even if I would allow the person who cleans the office to enter it in case I am not around; whatever I need is immediately organised; people are friendly and care taking - including the "guided restaurant-tour for a vegetarian", Emily (I am not sure, may be that she "invented" this English name for me, easing my life), vegetarian herself showed me the best places to eat; again and again the offer of using cutlery (so I do fine with eating my soup with the chopsticks), yesterday's cheesecake from Jaclyn (so sweet…, this cake) and the fresh tropical fruit Lillian, "my boss", brought today to my office before she left for the weekend with the family to the countryside and so many more things.

The other side: the permanent signs of respect of which one never can be entirely sure if it is just that or if it is as well subordination. But in any case: friendliness I experience does not seem to be diplomatic – if there is anything "unnatural" at all, it is at most that, looking at all these "exotic people" I mention that it is actually me, who is seen as exotic.

Well, I will try to explore as well a little bit the world around this (in terms of space) small city with the huge number of people living here (we have more people during the day living here in the city than you have in Ireland – in its the Republican part of the island – as citizens)….

But I'll stop here – before telling you more about what the day brings, and what I experience, living in one part of his one world.

I trust you are well – and I look forward hearing from you. Remember, it is not clear where the excitement actually is. Part of it may just be that we only see something as exhilaration if and when we experience it as different – taking *Erving Goffman* then, and his allusion to life being a theatre, we always have to take *Bertolt Brecht* as well: his *Verfremdungseffect.* The life of each of us is so exciting – and by occasionally stepping back, we experience it.

Thinking of you,

Peter

–

Well, *Jenny*, me again;

who should know the words if not you: Men make their own history, but they do not make it as they please; they do not make it under self-selected circumstances, but under circumstances existing already, given and transmitted from the past. The tradition of all dead generations weighs like a nightmare on the brains of the living.

This is what comes frequently to my mind – during the stay here, as it had been already the case when I travelled to other places. And actually it is in a way this sentence which brought me nearer to the question I stated as the unknown variable when I wrote recently: What is the *raison d'être* of my travel besides fulfilling a certain, defined task. There are basically only three options: First, following in the steps of others, as for instance in the steps of the amazing early companion *Matteo Ricci or* other early travellers as *Marco Polo* who travelled to a country, then known as *Cathay* or as *Jules Verne* who was going *Around the World in Eighty Days;*

second, trying to find new paths, simply looking for the exotic (which, of course, means that the paths have to close immediately behind us, so that they remain exotic); or third, finding ourselves, some possible core which remains the same in whichever environment we are. Well, if I take this together with the quote from our common comrade, it means as well to find the own history, personal and social. – By the way, and most honestly despite being a very personal matter for any being it is for me here as well a matter of the work I am doing – but later again on this subject.

Of course, ending the last letter by mentioning something from the office I had been, was premature. I forgot to mention the art of getting there. Well, at least for a country-boy as I am, *Taipei* is simply amazing. Sure, I lived in *Budapest (1,697,343; 3,232/km²), Hamburg (1,754,317; 2,324 /km²), Munich*

(1,332,650; 4,293 /km²), Paris (2,153,600; 24,783/km²)[42]... – and all these places had been at least for some time in one way or another exciting. Now, my "new home": 2,630,872 people, a density of 9,679.45/km. And this rather high density is actually very much a "felt density".

During the time I lived in Paris I always have had a little bit the impression of living in the quartier – and actually I lived in the middle of *THE quartier – the quartier Latin* – near to the *Sorbonne,* close to the *Jardin du Luxembourg*[43] and near all the other well-known places.

And as much as it is a very touristy place, I still have had the feeling of *living* there, of being amongst ordinary people like you and me (and actually so I was; rarely that I got in touch with one of the tourists around). I have had the same feeling of being more in a small quarter when doing some business at the *Place du Colonel Fabien.*

But here in *Taipei* it seems to be different – as said: felt density. I am so glad that the first day *Jaclyn* showed me the way from the University to the apartment building for visiting scholars and back. Before I go the first morning on my own to my new office, I had been jogging, of course. Well, perhaps I should not say "of course", as it is not really an easy thing to do. Sure, over night it cooled down – probably from 35 to 32 degree – won't tell you about my efforts to sleep, and the pain of failing despite the kind of *Adam'esque* clothing and the air-condition. However, the temperature is the one thing which amazes me; the other is that even in the early morning there are quite a lot of people around – not rushing to work, not hastily doing the shopping for breakfast or getting the news – it is just the use of the slightly clearer air, the way of beginning the day early, while it is still somewhat quite. And it is this buzz of a large city, the capital of a country in which...

Well, it proved to be a rumour – but it is a remarkable one and I am still looking for the background. Supposedly the state insists that every citizen who is covered by the health insurance has to reduce his/her weight by 1 kg/pa. Aim of the game: cost saving. Looking at the many slim people here, it must be a double strategy: the few who are really unhealthily overweight may come to a state of a healthy body stature; and the others will simply disappear – getting from the state of slimness to the state of skinniness to a state where they can just disappear from this world, leaving inconspicuous by walking through the little opening underneath the door – I will come back to the chasm in a while.

---

[42] figures (population; density) from *Wikipedia*

[43] photo from
      http://mlaverd.theunixplace.com/blog/archives/journees_patrimoine/Senat/resized-img_1097.jpg

But first: Getting there, making the way of that perhaps 10 minutes bike trip to NTU, coping with the traffic in this city. Entirely a child of Europe – and though even I would move here or somewhere else, I would remain being it, with that *nightmare on my brain while I am living* – I am not sure what is more appropriate to think about when getting ready for the road: thinking about *Irish fox hunt* or *Spanish corrida.*

I thought I would know what it means to see a congestion of two-wheelers – when I went last year from "my villa" in *Amsterdam* to the library to work in the library, I was again and again surprised by the amount of cyclists. Here now, the traffic is dominated by scooters – any photo is barely able to picture authenticity and no words can express reality.

Viva, si permaneces y esperas, morirás de hambre a la muerte – comenzar a luchar. Again I make the experience that learning the exact, the lived rules of traffic is one of the most important parts of intercultural learning. No book and especially no law book will tell us. And the knowledge of getting every single day one day closer to death has to be translated: *Come, Grim Reaper – I want to look into your eyes.* It is rather simple. 1st *rule:* pedestrian-ways are as well used by cyclists and scooter drivers (occasionally as well by pedestrians – usually seen, when walking to look out for their scooter, which parks at the side); 2nd *rule:* traffic lights have a meaning, and they have another meaning as well – try to find the one which is applicable; 3rd *rule:* hope that others find out the same; 4th *and by no means last important rule:* be friendly and (at the end) considerate and even amicable – as the others usually are.

There are two basic and simple tricks: standing at a junction, waiting for the green light, make sure that you start early enough: you have to try to be on the middle of the zebra-crossing before "somebody else" is – and by "somebody else" I mean, somebody who turns into the street which you are just crossing – but do not start the slightest second before you really see the green light. The second trick: if you see cars and scooters turning into the street which you are just crossing, just move on – in most of the cases they are so busy with avoiding to hit each other so that they won't trouble you. – It seems to be a high risk but the reality shows that it is possible to get away with it (I hope that I will not have to correct myself after a while – and what is convincing is the fact that one actually rarely hears that somebody is angrily blowing the horn).

Sobrevivido – I arrived on the other side, can cycle just straight away along the pedestrian way. Though the suffocating heat even early in the morning nearly forbids cycling fast, there is at least no pressure anymore, no reason for special attentiveness. So I am moving on, smoothly along the pavement;

it is early enough and the sides are not yet cramped by parking scooters. My thoughts are wondering, lost in the loneliness of a city with millions of people; it is a kind of daydreaming that accompanies me on the way to the.... – I harshly stop the bike within a second or two, but after a short hesitation I want to move on. *What are you doing here?* I am not sure if the question is asked by me or by the tiny bird, now safely sitting on one of the branches of the large trees at the roadside. Despite being such a large, densely populated city; despite being even in one of its rich parts, where I life, build-up with high-risers; despite of hosting the building which is at this time still the tallest of the world – the *Taipei 101* it is as well a city of some surprises. Somewhat squeezed in between the concrete blocks we find huge trees – it is only by the fact that the bananas around the corner of my apartment need some time to ripen, which keeps them safe from my desirous hands. We find little oases of tropical green where the kids play – provided that it is not too warm during daytime and provided as well that somebody has time to go with them to the playground. – Well, I still have to explore how people use the time. But I do know already: this little bird for which I nearly tumbled over the handlebar, has time and what is more: as small as the little fellow is, he has as well the right to sit there on the ground – perhaps even more the right than people sometimes seem have. You know, I am odd and so you won't be surprised that I bid farewell to the little friend before I cycled on, somewhat relieved: in the *German* language there is a saying: *Wo man singt, da lass Dich ruhig nieder.*[44] So, a city where there are even birds to sing, it cannot be bad altogether.

I arrived in my office – the door to the building is still locked and I have to open it with one of these "plastic keys", a swipe card which I got the other day, immediately together with the keys for the office and the bike. Well, priorities... – and one of the priorities is to provide appropriate working conditions. Is it just an expression of this enormous kindness, the devotion, the friendliness with which the guest is welcomed and maintained. I cannot believe else though a prospering economy like the Taiwanese and some kind of critical thinking can suggest that it is simply the creation of conditions under which high productivity is possible.

As said, it is still early in the morning. Nevertheless, on the square in front of my building, at the verge of the little forest there is a group of about 30 people (I just have a guess and you might know my talent in handling figures) doing some exercise. Directly in front of the window there is an elderly couple – exercising *Tàijíquán.* Already looking at these two people gives a

---

[44]   Where people sing, you should rest in a while

little bit of the feeling of the harmony of this sport and I am not sure if I should be astonished or take it actually from the contrary: it is a martial art.

My thinking turns to the books and papers – after such a short time already the desk is full, books are spread across the room, papers are on the boards and little post-it notes will be providing "the colour of my life" for the next hours.

Bewildering – being employed to think, just to think, not doing anything else than thinking. No teaching, no administrative work – being there just for thinking. Sure, there is some political will behind it though I am not sure at this stage about the complex setting of all this. Be it as it is, what I am supposed to do is fundamental research. It won't be widely seen – and it definitely won't be widely seen or least recognised in *Europe* as most of it will be made available in *Chinese*. What is striking and bewildering is that I am not in any way directly engaged in any of these considerations – perplexing, as I said. As I had been told the other day when I arrived: So you are entirely free to do what you want. Not least it is strange as at the end I will the moral and ethical control over it. In other words, it is not the "moral split" with the so-called value free research: *You do the research and I will decide how to use it.* Instead it is here: *I will do the research and will tell you how to use it.* But there is another thought. Is such fundamental research the rearing of the Cartesian *Cogito ergo sum? –* His *I think, therefore I am.* But didn't *Descartes* say as well *I doubt, therefore I think, therefore I am?* And what does that leave to somebody who is really just there: thinking, loosing the link, the foundation in and for practice? Does it leave anything else than the reflection *I think, therefore I discontinue to be –* and is this just another kind of exclusion from the real world? – Away from you, away from nature, away from the pulsation of the city and far away from the daily troubles? – Sure, we always complain about the endless meetings, the permanent quarrels, the useless debates. But how long can we actually live in the ivory tower where the world around us deluges our brain as idea, where we are only together with ideals of others and reflections of ourselves?

Now, please do not get me wrong – I am far from complaining. It is actually another great, most pleasurable and exciting experience. I am so glad and actually feel very honoured that I have this opportunity – you may remember my short reports and talks about last years' stay in *Amsterdam*, made possible by my good friends *Laurent* and *Marijke*, the stay in *Graz* with the new students and my friend *Sepp*, the opportunity to meet *Gertraud*: both partners for so enjoyable conversation in a most delightful environment... – Imagine, all these privileges are a little bit like living, really living in a garden house. Not just staying there, sipping a coffee, a tee or some hot chocolate with some biscuits, before returning to the main house. Really living there and being able to say: it is home, it is here where I am. The garden house; the house in the west of another island where I frequently live; or the ivory tower – just "normal abnormalities". – And the *cicadas* with their whirling communication and the permanent buzz of the traffic – day and night, this reminds us of such retreats not being a sign of standstill; nor is this buzz the total absorption. Standstill is probably the extinction of moving between the two sides – and we need to "complain" about each one to know about the privilege of each other. – It is like love that sometimes needs some kind of distance, allowing us to find our own heart, before we can give it away again.

Well, having talked so much about the ivory tower, I may have given a little bit a wrong impression anyway. As much as I am actually employed just to think, as much I am involved in debates. Interviews, discussions, developing concepts for workshops, discussing contributions to conference in Tokyo... – and not least the frequent kind visits, phone calls and offers: fruit, tea, lunch and just the help with a washing machine – even the worst translation of the user manual is of more use than just a couple of signs, as incomprehensibly as they are beautiful to look at.

What surprises me sometimes is that it is not necessarily the invitation for lunch, for a coffee... . It is not even the offer that I could get this and that if I would come... – Lillian supplies plenty of fruit, lovely fresh – frequently an entirely new taste for me; the girls from IHS offer me milk-tea: *Do you want just black tea or green tea?* I looked rather puzzled and after I learn that it is just tea with milk, I decide for the green milk-tea. Not much later I hear somebody knocking at my door – "the milk tea is being served", i.e. brought to my office and I learn of an entirely new taste – between ice tea, iced yoghurt, and something which I cannot describe.

– The last days I had been somewhat surprised – seeing me tasting things a good country boy from *Westphalia* would never even touch. Just experimenting? Trying something I might never be able to try later, after leaving in a couple of weeks, getting used to something that will be my surrounding for some time or the readiness to finally enter n one way or another this world? As said before, being here, I try to find the answer to this question: not *la raison d'être* but *la raison d'être ici?* I mentioned the three reasons:

> First, following in the steps of others, as for instance in the steps of the amazing early companion Matteo Ricci, second, trying to find new paths, simply looking for the exotic (which, of course, means that the paths have to close immediately behind us to remain exotic) or third, finding ourselves, some possible core which remains the same in whichever environment we

And being very occupied by the work, I mention how much this work is
actually part of myself. It is not the *workaholic* which may come to your
mind. Rather, it is the deliberation on the question of changing the world –
the old dream, of course; the search not only for the larger picture, but the
one detail: the own power – empowerment: *Who am I? What can I do and
what do I see as the commitment of my life.*

– Empowerment is actually part of the topic I am working on, and it is
difficult not just in terms of the theoretical discussion. What is more exciting
– and this is something I would never really get out of books – is the
following: This is a society which had been up to recently under martial rule;
it is a society which strives for a national independence which it never had
before; it is a society which paradoxically strives for this independence by
some form of subjugation – the global, and this is the US-American, world
seems to be the new, the future identity, the country follows to maintain its
own identity. Can you imagine...? The other day I talked with *Theresa Der-
Lan Yeh.* She told me about the consideration of some groups in the country
to have *English* as second official language of *Taiwan.* A country of which the
first official language is at least a "branch" of that language which most of
the people of the world name their own: *Chinese,* in such a country the use of
English, more exactly: *American English* as second official language is
considered to be a matter of emancipation. It is a paradox of history (though
barely the cunning of reason): The ambiguity of "freedom on the ground of
undivided power".

45

---

⁴⁵ *own photo, taken at the University in Florence, Italy*

The personal experience of it is coming the other day: I hold my "latest little baby" in my hands. I had been asked to produce an introductory text and I finally receive the text – the *Chinese* version. Does the text itself, the introduction into something which is by and large a European reflection, make more sense to the people here than the text in front of me – I hope it does. And it comes to my mind that it can only make more sense I we engage in a common debate and common action. And if we are not afraid to define mutual respect not least as respecting ourselves. The two previous pictures tell us about the consequence of denying one or the other.

– I am sure I will come back to this. But for day I will end with lighter note.

Above, I mentioned the chasm underneath some doors – and there is such crevice as well under the door of my office. One of the last days I return in the evening into the room – and a guest welcomes me. No, it is not a skinny person, but a little saurian. No movement – first I don't see the little chap. But I have to admit when I do so, I am a little bit irritated. Still, what can I do than accepting the small fellow – and prepared to engage in an eccentric friendship in this strange world, I call the little chap *Dino* – aren't we all a little bit odd? Isn't that what makes life amicable?

I send my love to the odd person in you,

Warm regards

Peter

—

Hola, love, ¿cómo estás? Trust you are well and ready to read a little bit more of letters between worlds?

I hope mentioning my new friend, *Dino,* didn't make you jealous. Or do you now think: at this point he went entirely mad? Actually my little Dino should not really be a surprise. Finally I am living in a country of which the climate is tropical. Trust your enemy – so listen to the *CIA* where you learn under climate for *Taiwan:*

> *tropical; marine; rainy season during south-west monsoon (June to August); cloudiness is persistent and extensive all year*
>
> *(https://www.cia.gov/library/publications/the-world-factbook/geos/tw.html)*

Guess this makes little Dinos likely as much as it makes me expecting things to see when I finally will decide: leave the office, leave the city and enjoy at least a little bit of what is said to be an amazing environment. I prepare myself already frequently – daydreaming. Cycling to the office, or coming back in the evening, I frequently look around. The little stand with the fresh fruit – peaches having the seize of mangos, mangos, having the seize of melons, melons looking like a huge pumpkin; the two mates sitting there as sales people look more like sitting at the sandy beach, following with their eyes to places of their dreams. There is often this strange smell – a lovely scent which reminds me at lemons and cinnamon. Some shrieking, strange noise. I look towards one of the banana trees, search in the palm trees, wonder if there is something in these huge green plants, looking like mammoth-*Ficus Benjamini (what a paradox – the Ficus Benjamini we know, is actually more a bonsai-variant anyway – but let the Westerners think).* – So I look around: is there a parrot? The yelping of a monkey? – Ok, it was just the jar of the breaks of the car, stopping at the other side of the road and if it is not madness that causes this kind of vision, it may be the suffocating heat. The other day I mentioned to *Cathal: It cooled dramatically down – from 38 to 33 degree early this morning.*

Finally, the most important of such trips and the reflections around them is the perception that we are, of course, the first who are exploring the world this way – nobody else went from *Europe* to *Asia*, the Caribbean, to *Africa...*, before we did. And if you do it again, don't get confused by seeing in any of these places as *Café* Bastille, *Restaurant Schwarz Wald*, a pub with the jolly name *Molly Malone's (if you actually find an Irish pub in such place the owner probably found the website http://www.irishpubconcept.com before you even thought of going some day abroad)* or the *Tropics* at *Ching Ming Road* – of course, all this strangeness is in its own terms weird – not because we are confronted with something that is outlandish but because it is there like a duck takes to water – and only this uniqueness of us, *You being the first* and *Me being the first*, makes the experience so exciting – we all know that any travel guide is simply a matter of fantasy. And if we do not accept this, the entire experience will not be any fun and, what is truly worse: we will not make any experience worthwhile to be made.

It is all about irritation – but irritation should not be one-sided. The other day I have to do some shopping. I pay what I have to pay; this time I am not brought to Court in order to sort out some legal issues – I may have told you the "little story" of the *Irish Dickens tale,* happening to me when arriving there. Still, irritation is needed, important to feel alive: the sales-person kindly and very explicitly gives me the business card – not the personal one, just the one of the shop – this ceremonial gesture: hand it over by holding it in both hands, look kindly at you opposite, and: take it with both hands, look at it, look at your opposite and say something nice: about the card AND about and to the person. A nice gesture, isn't it? – My hand glides into my pocket, I take my own business card out of the holder, still holding the other in my hand; I take my card in both hands... – well, sometimes respect, mutuality seems to be irritating. But it may help me to find a place in the memory of some *Taiwanese* people as *the professor, working there at NTU – You know, the guy who has these lovely business cards.*

– Above, I mentioned three options: following in the footsteps of somebody else, looking for the entirely new (and making sure that we do not really get used to it at any stage) or finding ourselves.

I envy you: having talked to you, you entered the world which was so new for you – really stepped into it and managed that it did not loose the entirety of its fascination. Not naivety but the ability to live dreams and life in a very conscious way.

But now you can see: I am not far from the same excitement. And despite heat and madness, despite being carried away by the fantasy, the excited expectation of going out there one day, even if it may be just for a couple of hours – despite all of this there is something else. It is the factual nearness of what we call exotic.

Exotic – Harmony by Estrangement

You want to know how close it is, this experience of the exotic world? – Back to *Bertolt Brecht* then, I mentioned already his work with the *Verfremdungseffect.*

First day swimming: The experience of arriving, though only at the margin of that area you liked so much. You didn't talk much about your stay, your move to the entirely different world of excitement – as you usually do not talk about your experiences, your life and your feelings though I can hear and read them between the words and lines.

Anyway, I could feel even in the few remarks the excitement, even if only listened to you on the phone, or read the few lines you had been able to send, looked into your eyes when we met: on all these occasions I could see the sparkle of exhilaration – and I am so grateful that you allowed me to get a glimpse into something which is so personal.

Having said I arrived at least at the edge of that stunning world means simply the experience of diving really into another world – and this is definitely a very personal experience though a very ordinary. Palm-trees and tropic plants with the full, large green leaves, the dabble of the water and the feeling of it when I dive into it – with this: dive into another world. It is another form of *loneliness* or *finding oneself* – not the one I mentioned before: the sense of being lost amongst 2 to 3 million people. No, the contrary feeling: I am alone, on my own - ownership of the entire world by feeling that I am really part of it. Conflation. The palm trees are not something "out there", they belong to me as I belong to them – this is the real fascination.

I have to admit, it is not quite correct saying that I have this experience for the first time when I go to this tropic place in the middle of the overwhelming power of the concreteness of the concrete. What I am talking about is something trivial – the public swimming open-door pool – despite the heat I am nearly the only guest (the privilege of not being bound to working hours; the privilege of having access to a pool which is used for competitive swimming and being separate from the more public and fun pool.

There had been three different occasions of really arriving in this new world.

The lunch on the second day – as said we all, the *Taiwanese* colleagues and myself, had been invited by *Tzong-Ho Bau,* the Dean of the *Institute for Advanced Studies in Humanities and Social Sciences* – had been the first time giving me the feeling of having arrived in an entirely different world. A long table – and in the middle of the long ends *Tzong-Ho Bau* and my dear self had been sitting opposite of each other. Without mention – and from my side without knowing all the people around – there had been an apparent hierarchy. Or should I better say social order of this figuration around the table? On both sides we exchanged some kind remarks about the honour, the pleasure, the excitement, the gratefulness – and the looking forward to a fruitful cooperation. The talk went on, exchanging some experiences, wishes,…; you may say small talk on a higher diplomatic-academic level. At one stage, after a placid meal (takes some time; before I went here I should have made a course in chopstick-handling), it was without saying clear that the gathering arrived at its close; *Tzong-Ho Bau* rose, so did I and so did all the others. He left the room, all following him with the eyes and – depending on their position – with bows of different distinction. And bows of different distinction does not necessarily mean the lower the position, the lower the bow. – Anyway, after he left the room, a couple of us stayed on, talking about the next steps, the steps for the next days and weeks and possibly years.

No, don't say it, love. It had been really a friendly, open and informal atmosphere. I know that it sounds strange for you, perhaps even… – unsavoury? Believe me, it had been friendly, open and informal. I do not believe anybody felt offended, felt inappropriately submissive… .

But there is something else – when I write it now it will come back to your mind – and you have to excuse my frequent sociological meanderings.

Didn't I occasionally say I would like to see *Norbert Elias* still alive, if not for any other reason than for writing a new *Court Society*, one about the chosen ones at the *Rue Wiertz* in *Brussels*, near the new *Government Centre* in *Berlin*, the... – well, even and not least the seemingly relaxed and informal figuration in and around the *Leinster House* in *Dublin;* the various forges of knowledge: universities and research centres; and of course, how could I forget last years meeting with the *emperors son* in *Budapest.* And as visible as it is in the major spectacles of the courts of old and new nobility it is visible in the small acts, perhaps the rehearsals of what remains to come. I have to smile when I receive a mail from a student – on this occasion she writes in her own language, beginning: *Buongiorno professore (in italiano non potrei mai permettermi di dire "ciao Peter" ad un Prof. universitario!),...*

C'est bizarre, n'est pas?/Ist es nicht befremdlich?/Non è sinistro?/ Nee, dat is bizar/Isn't is strange?... Many of such occasions, if they are part of our daily life, seem to be natural formations and figurations for us; we do not even see any need to ask the slightest question – *Norbert* always did and always would do, ready to pay the price, being ready to live very much in *The Society of Individuals,* where he personally had to bear the tension between *The Established and the Outsiders.* – Presumably you didn't read the books I just mentioned, possibly don't even know the titles. Amongst others, it is this what makes sociology an ongoing excitement, including striving for maintaining a similar obstinacy.

Similar and so different another opportunity of "finally arriving": the lunch, following a little workshop organised by the *Social Policy Centre.* We walked from the department's building across the campus, going to the university's restaurant – well, I can tell you, there is a difference between University canteens here and there. Not that the one is better than the other (though some are definitely better than some others).

Already the main room was furnished in what we imagine at least as traditional *Chinese.* Our small group, then, went to a little séparée – similar to my *One Thousand and One Nights*-escapade earlier the year in *Ankara* with *Sibel* and *Kezban;* and still entirely different. A rather large round table in the middle of the room, in the middle of the table a round tray – meals on wheels, one could say. We took place – the figuration had been "informally organised", in this case not least respecting language and thematic interests.

The waitress brought tea, various bowls with rice, veggies, fish, sauces, meet... – a seemingly endless supply, though at the end it had been a most beautiful collection of jigsaw of many delicious aces being offered on the tray which moved around in the middle of the table. I said *Meal on wheels.* Everything was offered on the tray in the middle of the table – and though everybody was equipped with an own bowl and plate and of course the own chopsticks, it was a little bit like having a meal out of a bowl for the entire group. – Sure, the waitresses had been…, well, not entirely ignored but in no way integrated. Still, it had not been in any way negative – not meant to be so, not perceived this way. For the *Stupid White Man* perhaps a glance of disharmony; their "inclusion", as Stupid White Men in their countries frequently pretend to offer to these people may seem from the other side as intrusion, as disturbing an otherwise given harmony. I am not talking about *Al Positano* where we enjoyed *being part of the family*; I am talking about the typical *EUropean* restaurant setting. Figurations, we cannot see them before we understand them. And we can only understand them by seeing them and being them.

The third "early arrival" – glancing the "real place" or the fulfilment of the expectation of the exotic. After using the first days the back entrance, I enter the campus the other day from *Roosevelt Road* – and showing some impressions I got from the internet I can only say again: photos cannot show it (well, your photos probably could, but that is another story).

Many of the buildings – one does not have to have much knowledge about architecture to see the shades of old *Japanese* imperial power, *Chinese* tradition and *Western* modernism [46] – are simply impressive in their uniqueness and in the mutual ignorance with which they stand side by side. But all this is only possible by… – did anybody ever say there are palm trees in Ireland? Believe me, this is not the truth; perhaps there are little "palm shrubs" but not real palm trees: the sheer seize, their slimness, carrying a their very end the leaves on the tall, peeled stems. Did I write in an earlier letter about the banana tree around the corner of my apartment? Gosh, here are trees, shrubs, flowers, gramineous plants…; here you reach a distance from the humming of the traffic of the city with its millions of inhabitants, you even dive away from the people around – walking, cycling, chatting, laughing, pondering, rushing or maundering, being caught between the leaves of which the seize is beyond imaginations of the *Stupid White Man;* and you in the middle of it: being bewitched by the sounds of birds, never heard before, enchanted by the humming of insects and snoopy gophers, scampering just in front of you; delighted by the sweet smell of the flowers and the blaze of colour. – Is it just an illusion that the air is much better, the suffocating heat is transforming into cushy warmth, could one even say tenderness. I dare to sit a little bit down, the pond, the garden, out-laid in the fashion of traditional Chinese garden architecture are too inviting, are nearly

---

[46]   More *Marcel Lajos Breuer* and *Bauhaus*-soberness than *Charles-Edouard Jeanneret's* environmentally integrity though this is surely my personal and lay view.

forcing me to sit down. It is quiet; I am the only one around. Sitting there, thinking about the need of going beyond mainstream *French* regulationist theories, linking it back to questions of socialisation rather than reducing it by descending from the accumulation regime...., or will *Michel Aglietta's* view on the *régime de croissance patrimonial* open a new perspective..., the work of *Robert Boyer* or from an entirely different angle *Marjolein Peters*, the recent presentation in *Brussels*, talking about different administrative regimes; should I get in touch with *Paul?* I will, latest next visiting him in *Ivry...* – ops, sorry. – I look across the water. Who is more puzzled: me, looking at my unexpected opposite or the fellow, glimpsing weary out of the water: a turtle, probably thinking *Stupid White Man*, sitting in the sun when it reaches its peak. Well, I leaned over to her – she was large enough to know, and she was protected by the firm shell, and by the fluffy cover of some kind of algae. I looked in the tiny eyes, saw her twinkle and heard some inmost voice asking: *Do you want to be adult one day? – You know,* I whispered, *we need dreams, and we need them during daytime.* And this moment I saw waves coming from all sides of the pond, a little legion of turtles, soon all stretching their heads out of the water, looking at me.

Thinking back now, while writing about it, I see you in front of me – your experience of seeing the first time something similar – a parrot in the primeval forest, a giraffe in the grasslands... – or just a little snail you may have watched in tender years of your childhood. And I can imagine you here in the middle of this, and as well knowing: what I actually see is only the entrance, the tiny opening of a window to an advanced different world of this one world. I am reminded as well at the dinner some time ago in *Gyöngyössolymos*, sitting there with friends, eating this beautiful dish, *Tamás* prepared – fresh pasta and mushrooms... It was so delightful: the nice meal, the pleasant company and the enjoyable "wild" garden setting. I praised the meal, the rally fresh ingredients. I mentioned as well that, in the morning, being out for a walk with *Abel, Lili* and *Zorka*, there had been other people, as well looking for mushrooms and already having succeeded before we started – having a huge bag. They would sell on the market. *Tamás* said something like *Well, this is at least one privilege which very poor people and very rich people have in common – they can get the best, the freshest vegetables, just what nature provides. The one get it from their subsistence economy and the others get it from the organic shop.* – I just saw *Bill* is looking at something like it, talking about the "voluntary peasants".[47]

---

[47] Jordan, Bill: *Rewarding Company, Enriching Life: The Economics of Relationships and Well-Being; http://www.billjordan.co.uk/pages/about.htm*

– It is only after travelling a couple of times across the campus, after getting a little bit around and frequently lost, that I really experience how large this campus of NTU is. – And it is only then as well that I see some remarkable fillips: stands for the bikes are protected from the blatant heat by trees.

It may be strange. Thinking about the exotic, another term comes to my mind: exorcist. Is there not some kind of parallel, indeed? The devil being driven out of each of us by stepping back from what we are drowned, absorbed: stepping back from routines. Allowing us to keep distance? – Many people say I would be workaholic because I frequently say that I don't really need holidays – may be they are right with the first. But the reasoning behind it seems to be wrong. I have at least currently with several jobs, despite the hasty life style, long working days,… one privilege: the privilege of distance. I told you often enough that it is not always easy – missing meeting people like you more often, the frequent lack of opportunities just to sit down for a chat, a certain loss of roots. No, don't say again what you once said: *But you have friends everywhere.* May well be – but that does not replace the loss of roots. Apparently there is no ideal world if both, distance and nearness, are privileges? – And it may well be that *Bill,* a colleague from *England* – just before I listed his latest publication – once said: *I had to stop – I was getting aware that travelling is like an addiction to me and this was the point from where I decided to decline.* (Well, just looked on his website where it says: *Bill has been a visiting professor at universities in the Netherlands, Germany, Denmark, Slovakia, Hungary and Australia.* Guess, I have to go some miles further before I have the right to get a detox-treatment – and before I have to miss the drug.)

Kitchen stories

At least Taipei seems to be a large kitchen. – Didn't we walk the one evening through Brussels – I said It is new for you, the first time you are here. So let us start with the touristy bit – later we will still have time to visit nicer places, not so busy, more genuine. And we walked from the Place du Petit Sablon, crossing the Grande Place, then going through the Petite Rue des Bouchers and along the other small lanes.

The variety of the colours of the food, competing with the shiny glimmering of the Christmas lights of the areas through which we walked before – colours and lights which no photo really can keep, so that it was not really a loss that you did not have your camera with you. People sitting around – chatting about their roaming during the day, continuing in a more relaxed atmosphere the debates from a workshop in the meeting room, more unlikely: perhaps some locals, just enjoying the evening there, after the usual business routine in the office. The colours of the food tries to compete with the colours of the various languages of people from around *Europe*, from *Asia*, from the *Americas* and all the other places; and the waiters trying to attract the favour of the passers-by. Anyway, the reason for recalling the lanes with all the restaurants is that I just saw the entirely different setting here: The lanes in *Brussels* are just like an exhibition of food – sure, beautiful, so exceptional that it nearly looks artificial. How different it is here: in many places, in the narrow lanes you find as well one restaurant next to the other. Still, it is actually more that you find various kitchens. You have the impression you walk into the kitchen of a household. Sure, I cannot really grasp the mood, the "familiarity" amongst the people. But at least my impression tells me that these are places where people come together, where... – well, I cannot really describe it. All this has a little bit of the atmosphere of *la fête* or a *bazaar* – fascinating and attracting by its prosaicness. – By the way, and perhaps part of the slimness of many people around: traditionally, here *fast food* means *small food.* Even a main meal is comparatively small, consisting of many small bowls with rice, exotic vegetables, meats, sauces and fruits – what occasionally appears to be an overloaded table is, as said, more like a jigsaw of many delicious aces. And though it is not necessarily everybody's gusto, it is a pity that the translation of *Asian fast food* tends to develop to... – *McD* or *The Large Yellow M,* you know what I mean? – Would be different to the bazaar-like setting, wouldn't it?

– Cameras and words are limited in what they can grasp, aren't they. And they still can make much more out of something than it actually is.

Part of this blindness of cameras is that it can grasp the moment, forgetting its personality, disregard that it is a very personal moment – all the experiences, expectations and sensations, if you want: the past and future history cannot be kept in this moment; they cannot be taken from us. And the muteness of language: well, isn't language always trying to generalise something, aiming on comparison, on description with the known: with what we know already and what we think others know, neglecting the uniqueness of the single moment: a moment which, taking that very moment, seems to be... – well, like laying on the ground, robbing close to the verge of a cliff and seeing something which is entirely new and will never come back to us: a snapshot, disappearing as fast as it appeared, apparently without history and without future – and nevertheless being with us as long as we are.

David and Goliath

The words *as long as we are* have another dimension going along with them. Somewhere I talked about travelling and "finding oneself", and I talked about letters between worlds; and right now, writing these lines, it comes to my mind that it is as well something as writing between generations. Much of the world here is for me not as unfamiliar as it may seem although, when I entered it the first time – not physically but with the feeling of empathy and solidarity – it had been an entirely different world. It had been names as *Vietnam; Ho Chi Minh; China,* the *Sìrénbāng (*the group within the *Communist Party of China: Jiang Qing, Zhang Chunqiao, Yao Wenyuan* and *Wang Hongwen);* the war mongrels especially from *France* and the *USA* and guerrilla war; party congresses and solidarity manifestations that now come back to my mind. It had been the time of questioning the power of mass media, of the "establishment" as we called it, the times of *Benno Ohnesorg, Rudi Dutschke, Daniel Cohn-Bendit, Bobby Sands...*

Is it this what makes me think these days not so much about *Taipei, Taiwan, China, Asia* but perhaps even more about general questions of life – its meaning, our meaning in life and life's meaning for us? Our own, personal development and "my world history"? The other day I got a nice note from *John,* encouraging me to continue dreaming:

> ***You should sleep nine hours without dreams.***
> ***Then you have the day for dreams.***

He then said: And as for dreaming, the trouble is getting those you dream about to share the dream with you at the same time. If you ever solve that one, I shan't be the only person to want to hear about it.

Is it a reformulation of what had been written in the *Economic and Philosophical Manuscripts of 1844?*[48]

> *Assume man to be man and his relationship to the world to be a human one: then you can exchange love only for love, trust for trust, etc. If you want to enjoy art, you must be an artistically cultivated person; if you want to exercise influence over other people, you must be a person with a stimulating and encouraging effect on other people. Every one of your relations to man and to nature must be a specific expression, corresponding to the object of your will, of your real individual life. If you love without evoking love in return — that is, if your loving as loving does not produce reciprocal love; if through a living expression of yourself as a loving person you do not make yourself a beloved one, then your love is impotent — a misfortune.*

---

[48]   3.4.

If I find the answer, I will let him know; I will let you know as well – and sometimes I would wish that this sharing is already the case and we just do not know it, simply because we do not talk about it.

Thinking about it, means as well to recall *Adorno's Minima Moralia,* his *Statement on Interpersonal Chill,* to reflect on what had been achieved and what remains to be done. – A paradox: Being so well aware of the antagonist character of the world, there was a world within, well able to manage some kind of forward-looking one world – *Woodstock, Joan Baez,* whom you liked so much when you heard the first times her *Diamonds....;* a world which was never to become true though it was needed to make other dreams to become true. Here I just remember some lines from the *Greek* poet *Yannis Ritsos:*

Whatever you hold in your hands

so carefully, wish so much love,

yours so totally, my companion,

you must give away

in order for it to become yours.

And now: we are sitting again in ivory towers, now we seize publishing houses by our own und tame publications on social policy in *Europe,* empowerment of individuals within the system we are forced to accept (talk shop slang for it is "agenda setting power"), and we occupy the offices... One world and one generation? – Sorry, seems that I got carried away again. Coming back to the region where I currently spend my life, we get caught by other thoughts and associations as during the earlier years. Today, we think of this area in terms of the miraculous *Asian tiger economies, Buddhism* and *Taoism,* yoga, SARS and perhaps sex-tourism and trafficking.

And it is probably the distance and still nearness of the previous world, of *my Asia* that makes it so difficult for me to cope with it now, just to live it and work here in *Our free (US-)China.* As I wrote in a mail to a colleague and friend from *Hungary:*

Hier ist es recht interessant - wenngleich recht kompliziert. Irgendwie hat mir letztes Jahr in Budapest weitaus besser gefallen: nicht weil es vertrauter war, sondern weil es mehr eigene Identitaet hat. Paradox? Ja: hier kann ich von den Schriftzeichen nichts lesen, kenne viele Dinge nicht und habe teils selbst beim einkaufen Schwierigkeiten. Aber: es ist alles sehr stark vom "grossen Bruder" gepraegt: "Schließlich war Taiwan früher unser freies (US-)China." So schrieb mir Hans-Uwe in den letzten Tagen aus Bielefeld. Ich habe ja seinerzeit, als ich dort war, lange mit Zsuzsa geredet, vor allem an dem Wochenende, als wir zum Balaton See fuhren; sie erzaehlte mir auch von den Veraenderungen, vom massiven Einfluss aus dem einen oder anderen Westen, den oekonomischen und sozialen Verwerfungen. Es war ein schoenes Wochenende, hat mir vor allem menschlich, aber auch mit Blick auf die Arbeit viel gegeben. Trotz der Einfluesse dort bei euch gilt aber doch: dort ist es ein Entwicklung. Dies bedeutet ja auch, dass man noch etwas aendern kann. Hier? Es scheint viel festgefahren, der Einfluss ist so massiv, die Strukturen und Linien scheinen so festgezurrt. Und ich haenge ein wenig dazwischen mit der Arbeit: die beiden Chinas, der Rest vom Asiatisch-Pazifischen Raum, die USA, die Querelen, die wir im Lande mit den VN haben – und da bin ich nun wie ein Stechtier am flattern. Nicht wie eine Muecke, denn sie will das Blut für sich saugen. Ich will zumindest einen kleinen Beitrag leisten zur Entwicklung der Sozialpolitik hier. Ob lange Arbeitstage mehr bewirken, als mich zu erschoepfen? Nun, was ist es anderes als das, was ich sonst mache? Was ist es anderes, als was viele von uns machen: der Alltag von David und Goliath. Und es ist noch etwas, was mich hier irritiert. So skeptisch ich gegenueber dem ganzen EU-Zauber bin, im Unterricht in Irland oder wenn ich in Bruessel bin oder auch bei Veranstaltungen wie jener kuerzlich in Debrecen, so sehr ich letztendlich EU-Kritiker bin, so sehr fuehle ich mich hier doch als ihr Vertreter und die EU als eine Art Verbuendete. Du siehst – wenn Du kommst und wir sonst nichts zu sprechen haben, so bleibt hier ein weites Gebiet.

David and *Goliath* as individuals and historical agents – sorry, the sociologist barely comes to a rest.

I was just reading a text from *Giovanni Arrighi*, fitting well into these thoughts; he states:

> *In sum, Huntington's claim that Western civilization is the bearer of a heritage of liberalism, constitutionalism, human rights, equality, liberty, the rule of law, democracy, free markets, and other similarly attractive ideals-- all of which are said to have permeated other civilizations only superficially-- rings false to anyone familiar with the Western record in Asia in the so-called age of nation-states. In this long list of ideals, it is hard to find a single one that was not denied in part or full by the leading Western powers of the epoch in their dealings either with the peoples they subjected to direct colonial rule or with the governments over which they sought to establish suzerainty. And conversely, it is just as hard to find a single one of those ideals that was not upheld by movements of national liberation in their struggle against the Western powers. In upholding these ideals, however, non-Western peoples and governments invariably combined them with ideals derived from their own civilizations in those spheres in which they had little to learn from the West.* [49]

---

[49] Arrighi, Giovanni: "Beyond Western Hegemonies": 69 - http://www.marion.ohio-state.edu/fac/vsteffel/web597/arrighi_hegemony.pdf

While I am reading texts on world systems theory, while contemplating about Hungary, I listen to *Agnes Baltsa's Songs my country taught me* – does the actual country matter; isn't it more this *something of identity?* Identity that cannot be identified – and identifying with something that, taken seriously, does not exist?

– Gosh, my friend, there is something I write to you now – and although it is something that I want to shout, so that the entire crazy world can hear it, I can only write it to you, in this confidential epistle: I have the impression – and you know that it is not the first time that I have it – that there are only three kind of people who can really be open, honest; who can be so and who actually are this: old people, who do not have to think about their carrier anymore; young people who do not think about such career yet, who just live and do what they are doing because they are curious and intelligent, looking for the real future; and people who are.... mad – mad enough to resist thinking about a career, made enough to resist the craziness of a world in which everybody seems to be ready to act like *Dr. Faustus.*

Well, perhaps all this is one reason for having forgotten my age: avoiding to admit to belong to one of these three groups in a world that does not want to know about any of them: not the old, not the young and not the mad. – You ask if I am talking about *Asia* and the people here? Please, don't ask this question – just take it as remark by somebody who is living very much between the worlds, who is living in several worlds at the same time, seeing many beams of the light, as the good old doctor; but who still does not want and cannot believe that there is only the one. who holds it in the hands, namely *Mephisto.* All this, and it seems to be somewhat universal, is about swimming, being made swimming and the control of directions – and all this in a turbulent environment of a nation which actually is two nations, *Asia* as region, the *US* as dominator and the *United Nations.* – To the best of my knowledge it is only the salmon who is able to swim completely against the odds.

Part of what I definitely mean – and just the other day *Lillian* confirmed my impression: It is an entirely *US-Americanised* and commercialised city. And in many cases and places it shows that the amalgamation, as long as it is superficial, outward, does not lead anywhere. It is somewhat frightening if you see people not being allowed to have their own life and being thrown into something where they cannot swim – I know this from *Ireland,* and I think I can honestly say that I know it as well from *Germany:* from the *old Germany* in which I grew up; and from the *new Germany* – two countries, over night being forced together by the assurance of blossoming landscapes, which could not develop because the fertiliser that had been used did not match the soil which had been already rich enough, though in another sense.

It finds a striking parallel in history – the liberty statue, usually thought as the landmark of *US*-liberalism, but in actual fact a generous present from *France*. And it is exactly this what happened: liberty perverting to liberalism; empowerment distorting and developing as power:

But I just remember as well a nice poem – not from any *"Nowhere Land"* but from *Greece*, again from *Yannis Ritsos*, if I am not mistaken written in 1968:

> *"Go on down," they told him. "Don't be afraid. Coming back*
> *up will be glorious.*
>
> *Your future crystal clear in front of you. "He hesitated.*
>
> *Still, he got himself ready in the chapel of Good Luck,*
> *passed by the abode of*
>
> *Forgetfulness and Memory, offered sacrifices on the tomb of*
> *Agamedes, washed himself in*
>
> *the Hercina, guided by two charming twelve-year-old boys,*
> *rubbed himself down with oil,*
>
> *and went ahead. At the last minute, in front of the black*
> *mouth of the oracle - the sacred*
>
> *place, closed off by an intricately decorated brass railing - he*
> *stopped. "No, no," he yelled.*
>
> *"No, no." He drew back, frightened.*
>
> *He may have remembered the unfortunate spear - bearer*
> *Dimitri, who never came back up.*
>
> *Of course they say Apollonius brought up two metal plaques*
> *from there. But he - what use*
>
> *did he have for Pythagorian verbs, the past and the future ?*
>
> *The present was preferable, however meagre and*
> *insignificant. The unknown was*
>
> *preferable. And suddenly he left all the moment's dazzle. He*
> *cut a laurel leaf, bit into it,*
>
> *and left on the run, while the admonitions and curses of the*
> *priests roared behind him.*

Escape

I am reminded of this, though from a different perspective the other evening. Coming home, I arrive the same time at the gate as one of my neighbours – I frequently said *Hello,* once asked if he would work as well for the university but had been left without answer. This evening I say as well something: *You are here as well for a longer time?* In broken *English* he answers: *Yes, a couple of month* – and in not less broken tone I reply *Così provenite dall'Italia?* All usual shyness, speaking this beautiful language, is forgotten. All restraint is forgotten. *Piacere. A che cosa state lavorando a NTU?* Despite the kind of distant question I nearly would like to embrace him – indeed, he reminds me a little bit at my friend *Marco. veni, vidi, vici* – the same strange immediate closeness, as I felt when I met *Marco* for the first time in *Berlin,* later then in *Firenze.* We converse a little bit, changing between languages. I do not mind the mistakes I make. It is just nice to see somebody from the *same country* as I am: from *Europe.* Don't grin – I do not pretend to be *Italian* – far from that although I like them. It is from here that *Europe* seems to be one country. What is at stake is that I am happy indeed to see somebody from the *old continent* and somebody with whom I don't talk really about business. It is not any loneliness; it is more the longing to escape at least briefly the dominant *American* culture and a straining job that impends to grind me and my thoughts between the various superpowers.

Despite such short encounter, there is only one way out for me – and at the moment it is the way out of town, leaving at least a little bit the city; the dense centre which hides the loss of power by exhibiting superpower and hiding the loss of the capability to act by the hyperactivity of a never-resting buzz – I need distance to be able to come back to it again; need distance as well to answer the question if I really act different, without selling my soul to the devil – if not consciously so at least by falling into the traps around me, getting caught in one of the nets, some of them nearly invisible. There is only one way out – and the few meaningless words are so meaningful when we arrive at the edge of 16 hours working days; you know the words:

> But currently I do not work much, but enjoy the summer; during the last days I made some extensive walks, did even a little bit of hiking – the meadows with the flowers, little villages, orchards and beech groves – it still is an idyllic landscape.

And I want to find this idyllic place now and here – a little bit of it at least, getting more of the glimpse of this simple excitement of the nature around.

So, let's go then – just join in thoughts, and another time I will write how I experienced it – perhaps in this part of the world the meadows with the flowers, little villages, orchards and beech groves turn into flower birds and eagles, monkeys and animals of which I don't even know the name – spiders, snakes and butterflies as large as book pages,

¡Venido, hagámoslo! – Come, let us just do it...

Peter

–

Jenny, it was so good to hear from you – you had been rare, you said and you mentioned as well something that you hesitated, writing in the language, which is foreign to you (though I barely believe that it is foreign to you). And then you simply didn't care of the language, just assumed it will be OK. Well even more so, you finally saw the situation, our situation – and perhaps the situation of life? – as it is and as I wrote on another occasion: the position as tourist in matters of every day's life, living as seafarer and going through calm, deep, shallow, wild waters – one at a time and sometimes even all at the same time. It is something that deserves its own language and so I got this strange feeling of being far away and 'home', reading your words *Mooi dat we in de 'mondiale taal' (van zeevaarders) kunnen communiceren.*

Natuurlijk kunnen wij – maar u weet het: het werkt slechts schriftelijk, in het luisteren - maar niet in het spreken. Nog niet.[50] And so I will continue in my language – in the language which is currently my language – and in the background I listen to another language we have in common: music. Music and thinking about seafaring must at one point end here – at least at the waterfront: Bedřich Smetana's cycle Má vlast, and especially the episode on the Vltava.

On the waves I am listening to, I am carried away – to the waves I was looking at when... You know the words, ending the last letter? *Come, let us just do it...; let's go then.*

The way led me... – well, first simply out of the city which is already something, isn't it? And actually it really is. When I arrived here the first day, being driven in the University's (?) Cadillac from the airport, I didn't see much. It had not been dark as the first time, when I had been here in February. Still, I was tired, I was exhausted from the heat, and I had been asking some questions, answering as well some questions about matters to come. Now being more relaxed, being eager to see something of the surrounding, I relax, just sit down (though I do not have the Cadillac at my

---

[50]   Nice that we can communicate in the 'universal language' (of seafarers). – Of course, we can. But you know I can only do it in writing, I can listen as well, but I cannot speak it. Not yet.

disposal anymore). *Linda,* the young women from the *Philippines,* is sitting next to me and I am torn, wanting to talk to her and wanting to see this… – wonder around me. Is it a wonder?

In a way I could have seen it everyday, a little bit of it, just around the corner – later, being back I will see it, being more attentive.

Linda is another seafarer though she on the land-side: at a weather-station. More precise: a social-weather station – so we have much to talk about, and I am brave enough to accept her invitation. *Yeap, will come around when I'm back in Taiwan again.* – A friend once said, *You're great in island hopping –* alluding to the frequent trips between *Ireland* and *Mainland-Europe.* Am I just starting continent hopping?

Be it as it is, we talk about 'social weather' and problems of positivism; the weather in her country – as warm as here, but not so heavy; the life in the country and her feelings about it: being proud (not nationalist) when talking about her country, being angry (not envious) about the wealth she sees around, being ashamed (not embarrassed) about having such a long way to go… – but the way she wants to go seems to be clear for her, navigating between 'modernity' and 'tradition': staying in the country and not leaving as so many of her fellow-country people and especially the women; working though admiring the family; appreciating the own countries wealth of nature and tradition and enjoying the opportunities to visit other countries; striving for affluence of the country and wanting to avoid its destruction by it. Her open character, her energetic spirit makes me believe that it is possible. Or do I just hope it – one of the dreams for daytime.

Although we are talking about so many things I look around: multi-story roads – the architects building it must have been dizzy after thinking this to an end; and they must have been puzzled seeing later that this coppice of roads actually works. The houses – thinking from here, it is a strange to look at what people in other places think should be knocked down: in *Dublin,* in *Lille,* in *Hamburg;* but not in *Amsterdam.* The buildings as such do not really play a role. Moving on, first to the *Academia Sinica,* we pass areas which seem to be a contradiction in terms – and which I always overlooked in the immediate surrounding of my apartment: tall buildings, skyscrapers even and narrow lanes, with the old cottages, or entrances with the character of what we usually think as being typical for these *Asian* areas: little hovels; the washing hanging in front for drying; people sitting under the palm-trees on the veranda, barely clothed as even in the shadow the heat is unbearable; lemons, spread out on the windscreen to ripen; the dogs, at most indolent lingering around; somebody strained by moving the heavy transport-bike, protected by the straw-hat with the broad brim; somebody pouring out the water after it had been used for cleaning something; people chatting and others trying to sell something from their little shop that looks more like a stand on flee-market – old books displayed on a table, t-shirts hanging under the little roof, leaving it to the outsider open if they are for sale or just hanging there for drying...; and of course the many kitchens, open to everybody – and all side by side with the modern shops and the buildings with the clean and clear glass fronts. In between the traditional *Asian* or even *Chinese* buildings and statues: little palaces and temples, *Buddha's*, snakes, dragons... . Little parks, sometimes with equipment for the kids to play – but occasionally they play just where it comes to their mind: under the arcades, in the entrances of the small yards... . Contradictions? Contrasts? Idyll? Harmony? It is actually difficult to say as the poverty does not look like poverty; the wealth does not look lie wealth – not here, not necessarily, not for me, the White Man, stupid or not.

In the meantime we left the densely populated areas behind and entered areas... – *Ireland,* the green island. Supposedly there are forty different shades of green – something like a propaganda-counting from *Fáilte Ireland?* Anyway, it seems that here are already twenty different shades on each single square meter. And it is not only the different shades. It is as well the density. I know the intensity of green from my little mountain back home – and every year I see it, especially in springtime or early in summer, I am simply impressed. Sitting back here in the office, writing about it gives me already this languorous feeling: no a deep breathe of that. But density is another thing – and that is something probably in need of our tropical climate as we have it here. One has the impression of touching the plants would be like touching something very soft; something spongy and still firm; one can nearly see the juice flowing through the large leaves. The trunks of the trees are quirky, turned around in themselves, the roots are growing across the ground – hide again to come up a little bit later. – It is again something so usual, here at least, that I need distance to see it.

There is another density: even here, moving away from the city, and after freeing from the impressive, truly overwhelming density of the green, houses, 'flats' in the mountains. We had been already driving through this area for a while, but only then I am getting aware of it: I am not looking at some rocks afar but at the cottages or summerhouses or any other smaller buildings – not immediately recognisable as such. It seems a mixture between mud huts, for me perhaps known from some *Spanish* shores and the *Italian* villas in *Tuscany.* From here at least, from the distance there is an appealing charm.

Much later, when we left the vehicle, sitting down amongst the trees, I take a large leaf – I do not know the name of the tree from which it had been fallen down. It is not green anymore, after being there on the ground for some time already. Still, it is a nice feeling – the feeling of holding some nature in my hands.

Using it as fan, it spends some fresh air. Looking at the yellow, moving the view on to the rocks of the coast at which we are now I ask myself that, if there is any point in counting the shades of green there must be a similar point in counting the different shades of brownish-yellow or yellowish-brown. Already when my eyes move out to the cape, it is not only the colour of the leaf that pulls me away from the green. Some distraction is coming as well from the midst of the green trees. First the distinct green little spheres with their rough crown, some of them however, turning to a brown colour and others looking like little golden orbs. They invite to nibble – like the apple tree in neighbours garden: but here it is fresh pineapple. Not sure if it is allowed, I pick one – as far as I know, biblical *Adam* convinced *Eve* to take the apple. I am not opening a new chapter of that script; there is no snake needed to convince me to pick a fruit. It is difficult to peel it without knife but...: the taste is wonderful: the freshness, the fruity juice, the light breeze from the seaside and the view along the cape. – Is it not strange that one forgets the entire world just by being and feeling right in the middle of it?

The browns and yellows are not attracting simply because of the variation of these two merging and differentiating colours, but as well because of the different shapes of the rocks – truly a spectacle in stone, a rigidly-standing movement – the visualisation of a contradiction in terms. One can visualise the years of water and wind, which played with sand, rock and whatever material was available to form this unbelievable peculiarity – forms which inevitably remind me at the paintings of *Salvador Domingo Felipe Jacinto Dalí y Domènech*, especially the period which I tend to call 'loss of time' or 'melting time'. Rocks with their bizarre forms, evoking the feeling of stepping out of reality without leaving it, stepping into a new reality, getting lost in its variety without ever arriving. Going nearer, melting at least on the surface and the attention being caught by something that appears as untouchable treasure of nature with its obvious life, one can see the details, without understanding them: the rocks appear to be made from sand – sandcastles for eternity; forms pressed into the surface – flowers stencilled on the seemingly soft surface, captured for infinity... until we reach the blue water. Blue? One shade of blue, forty shades of blue, every single movement seems to induce a new variety of the one colour – shades as movement, something roving and permanently redefining borders, marking them and taking them away.

We are already on the way back, moving to the vehicle to go back to the city. It is entirely unprepared, without any warning. First a few drops, a couple of minutes a soft rain and then: bucketing is not true, it is more like standing in a pond, one nearly develops a longing for a snorkel, yearning for free and deep breathing. Did I just ask *Is it not strange that one forgets the entire world just by being and feeling right in the middle of it?* Another question has to follow: Isn't it bizarre that under certain conditions, after a nice encounter with nature, with genuine life, one can easily overlook what would drive one berserk another time?

Next day, being back in the office I face another matter of continent hopping: I am meeting a colleague – being here briefly in *Taipei* between a meeting in the *PR* and *US* and *UN:* The *Peoples Republic,* the *United States* and the *United Nations.* I am surprised, really feel honoured: This person, after a lengthy talk, is honestly thanking me for being ready to talk about the work I am doing, our work, showing interest and readiness to support. I feel honoured myself – and I do not have any problems to say it and mean it. Actually, I nearly mention it only after having it done: a slight bow underlines my honest appreciation.

– Isn't it weird, bizarre indeed: *Stockholm* comes to my mind, the *Kungliga Operan* and visit to that beautiful opera house in the *Staden på vattnet*[51] as business affair.

Is the reason for this perhaps simply the quote from the review I just finished before the meeting, where I quoted that the actual topic would be *balancing work and being-out-of-work/non-work.*[52] Or does it come to my mind because I quoted during out talk the famous passage about conditions under which

> *nobody has one exclusive sphere of activity but each can become accomplished in any branch he wishes, society regulates the general production and thus makes it possible for me to do one thing today and another tomorrow, to hunt in the morning, fish in the afternoon, rear cattle in the evening, criticise after dinner, just as I have a mind, without ever becoming hunter, fisherman, herdsman or critic.*

Or is there another reason behind it – behind *Stockholm* and its pleasant opera house?

Seems that Irishness has me well in its claws – for me the weather is an issue whereas here it is just taken as it comes, is and goes. Barely that somebody talks about it; and if so it seems to be something which is done for the poor

---

[51]   City On Water
[52]   Balance zwischen Arbeit und Nicht-Arbeit – it is nearly impossible to translate the term Nicht-Arbeit.

guys from abroad. There is one exception – well, not really. It is an exception only as I get the impression that people feel obliged to talk to me about it. In the perspective of factual information – I look it up later – everything seems to be very clear – wikipedia informs me:

> *A tropical cyclone is a meteorological term for a storm system characterized by a low pressure center and thunderstorms that produces strong wind and flooding rain. A tropical cyclone feeds on the heat released when moist air rises and the water vapour it contains condenses. They are fuelled by a different heat mechanism than other cyclonic wind storms such as north-eastern wind storms windstorms, and polar lows, leading to their classification as "warm core" storm systems.*

More or less as clear as what I read in my policy book:

Linear: $\qquad Y=a+bX$

Diminishing effect: $\quad Y=a+b \, LOG \, (X)$

Changed direction: $\quad Y=a+b_1X+b_2X^2$

There is another language for the first, i.e. for the weather at least – Friday afternoon, I didn't see *Jaclyn* and I didn't hear anything before. But that doesn't mean anything – she is doing her business, always being there if I need her but not always being around. For my part, I didn't manage to leave the office, not even for a coffee around the corner – the rain is two heavy. – It is going towards 4 pm. and I receive a mail from the neighbouring building: *Jaclyn* writes:

> *… Hope you are well in these rainy days.*
>
> *You may already know there's a typhoon coming in tonight, and the whole island will be covered by this storm for a few days. The storm is huge and the wind will be very strong when it hits the island, so want to inform you that be careful of the flying object outside; it could be a fell-off fascia, a falling branch, etc. Also, you may want to prepare some more food at home just in case stores closed for the storm.*

Not entirely sure what I have to think about the last line now:

> *Have a nice weekend.*

I know that she doesn't mean it this way, but it sounds somewhat cynical.

Somewhat later another mail – from *Theresa*, concerning some workshop I proposed; the mail ends:

There had been already one typhoon – well, it had been a day which could have been better; but nothing that was really worth mentioning. But these warnings... . I want to leave the office early – after trying to comfort myself, writing to *Jaclyn:*

...

Thanks for the news - though it is not the best one. Will take your advice on board. I'll try to be brave. But at the end of the day I managed in my house for couple of days - being cut of by storm, heavy rain, not having heating (as I didn't have any electricity due to the storm) – and that was during a rather cold winter.... The only room where I have had a fire place..., well I couldn't use it as the wind destroyed the glass in the window. So I hope the experience in this case will not be too shocking.

Will leave soon (if rain allows), getting some stuff for the fridge.

I really leave early, it seems to be quite, at least no heavy rain – just the right time... – the right time to cycle cannily to the near *Roosevelt Road.* – All is quite and I consider that it may be perhaps just fact that *this something* has a name, making it more imminent. Wind is wind, storm is storm, but here we have a typhoon – the 'a' makes the difference. And real storms, hurricanes, get even a 'personal' name: *Andrew, Ivan, Katrina, Rita, Wilma...* I park the bike, walk under the arcade to the bakery, leave the shop again and... even under the protective roof of the walkway there is now barely hope to stay dry. Amazing. I would have thought there couldn't be so much water in the sky for such a rain to persist more than 5 minutes. But it seems that could well last another hour, or two, or... – I recall the words from the mail: *you may want to prepare some more food at home just in case stores closed for the storm.* – OK, it is warm enough; I have my trunks with me. Why should I not do in *Taipei,* what I did some twenty years ago in *Hamburg?* Fortunately the rain calms down so that I can get home – not dry, but in a reasonable state. I said *The rain calmed down,* didn't I? Moving on, I mention actually that it is – for what I am used to – quiet, in a strange way quiet. The *cicadas* stopped for a long time again their whirling communication; but as well the traffic was kind of distant, unreal. Though a few cars had been driving along the street, some people were walking around – or even rushing from one protecting corner to another and even the police stood in the middle of the junction, regulating the little bit of traffic, there was something that gave all this the glance of a ghost town.

Later, I have had dinner as usual at home and after talking to *Lillian* on the phone, I went another time to the office. Around 7 pm., the rain ceased, there was barely any wind but there was still this strange, somewhat frightening silence. Was it really different to other evenings? Or had it been the idea and the lack of knowledge of the *Stupid White Man* that gave the impression of something special going on? In *Aghabullogue*, the birds would tell; and in the evening the cattle would do so – another language which is not spoken here and so I just wait for things to come. Finally it would not be the first time that I end up in sleeping in any office.

I have to finish the book I am working on – at least I have to build a sound scaffold while I am here. Getting the question right, getting the fundamental information; getting it at least to that stage that somebody else could continue and fill in the little bits and pieces. I know I have to do that as myself – but still, the scaffolding should be ready. Outside it is still quiet – and dry. Finally I go around the corner for my habitual Cappuccino in the evening, carrying a book with me. I sit down in the comfortable armchair, open the book... and close it again. *Kang-ren* comes: *Ní hǎo. – Good evening to you;* and although I do not have time, I am grateful for the distraction. We talk about god and the world – not *Benedict's* version but our own. Both academics, living in the world of social science and knowledge, both atheists, not believing in any metaphysics, our worlds are so different and especially: it even matters that the god in which we do not believe, is a different one. – Well, actually, in *Kang's* case I should say: *Chinese* religion not being simply monotheist, she does not believe in the various gods on offer. – Near our table three *Chinese* people are sitting together, their loud voice, the exhilarated behaviour makes me feel uncomfortable – or is it the broad *American-English accent* they use which gives me this feeling?

Later I move back to the office. After a little bit of further writing I switch off the computer, air-condition and light... – and, if not the brain, so the concentrated and focused thinking on the topic I am working on: *Social Quality – Looking for a Global Social Policy. A Contribution to the Analysis of the Development of Welfare States.* –It is only now that I hear the storm – the wind breaking at the corners, soughing. As usual, it is late. I am leaving the office and a little bit further, away from the houses it is actually not so much the wind, but again the strange quietness. Though I am not really the only one who is still moving outdoor, it is the first time that I feel that even this city with the million people living here can be calm. It is the first time as well that I really see it: even here, in the midst of the city is a sky, strangely coloured – and paradoxically it is just this day, after it had been getting dark very early, that the different reflections of light give the impression of a strange brightness. On the short way to the apartment – fortunately it is not raining – I begin to translate the language of the birds. There are only a few; they are rushing from tree to tree, hastening just to the next one and rarely going further – as much as there is safe distance there is now safe nearness. It is only few minutes later that I experience the wisdom of this behaviour. I arrive the apartment, open the large gate with the bright colourful blue glass mosaic. The heavy gate falls into the lock, I fasten the bike, make the four steps to the door, open it and the very same second the sky seems to open like a sluice, it would be enough water to make one soaking in less then a minute.

As said, *Theresa* ended her mail with the words

and take care of yourself during the typhoon. Get some food and water first

It was a couple of times while being here that I thought about the sincerity of supply with water as one of the fundamental rights. We take it for granted – and even here it seem not to be a problem. The reason why I get so much aware of it, is simple: Usually I neglect drinking – too much coffee with its counterproductive effect and then at one stage mentioning, or being in an unedifying way reminded, that I need these two litres or something like it to allow the reproduction of the some 90 % of which the human body is made up. But here I cannot cope with that behaviour, I am naturally drawn to it: drink something, drink water – it seems to be a voice that insists and will not be quite before the body gets its right. And there is another reason. Going into a coffee shop or a restaurant, in many cases a glass of water is offered – and the glass barely remains empty. Here in the University there are modern providers of water: ice-cold, tepid and hot, so that one may even speak of implementing the fundamental right for choice – blunt American-style capitalism which is so much dominating the life-style here, did not take it away; not yet, and not in all places though there are some places where... – fundamental rights in contradiction: the claimed right to private property, claimed by few, and the right to avail of water. *Anatole France* comes to my mind

The law, in its majestic equality, forbids the rich as well as the poor to sleep under bridges, to beg in the streets, and to steal bread.

Doesn't the cynicism of this genius of a writer grasp my entire task here – as I wrote earlier the task is *developing an integrated framework for the future social policy in theory and practice:* Water as material condition: as matter of socio-economic security; its easy and free accessibility: as matter of cohesion; the accessibility for everybody and everywhere: as matter of inclusion; its availability as matter of giving people the right to live their own life, independent of mercy of others: as matter of empowerment. The variety of what is available, not variety of the same but variety within the fundamentally equal: as social quality, something even individual in the understanding concrete which

> is concrete because it is the concentration of many determinations, hence unity of the diverse.[53]

Sunday, the wind ceased, it is not raining anymore and the usual buzz took over. Sunday morning, not part of the buzz, but of life in *Taipei:* in front of the window of my office a group gathered for a session of *Tàijíquán.* The coach is just an startling beauty – I guess the ideal of a man in terms of prettiness – he could stand as model for the *Chinese Michelangelo* of our times: slim, strong, following his slow movements one can see the 'relaxation of tense muscles', the 'tightness of entertainment', the 'extravagance of ordinary movements'. Then the two salience young women in the group of perhaps ten people: just looking at them seems to ample to decrypt any code behind the *Asian Leonardo da Vinci* of our days: Slim, of course; the long black hair underlining the perpendicular, straight posture; the movements showing an elegance that seems to be artificial, and even in that it expresses nativeness. – Indeed, especially these little things are probably only visible to us when we travel on our own.

Still, there is something strange; looking at the group and the individual dancers, being magnetised by the three beauties... . Now, earlier the morning, the time I arrived, I looked at somebody else, as well standing in the green area which I can see from the office – a man from the street, may be forty, fifty years of age. His street clothes are more than casual; one may say that he is even a little bit chubby; his face is covered by a beard, to be more precise: he simply looks as he didn't shave yet, just arriving there after getting up. He is performing as well the *Tàijíquán.* But strangely, it is more fascination in watching him than in looking at the three beauties. It takes some time for me to find the reason. Is it because the others are 'training'? Is it because the people in the group are looking so different, only the three of exceptional beauty, in these extremes strongly underlining the contrast to 'normality'? Is it because I can see the face of the one who is actually standing nearer to the window – the face, completing... ? Yes, it is this completeness, the completeness gained by the face that is obviously part of the entire exercise; but as well the completeness of something else. I can see it later, when most of the people of the group left, only the coach, one of the young women and somebody else remaining – I did not really recognise the other before, he was just part of the group. Now, a few small exercises give

---

[53]   From the Grundrisse

evidence of what harmony of a group is – it is still difficult for me to grasp; it is something I see as well in the park, when I am jogging, seeing the many people around, the groups exercising *Tàijíquán* or employed by other group-exercises. Is it this what is so difficult for us when we try to look at *Confucianism?*

I recall a passage from one of the books on my desk.

> *It is the group not the individual that matters. The groups in question – families, corporations, entire societies – are structured hierarchically. They rest in principle on ascending orders of duty and obligation, and descending orders of responsibility and care. There is (or should be) a place for everyone; everyone should know his or her place and behave accordingly. It s only in the unique combination of his/her relationships to others that the properly exists.*

> *So individuals are deemed to be possessed of roles and duties, never 'rights regardless'. Entitlements are a function of performance and position within the group. Seniority brings its just rewards with advancement up the hierarchy. Thus the individual's position is forever evolving, not static.*[54]

Perhaps all this can only be understood after looking at individuals and groups doing their exercises.

Without doubt, there is still much on the way ahead what I have to understand – what I want to understand. So much – and so much work already to process from what I understood already. I continue writing – some old stuff which should be already for a long time at press; some stuff which can easily be done in between – small things of which the most difficult part is just to decide: *Do it, and do it now!* There is so much other distraction. Thinking back – the last time we met; thinking about the future. The question if we will meet again. How will the different projects and jobs evolve – alone and working together. All these silly questions of who, and where and when. And the one question which is even more silly: Who asked this question in the first instance? Even more silly – and perhaps even more important than all the others though I am not sure which of these question is actually relevant at all; meaning: the answer on which of the questions is actually a matter of our personal, active, controlled and conscious decision.

It is calm – no wind, no rain. Sunday, meaning as well not really day-to-day's business – today people are not at work. I follow my Sunday's entertainment and continue the correction of a script. That the Internet connection, the

---

[54] *Jones, Catherine: The Pacific Challenge. Confucian Welfare States; 198-217; Catherine Jones (Ed.): New Perspectives on the Welfare State in Europe; London./New York: Routledge1993*

mail program is working in the background is more a routine: starting the computer, automatically launches some standard programmes from the Dock. While making a note on the margin of the script, I hear the chime, announcing the arrival of a mail. I briefly look up; a known sender – so I begin reading:

> *I am busy doing my thing as usual – I try not to get overburdened by work since I haven't done any for about 40 years – publishing is fun and can't be considered work. I do the treadmill now and walk outside on brisk walks....*

The editor of a Journal on European Economics and Politics approaches me, inviting me to join the editorial board. It is, of course, a pleasure – though I do not know exactly why. Because the invitation is coming from somebody who approaches work in the same way as I do: as 'fun'? Because it is something from which and with which I can develop more contacts? Because it gives me some place which I can call 'home' in what some people consider a postmodern world and of which I still think it is very much a pre-modern society? At least I am sure that it is not a matter of taking part in this most absurd race for scientific standards – a race that uses all means which can only have one result: perversion and undermining of scientific standards. In this regard I feel more and more that these systems of peer-reviewing, quotation-indexes, of Power Pointing presentations etc. are the best way of producing meaningless, monologues rather than the claimed debates. In this light, the invitation is in a way not necessarily a reason to be proud of; but at least a reason for opening a large array of deliberation. Having said the invitation is a pleasure, as this and many of 'my personal listings' are probably more listings that are dealing with something that is contested; some are possibly even a kind of blacklist in the view of traditionalists and mainstreamers and SSClers.

So I can be equally satisfied about some other voluntary work: After more or less difficult communications with a Dutch publishing house, negotiations about acting as editor of a book-series seem to come to an end – *terug naar Europese aanwezigheid in termen van het publiceren.*

I could be carried away right now: post-modern, pre-modern – and I saw in the text I am proofreading, my elaboration on re-feudalisation and the development of education and research. No, I will not allow this distraction – enough that I do some final work on a publication on this topic. And I don't even allow myself to answer the mail. Instead, I am forcing myself... – forcing myself to leave the office, to get carried away at least for a couple of hours by something else.

As said *It is calm – no wind, no rain.* Now, finally I really know as well why, when it is humid, we use the expression *It is heavy.* I make it out by feeling that the burden of the warm air is taken off my shoulders and it is obviously possible to move, to walk freely.

Sunday, meaning as well not really day-to-day's business – today people are not at work and after the typhoon the air is somewhat clear, with around 30° it is not too warm and the *RealFeel*® (*didn't even know that my feeling is now as well a registered trademark – Oh, Naomi, if you have any genius it is to think about the title NO LOGO in a world where even feelings are trademarked and bear a logo*) temperature of 35° invites for a little spin. Finally, there is not too much time left – this year; and some days ago *Hsiao-Hung Chen* told me: Just five years ago *Taipei* had been the most liveable city in *Asia.* So, it is time to look at the *Tàijíquán* of every day's life, at least of a probably quote ordinary Sunday.

It is a short trip only from the office – cycling for about 4 minutes across the campus, crossing *Roosevelt Road,* moving through one of the small avenues and after perhaps 10 minutes I am at the river – the cycle lane in front of me. Another small jolt: Don't stop here; later you can sit down, do a little bit of writing. Now it is time to move, explore the *Tàijíquán of every day's life.*

Convinced, I move up, role down the small bank, turn sharp to the right – now I am really on the lane, in the middle of two jungles. The one welcomes and absorbs me like a little cocoon. Though there are people around, they don't really reach me. Everybody is doing his or her own thing. Some of them overtake me on their modern racing bikes; I overtake others. Under the first bridge some people are simply resting – kids are playing; some people are entertaining themselves at the climbing wall. Another bridge, converted to a tennis-hall – there is space enough for at least five tennis courts; this richness of nature in the middle of the town is somewhat disturbing. The irritation is not the fact of being there; it is more because it is so easy to forget – or should I say come to oneself? The dragonflies performing their love dance before mating; the little birds jazzing in front of blossoming flowers; the cattail moving gently in the soft wind – and the lane curling through the river meadow. I want to move on and on and... –... and I want to sit down, sit down in one of the little fields of rocks, being piled up as invitation for a rest. That a young couple is resting there, listening to the various sounds of the birds, looking at the river, probably exchanging sweet nothings – makes me following the other temptation: rather than sitting down I continue cycling. Being caught in the green, subtropical cocoon, I get occasionally nevertheless glimpses of the other jungle around me: 2,630,872 people, living in the huge buildings which are visible across the riverbank. Although they are so close, it seems as if they would be far away, part of another world. And with this distance to the large houses I see probably the first time the tiny architectural adornments. Nearly not visible, they make suddenly such a huge difference. I arrive at the outskirts, the buildings are lower now, there is more variety – or is it more visibility of variety. I sit down for some time, having my simple lunch: some bread and fresh fruit. Cyclists are passing, children humming their little songs, people chatting or simply enjoying the day, taking the pleasure in moving – for people for whom work is burden and for people for whom it is just fun this fusion with the nature, this kind of activity is irresistible – the ease of fresh air, the nature's own buzz and the ease of mind.

Time to return – and brave as I am, I move just at some bridge back into the city – the Sunday buzz of people doing some shopping, sitting down for something to eat, standing at the corners for a chat... – what a difference to the surrounding I just left a couple of minutes ago. Though I see some cosiness and contemplation here as well, it appears as foreign matter.

The world, the environment in which people live mirrors so much the need of

> *both a new mode of production and a new object of production...: a new manifestation of the forces of human nature and a new enrichment of human nature. Under private property their significance is reversed: every person speculates on creating a new need in another, so as to drive him to fresh sacrifice, to place him in a new dependence and to seduce him into a new mode of enjoyment and therefore economic ruin. Each tries to establish over the other an alien power, so as thereby to find satisfaction of his own selfish need. The increase in the quantity of objects is therefore accompanied by an extension of the realm of the alien powers to which man is subjected, and every new product represents a new potentiality of mutual swindling and mutual plundering. Man becomes ever poorer as man, his need for money becomes ever greater if he wants to master the hostile power.[55]*

It is especially here in the shopping malls where this gets so clear – especially by feeling the contrast to the still existing debris of different histories, the penetration of ongoing differences in culture and lifestyles and positions... – and respect. Apparently not known anymore, but still present, hidden behind hectic and logos. In corners, in gestures, in gazes that occasionally meet the wanderer, being hidden for the occupant.

This *Tàijíquán* is so far from the one to which I know. The *Tàijíquán* – once I walked with a friend through *Paris.* She was born and reared up in the *Pyrenees* – and whenever she talked about that part of the world one could feel with every word how much she still loved the place – one could imagine

---

55   Economic and Philosophical Manuscripts, 1844: 3.3

her, as little girl playing and dancing in the fields, one could see her vividly sitting as young women with her friends in the village, at the foot of one of the castles... . But meeting her in *Paris*, walking a through the quarter, the famous quartier, *her Quartier Latin* and talking with *Marie-Laure* about all the places as if we would talk about common friends, it was as if she would have lived there not just for one life time – I know this identification with a place, with space, with its history especially from many of my *French* friends who live so much in their life in their communities in their societies in their history. I know it from many of my *French* friends. And I know it as well from *Italian* friends. Standing there, earlier the year with *Marco* on the *Piazzale Michelangelo* above *Florence* and listening to him, talking about *Leonardo da Vinci, Galileo Galilei and equally about Giovanni Spadolini,* the two living for us from history books, the one living as part of personal history, walking later with *Marco* and *Michele* through the town, enjoying a most beautiful meal in one of the historical buildings – a kind of family-restaurant where I felt so warm-heartedly accepted by the owner and the chef, conversing so nicely, so that it was like merging with the city, country, history, presence and future... – and from *Andy*, my neighbour, when we sit down on the rock in the field in the *Jasjana Poljana* and he talks about the All-Ireland Championship in which the village played an important role, the development of farming, the third-level education in Ireland, the fights in *The Rebel County...*

Unforgettable moments, for me at least. Unforgettable because they are not forgetting and opening doors to the future. It is this merger of people, time and space – so different and still so very much the same, being about acquainting with each other, with place and times; and it takes time and personalities in every day's *Tàijíquán;* difficult to learn as it is at least seemingly for many times learning and standing against the odds.

Now it is time to end of writing, end writing to you. Colourful greetings and be good – against the odds if needed,

Love from Peter

–

Hello, cherished one,

I thought about it. Perhaps it isn't really important from where people come, maybe that the nationality doesn't really matter and probably it had been just by chance that I made these beautiful experiences of a merger of people, time and space especially there in *Italy* and *France.* After sending the letter and after thinking about it, I remember similar occasions with others, people from other countries. *Budapest, Dnipropetrovsk, Munich, Skriketorp* and some others, not too many; and, of course, I remember this impression as well from being together with you. And so the few words at the end of the last letter are probably much more important than I thought when I scribbled them: *it takes time and personalities in every day's Tàijíquán; difficult to learn as it is at least seemingly for many times against the odds.*

Last year when I had been in *Hungary*, *Steph* sent me this nice poem: *Children and Jesters.* And now *John* sent me another poem, he got it from one of his *German* ancestors; it is written by *Theodor Fontane.*[56] The second stave goes as follows:

> *Das gibt dann eine glatte Fläche,*
> *Man gleitet unbehindert fort,*
> *Und „allgemeine Menschenschwäche"*
> *Wird unser Trost- und Losungswort.*[57]

Answering John, I am asking if these are just the words of the settled, middle-aged, prospering citoyen, for children and *jesters* and people who are old enough to understand the world rather than assuming that they understand their own life – for the latter the poem may be different, reading:

> *Da gibt es keine glatte Flaeche*
> *Nichts geht ungehindert fort*
> *Und allgemeine Menschenwuerde*
> *Wird zum Stachel und zum Kampfeswort.*[58]

Talking about *spike* and talking about this *want* – it is as well something which exists for me in a nearly mysterious way: I want, well: I feel I have to know more about this surrounding, this current home – not just the physical environment or anything tangible. I have to know where I am – to know finally who I am.

It seems to be farfetched to talk about the imprisonment of which I hear – a colleague was imprisoned. Political considerations had been mentioned as reason – lack reliability and the strong suspicion that he would be terrorist

---

[56] *Theodor Fontane:Gedichte. [J. G. Cotta'sche Buchhandlung Nachfolger, Stuttgart und Berlin, 16. Auflage 1911, Seite 23]. Sprüche. 10*

[57] That then is a levelled surface
unhampered one slides forth
And the saying of "general weakness of us all"
Is comfort and the opening word.
(translation P.H.)

[58] There is no levelled surface
nothing can just slide further
Now, human dignity works like a spike
Something we want to reach for all.

activist. Saying it is a colleague actually means that he is working in a similar field as I do. The *Guardian* writes:

> *Dr B is alleged to have used, in his academic publications, "phrases and key words' also used by a militant group, among them "inequality" and "gentrification". The police found it suspicious that meetings occurred with German activists in which the sociologists did not bring their mobile phones; the police deemed this a sign of "conspiratorial behaviour".*

You are wondering? You heard that *Taiwan* is a democracy and these things would not happen anymore? Look, I am not talking about *Taiwan* – may be such things still happen here as well; but this case happened in *Germany*, the colleague is imprisoned in *Moabit*, in *Berlin*. I get the information from colleagues somewhere in *Germany*; but I get it as well from *John*; I sent it from here back to colleagues in *Europe* – amongst others to a colleague in… – yeah, in *Berlin*, he being a stone's throw away from the nick.

I am not writing this here to talk about the case, though it awkward enough to talk about it. The reason for writing about it is that I feel, and hope *Andrej* felt during his time in detention that he was not alone, despite sitting there not only in prison but under conditions which had been compared with *Guantánamo*. Sure, there is some speculation about his feelings – and his feeling of not being alone. But it is actually this – being alone, feeling togetherness, being together with others, being alone – that is so suspenseful, so tantalising. I wrote about the huge number of people doing their exercises every morning in the parks; the huge amount of scooters; I wrote about the way of living, of accommodation – and I mentioned the difficulties I have with it, at times feeling suffocating, the feeling of these masses encroaching on me like the heat lacing up my throat. But it is not really the density – it is more…

You know, I would like you being here anyway – exploring this world, new for both of us. I think I know you well enough: your individualism, perhaps reclusiveness, independence, own will-power – the right word is missing; and at the same time your openness, so ingratiating, charming. Being enough reason to enjoy your presence, there is another reason for liking you to be here with me. Back in *Europe*, I frequently talked with *Laurent* about the situation here, in the *Asian countries*. And he said something like *The social is entirely new to them – they do not even have a word to properly translate it.* And actually it seems to be true as the difference between *social* and *society* seems to be only the difference between an adjective: 社會的 and a noun: 社會.

I stumbled across this question today again, taking another entrance of the campus, passing the sports grounds. It is again and again amazing... – and I am wondering how you would feel about it, how you could live it. The actual reason for such a question is that there is a similar kind of ambiguity or ambivalence as I just mentioned thinking of you: independent and included, opposing and coherent... . A couple of days *Gertraud* wrote that it may be this 'mass society', the density people experience, that gives them need and power for meditation, for *Tàijíquán*. Seclusion rather than *The Lonely Crowd* of the late 1950s *Changing American Character*. Don't be afraid – or do not hope I might return as any kind of guru, bringing with me any *Asian* wisdom and teaching of new spirituality; nor will I come back as renascent *Christian*. But philosopher as I am by training, it is inspiring to think about it. Of course you know 陰陽; well, if not this way you may recognise them as *yīnyáng*, or as... – well, here they are:

right, *yin* and *yang*. After reading a little bit in the *Chinese Classics* and *Kǒng Fūzǐ, Xun Zi, Wu Xing* and as well again *Matteo Ricci,* I first approach them in the common way – finally I am Stupid White Man although I should know better from the reading of the 50 or so volumes and already from the reading of *Hegel* without which the others cannot be understood anyway: the dichotomy of good and evil. Reading further, I see that this is much more – something *Alan* and so many others who are looking for *a levelled surface, on which unhampered one slides forth* is apparently not able to grasp: it is the simple idea of dialectics: ancient *Greek* philosophy knows it, ancient *Chinese* philosophy knows it, modern philosophy knows it – only real life, especially real *American*-style seems to have difficulty with it. Societies based on strict competition are limited to think in dichotomies, in terms of opposition, in terms of exclusion – a binary-code-society; 陰陽 suggests another time the unity of contradictions: *yīnyáng* as matter of change. – The immediate interaction of micro- and macrocosm, or in the understanding of *Nicholas of Cusa* that *God is at once the greatest and the smallest, being present in all things as all things are present in him* or in the words of a modern philosopher: *god being permanent and the world being fluent but as well the world being permanent and god being fluent.* Leaving deism aside, here, in daily life only seeing the stroke of the broad brush, it remains striking how we manage this macro and micro in so different ways. Is there one single solution for 陰陽 ? Is there one specific *yīnyáng* for every society? Is *yin* and *yang* a matter everybody has to find for him and herself? I try to imagine turning this

around with a very high speed – what will happen to the two colours? What will happen to the forms? What will happen to the entire shape and its dimension? It may be left for another time to decide if it is correct or not, but there is definitely a good reason for thinking in circles, cycles of balance and imbalance, for considering generating and creating *(shēng)* as well as overcoming and destructing *(kè)* and an overacting cycle *(cheng)* and an insulting cycle *(wu)*.

Do you remember? When I wrote about the Typhoon I said it may appear particularly dangerous as it has a name; the hurricane being even more dangerous and having even more a name. On the other hand, the fascination does not need a name, it is even destroyed by it – it maintains it only by its mystery, by the possibility of delving into the unknown, delving deeper and deeper, first snorkelling, then moving deeper, gaining independence by the oxygen cylinder as a kind of handbook, methodological guideline between the worlds.

– Thinking about it, sitting on the bank at the little pond, reading in the book which I hold on my lap, the letters begin to blur: *Confucius* – confusius – confusios – confusion. Dozing in the sun of the early morning, I recall a poem from *The True Tao* – it is written by *Chuang Tzu:*

> *Creation and destruction*
>
> *When you break something up, you create things.*
> *When you create something, you destroy things.*
> *Material things have no creation or destruction.*
> *Ultimately these concepts connect as one.*
>
> *Only the enlightened know that they connect as one,*
> *So instead of debating this with your preconceptions,*
> *Approach it in an ordinary way.*
>
> *Those with this ordinary approach, simply apply the idea.*
> *Those who apply it, connect with it.*
> *Those who connect with it, attain it.*
> *This easily attained understanding is not far off.*

I hear the clear voice of the birds in the trees around me, do not know their name, cannot imagine that I ever saw the beauty which their voice wheedles. For me, they do not have a name, they do not have a face and they do not need it. And by this they tell me something I have to try to teach *Alan* who has this fundamental 'dislike' of dialectics as he apparently never understood it. And I have to maintain at least in all these debates on EUropean streamlined thinking, when sitting in one of the heavy chairs in political and academic ivory towers, that we will not be able to overcome contradictions by putting a new name on them. We will not succeed by over-adapting =

submitting ourselves. *Shēng* is not *cheng* and will never be so. 陰陽 is dialectics, is unity of contradictions.

I continue to listen to the birds, hear their strange voices – hear that they are telling me to go on, not to capitulate before understanding the next mystery and the next mystery and...

–... and it needs in any group this specific understanding and maintenance of self. A little bit later, leaving the cosy place to return to my office, I continue these thoughts in a rather different way. The old man who walks aside of his wheelchair which is pushed by his much younger companion: slightly trembling, he folds his hands and makes several bows towards me – then: thumbs up; I automatically slow down in my jogging and bid him well, make also a bow, not only nodding the head but bending the upper part of my body. Passing another time the sports ground – the young lads training volleyball, playing cricket before they go to work, before the suffocating heat competes with the overpowering rivalry. In front of the office building the group dancing to American music, following the rhythm of the music and moving in an elegant, swinging way and only a few yards away the old woman – barely able to stand upright, holding tight to her..., yes, the wheelchair, dancing as well, peppy in her own way; ... all such experiences seem not to be 'time out' – and it seems not to need such 'time out', the few moments that I feel even in this for me so alien environment as well a kind imminence, of nearness of respect despite the distance – there seems to be only a tiny difference between immanence and eminence, but it is a huge step to overcome it.

So, the home is not least: 'the self', independent of space, knowing that there is always a way back to that: to the self. Nearly always, as it is probably just this what causes some trouble for me: the loss of control. And yes, others need it in terms simply of the permanency of being somewhere, sticking to it: The famous *Sauerbraten, Cheddar, petit sale, kutja, olla prodrida, challa...* . – Sure, I shouldn't talk about eating and sticking to the same – stubborn country boy, once coming from Westphalia and very little adventurous especially when it comes to eating. Just a matter of *Aodhán's little tea kettle* of which I wrote from *Hungary...* . Or just something I frequently excuse by being vegetarian? – definitely a limitation in experimenting with food.

But actually, I am not as stubborn as it sometimes seems to be the case. I went with *Der-Lan* to lunch, a young *'American'* woman in the sense of having her PhD from there and being there as well for frequent teaching... . Nevertheless quite nice – perhaps because she once said that she thinks *Taiwanese* society and *Taiwanese* people are too *'American'* and she would try to get away from the connections she has ex officio to that country at the other end. Anyway, she is vegetarian as well and so we went to a special restaurant when she invited me for lunch: 春天素食餐廳 – *Spring Natural Vegetarian Restaurant*. For me it meant security! I still didn't go for the faked meet. So many other things: flowers,… – well, I could tell you if my memory for all these things would be good enough. Sorry, for these things it is as good as for dates, pin-numbers and ways to the hotel. But the texture and taste will remain engraved in my memory. Bizarre – the impression of entirely new flavours: not sweet, not acetous, not even sweet-tart but a real and strange merger. Not bitter not dry, but a new taste of acerbity… – it, not the taste but this strangeness of experience reminds me of…, well: perhaps of ski-touring, the most exciting thing I experienced not long ago: The exhilaration of one year holiday, condensed in one day. I knew all different kinds of skiing, of walking, of climbing, of hill-walking, and with ski-touring, a little bit of everything I entered a new world, the only word coming to my mind is: sky-touring, both ways feeling like being in heaven. Similar here: eating one of these dilly things, a reminder of many things known from before and still an entirely new world – a heaven of a special taste.

Ah, talking about heaven, I think I never told you… – well, the other day I got a mail from a friend, from *Hungary*. May be you remember, I mentioned her on another occasion. She wrote about the harvest, the hard work and that next day they would go to a traditional wedding. And this brought back to my mind another story which is at least for me something very special. Though I love music and actually love dancing, I never did it again after leaving the traditional 'dancing school' probably everybody attended at the time and age – guess I had been at the tender age of fourteen or so. I just didn't do it anymore, perhaps being too much caught by the idea that dancing is about rules and very definite steps rather than about rhythm. Now, having been in *Debrecen* earlier the year – I had to give a speech there during a conference – *Judit* organised for the evening some entertainment, part of it: *gypsy*-music – the *cigányzene* and dance. (You remember my letter from *Budapest* last year where I mentioned the reason for saying *gipsy* rather than *Roma* and *Sinti?*) Anyway, after the performance the head of the group prompted… – well, I had to join, everybody was dancing and probably I have had this furtive bliss: no excuse. It was simply gorgeous, especially as I of course allowed the change of roles. It was not so much dancing as couples but the entire group was moving, flying according to the rhythm that drags everybody along, even while sitting. Although it had been mainly this group-dance occasional 'pair-dance' had been part of this entertainment. First I was dancing with a colleague from *Finland* – great fun: two pupils, being directed by the *cigány* – and the rhythm. And then the young women from the group came to me. Ok, Ok – prejudices, I know: But shall I tell a lie only because part of reality is like the book of fairy tales? She had long black hair, she looked at me with her dark eyes, her dress was one of these beautifully coloured long dresses, the attire glittering in the light of the floodlight reflecting the sparkle of her eyes. I left the guiding role during the dance to her; after speaking first for a while *German* to me, she later explained me in her flawless *English*... – no, not the sequence of the steps – this had been explained just by dancing. And I simply enjoyed it, little bit strained and cramped while she was talking about her life – the life of a young woman, standing in the middle of an exciting life. Feeling responsible for making something out of this life, but as well: feeling responsible for a role in... – well, in society? in history? in the history of her country? of her own people, the *cigány?* And in maintaining as well at least some good, some simply nice parts of the tradition.

All this sounds probably terribly pathetic. And she did not use a single word which sounded pathetic, rather, she talked in simple words in a seemingly simple life. But still it had something of this greatness. Later, after the dancing, after being left to the group, meeting her again and leaving again... we have had a little bit the opportunity to sit together during the dinner. She, studying there at *Debreceni Egyetem,* talked about her plans. But she talked as well about the difficulties and the joys of being 'one of them', a *cigány* – highly qualified as many 'of them'; highly discriminated at times as many 'of them'; and willing to change: change herself by changing her environment, changing her environment by changing herself. Listening to her, it was even more a pleasure having accepted her guidance during the dance – and it was a pleasure as well knowing that she takes some guiding role, perhaps in the village to which she may return one day; or in *Budapest,* the capital of the country where she may go one day; or in *Brussels,* where she may play a role one day in the capital of *Europe* – just in life wherever it puts her and where ever she looks for her place.

She reminded me at somebody else from *Hungary,* I dare to say: a friend, I met earlier that day: *Zsuzsa* – I definitely mentioned her at one stage. Once, when we had been sitting in her home she said, she could well be my mother; this means as well she then could be the grandmother of the young dancer – and in a way we probably could really be or even are in a certain way something like a family: mutually respecting people, interested in the other and thus having very much in common despite and because of the differences. Perhaps it is for some already the reality, the solution:... *getting those you dream about to share the dream with you at the same time.* Sharing the dream at least in some way, and dreaming it at the same time: every day though we may not know it and we will never know it – the good thing then:

always looking for more to join in this common dream and knowing that they are there, somewhere – the excitement of names still to be discovered.

Now, back from dancing, from heaven and dreaming, returning to reality – and despite simply enjoying the memories of what I just wrote about, the memories of a simple, ordinary pleasure being such a memorable exception – there was another reason for writing about it in such length.

Before I said, for people like you and me *home is not least: 'the self', independent of space, knowing that there is always a way back to that: to the self.* But I know as well that this is at most half of the truth, probably not even a quarter. Yesterday evening, before falling late at night into a deathlike sleep, I was reading again in *Erasmus Schoefer's Sonnenflucht*

> *What they have build is as well their presence... .Most of them don't know it, they live without history. Why they live without history? Well, their history tells it. The spirit of their presence is their past – it doesn't matter if they know it or if not.*[59]

I know, while being in *Taipei* I think quite a lot about here and there, home and being far away from it... And it is more and more that I feel another notion creeping up – still not being entirely sure if it is just my lack of insight or a general mark of this society. As I write to a friend:

> *...I have to admit there are other things to which I cannot get used as easily as the typhoon: Actually I have the impression that it is the first time in my life that I really left home....: recognise = deeply sense for the first time that one is not only a social, but with this a historical being. And here, history is alien for me –not just the history in the long durée but as well the more recent history... - it is strange: dictatorship in Greece, in Portugal, Spain – and of course before in Germany. But still: it had been "own", "home made" authoritarian regimes. On the other side: here, the Kuomintang had by far not been as brutal as German fascism, but Chiang was as well conqueror here on the island, and declared it actually before his arrival as not more than another Chinese province. He arrived in a similar way as subjugator as before the Japanese, and with them and after them the United States of Northern America – not dictatorships in the strict sense, but nevertheless defeaters. And with this in a nutshell: what I see here is a far-reaching loss of history – and part of what might be called at least for some the 'own history', the own history of the conquerors had been stolen and can now be seen in the museum.*

> *...*

---

[59] Was sie gebaut haben ist auch ihre Gegenwart ... . Wissen die meisten nicht, leben geschichtslos. Warum sie geschichtslos leben erfährst du aus ihrer Geschichte. Die Seele der Gegenwart ist die Vergangenheit, bewusst oder nicht. (*Schoefer, Erasmus: Sonnenflucht. Die Kinder des Sisyfos; Berlin: Dittrich Verlag, 2005:* 300)

At least in my daily life and in the daily life of many people around me it seems a common sentiment: the loss of history, much worse than its end would be.

I have to dive, change the scene. Come, join. Hop on the bike.

Love, can you tell me why the scooters around are beeping their squeaking-beeping horns? Is it because we are driving amidst the stinking roaring crowd? or because the one little scooter in their middle is not fast enough? *Beinginthatthongofseeminglyfortheirlifefightingdrivers* – they just turn sharp in front of a car on the other lane in order to overtake another car, parking or at least stopping in the middle of the lane, turn to the right again, further to the right, overtaking another scooter driver – *themainthingbeingtostay-infrontofall, itdoesn'tmatterhowtogettheir.* The person standing, trying to cross the road is being ignored, and ignores – obviously not afraid of being hit. *Calm down lads, a minibus.* Indeed, the little old scooter has to do hard work, carrying four people. *Andinthemiddleofallthis* hullabaloo – I only see it when stopping at the next traffic light – a mother on a scooter, the child standing in front of her, leaning against her lap, the head bedded on the soft jacket which is put on the handlebar, sleeping, snuggled, smiling. A reminder of TLC *inthisworldofhecticandfight.* – Although it is not healthy, it is great fun at least to join once – like a fish in the bowl, knowing that it is likely that food is provided at the regular hour, still feeling like fighting for life: *withtheothersagainsttheothersandeverybodyagainsteveryoneandeveryoneaga insttheothers,* and at heart knowing what is not said: that the *although* is actually very much a *because.* Another reason for seeing it as fun is that I left the office with a good reason, with a goal: the *Taipei Fine Arts Museum.* I visited the *Museo Reina Sofia* to see – amongst other great artworks – *Picasso's* famous *Guernica,* the exhibition of works by *René Magritte* in de *Koninklijke Musea voor Schone Kunsten van België* is not unknown to me, you may as well remember the exhibition of the artists of *Die Bruecke* in *Berlin…* – and now I should miss this one? Impossible I guess though it is not especially famous. But I have to admit that there is another reason: I do not want to leave the city without actually having seen a little bit more of it – and actually it is not really or not alone the museum, it is more the town – a town which is not inviting, in which at least I need a goal to which I go rather than just strolling along.

It is quite easy to find the museum without getting lost. Point of departure: The college and just following *Roosevelt Road* – moving through the city, *Shelly Rigger's* words come to my mind:

Through and with the traffic, just following the main road, cycling, cycling – stopping at the traffic lights – cycling... and: there it is: Seems as if I arrived another time in *China*.

It is not yet the museum though it is another museum: *Chiang Kai-sheck Memorial Hall*, now: *National Taiwan Democracy Memorial Hall*. Is the space, the generous outlay of the arrangement with the Hall and the two other edifices aside? – for here it seems to be colossal, though it is probably not larger than at home the *De Dam (Dam Square)* and much smaller than the *Hősök tere (Heroes' Square)*, not to mention the *Jasnaja Poljana – the wide field*. Is it the cosy, I always think: belittling style of *Chinese* architecture even of monumental buildings? Or is it the representation of imperial power, the 'something' which is capturing even for its enemy? Be it as it is, in front of my eyes history unfolds. About thirty years – the hall had been build after *Chiang's* death in 1975; little bit more than sixty years: *Japan*

'retrocedes' Taiwan to the republic, but now under the ruling of the dictatorial president; history of about hundred years, as the Hall reflects architectural elements of the memorial of *Sun Yat-sen*, the first provisional president, when the *Republic of China* was proclaimed, after overthrowing the *Qing Dynasty* in 1911. – And how many years is it of personal history? When the name *Chiang Kai-sheck* played a role in my life, during my lifetime when this region was possibly closer to me then it is now?

What do dates, names and places matter. You may say, at the end, my eyes are facing a condensation, are looking into the mirror of what I began to study a little bit already and what I have on my working plan for the next week: getting familiar with the history of the country and region – the last hundred years and with that more then the last 2000 years. Can that be? 2000 years, going back to the *Kong Qiu*, known as *Confucius* and supposedly so different from our forefathers and here still as important as for instance *Plato* in *Europe* of which *Alfred North Whitehead* supposedly said in 1929:

---

[60]   Rigger, Shelley: Politics in Taiwan. Voting for Democracy; Ldn./NY: Routledge, 1999: 4

The safest general characterization of the European philosophical tradition is that it consists of a series of footnotes to Plato.[61]

Well, a lot to do then. Moving further to the museum, cycling through the heavy traffic, I am thinking about the last paragraph I wrote before I left the office, standing provisionally there for as part of my coming work:

It had been said that it would probably be uncontested that KMT was the first intruder that really and fundamentally occupied key positions, not only building a new elite but as well fostering a new stage construction of collective identity (see page 54). At the same time we have to acknowledge however the following paradox – a fact with major consequences for the later development not least of welfare and social policies. Connected with this step is what we can define as first stage of a loss of identity. One can but doesn't have to 'agree' with the historical development: the victory of the Communist Party – either way one has to acknowledge this victory as historical fact and way of national development. Not acknowledging this fact, KMT had to disengage in some way though not from the national tradition, so at least from the national identity. In other words: KMT had to build its identity on finding a way of legitimising its exceptional path. – A symbolical expression can be seen in the fact that Chiang Kai-shek dislodged many treasures from their historically authentic place, thus separating them in a way from life by hiding them behind museum doors. Sure, the Forbidden City in the middle of Beijing has as well the character of a museum; but at least it remained in its position, serving in this way as living example from which to depart.

Another dimension of a loss of identity can be seen as being closely linked to this: Although Japan did not place a rubber stamp on the country, one has to qualify such a remark. Japan had been an imperial power and used Taiwan, steering strategically the development of the future structure in its specific shape of an early stage of industrialism coming to age.

The pattern of agricultural and industrial development had the effect of weakening established landed groups without the emergence of independent industrial or working class groupings. The territory developed firmly within the orbit of the colonial system.

(Preston, Peter W.: Elite Political-Cultural Projects, Economic Growth and the Achievement of Social Welfare in East Asia; in: Finer Jones, Catherine (Ed.): Comparing the Social Policy Experience of Britain and Taiwan; Aldershot et altera: Ashgate, 2001: 307-332; here: 326)

With this, in principal a third stage of loss of identity is reached due to the particular – and peculiar – international situation. The international isolation on the one side, and the identification as welcome anticommunist spearhead

---

[61]   http://www.newphilsoc.org.uk/Plato/plato%20home.htm

created from both the US American and the Taiwanese perspective a symbiosis. However the character of this symbiosis is contradictory:

* *its mutualism is given by the US having a safe base in the region – a base of which the limited own power secured a certain degree of US-hegemony; and by the gained indirect re-entry of Taiwanese which somewhat compensated for the loss of international recognition*

* *its parasitism given by the additional mutual gain of economic development, parasitic however as it meant the further loss of identity due to the externally controlled growth which did not leave much space for upholding genuine identity (but see for qualification below, especially sections b.ii. and c.)*

Also a few lines from *Victor Lippit* spring to my mind:

... the first question that must be asked is "Who benefits from it?" When we speak of "China" as thought it were integral in every respect we are in one sense creating a metaphysical entity, for "china", like other countries, is or has been composed of groups and classes with sharply differing perspectives and interests.[62]

– A bromide, still worthwhile to be mentioned as in daily life and even worse in social science and politics we go straight into the trap – celebrating unity from our small immediate community to the global village.

A bromide, still worthwhile to be mentioned, as the trap means as well a serious distraction from things worthwhile to be seen. Looking at this country (and I dare to speak of a country and even a nation), I am wondering again about *Europe's* and *Ireland's* new friendship to the so-called *PRC* – well, one meets people there from business, the clean up by advisers for whom any history is only the history of share prices and currency exchange rates. Basically, the supposed support for *PRC* and the rejection of relations to *Taiwan* is nothing else than capitulation and leaving the *Asian* field to the *United States of America* – the unprecedented end of history, not as it was predicted, but by allowing global dictatorship. *Taiwan* is frightening in having gone some way ahead – a way *Ireland,* the tiger of the *West* may well follow if failing to look at her own history in comparison with the history of this sister-island. Big brother, if he just would watch, it would be bad enough, but allowing him to determine the route while he will be already there when we arrive, after taking the direct way, is definitely not a solution. Well, all this is of course a complicated issue. The only thing that can be briefly said is that, being here and doing some 'local' research, I see issues

---

[62] Lippit, Victor D.: Development of Underdevelopment ; in: Modern China, vol. 4, no. 3; July 1978: 251-328; here: 295; see as well Krader, Lawrence: The Asiatic Mode of Production: 5 f.

here that make the comparison *Taiwan-Ireland* an extremely interesting lesson for possible learning for *Irish* policy.

But the *Irish* government is already sitting on another horse-back, rides the *PRC*-card. May be that *He who comes too late will be punished by life;* but up to now it seems that those who left too early have already been overtaken by others who watched out for the goal before they left for the race.

Sorry, love, I am so boring – but sometimes this is so exciting to me that I am simply being carried away. And you have to allow me these bloopers, please; as otherwise I feel sometimes caught here in the city. Actually I am more and more getting aware of the reason: it is really this lack of history. The same I mentioned before but in a different way. On the way onwards to the museum I see only few old houses, I see only few and sometimes tiny 'marks of history'. Don't get me wrong – I surely do not want the imperial powers being reinstalled. But...

Being now back at the desk, now continuing writing this letter, I look out of the window: one of the parks on the campus, it is still Sunday. Only a few people doing some exercise as it still too warm; but several people are there just for a walk; playing with their children; or the children playing on their own, just enjoying moving around, exploring the unknown of the surrounding, chatting, shouting, laughing – making, building their own histories. And of course, everybody out there has a history; they have been and are building their history; every house, every flat has a history – they moved in, left their parents, perhaps because they wanted to be nearer to their workplace; or they just preferred to be on their own; may be as well they moved because their parents – ah, no, I won't write it, not here, although I do not believe in any way in this idea of awakening any ghosts by talking about them. Every single person has a story, he or she can tell. But how many of these narrations make history? How many anecdotes have to be lived through by ordinary people in order to bring to real life what we only see as the history of 'great men'? And what kind of 'great men' is it, really making a difference not on any battle field or industrial building site but in the living room of *Xie-tian, Kong-Ning, John, Sean, Sheila, Walter* or *Adélaïde, Franco Boldoni... ?* And will *Aaron, Dolores, Hugo, Nigel, Elisabeth* or *Yu-wen* be allowed to keep their history?

Finally, I am arriving at the museum, I lock my bike. I kneel down, looking at the centipede – quickly walking out of the way. This little animal, sliding over the ground smoothly like a piece of silk moving in a soft wind. – The centipede in the middle of the city with the millions of people – history seems manageable; the middle of the city with the millions of people a centipede – history gets lost. And as much as it is in the one case manageable because it is reduced on the presence, as much it is for the very same reason getting out of control when it looses the beginning and the vision.

I sit a little bit down in the park – distancing myself from the noise and even more so from the exhaust of scooters and cars. I have a headache – the price I have to pay for such real life exploration – as real life should sensibly not leave air-conditioned rooms, taxis and the MRT (Mass Rapid Transport) which however mean that that real life is unbearably diluted to nothing.

Entering finally the museum I am impressed – sure, the *National Palace Museum*, which I will visit later, is impressive. But the two special exhibitions *Meng-Tze Cheng's Looking Through* as another way of *Exploring the Possibilities* of *Mind-Space* are not only explorations but keys, opening the traditional world by using contemporary views; or looking with traditional means at the contemporary world... . *Buh-ching Huang's Documents III* seem to be something I believe to have seen, somewhere in..., was it a coffee shop or when I visited colleagues? Or somewhere in my own house in *Aghabullogue?* Was it a living room or an office? And still these *Documents III* are not simply some exhibition of any daily, contemporary triviality. On the contrary, the colours, shades of green, beige and red seem to open in their simplicity a world of the condensation of history: life in a wooden frame, movement of something that is beyond any question static. And as much as I think I may have seen it anywhere it seems to be so unique for here: the material which had been used, the different colours – including a shade of green which I am sure is not one if the forty *Irish* shades. *Ren-Ho Huang's Harmony*, made from 'mixed media', though being static, a matter of movement again: in this case represented by the conflicting spheres which are necessary before any harmony can develop, the movement of light and darkness, of change and stasis... .

The new generation for a new republic – or the new republic for a new generation? For a while I am caught by *Hsing-wan Chen's Stroll* – feel invited to stay, to walk, to explore – to look if there is and if so: where there is real life despite the invaders from the different sides, regardless of the incarceration of tradition and progress.

After having visited the art gallery, I sit for another while in the park surrounding the building. A little bit in the background I can see a large building – temple-like though I assume it is the *Grand Hotel*. It is as strange as the park is alien here, being too aware of the large city just around the corner. I skim through the book I bought – modern *Taiwanese* artists with their new views on the country. Is it their country they look at? Can they make it being their country – the country as well of those people I see when I walk a little bit later through the streets – luxurious shops and hotels and side-by-side people selling some goods: a flee market? a market of the shadow economy? the same as the activities as I saw in *Florence:* selling the designer goods?

I take the MP3-player – *The Songs of the Capeman* are attracting again my attention as so many times during these days – I hear the words from another world – from *Puerto Rico,* a teenage gang and the killing in a society which... I hear the words

> *I mean you either belong or you get hurt.*
> *– That is for me to know and for you to find out*

> ********

> *Virgil*
> *This boy used to be on death-row*
> *Will his violence return?*
> *Will he call out to his mother,*
> *mama, you can watch me burn!*

> *Inmate*
> *Killer wants to go to college*
> *Another bullshit degree*
> *Tell the little town of new paltz*
> *you aint got nothin to be scared about with me*

While cycling back these words are getting deeply engraved in my mind – the melodies and rhythms are mobilising and comforting, want apparently show a way and give as well the feeling that there is a way though and out of the jungle.

Now, I have to leave you – still, I love you,

Peter

Ja, Griasdi (I guess this is the way how to spell the *Bavarian* for *Hello)*

Griasdi, mo(a) Liabe – Well, Hello to you, of course.

But *Griasdi...,* well it is the beginning of another little story of me, living in *Taipei.* – Just returning the one day to my office, I see a man, the same age as I am, arriving the same second as I do. I can't stop myself using this salutation – a little bit unsure, enquiring: *Griasdi! Ming-Cheng?* We never saw before but it must be him: *Ming-Cheng Kuo,* my *Chinese* brother. Life is full of surprises, isn't it? I am sure that you didn't know that I have a brother in *Taiwan* – and to be honest, *Jenny,* I didn't know it either – and even the minute we meet, I am not aware of it. OK now, I will tell you – if there is not anything else with what I could awake your curiosity yet, it must be finally these few lines.

You know about my connection to the *Institute for Foreign and International Social Law* in *Munich*, don't you? When it had been finally confirmed that I will go to *Taiwan, Roswitha,* a friend of mine who works at the institute, told me about *Ming-Cheng* – no, she didn't write to me in *Chinese,* though she could have done so; nor did she write in *Bavarian* though that wouldn't have been a problem for her either – just plain and simple *German* for the Stupid White Man, who is only occasionally in the capital of the free state *Bavaria* and whose knowledge of *Bavarian* language is rather poor to say the least, limited to the touristy variation that tries to be funny. *Ming-Cheng* is working as well at the institute, actually having much stronger links than I do as he studied there as well and holds a PhD in law from the University in *Munich.* He is not aware of who I am and about the background – we never met in the *Amalienstrasse* in *Munich.* But as soon as he knows, as soon as I mention *Hans Zacher* and talk about my relation to him... *Ming-Cheng's* words effervesce and so do mine. Talking about the development of social legislation, philosophy of law, talking about the institute – and most important I think for both of us: we have common friends, in particular one common..., I am hesitating: friend? So we talk about dining at the *Starnberger See,* the little Pizzeria at the verge of the *English Garden*... - philosophy of life is not something we talk about, we just practice it. *Hans, Roswitha, Martha, Barbara,...* - in a way we walk together.

Well, later at least. First we drive to the *National Chengchi University,* its *Law Institute* and here only *Hans F. Zacher* is with us in mind – finally a little bit of serious talks cannot be entirely wrong.

More interesting is the drive to the restaurant in the near mountains; and as I said: *Hans, Roswitha, Martha, Barbara,...* - in a way we all walk together. When we arrive, the lady just plays the last little bars – bewildering, not because of the strange sounds but actually because the tones catch the mood of the primeval forest: the density, the impenetrability and still a certain ease of the skilled rambler who walks through it without hesitation. Gosh, this difference between the worlds of large politics, the academic debates and organised meetings – and the enjoyment of sitting in this rather large but still cosy restaurant. It is the immediate talk; it is the respect for the detail; it is the appreciation of small things: taking of the shoes and slipping into the specially provided slippers; somebody being there and offering us..., no: talking with us about where we want to sit, depending on our wish for light, for fresh air, the view...; the joss sticks, not least to keep the mosquitoes away – and all without, well the *Germans* say: *aus einer Mücke einen Elefanten machen;* we say all without *making a mountain out of a molehill.*

After a while, the smell of the tea, made from the blossom of a flower is augmenting the air and mixing with the aroma of the joss sticks, the meal, the variety of little dishes served and the lady recommences playing music again – the *Chinese* music always so far away from me, now coming closer, close even, merging with the entire environment and more: inviting to enter in a really new world – the world of a living past.

Ming-Cheng tells me about his tea farm – how he developed a little farm from just having a garden – another, a personal *Zhōngguó. China,* a long time ago having been known as *Central Country:* the country of the middle, not located at the edge of the earth, at the time being imagined as flat and having a final end, not located at the margin but located in the centre; the central power as well, being surrounded by peripheries – dependents and minors. Finally *Ming-cheng's* tea-farm – coming from the periphery, first being a little garden, being extended and gaining force, one day perhaps emerging as the sole place of retreat, of real treat – from the peripheral leisure time retreat becoming the focus of life? Flat or not: *E pur si muove – And yet it moves.*

And of course, being amongst us we talk as well about policy – the new democracy here, the old democracy there; the tiger economies, the need of rights, the question of living in a country which... - ah, can we say it is still a developing country? I mention the case of which I read the other day:

> *A young woman (under 18) worked in the catering industry and was paid only little money. She received no extra pay for Sundays or bank holidays. Her hours varied from 60 -70 hours per week. She was in this job almost 2 years and asked on numerous occasions for the minimum wage and proper hours (she was legally entitled to 70% of the minimum wage). She was told if she did not like the conditions, she could leave. The case had been taken up by an advocacy organisation with the employer and his attention was drawn to the legal regulations and the fact that she would have a case for unfair dismissal if she were sacked. The advocates also established that no social contributions had been paid on her behalf.*[63]

Ming-Cheng says again: Yes, yes; that is what I mean. We have a long way to go. There is this injustice and we need rights, basic rights. We are so far back here with our social system. – I move my hand across the table, answering embittered, Ming-Cheng, this case happened in Ireland, the now rich country, the country which first programmed National Recovery, then Economic & Social Progress. The country went the way of Competitiveness and Work, failed to achieve the first of the three goal: Inclusion, Employment

---

[63] Slightly modified from *Citizens Information Board: Employment Rights from Information to Redress Dublin: 2006: 35*

and Competitiveness it set itself; Prosperity and Fairness being for so many more a kind of tragedy. Sustaining Progress?[64] Well, yesterday we stood at the margin of the cliffs, perhaps two steps away; today..., yes, we are progressing.

If you want these rights here, don't look at the Europe you know from the library at the Amalienstrasse. Don't be embarrassed when talking about the DPP and the growing dishonesty. No, I should say: Be embarrassed and talk about it and do not forget the books. But that is only part of the reality – and I know that you are well aware of it. There is only one way, and that is the way of going together.

I am personally embarrassed – not only about the *Irish* case I just mentioned. I am as well and perhaps even more embarrassed about the many words that remain unspoken, the many steps not being made as we are all and permanently talking and running – like the hamster in the treadmill: Standing still by movement. And if I learned anything during my time here in *Taiwan* it is to see more about the *US-Auropean* treadmill. And I feel challenged: Human rights, Social Quality, living standards, human security – *Tell me, Ming; tell me how we can proceed in this tight walk between influencing, making progress and being overwhelmed by dishonest proposals of third ways....*

We talk about lighter things again. It is so nice to laugh, candid, forgetting or no: remembering: remembering the ease of the own ideas, the own life: dances, the joy when we talk about our children, the pleasure of listening to music – of making music... It is rather late when we leave – walking to the car I glimpse through the dense, thick leafs of the trees, taking a final look on the city. From here it seems to be far away now – and it looks somewhat peaceful. *Mind!* the second I hear the word, I feel *Ming-Cheng's* ungentle grip, pulling me aside. He points on the ground: the snake in the grass. I only see the end of the snake, moving with a sharp sibilance out of the way, now looking from the tree; back to field one, so much I know from the scripts. – So we are leaving this little paradise.

It had been a nice evening – in any country is something you have to look at, to visit, to delve into before you can say: I arrived. Not sure if this is really true, if there are not more things than just one. Be it as it is: One thing one has to visit while being here is surely the tea house – it is like the real coffee-house in *Vienna,* although that may well be "our *Italian* pizzeria" which still is so *Viennese.*

---

[64] Referring to the titles of the various Programmes of the so-called *Social Partnership Agreements.*

So it was that evening this atmosphere of this beautiful restaurant – remote in the mountains though very close to the city. But my feeling was more that the remoteness actually allowed a very special nearness – dialectics of and for every day's life. It is a kind of immediacy that requires and makes possible to communicate – giving us the impression of communicating even if we do not have the language. Inching forward, guessing, communicating by solely approaching the hidden meaning of gestures, mimicry, behaviour…, the meaning of words remaining in any case veiled. There is in any case enough space on the backstage – the place where life actually happens and where words play only a small role. Do you remember, some time ago you mentioned *Erving Goffman,* his mention of the backstage.

In every day's working life it is at times difficult: the backstage is actually brought onto the main stage – and vice versa. You suggested in these countries, the *Chinas, Japan…* things would not go the direct way, one has to take detours. Being now here I learn quite a lot about the detours – the detours I walk every day. I walk them here in *Taipei* and equally in *Cork,* in *Brussels,* in *Berlin…* . The detours here, well, I am not sure how much I learn about them, but I am getting definitely more and more aware of the *European* one's – the barred ingenuousness and the unwrapped ganiess xyz I experience here is a mirror, a magnifying glass. *Erving Goffman* said

> Man is not like other animals in the ways that are really significant: Animals
> have instincts, we have taxes.

What appears here and for me as hierarchies, as submissiveness… - or just as seniority based on experience, respect… ? Is there any way to find it out? To find out what is instinct, what is tax? Probably we talk too much about the getting the correct currency, forgetting the more important question: *Do we have to pay these taxes at all?*

Of course, much of the questions coming up with regard to life here is just a matter of the stupid white man, who left the safe place of the own stage of alleged security, being sure about and caught in the codes used on the backstage. Here it is now about moving on a new site – being ex-sited, ex-citing just because of its newness. I remember, once being criticised for a report I delivered to an *Irish* government agency. The reason for the rejection was that the report was considered as being *outlandisch* – gosh, my friend *Laurent,* at that time we didn't know each other: now I know we would have laughed together about the thorough implications, the rejection of *German* philosophical approaches and its acceptance of complexity on grounds of the narrow-mindedness of *Bentham's* ancestors, not capable of bearing the strange, not willing to merge with the weird and wonderful. And does this possibly mean as well that opening its own culture is incarcerated into multiculturalism, allowing multitude, allowing difference, but subsequently leaving the stranger always being exactly this: a stranger? Not allowing him or her to join? Not allowing her or him to change?

For sure, this does not claim any *German* openness. *Nietzsche's* master-slave morality and the *Uebermensch, Kant's* legendary rigidity of daily habits, *Hegel's* and *Schopenhauer's* crankiness in academic competition, which nevertheless allowed the first to elaborate dialectics, possibly only because he accepted to remain in the iron cage of idealist thought; and not least: it had been another, very much *German*, iron cage – the one of bureaucracy and submissiveness, of law and order that allowed translating *Wilhelm Voigt's* written comedy into the real tragedy of *Adolf Hitler. –* And as you told me the other day, today people in *Switzerland* name behaviour which is sticking very much to rules, which insists on formal obedience, as being *German.*

For me it is difficult to think, to write about it, sitting here in *Taipei,* being advisor in distinct positions (distinct actually having a front and backstage in its own terms). Never forget, it is a country which had been up to recently under martial rule, another country that had never been allowed to be a country and a people: torn between and submerged under *Chinese, Japanese, Americas.* As *Marc J. Cohen* writes right at the beginning in his look on Taiwan at the Crossroads

> *If the history of Taiwan (or Formosa) had to be described in one single sentence, it would be the following one: the people living in Taiwan have always had to cope with the consequences of decisions that had nothing to do with Taiwan itself.*

And as such it is an 'underdeveloped' country – underdeveloped in the sense that the development was to some good extent determined by these interests of the occupier, not the interest of the country or its people. Sure, another difficult one, as the people's interest is rarely a guiding force anyway; but there are differences going beyond tiny nuances. Rejecting the term 'underdeveloped country' has, despite it charm of empathy the menace of justifying colonialist heritage. Accepting a qualified term might as well help to qualify expectations, accepting as well that it is at the end a country with most beautiful sides to it, and many most beautiful, ops... I meant nice people. And yeas, many beautiful people as well – remember what I wrote about the session of *Tàijíquán –* the models for the *Chinese Michelangelo* and the *Asian da Vinci.*

Having thought about history, I now have to think about this mergers of stages: As noteworthy it is that animals have instincts, and we have taxes, it is perhaps more vital that at this stage taxes and all the things around them actually are our instincts, determining stage and backstage.

En passent a funny thing – probably one could make a joke about sociologists from it and perhaps it is just the odd humour of an odd sociologist that finds it witty: While *Goffman* talked about the backstage, *Luhmann* walked on it – *Niklas* and his pub in *Lueneburg*, the town of his birth.

But it is not only my odd humour that makes me smile – just let me introduce a crash course on one of my teachers and later colleagues *Niklas Luhmann:*

- he studied law;

- he began a career in *Luenburg's* public administration;

- he finally concluded that societies are only about communication, moreover: that they are communication;

- saying that it is about difference that has to be communicated

- and... he owned a pub: *The Pons.*

Wiki may be frequently at least a good point of departure, so lets start there – and at *http://en.wikipedia.org/wiki/Pons* we read with regards to pons

> *It is part of the central nervous system, and relays sensory information between the cerebellum and cerebrum. Aides in relaying messages in the brain, and contains the pneumotaxic centres that help regulate respiration. Some theories pose that it has a role in dreaming.*

As well, *Pons* is the name of a series of dictionaries, language courses and, trusting the advertisement *everything concerned with learning language.* But of course most basic and important – humanist education must come to a meaningful application: *pons* is the *Latin* word for *bridge.*

The pons, the pub as place of communicating between the different parts of reality or finding a place in the world – public places always depending not least on the relation to others, everybody of us being the other, wherever we are.

Another thing, so far it is funny, moving around – it is not only once that people gaze at me: the white man. Not less funny, it is rather frequent that people say *Hello* or at least they nod towards me: other white men; getting most funny when the other white man is actually black – but here the black and the white are both white and black. One day in the *National Palace Museum* the guide, *trained American,* uses the term 'barbarians', when talking about the *Chinese* history. Knowing about the different uses of terms,

I ask *What exactly do you understand under this term? –* She answers: *Well, everybody coming from another country, not from what had been seen at that time as the centre of the world as which China had been seen.* Frankly she adds with a smirk: *You would be one as well.*

– 陰陽, *yīnyáng*, black and white are here just getting one, merging into one, the none, the not one who is the one; the other as the one is none as being of the some.

Anyway, here, just being one of the some which is not someone but me, it was the most pleasant environment to talk and contemplate and trying to find the own determination rather than living up to standards of others.

> *Wagner: ..It does seem so sublime,*
> *Entering into the spirit of the time*
> *To see what wise men, who lived long ago, believed,*
> *Till we at last have all the highest aims achieved.*
> *Faust: Up to the stars -- achieved, indeed!*
> *My friend, the times that antecede*
> *Our own are books safely protected*
> *By seven seals. What spirit of the time you call,*
> *Is but the scholars' spirit, after all,*
> *In which times past are now reflected.*
> *In truth, it often is pathetic,*
> *And when one sees it, one would run away:*
> *A garbage pail, perhaps a storage attic,*
> *At best a pompous moralistic play*
> *With wonderfully edifying quips,*
> *Most suitable to come from puppets' lips.* [65]

Such experience, for me, is probably more important than much of the studies I undertook in the library – it is the living history.

Now it is brighter in the mornings; the time I get up it is still dark; but it is getting lighter: it is cool, the temperature goes down as far as 28 degree and it is not as humid as it had been during July and August. You can imagine, it is truly a relief and makes it rather pleasant to stay occasionally outside, doing some reading on a bench near one of the lovely ponds. It is getting lighter and so it is amiable just sitting there, watching at least for a couple of minutes lazily the frolicking children – another experience of daily *yīnyáng:* old and young, laziness and romp, adrift in thoughts and lost in play. It is getting lighter, soon the courses will start and the students are returning to the campus – another buzz, a brighter buzz. Is it just the youthfulness which gives all this some optimism? The feeling of light-heartedness? Is it that one

---

[65]   *J.W. Goethe, Faust, Part One, 1808*

160

sees people laughing, playing, chatting, rather than people in stubborn straightjackets of overcome rules, people with disrespecting respect, asking for respectful disrespect – the feeling of history: people not being entirely caught in roles and a history which had been entirely out of control, a lost history? It is getting lighter – cycling to lunch or to one of the shops, cycling across campus to the library is getting easier, more pleasurable; when I have to cross the way of others, my previously probably rather grumbling thanks is replaced by a friendly 謝謝! It is not a spoken language, and I don't say it because of the picturesque letters of which we have supposedly about 30.000; when we talked about *Italian, Swedish,* and other languages, I once said to you that in my eyes the most difficult is to overcome the compunction of speaking in the same melodious voice as the natives do – and these lighter days here I tend to join the choir: 你好 *–Hello!* 謝謝*, Thank You! –* And the bow is like the move of a dancefigure.

It is getting lighter and so I say 你好 when I meet *Tsu-yu* and *Mei-yu* – they asked me to join them for *The Dance of Cherry Blossoms.* Ah, you think after the little story I previously told, I am now crazy for dancing? No, it is not really about going dancing again – would be afraid that I don't find somebody taking the lead, anyway. Nor is it about Cherry Blossoms though I admit that it is nice to see not only the fruit that is plentiful here on the tables; it is nice as well to see where and how they grow.

Now, join me for the real *Dance of the Cherry Blossoms:* One day I receive an e-mail

> *... Since the last trip to Shi-Tou, Dr. Du wants to introduce a CD album for you, which is called "The Dance of Cherry Blossoms". The music in it is composed by many Taiwanese artists, with piano, bamboo flute and electrical sounds. This album is the best-seller of "mind-soothing music", and is widely praised. Because that Dr. Du is busying on the school's affairs, therefore, I am honoured to accompany you to enjoy this album. I also invite another student, Mei-Yu Liu, to join us. She is an undergraduate of Department of Foreign Language and Literature, and love music deeply.*
>
> *I wish Dr. Harrmann could make some time from your schedule, and go to the CD store with us. Please choose the time you like, and reply me.*
>
> *Thank you a lot for it!*
>
> *Best wishes,*
> *Tsu-Yu Hsu*

I feel pleased not only to have the opportunity to get this recommended CD but perhaps even more to meet some 'ordinary people', getting a little bit out of the golden cage in which I sometimes feel caught. I do not know what it is, but there must be something in the mail that gives me the impression that it will be nice and casual to meet two young women or the one young woman and the young man – what do I know about *Chinese* names. It must be nice – finally it is getting lighter for a brighter life. We arranged to meet at the main gate. When I arrive I see already from some distance somebody smiling, waving at me – of course, the white man is easily recognised. Though there are a couple of them around and the number is increasing, it is still no problem to spot the odd one amongst all the others..., ops, in this case the acronym is ordinary ones.

你好 – *Hello Tsu-yu* and *Mei-yu*. Having a bike seems to make some impression – the impression of being..., ordinary? Of joining in a lighter atmosphere? The impression of not only driving in black limousines, the notion of... well, here we are and let us just see how to get on. The lightness is especially meaningful as poor *Tsu-yu* is somewhat struggling with *English* – not as much as I am struggling with *Chinese* but she is fighting – I gave my fight up after the first couple of words.

First, we go straight to the CD shop – I would never have found it. Well, I would never have gone into the little leeway, more or less hidden, not in accord with the standard *European* shopping malls nor matching the expectation of a snugly back road. It is one of the places similar to spots in *Brussels, Amsterdam, Cork* – one which is probably even not really known by locals if they don't happen to live nearby. A very kind salesperson, the talk amongst the locals – it is apparently something like a scene shop: alternative music, spiritual music...

So what are you up to? Do you have time? Do you want to see something special? – Don't have a clue. What do you think, anything of a must around, something I should really see? After strolling through a couple of shops – though Tsu-yu and Mei-yu don't want to say that these are a must, we end in a coffee shop. It is one of the small places in one of the back streets, unimposing but even nicer because of this. We sit there for about two hours or so – two hours as a quick glance into the life of young people, who are looking for a place in a lost world – a world they lost and a world which lost them. They are in conflict with the Chinese, the Japanese, the Americans – their parents wanted democracy and the young people with whom I am sitting there, know that they didn't get it. Looking for spirituality, searching for Taiwanese-ness today, doing what Shui-bian Chen, the current president, asks them to do; but did he want them to find the Taiwanese-ness in the life of what we call 'The Mountain People', the aborigines, the indigenous people – people who – many, many years ago – lived in the coastal areas, harvesting the fertile soil and being pushed back by those Chinese immigrants who arrived in a first wave, hundreds of years ago – Chinese, who today claim to be natives?

It is difficult and sometimes I am asking myself where actually history begins, which part of it is relevant – is it the dreams that help us to reverse nightmares or is it the nightmares that allows us to dream. Be it as it is, 謝謝, *Tsu-yu* and *Thank You, Mei-yu*, it was a pleasure to live for a while…, should I say 'off record'? It hadn't been often that I had been allowed to cross at least a little bit the inner borders of blurring identity for an open talk – taciturnity here and there, only that I have some key there, a key that barely works here.

– I cycle back across the campus, it is late afternoon. In the meantime I ignore the guy who frequently walks across the Campus, taking his little pig for a walk. Did I ever write it would be busy here; did I say before there would be many people around? Gosh, the beginning of the terms approaches. The first students are already on the campus, surely many fresher, moving timidly around, not yet knowing where to go, and not yet knowing how to move; and some perceptibly not even knowing who they are – the entire way laying open in front of them. Or is it more that they just approach a huge cabinet, containing all the different keys which may make it possible to open the doors, to find the ways? – Though it is such a huge crowd, it is not frightening me now; on the contrary, it is comforting, giving hope that some may actually not be looking for the key only but before doing so exlpore the door which needs to be opened.

Moving along, I am humming the lines from *Angelos Sikelianos'* poem *The March of the Spirits*, slowly moving home through the mild air of the evening.

> *II. (Second singer)*
> *Gigantic thoughts,*
> *Like clouds of fire or islands of purple*
> *In a mythical sunset,*
> *Lit up in my mind,*
> *Suddenly my whole life flared up*
> *In concern for your new freedom, Greece!*
>
> *IV. (First singer)*
> *Fate and your Fate is mine threefold*
> *And from Love, the great creator Love*
> *Now that my soul has hardened and penetrates*
> *Right into the mud and on to your blood to mould*
> *Today I call with it to all comrades:*

V. (Second singer and choir)
»Forward: Help us raise the sun over Greece
Forward: Help us raise the sun over the whole world.
Look, its wheel is deeply stuck in the mud,
Look, its axle is deeply sunk in the blood.
Forward lads, the sun cannot rise alone
Push with knee and chest to get it out of the mud
Push with chest and knee to get it out of the blood.

Look how we blood brothers lean upon it
Forward brothers, it has surrounded us by fire
Forward, forward, its flame has engulfed us.[66]

Leaving the Campus at the other end of the huge area, I feel something strange happening: The usual embarrassment by straight lines of streets, the city, designed in squares: logical, cold but seemingly clear, lost something of its pressing, depressing, disorienting character. With the chatting people around, with the increasing buoyancy... – there is something that seemingly lowers even the high raisers. I think of the recent talk with *Hsiao-hung;* the insight into another history which this long conversation on world systems theory, the *mainland-issue,* the *United Nations* partly being an *US*-branch brought to me: can this impression of freedom, I praised before, be just the expression of a new nationalism – the young people watching out for a new history – the rejection of a life without history, and the 'start of history from the scratch', under the leadership, *Shui-bian's* claim of democratisation as nativization, as gaining openness?

Supposedly there is something very special in the way of traditional Asian dealing with history – the Imperial interpretation of history, clearly being history of the ruling classes and as well being interpreted by the next generation of rulers. So I read:

In China and Korea, it was standard practice that, once the state's historical
bureau had finished compiling the official history of the previous dynasty,
the bureau destroyed all sources it had collected.[67]

Was the history of this country already destroyed before anybody could really compile it – officially or not? Are the young nationalists, better to say: the new nationalists on the way to a new victory?

Every page a victory.
Who cooked the feast for the victors?

[66] *http://www.mikis-theodorakis.net/marchetx.htm*
[67] *Stato, Masayuki: The Archetype of History in the Confucian Ecumene; in: History and*
     Theory. Studies in the Philosophy of History; 46, 2, 2007

Well, changing scene now – may be that you are with me in mind, but this time I have to say it is good that you are not really here. Anyway, one has to make all these experiences, personal, first hand...

I know, I am rather nervous the last days – and it is a long story, part of which you may sense through the letters. All the questions, miscommunication, non-communication, political issues with the *US*, the *UN*, academia; working again on different stages: writing here on global and *Taiwanese* policy issues, correcting a thesis, I receive from a student in *Cork*, sending out questionnaires for a project on child labour in *Ireland*, finishing an article for a book to be published in *Germany* – all this sometimes demanding extreme concentration; then the thoughts about the work in the immediate future, soon being back in *Ireland...* .

And as usual all this effects my health: being nervous, somewhat restless, extremely tense; of course it effects my sleep as well. I wake up in the middle of the night although I only get a few hours anyway. So I am waking up the one night, angry with myself: I feel this tremor, shaking my entire body. I am drowsy, only feel this tremor and some thoughts coming up – work issues creeping up the light duvet, laying down with my head on the pillowcase. Am I really so nervous that my entire body is quivering? *Oh, shut up, turn around I* whisper angrily to myself, *You're an id...* I hear some noise, the door is rumbling in the frame, the bed... – yes, it is not me, it is the bed that is shaking, and still my only idea is: is it really necessary that I wake up in the middle of the night. Not sleeping makes things even worse, I'll be even more nervous after that. Just leave me alone these few hours of rest.

I do not know, how long all this takes; I am getting aware that it is easier to move the world than to move its policies: an earthquake. Strange, that with this awareness I find easily back into sleep, despite the entire building still being shaken. Perhaps it is the awareness that I won't be able to change anything here, still having the frequent illusion to stem the tide in other ways of life.

Leaving the house the next morning, after first hand experience I do not see any devastation and so I look for information on the web – not so much as I think it was a dream; it is more that I want to know if this kind of incidence is

---

[68]   *Bertholt Brecht: Questions From A Worker Who Reads*

taken notice of or if it is just like rainfall in *Ireland* – something that comes and goes.

> *A magnitude 6.5 earthquake shook Taiwan a few minutes ago, according to the U.S. Geological Survey.*
>
> *Seismographs detected the quake off the island's eastern coast. Initial reports suggest that the quake occurred about 40 miles below the surface of the ocean.*
>
> *Update at 2:39 pm. ET: Reuters says a journalist in Taipei reported that his building shook and pictures fell off the wall during the quake.*
>
> *Deutsche Presse-Agentur reports: The quake was felt all over the island, causing bottles and cups to tumble off shelves and window frames to rattle. Many residents living in high rises in Taipei ran onto the street, fearing their buildings might collapse.*
>
> *http://blogs.usatoday.com/ondeadline/2007/09/big-earthquake-.html   - 06/09/07*

Sometimes good, not to know too much, isn't it. For me sleep doesn't have the effect of beautification; still, I love my little respite. And as during the day nobody mentions the night's incidence with a single tone, another riddle opens: Is it a matter of *not talking about the ghosts* or simply: *Things happen, why talk about them?*

If we want the nature, we have to take it as it reveals itself. I see its beauty when I visit one of the afternoons the *Yangmingshan National Park* – we defined it as working visit as *Joanne* and *Pei-shan* wanted to talk a little bit about social work issues, social policy developments and other things; more a matter of general exchange. Going up the hill, immediately bordering the city I enter an entirely different world. The mere sight is a treat – looking across the dense green, the full plants and the single blossoms. Finally leaving the car, I smell the air fresh air which carries a rather strange aroma. Before I can say anything, *Pei-shan* asks *Do you mention it? The smell of the hot springs.* We climb down the stairs: another simple restaurant, an open atmosphere where we sit down for lunch. Although there is a menu, the meal seems to be more a matter of negotiation. A little bit of this, little bit of that – the young women is very open, and she is in no way grovelling. While we are waiting for the meal – we talk about the different experiences and working areas – there is no interruption by any tiny bell of a microwave; everything is freshly prepared and when it is finally served there is no shortage of anything. Fresh vegetables, fresh flowers, fresh mushrooms, some soja-dish – the only thing I recognise as known are the mushrooms in some kind of egg-breaded cover. I am distracted by the mere view – even if we are not on the top of the mountain it is a wide outlook; the landscape varied and some ugly buildings in the middle of it are absorbed by the splendid perspective. A compact forest – but the density underscored by the density of the brightly coloured variation of green; occasionally interrupted by spots of large dark-red plants. Where there is space left, it is filled by climbing plants and bushes crawling on the ground. Looking as closely as I can there seem to be spots with not the slightest trace of men ever having been there. Though mostly covered by trees, some areas are clearly showing signs of volcanic influences. This beauty, this power – I do not want to think about the night when my sleep was interrupted. After the meal we go further down the mountain, enter the bathhouse. The warm water is pleasing, deeply immersed in the warmth, just leaving the face outside – it is fondled by the light breeze as the eyes are praised by the view across this landscape. The icy water when I leave, awakening the body, the most peripheral cells being stimulated – I nearly stop breathing..., and return into the hot water, another time being the body is stirred. – I look through the window: an eagle is circling in wide loops, only occasional flaps with the strong wings show the strength of this animal – sovereign of itself, being able to move as it is in total command over itself.

I am – another time – angrily thinking of a colleague from *Germany*. He was briefly in *China* last year, in the PRC. When we met after his visit, he was talking about the progress of the country, the way of overcoming poverty, the shortcomings of the ancient regime; the efforts there to combine progress though still keeping the traditional values, the old spirit.

I remember reading in the middle/end of the 1980s in a newspaper which I got for many years from *Moscow* a short article: McDonald's would soon open its first store in *Pushkin Square*[69] – lucky *Alexander Sergeyevich*, he could not see that going to happen; poor *Christoph*, he didn't want or could not see in his *European* jaundice that with the establishment of the 27 cash registers for which, lets be optimistic: 81 jobs (most likely badly paid, precarious) would be created, probably 243 people would be pushed into poverty, and many people would be caught in the traps of eating junk food, rubbish. And today it is him who does not (want to) see the consequences, coming along, creeping with this wealth into the remaining and hidden corners of that new world – the previously peripheral Taiwan, now being

---

[69] 1990 McDonald's Canada opened Moscow-McDonald's, the first McDonald's restaurant in the Soviet Union, serviced by 27 cash registers and seating 700. This restaurant in Pushkin Square is still the largest McDonald's in the world. – From: *http://www.mcdonalds.ca/en/aboutus/mcdCanada_milestones.aspx*

nearer to the centre, now integrating the PRC into the world economy by exploiting it as its periphery.

Right now another quote comes to my mind, supposedly it was on a sign in the office of the one who was not interested in details but in the universe – I am sure you will like this as well: Not everything that counts can be counted, and not everything that can be counted counts.[70] And it is still the question if the progress is real, or if it is just another step of the *McDonaldisation*. Here at least, in *Taipei*, I see new shadow economy; stands, selling designer stuff under the claws of the tiger, the owners of the local teashop, an enterprise which is just another precarious family-business, the 'bike-trucks': people living in poverty, collecting with the transport bikes, so well known from many pictures, the rubbish of this tiger economy to recycle it. Well, some tradition left; tradition maintained by people who protect themselves against the sun by traditional straw hats with the broad brim, living in the timber houses, not yet totally ousted by the modern concrete buildings – hidden there but even more veiled in mountains of data that aim on showing a democratic and well-being society. And I can only see from the data that the rich *Taiwanese* people now inundate the *PRC*. As said, what many people still call Mainland-China takes over the peripheral role of the capitalist world-economy, before held by the *ROC*.

– People. Countries. Sovereigns of themselves, being able to move because they are in command over themselves?

Isn't it strange? – So easy to talk and write about globalisation, about the freedom of moving around, possibly speaking different languages, being connected via Internet, phone… . And then sitting there in an office in *Taipei*, 6 hours, 7 hours, 12 hours time difference between here and there. What is this difference about – even if I would be 'there', we are not really, or rarely really together. And sitting here in the morning, writing the letter and looking at the world clock, I sometimes think it is like sitting there, narrating a bedside story; or in the evening, when I leave office, and you just arrived in your office – the one of us being still a little bit drowsy, the other being already little bit sleepy. What is this difference about, a difference that does not really exist? If I am in Aghabullogue and you in your place, still European, we seem to be together. With the more 10.000 kilometre between it seems as if we would live in worlds that are more different than the worlds within a distance of about 1.000 km. What do 9.000 kilometre matter? Is it really what we frequently say: it is just in your head. Just the idea of something. Or

---

168

is it something 'real' – even if it is only the *real opportunity* of synchrony and synchronism?

Sure, it is just another game, playing with words and ideas – just the ordinary day-today work of somebody like me.

But it is another dimension to it. As much as I just enjoy delving into my living space, living is again and again delving into work – sociology, philosophy..., all this makes finally only sense, if it is concerned with real life, although it frequently may sound as if pure reasoning has nothing to do with today's practical reason.

When talking about globalisation, modernity and postmodernity, do we actually think as well about *Oma Ursel.* – Right, you don't know her. And when I saw in *Taipei 101* a china mug with a sheep (believe me, it was definitely an Irish sheep) and green shamrock, reading *made in Germany* at the bottom; when I saw the strawberries in one shop, the label telling me 'from USA, E.U.', what role does *Oma Ursel* play? Perhaps we think more about her, when sitting in *xīng bā kè* for a chat, in *Starbucks*.

I get known of *Oma Ursel* when I stroll one day through the city, being greedy for a coffee, a real coffee. I am on the best way to start of a new revolution, the storming of the *Bastille* in 2007. I hope getting what I want in the little coffee shop with the name *Bastille*. A gracious *Chinese* person tries to communicate to me – in perfect *Chinese* – that there is not a single space left (and I don't even try to communicate back that it may be possible to join somebody, sitting alone at the table, that I might storm the *Bastille).*

So I look out for another place – in short distance only I see a silhouette at a house – and I know who is pictured before I read the letters: *Oma Ursel's Cafe-Restaurant and Goethe Gourmet Gasthaus.*

To be honest, it costs me quite an effort to enter – don't really like the idea of entering a *German* or *Irish* place. But coffee is like a magnet and though *German* coffee seems not as promising as *French,* I open the door. Finally, good old *Johann Wolfgang* had definitely not been the worst of all times – and finally he had been long enough in the other coffee loving country: *Italy.* He knew

> *... das Land,*
> *wo die Citronen blühn,*
> *Im dunkeln Laub die*
> *Gold-Orangen glühn,*
> *Ein sanfter Wind vom blauen*
> *Himmel weht,*
> *Die Myrte still und hoch der*
> *Lorbeer steht,*

Kennst du es wohl?
Dahin! Dahin
Möcht' ich mit dir, o mein
Geliebter, ziehn.[71]

lived away from the *Winter's Tale*, where

Sie sang vom irdischen Jammertal,
Von Freuden, die bald zerronnen,
Vom Jenseits, wo die Seele schwelgt
Verklaert in ew'gen Wonnen.[72]

And he wanted

Ein neues Lied, ein besseres Lied,
O Freunde, will ich euch dichten!
Wir wollen hier auf Erden schon
Das Himmelreich errichten.

Wir wollen auf Erden gluecklich sein,
Und wollen nicht mehr darben;
Verschlemmen soll nicht der faule Bauch,
Was fleissige Haende erwarben.

Es waechst hienieden Brot genug
Fuer alle Menschenkinder,
Auch Rosen und Myrten, Schoenheit und Lust,
Und Zuckererbsen nicht minder.[73]

---

[71] Know'st thou the land where the fair citron blows,
Where the bright orange midst the foliage glows,
Where soft winds greet us from the azure skies,
Where silent myrtles, stately laurels rise,
Know'st thou it well?
'Tis there, 'tis there,
That I with thee, beloved one, would repair.
(from: *http://www.gutenberg.org/dirs/etext98/tpgth10.txt*)

[72] She sang of love and sacrifice,
of pain and a tomorrow
when alt shall meet in a better world
beyond this vale of sorrow;

[73] A different song, a better song,
will get the subject straighter:
let's make a heaven on earth, my friends,
instead of waiting till later.
Why shouldn't we be happy on earth,
why should we still go short?
Why should the idle belly consume

Yes, I know you think *Goethe* was a macho and you know I do agree – still, as much he was a child of his time in this regard he was very much ahead in other regards: besides being an idealist, besides – well, in terms of his time he surely was a democrat and fighter for human rights. So, I go to *Oma Ursel*, locally known as *Qiu Daiyu*. As soon as I sit down, somebody comes up with the menu – and a carafe of water. I look at the t-shirt, see the silhouette of the *German*, more correct probably: the *cosmopolitan* poet. While I look and get hopelessly lost as the menu is in *Chinese* only (a strange kind of relief), the glass is filled with fresh and cold water. I order a cappuccino – even if I would not be disrespecting alcohol anyway, it is not time for a *Koestritzer* which is advertised with the experience of more than 460 years experience in the brewery of dark beer, experience from *Thueringen*. The *Koestritzer* brewery, located in a spot in the *Federal Republic of Germany*, which had been located in the *German Democratic Republic*, which had been located in the *German Empire*, which had been...

Later I talk with *Qiu Daiyu* – she lived for many years somewhere in *Bavaria*, she admires *German* bread – and later, when leaving, I buy a *bretzel* for my dinner. She loves *German* cake – and after she convinced me to get a slice – *come on, it is teatime* – I can understand her gusto. The recipe for the cappuccino however, seems to be from one of the chapters of *Goethe's Italian Journey*. And what she loves most: Life, travelling, being together with people – being a stranger amongst strangers. Globalisation as matter of multinationals in the late 21st century? Postmodernisation of life: options, choices...?

All these processes are permanently taking place, since long periods. And perhaps I find it here occasionally particularly difficult to live not because I have the impression that certain doors are closed but because I do not know if and why I actually should open them. Because I do not want to open those doors which had been opened by others before me, determining the stars under which I walk and marking with their stripes the lines I should follow. *Johann Wolfgang* – with all qualifications – simply could walk; *Qiu Daiyu* probably simply had to walk; *Ricci* wanted to walk, fulfilling a mission; so many others just moving around, too sure about their coming back, moreover even while moving they only approach rather than enter the places where they go; it seems that for *Peters*, in a world, in which the want for understanding is officially banned at least from learning-outcomes set for

---

what working hands have wrought?
There's bread enough grows here on earth
to feed mankind with ease, and roses
and myrtles, beauty and joy,
and (in the season) peas.

Irish students, *Peters,* facing hierarchies here and there without fully accepting them, it is difficult then to walk – cross-country journeys are barely comfortable though they are the most exciting, indeed; thinking beyond instrumental reason is never a simple task but it is probably the most awarding when it is finally showing tiny germs growing out of the rough grounds. – It is still good then to know that you will join at least for some part of this way, that you will share some of the dreams of a simple peasant.

It may be a dream, a vision, still it is worth these exercises – being *Don Quixote* here, *Jester* there.

> *We're the children of the 80's, haven't we grown*
> *We're tender as a lotus and we're tougher than stone*
> *And the age of our innocence is somewhere in the garden*
>
> *(Joan Baez: Children of the 80s)*

Having mentioned above my *Taiwanese brother,* I brought up this very special encounter with history. But actually I bump into some part of this living history as well there: in the library. It is this love for books not in terms of memorabilia, of bibliophile reminiscence.

It is rather real life that opened its gates the first time for me when I visited *Shakespeare's A Midsummer Night's Dream;* it was not only the play, it was the occasion, sitting together with many others, the many like-minded: a long time ago, on occasion of the *Ruhrfestspiele* in *Recklinghausen/West-Germany.* An undertaking which brought arts and workers together – a Midsummer Night's Dream in its own terms, one of these daydreams mentioned.

Well, this appreciation of books and the library; novels, poems but as well... – Now, the one day I got a mail from *Bob* and he sent me his recent book *Beyond the regulation approach: putting capitalist economies in their place.* I browsed through it – his previous work, thinking of my previous discussion, see *Paul's* works referenced: *Capitalisme monopoliste d'État* and *Une sécurité d'emploi ou de formation;* long discussions we have had in *Kinsale,* in *Ivry,* I leave the book on the desk, move the beautiful, heavy chair back. The furniture – chairs, tables, shelves, little desks for making notes while standing – could well fit into a comfortable library of a private bibliophile collector of books, respecting, or should I say: celebrating in a special way the value of the books, of the people who wrote them. For serious conversation we invite people if even possible in a nice and comfortable environment, don't we? So, don't books deserve a similarly comfortable environment? I pass the other tables – students sitting there, making notes, reading or simply having a nap – *Latin* Grammar; chemistry; social work with parents of drug addicts; *Kant* in *Chinese*. – It reminds me that I once heard that somebody read *Kant* and didn't understand it. In a second attempt he read the *English* translation of the same book – and supposedly he understood. What would *Chinese* language make out of *Kant?* I walk through the long rows with the shelves: tend to pick haphazardly books but resist... – until seeing a huge collection: *Honoré de Balzac's La Comédie Humaine.* Of course I do not know every edition of this opus magnum, but I cannot resist, there is something tempting. I take one volume – a very simple, modern binding. I open it: What appears from the outside so recent, even a disrespectful binding, proofs to be an edition from the 1860s. I nearly don't dare to open it further. Still, I cannot stop myself to start reading:

> *J'étais plongé dans une de ces rêveries profondes qui saisissent tout le monde, même un homme frivole, au sein des fêtes les plus tumultueuses. [...] Assis dans l'embrasure d'une fenêtre, et caché sous les plis onduleux d'un rideau de moire, je pouvais contempler à mon aise le jardin de l'hôtel où je passais la soirée. Les arbres, imparfaitement couverts de neige, se détachaient faiblement du fond grisâtre que formait un ciel nuageux, à peine blanchi par la lune. Vus au sein de cette atmosphère fantastique, ils ressemblaient vaguement à des spectres mal enveloppés de leurs linceuls, image gigantesque de la fameuse danse des morts. Puis, en me retournant de l'autre côté, je pouvais admirer la danse des vivants! [...]*[74]

I put the treasure back on the shelve, resist to take another volume; leave *Romain Rolland's Jean-Christophe* where it is; my way is bringing me finally to the *compact store* – the old treasures, closed for me as written in the language which is for me still secretive though hugely seductive without its 'real name', translations of books, documents. *Chinese* history and philosophy by *Chinese* writers, *The Analects, The Great Learning; Chinese* history by early explorers of different kind: *Ricci, Polo...,* another insight by *Asian* people moving towards the *West: Xuan Tsang, Cheng Ho... Aristotle's politics, Maine's Ancient Law, Sun's Mínzú, Mínquán and Mínshēng* – and back to *Jessop's Beyond the regulation approach.* Of course, I admit that I dare to think as well if my recent work on *Social Professional Activities and the State* may play any role here – and already thinking this, I fell going beyond appropriate modesty. And then again: at least I take part in something, can perhaps make some contribution...; being here it is in some cases as continuing the conversations from *Kinsale, Ivry,* the *Balaton...* – Again, I have to thank you... .

– The remote restaurant and the smell of the flower-tea; the library and the smell of old books – as different as these worlds are, they remind me at you:

---

[74]   *de Bazac, Honoré: Sarrasine*

Do you remember, you once said – leaving the city, going to live in the countryside – that you would be so glad, not least because you would be going to a place where there is night, where there is real darkness? When I heard you saying these words, I had to grin – as I thought it was the beam of a somewhat 'wise person', the older one of us. I learned later to correct myself. It was after having been made attentive by the words of your youthful wisdom and while experiencing what it means to live in a large city. Then it had been *Budapest* and now it is *Taipei* – in cities there is neither darkness nor moon and stars; neither dawn nor sunset; neither sunbeams nor clouds. Sure, there is a certain fascination in both sides: cities and countryside. And there are huge differences – cities like *Budapest* and *Taipei* should not really be mentioned in one breath; and the wide field from *Aghabullogue* is so different from the jungle of the mountains of *Shi-Tou* – so fascinating in it is density of green and difference. But you know what I prefer, at the end.

Why I remember your words: darkness and sun…. when talking about such places as the labyrinth of real and exploring, interesting communication and getting lost in the warren of a library that allows to find history and a place within it? It is a simple connection, not only by knowing that you like such places as well. It is more that on such occasions one can see that it is only by this darkness that we can see the next sunrise.

After my encounter with *Balzac* during the day I feel it as special obligation to go in the evening, when leaving the office for my habitual evening-cup to the little coffee-shop in one of the side-lanes – the cosy place has a little bit of a grotto, emerging – or do I have to say absconding – in the middle of the jungle of high raisers and concrete buildings. I sit down, and although I should be reading something for my work, I take one book from the shelves with a varied small collection of books in various languages, possibly left there by the odd passers-by. I read on the back of the dark-red cover *Les Fleurs du Mal* by *Charles Baudelaire*. It is not least the attraction by the illustrations: *la peinture symboliste et décadente* as the cover promises. It is another treasure, a pleasure, allowing entering another world which seems to be so much this world – this globe of contradictions. I skim through the book, enjoy the pictures: *Eugene Delacroix, Gustav Klimt, Xavier Mellery* – a little note paper slips out between one of the pages – it is difficult, though especially tempting to read the handwriting:

<blockquote>
Ou, les mains sous la tête, les yeux fermés, il écoutait l'orchestre invisible, les rondes d'insectes tournant avec frénésie, dans un rayon de soleil, autour des sapins odorants, les fanfares des moustiques...[75]
</blockquote>

Romain Rolland followed me – I could leave the book in its place in the library, but here, in reality *Jean-Christoph* wants his recognition, the just recognition of youth.

Though the smoke in the room is pressing on my lunges, I stay and as it is not too bad I still like it: the cosiness of the light, the decoration – which actually is not just decoration: apparently it is as well a coffee-trade: huge bags with coffee beans leaning against the shelves, some instruments of which I do not know the use, pictures from across the world and the old radio receiver – instead of looking at shiny LCD-displays, I see the old tube with the red shine – still, the music comes from a CD-player which I do not see; I only have a glance over the CD-collection: *Western* classical music; Jazz music: *Bonafede, Getz, Davis, Coltrane, Metheny, Contreras...* The furniture is a variegated collection; just the same as the people: many ages, many ways of life – the only thing they share, is their variety. A white man sits in the one corner with a local girl, apparently students, for her being the welcome stranger – interesting because he is so exotic; and he apparently savouring the respect and perhaps even admiration – a new golden cage? A real togetherness on the way? Finding history? On the way of making history? A couple at the other table is speaking harshly, interrupting each other, the words sounding hard and full of anger – A quarrel? A love story? At least I remember *Peng* saying that one of the *Chinese* dialects always sounds full of anger, even if the words are full of kindness. When going to the counter, I pass the table with the two other white lads, pick up the words *Wir in Hamburg...* – Ah, you in *Hamburg*. You are in *Taipei* now, and you have to face the border that you didn't cross when taking the plane that brought you here – the border which is or is not here, its existence and non-existence, its crossing and non-crossing just part of every step. As much as we may occasionally try, for my part I learned at least one thing: neither to hide myself (now being the other) nor hide the other (now actually being the "me") behind the exotic. Exotic and exorcism can go very close together.

Then, paying at the counter a coin slips out of my hand, falls onto the little board, stretching long across the counter and holding the sacks of different kinds of coffee: *Colombian, Kenyan, Ethiopian* – to get the coin I have to move one bag: *Costa Rican Tarrazu* — from the *San Marcos de Tarrazu valley* in the highlands outside of *San José*.

---

[75]   From the third volume: *L'Adolescent*

Beginning these letters I wrote

> *The question is What actually matters? The permanent difference and newness? The position from which we approach the situation or the general position, the actual power we have in life? Or is it just the beauty and pleasure of occasional experiences – people with whom we enjoy nice experiences (the sharing of something as it is more a typical US American expression), just personal adventures a place gets identified with?*
>
> *I know, it sounds as much academic as much as the Caribbean and the Taiwanese shores and forests are actually exotic – and as much as academic and exotic notions are real they are as well…, now, matter of dreams and reality (I know you are aware of the shift of the 'expected' sequence).*

After having been here now for quite a while I only feel confirmation of what I always said: at the end it doesn't matter where you are. What matters is to find people to talk with, to link – and live – with. And what matters is as well to maintain a certain way of alienation – not accepting that communication silently withers in routines and nothings of truly alienating matters, alienating in terms of uncontrollable. – When I left one day the city here – we own from the University a huge forest in *Shi-Tou* where they brought me as special treat after a workshop – I have had a little bit time; well I took it. Walking around through the little Bamboo-village, standing at the bridge of the little traditional garden, being surrounded by al the exotic plants, the giant tree, the most exotic was… – well, I gazed at a little butterfly, strolling from one leaf to the other, finally reaching the blossom. Such a tiny being, such a long trunk, looking for the right opening, slurping the sweet juice – the last time I did something similar was when I grew younger with *Franziska,* she being perhaps three and I… three again: we both had been fascinated by a little snail crossing a narrow pathway.

Isn't the true fascination again and again the exotic of every day life, the ability of communicating – if we are not doing it, we have to blame ourselves. *I am so busy, I have so many things to do* – why don't we say: *I am afraid to take at least that little bit of responsibility I can take.* I am not afraid to face myself – accepting as well my limitations. I know it is not much but I won't run away and hide myself by just following the run in the treadmill that brings me around, but not forward. I won't hide myself by speaking the language of others: of business, of ill-defined evaluations, of superficial successes, a language of figures rather than words – a language that does not allow me to talk – the *American* language. I want to have dream during the days rather than getting disturbed by nightmares during the dark hours.

– Leaving the coffee shop, I look for the name of the place: across the window I read *Chez Che* – the moment I read the letters across the window I am irritated: repercussions of earlier times of globalisation: *A spectre is haunting Europe –* the spectre from 1748: *Charles-Louis de Secondat, baron de La Brède et de Montesquieu* publishes *De l'Esprit des lois;* 1848, the spectre which is feared by *All the Powers of old Europe [that] have entered into a holy alliance to exorcise this spectre: Pope and Czar, Metternich and Guizot, French Radicals and German police-spies,* 1917, the spectre arising from the rubble and ashes the war across the world left behind, 1968, the spectre thawing away the ice the cold war had been left behind. – I unlock the bike – the coffee houses, the tea houses, the libraries... - why do we never think about them when talking about globalisation. I know that we can move forward only by moving together. And I recall as well this poem – it is written by in 1895 by *Rudyard Kipling.* Listen to the words.

> *If you can keep your head when all about you*
> *Are losing theirs and blaming it on you;*
> *If you can trust yourself when all men doubt you,*
> *But make allowance for their doubting too:*
> *If you can wait and not be tired by waiting,*
> *Or, being lied about, don't deal in lies,*
> *Or being hated don't give way to hating,*
> *And yet don't look too good, nor talk too wise;*
>
> *If you can dream — and not make dreams your master;*
> *If you can think — and not make thoughts your aim,*
> *If you can meet with Triumph and Disaster*
> *And treat those two impostors just the same:*
> *If you can bear to hear the truth you've spoken*
> *Twisted by knaves to make a trap for fools,*
> *Or watch the things you gave your life to, broken,*
> *And stoop and build'em up with worn-out tools;* [76]

I have to tell you about another encounter with culture – knowing that it is not really possible to grasp it with words. One evening I went to the *National Concert Hall.* Already the spacious setting – the memorial monument and the two Concert Halls with their traditional architecture is impressive. When I finally enter the hall, the bounteousness continues. Selected pieces from the *National Palace Museum* are exhibited – looking much nicer in this kind of natural environment – looking like *ordinary furniture.* I know, my like of this pageantry is not least a matter of feeling the use of it, felling that closeness actually depends on this kind of distance. I want it for all!

Anyway, the inner hall is very modern, still showing its origin – clear lines and the playfulness of life that has security behind it.

---

[76]   *Rudyard Kipling's* poem continued

The light is dimmed and it is getting quite – although the orchestra is not yet on the stage. There is some magic tension, and it swells with the time – with the smell of joss sticks, with the musicians walking in a row, everybody to her or his place, putting down the little light and taking the instrument. The one side of the stage is nearly entirely occupied by the players of the main instrument of the evening: the *èrhú (erhu)*. The other side with traditional *Western* instruments. At the back: percussion instruments, a huge variety, framed by the two exceptionally large timbals. They show beautifully drawn pictures. The organist is entering as the last on, sitting down – the first tones, but not coming from the organ but from the left. The drummer, or is it: timbalist, dances the tones out of the instrument, from the right now – and the organ, the first tones mixing with the deep and reverberating sound of the timbal, ascending, reaching the height of the glockenspiel, seamlessly passing over to the èrhú, seamlessly mixing with dance, light and the fall of silk clothes, falling down and being moved in a light breeze, mixing itself with smoke ascending front he upper stage. The dance is changing between 'direct performance' and the artfully performed shadow play. It is a mix as well from arts and the artfully produced voices of birds, the movement of work of the instrumentalists and the playful dance in the background, its bouncy character underlined by the changing light – a soft light, gliding from one colour to another rather than aggressively flashing. Colours are flowing into one another but as well into the events on the stage and the events absorb every single beam – flowing into the event, being absorbed, in-fluence, in-flow, flowing… Although the entire event is not harmonic in the way as we *European* would understand it, having more in common for instance with the dodecaphony of *Schoenberg, Berg, Dallapiccola* and others, there is nevertheless harmony in it – the harmony of mastery. Mastery of something new, by possessing the old.

Friday, the last working day of my stay here in *Taipei*. I am going another time to the secretariat's office – and without knowing, I had been expected. The six girls are getting up, standing around *Jaclyn* who is in the centre. I look into the faces of the six girls in the *IHS-office*, being a little bit surprised – what will be happening now? *We have something for you* – the young woman hands a fruit over to me. *It is as a present, a special fruit we eat on moon-day – moon-day* is a special day we celebrate here, but that is another story, and I might tell you another time more about our holidays and customs. The girls look at me, I look at them *Thank you* – I could hug them. I get the impression of a heavy chain link opening, one of the inner doors of the cage, I faced here more than in other places. I am not sure if it is just a matter of perception; nor am I sure at which side I stand: inside or outside of the cage; or if it is about two cages with one wall. Anyway, now it is much easier for me to leave, as I arrived just in time, just before I left. And of course now it will be as well more difficult to leave. Of course, I do not hug them – one chain link is not a chain; instead I just say 謝謝, *Thank You!* They smile – more, warmer than they did all the time during my stay.

Later then a last informal official meeting – the colleagues from some *IHS-projects*, and of course as well *Tzong-ho Bau, Chien-fu Jeff Lin, Der-lan Yeh*. Some of the girls from the secretariat are also there – the order around the long table closing a circle, bringing us a little bit back to square one: me sitting opposite *Tzong-Ho...;* short speeches, a discussion with *Chun-chieh Huang....* I try to get the talk away from its dialogical formality. Human rights, education, the young people are mentioned – and I hate myself for not asking: *Jaclyn, you are young. What are you saying to this? Just say your opinion.* I don't dare it – and possibly it is better, better for her – a chain link is not a chain; and breaking it within a cage does not provide a single inch leeway.

Sunday, the 16th of September. The last day. It is silent in the library. I am doing a little bit of reading. The light noise of the air-condition does not disturb me; nor does the lyrics of the birds outside; I note the laughing children, their singing – and then, at half three the tiny bell, a soft melody, making the visitors of the library aware that there is only half an hour left. It is Sunday and the library closes early so I have some time to sit for a while down at the little pond. I watch out for the turtle. A group of fish is stretching the head to the water surface, the yap widely opened. Six or seven of them, and in a second row larger ones – it looks like a choir. A child is playing next to me – the soap-bubble moving its way in front of my eyes, the different colours gratifying me, colours that are created by the same light that lets them now shine. I enjoy the last tropical sunbeams before returning to *Emerald Island,* well known as well as *Hibernia*[77]....

Yes, the *Emerald Island* is more miles than hours away – and I will be expected by some

> *The weary traveller will be returning home from his voyage.... . I was delighted to hear that you will soon be returning to the Emerald Isle sometime next week and you must be looking forward to getting back home. Too much of a good thing can also be tedious and it will be nice to hear about your adventure in the other side of the world and your collaboration with the secessionist and illegal province of the People's Republic ? I am sure they have another view on things over there.*

---

[77]   *hibernus (lat.) – wintry*

They have another view. Personally I never believed in *China* being a Peoples' Republic under *Mao Zedong,* but that is another question. Today's question is that by now *China* lost its *People's Republic* to the dream of an economic miracle; the question is that the *Republic of China* is loosing more and its *China* to the nativisation and *Taiwaneseness.* As the title of the book, *Chun-chieh* gave me as present says: *The Challenge of a New Democracy to an Old Civilization.*

Tomorrows question is another again – and it is not least a very personal question that will probably follow me for several weeks now, or that will follow me even longer, until another 1968, which finally completes our first and failed attempt: Being here in the *Far East,* the *Central Country,* I learned much about the *West:* its hierarchies, its taciturnity, much of the mendacity of new democratic claims, co-determination, the pretence of governance and openness – politically and personally. A bow can, but does not make a person necessarily a subject; and equality may be easily a duplicitous comedy, of which the tragic remains hidden, though temporarily only. – *Europe* as *Hibernia,* now hiding its harshness behind the tracery of frosted windows? Nice to look at, painful to touch, and melting away when warmth lays a hand on it?

I will come back to the window, the Tropical and the Hibernian – looking with *Jaclyn, Han-jung, Shih-jiun, Ming-chen, Pei-shan, Hsiao-hung, Yeun-wen* and others; looking with the musicians of the beautiful concert in the *National Concert Hall* I mentioned. Looking with the many with whom I could not speak – not being able to speak their language, they not being able to speak my language and with whom I nevertheless exchanged so much. And I will come back as well to those with whom I share the language, a matter still not fully allowing to communicate. I know their honest and deep felt respect – and I respect and appreciate it, and I know as well… . Let me say it this way: you probably heard that in this culture one 'looses face' if a dish is offered and you reject it; if you heard as well how far this forces us to loose face, please let me know. Or find it out with me before we all move around without face – only with façades.

… Monday, 17th of September, four o'clock in the morning. The heavy door with the stained glass falls into its lock – at least for me now for last time. It is only few days ago that I recognised the sign near the door: The stained glass, beautiful in the various blue shades, evoking the association of a kingfisher is especially designed, a beautiful mark of respect for us: scientists from other countries, coming to visit the *National Taiwan University* and work here. It reminds me at the time of me being a student in in *Bielefeld* and later shortly returning: The *ZIF – Centre for Interdisciplinary Research* gave guest researchers such exclusive place to undertake their work. It was the place of which I thought it must be the most delightful experience to be allowed undertake research – the hope probably most of academics have – just a dream of which one thinks it never will become truth. Do you remember what I wrote earlier, after arriving here? Right: *Bewildering – being employed to think, just to think, not doing anything else than thinking. No teaching, no administrative work – being there just for thinking....*

The door falls into the lock – one can feel a light reverberation. The black car again; a comfortable drive will bring me to the airport where the *Boeing 747-700* will be waiting. I appreciate the secure drive, indeed. In a blink of a second all the views of three month are passing my eyes, the smell of the mornings, daytimes and evenings are touching my nose, I hear words – whispered, clearly spoken, official and informal chats... The taste of the strange fruit comes on my tongue – the fruit the young women from the *IHS-secretariat* gave me on my last official working day...

– An impressive time – and a difficult time. It will cost me some effort to sort things in my little brain. I know already now the most difficult part of it: establishing normality. Or better: arriving is always a matter of leaving part of yourself behind without denying yourself and accepting arrival without denying from where you come – and even less to where you want to go.

> *If you can make one heap of all your winnings*
> *And risk it on one turn of pitch-and-toss,*
> *And lose, and start again at your beginnings,*
> *And never breathe a word about your loss:*
> *If you can force your heart and nerve and sinew*
> *To serve your turn long after they are gone,*
> *And so hold on when there is nothing in you*
> *Except the Will which says to them: "Hold on!"*[78]

Surely arriving in reality of a country is made difficult, if stained glass is the entrance of a golden cage. Arriving in a country is not simple, if the country bans part of itself behind the doors of museums. And even for a society, arriving in reality will not be possibly by denying its history and future. Riding on tigers – *Asian, Celtic* – doesn't make landscapes blossoming. Cities can be forbidden and histories hidden – but just leaving, leaving all this behind by running away only means leaving – leaving it to others.

> *If you can talk with crowds and keep your virtue,*
> *Or walk with Kings — nor lose the common touch,*
> *If neither foes nor loving friends can hurt you,*
> *If all men count with you, but none too much:*

---

[78]   *Rudyard Kipling's* poem continued

And a women, a daughter, of course!

Monday, the 17th of September. Crossing the strait, a short interim stop in Hong Kong. People mix – and here it is not obvious who the white man is: the White? the Yellow? The black? – At least it is for me somewhat strange to see 'the white man' again – the first appearing as stranger, then getting used to them. The *Asian* news agent and book shop side by side with the one I know too well from Europe. A new flight – the same airline and the same aircraft. Some of the board assistants look as if they have been taken out of a picture book – make up, made up, a glance of *Chinese* classics in look and behaviour, including a very obvious hierarchical order: without knowing exactly its meaning, one knows instantaneously the existence of seniority: clarity and honesty. However, there is now as well other change: though most of the board assistants are still *Chinese*, they are now joined by others: Koreans, Indians, Europeans...

I am lucky, having plenty of space. And plenty of space underneath, nearly 10.000 meter. About 10.000 meter underneath; about 10.000 kilometre to go at least until I arrive *London*. The little monitor shows the route: aside the route *Ho Chi Minh City, Hannoi, Choinqing, Nowosibirsk* – crossing the *Ural means that English* tea is offered rather than the *Chinese* tea which had been served before. We move forward: *Lenin...,* no: *St. Petersburg*, it seems more and more peanuts: crossing *Finland, Sweden, Denmark, Germany, The Netherlands* before arriving at *London-Heathrow*. The various flight information interrupted by the advertisement: *Crédit Suisse*. The reading and writing, the thinking the dreaming interrupted by meals, drinks and snacks or at least the frequent question: *Sir, is everything all right. – Yes, everything is allright.* I smile. Not really everything is all right: I have to dream as I cannot sleep despite not having slept last night. About twenty hours flight altogether. I will have a little bit more than twenty days in *Europe* before I go back to *Asia*, go for another twenty hours flight though that time will be for a brief stay only.

It was early in the morning that I started in *Taipei*, it was your evening; I arrive in *London* the late afternoon – our late afternoon. And still, we are apart. After passing the most stressful procedures, supposedly for security, I will have to wait in the dirty part of *Terminal 1* while you will be still at work,

---

[79]   *Rudyard Kipling's* poem continued

preparing for going home and then enjoying a nice evening. At least it gives me time to get used again to be... - well, white amongst white. But does it mean to be 'home'?

Monday, 17th of September the *Airbus A320* of *Aer Lingus (EI) Flight 725* touches ground in *Cork* – back in *Ireland,* away from all extensiveness of *Taipei, Hong Kong* and *London* airport and the grandeur of the *Boeing* world – it is nearly midnight.

Not having been here for a while, the lovely landscape springs to my mind – though it is already dark, I visualise the tiny palm trees, the gorse, the ivy and the wide fields with the different shades of green... – already now I think back: the parrots, the huge palm trees, the bananas, the cornucopia of fresh fruits and the various dense greens...

At the end, the regained provinciality, the bluntness still hides something: the fact that there is a similar strain and stress, a comparable dependency as I experienced it during my stay in *Taipei.* And the involvement in day-to-day business, the routines of offices, meeting rooms and 'local' airports hides as well that we have exotic worlds at both ends of the journey – here in *Asia,* here in *Europe,* the *Americas, Africa* and *Antarctica* – here on this one world, depending from where we arrive and depending how long we stay before the exotic gets toxic.

There is only the one challenge – not to loose the rotundity while unfolding this world, while engaging in it; and not getting lost in circularity while looking for a straight way. A quote from *Andre Gunder Frank* comes to my mind – during the time in *Taiwan* I had been reminded frequently of his work – and of my contacts to him during the last year and these extremely hard months of his life. He once wrote, harshly criticising shortcomings of world history analysis

> *They (have to) suppose a hypothetical never never land in which development and underdevelopment would be or might have been different – "independent" development? – if the world were square instead of round...*[80]

---

80   *Development of Underdevelopment or Underdevelopment of Development in China; in: Modern China, vol. 4, no. 3; July 1978: 341-350; here: 347*

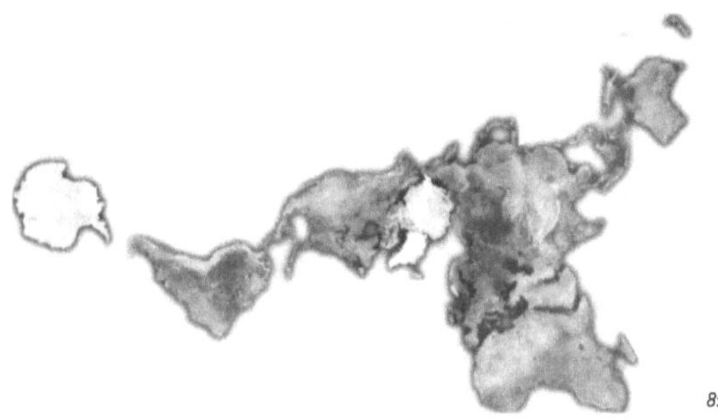

The world is not square – and it is not flat; and today nobody will deny: *E pur si muove.*

I know, it is a strange end of a letter which is something like a love letter. Still, it is an end to a letter only – come, let us move with it, though sometimes it means to move against it.

> *Amor già mia conscienza non acerba,*
> *Ma ben l'invita, e'l vero mi constrigne:*
> *Ché tanto i lice l'esser meno acerba*
> *quanto fortuna in alto più la spigne*[82]

I embrace you, and hope that we will see soon again,

love,

Peter

Postscript – To be Read as Prolegomena.

My biography – a biographical note? Sure, not as exciting as for instance that of *Immanuel Kant.* But the life and especially the mind of that great philosopher in his small world in what was at the time *Koenigsberg* and is now *Kalinigrad,* was definitely much more exiting than my wee existence in the and between the formally large, even global world. But a small mind in a large world is prone to get lost. And, definitely not claiming a fame of similar genius as he had, there is possibly another aspect that makes his biography

---

[81] *http://ca.wikipedia.org/wiki/Fitxer:Dymaxion_map_unfolded-no-ocean.png*
This is an unfolded dymaxion map, unfolded to show the land masses of the world as nearly continuous

[82] Love does not make my conscience harsh,/ but the good invites it and truth drives/ me, so that it is allowed/ to become less harsh
as fortune leads it to greater heights
(Francesco Petrach)

more interesting: He didn't have to write it himself. If you would have written the biography for me, perhaps you would have detected similar amusements as his inescapable punctuality, supposedly only once interrupted. And if I would write yours, I am sure, there would be much that is worthwhile to be known, memorable, inspiring, amusing and amazing not only for me.

Who you are? Perhaps you found yourself in the text – perhaps with a direct quote, with something that brought me to what I thought, I wrote, I am. Perhaps you didn't find yourself, you had been somewhere hidden in a global jungle. Or you saw others you know, glimpsing around the corner. May be, you thought this is written only for you – and…, yes, it is indeed only written for you because you will have to read it in your own, personal way.

Now, at the end, I have to admit something.

> *Men make their own history, but they do not make it as they please; they do not make it under self-selected circumstances, but under circumstances existing already, given and transmitted from the past. The tradition of all dead generations weighs like a nightmare on the brains of the living.*

Everything I wrote is true, everything is just describing what life during this time in *Taipei* and *Taiwan* on the *globe* in the *universe* was like – but that does not mean that everything happened this way, that all this is just like a photography. Imagine the view I have, sitting on my little mountain in *Aghabullogue*, looking out of the window across the valley, towards the mountains of *Kerry…* ? Just think of it – and then imagine – everyday this view is new, everyday it is different, depending on the light, the air and how it mirrors the beams, how it brings the tint to life; depending as well on the colours embossed in my brain, the feelings – pleasure and discontent, gratification and frustration, and not least the experiences and expectations.

I wrote that one of the days in Taipei I received a very nice mail from John, amongst others stating: And as for dreaming, the trouble is getting those you dream about to share the dream with you at the same time. If you ever solve that one, I shan't be the only person to want to hear about it.

A biographical note: about perceptions, being and dreams. And…– well: and a love letter; a love letter to you, if YOU think you are YOU; turn it around: if you think, you are me. See yourself in a group, a small, nearly tiny group and somebody says just one word: You! Will you ask ME? Will you ask WE? And the soil you are standing and moving on, would that have a similar question, asking: HERE? And hours, days and years you and I live in, would they ask NOW? – Wherever in which way ever and when you say this is ME, this talks of US, this is concerned with HERE or tells something about NOW or perhaps even if YOU feel NOW being HERE with ME being US…

... it is a love letter written to you by an eternal tourist who will never leave. A tourist wanting to solve that one great question:

getting those... to share the dream with me at the same time.

– Perhaps a first step is to look together at the rich colouring of the world – including the various shades of grey. The *Malaparte*, 'he of the bad place', may become *Bonapartes* – and so much as one *Malaparte* is always possible, *Bonaparte* can truly be thought of only in the plural.

Wer nichts infrage stellt, traegt nichts bei zur
Entwicklung des Lebens.[83]

---

[83] Those who don't question things, do not contribute to the development of life. (*Schoefer, Erasmus: Sonnenflucht. Die Kinder des Sisyfos; Berlin: Dittrich Verlag, 2005: 192*)

Rome, November 2008

Lost

Isn't it strange - rightly or wrongly many people didn't accept when and that the Irish language was literally beaten out of the heads and minds of the Irish people. And whatever you think about "the Irish question": beating something out of the consciousness is surely is surely something "questionable".

But...:

... well, Starbucks has in many places free internet access; and since I know this I am occasionally going there - finally I want to stay in touch with the world: not least with my friends and colleagues at home (ah, gosh;

don't ask me if I have one, let alone where this may be). And I want to stay in touch without paying huge amounts of money for roaming charges. So I went there when leaving Brussels - at the airport. Though I had been there with a friend I just had to send a mail to complete one of these nasty bureaucratic tasks.

Sure, you may think I am a snob - and I may even admit that I am: but despite liking my work (or parts of it) I am admiring this "flair of the world"; allowing me sensing the richness of history and diversity of life, its variety, vividness, and forcing me to really face its dangers and injustices..., letting me often feel the real distress with others - in any case: people with their different lives, their traditions, their individuality and individual power and powerlessness - the difference of the skin, and gestures and expressions just being one moment where real life is getting obvious; and now all in the global village - where distances do not exist anymore: just one mouse-click away, just one tiny lodgement into the account of airmails: Beijing, Rome, Johannesburg, Porto, Berlin, Delhi, Cork... - And people from all these different worlds everywhere: from Nanjing in Bratislava, from the Balaton in Washington, from Cobh in Kaoschiung - and of course on the airports, these melting pots of diversity...

... for instance here in Brussels... "Bonjour, pour moi..., ah... Je prend... " - I asked for a cappuccino... - "And which seize do you want. We have three" - the young women, I guess from the Philippines, asked. Not speaking her language; and not even speaking one of the languages of the country which she currently calls her home country. I switched as well to English. I love to have something in common. - But sometimes I am wondering if what we have in common is not much more then estrangement, alienation.
It is not always necessary to use violence, to beat something out of the minds of

people. Brain washing doesn't need electroshock. Sometimes just a small salary does the trick.

- Recently I heard a poem, better a short story. It had been about a group of three in a prison cell. A large linen bag had been thrown into the dark room, and one of the prisoners said: well, perhaps it is the post? – The post? But we do not get post here. - Well, perhaps we get: all the invoiced for the electro-shocks. One letter, one invoice for each would fill a huge linen bag.

It is a quite touching story as it had not been filled with letters - it had been filled with... - well, there had been a child in it. There is a not less touching end to the story. To cut a long story short: the child had the nick name "the captain". And at the end, all prisoners, not only the three, "played". The captain standing in the middle, all the adults gathering around the child and moving on and on and on - leaving the guards behind - alienated, not being able to take their guns and do what they had been obliged to do: to shoot.

There had been another language, spoken by all: diverse, everybody pronouncing it in his own way; and still speaking one language.

I send this to you - and perhaps you can tell this story to a young women from the Philippines, a boy from Italy, a man from the Congo or a woman from Brazil. But don't forget: you cannot press the reply button. You have to tell it in your very own language.

Ciao - va tottu bene a Roma,

Peter

... and found

On 20/11/2008 20:23, "..." <...> wrote:
> 		DUE TO RECENT BUDGET CUTS, AND THE RISING COST OF ELECTRICITY,
> GAS AND OIL, THE LIGHT AT THE END OF THE TUNNEL HAS BEEN TURNED OFF.
>
> 	WE APOLOGIZE FOR THE INCONVENIENCE.
>
> 	Sincerely,
>
> 	The Government
>
> I couldn't resist!! Aoiffe :)

But why should should you resist – I actually heard this quote yesterday as well here in the Chamber of Deputies here in Rome where we have had our meeting. Actually presented by an old colleague from Russia who said as well something like "Marx hadn't been wrong in several things".

Got recently a nice poem from a colleague:

> DER SOZIALISMUS
>
>
>
> beweist uns, wo man ihn in neuester Zeit
>
> Abschaffte, seine Unentbehrlichkeit.
Translates to something like:
Socialism
Shows
where it had been overcome in recent times
How necessary it is

Definitely frightening where we are going – and if you are not sufficiently aware of it: latest if you sit together with people like this Italian "Mr. B.", if you hear from a meeting that took place just two days before, a meeting where where one of the relatives of Mussolini continued what her ancestor started: fascism, soft, if compared with the German version, but stil... fascism.

While I traveled here I was reading in a journal the story about somebody with "the absolute memory". You name a date and the person knows everything what she experienced that day: the joys, the events, the meals... – the pains, the battles, the discrimination... - everything. The presence of history...

... Rome: you walk through the city: getting aware of the greatness, the great histories, the values from classical philosophy, the middle ages and renaissance... enlightenment... - the poor people living in small houses, one-room apartments, not having much more than just this: a roof that kept the rain of their head and walls that let the water through - the dampness, slowing killing them. The greatness of the Pantheon, a present from the earlier East Byzantine empire to the west - a roof, open to heaven as expression of something higher, and as such providing shelter "for all gods".

The presence of history...

... If you walk consciously through the city, if you are jogging in the day's early hours along Vatican City, if you allow all the impressions and memories to touch you... The presence of history...

... You have new impressions: the greatness of history and its greatness; the power of humans and the de-powerment by actions and structures. And you may get aware of things you do not see: the hijab discussion in Turkey is a matter you see reflected on the streets; the "hijab-discussion" of Christianity is locked behind heavy doors of monasteries. And you may get aware of a kind of absurdity: The huge shop where the cardinals and the pope buy their special gowns next to the small tourist shop or the marketender who sells small kitschy replicates of the most impressive monuments... You may get new thoughts, while you are passing the old man whose fingers are moving the rosary further, around and around while you listening to the music from the MP3-player in your hand, the party shuffle created on a randomly though following a specific pattern of a "life mix".

Monuments, moments – the German term for it is: denkmal – Denk-mal; you may translate it as: Stop and think. And if you do, you may know the deeper meaning of the words a colleague once wrote "Now as for myself, I do not claim to have discovered either the existence of classes in modern society or the struggle between them. Long before me, bourgeois historians had described the historical development of this struggle between the classes, as had bourgeois economists their economic anatomy. My own contribution was 1. To show that the existence of classes is merely bound up with certain historical phases in the development of production; 2. That the class struggle necessarily leads to the dictatorship of the proletariat; 3. That this dictatorship itself constitutes no more than a transition to the abolition of all classes and to a classless society."

(Marx, Karl, 1852 a: Letter to Josepf Weydemeyer, March 5th; in: Karl Marx. Frederick Engels. Collected Works; Volume 39: Marx and Engels: 1852-55; London: Lawrence&Wishart, 1983: 60-66; here: 62/65)

Take care - and accept my sincere regards from this great city, where you meet great people - in the streets where you may enjoy life, looking around and talk to them: friends you didn't see for a long time, learning about their new projects while you are sitting down for a lovely meal; with whom you are discussing new conceptual ideas for a new publication while you have an ice-cream next to the Pantheon, listening to the music of some buskers; as well in those places where Mr B. may sit next to you, but where you find as well people who know what it actually means: to fight against certain hegemony; and where you find great people – great though they may be forced to sell faked designer bags, great though may have to look for "left-overs" in the bins of society, may have to sleep next to the Vatican – rough, on the stairs, supposedly leading to truth and heaven; great people as well who are not amongst us anymore, not visible - because they lived even in our times in houses where dampness slowly killed them or people who said something against hegemonic powers - even today, in democratic societies not free to say and act as they think it necessary.

– People, what else could see even if you look at the buildings, monumental – with their momentum; Denk-Male, asking us and allowing us thinking.

Socialism

Shows
Where it had been overcome in recent times
How necessary it is

Socialism

Shows
Where it never existed or even could have been thought of
How necessary it is

May be they can switch off the light at the tunnel – may be we can lit a fire by the sparks of bright minds of people who gather, who build relationships and develop processes – in practice.

Take care – and do not get lost,

Peter

A Study visit to Austria

A lovely country, a lovely trip – and some "buts"

Dedicated to my travel companions

Tu ne cede malis, sed contra audentior ito.

(Publius Vergilius Marco)

Monday, December 15th, 2008. I am sitting at the breakfast table now – preparing some work for the day: meetings, a phone conference with colleagues in Cork, some writing. At the end a small world of which the obscurantism can be easily overthrown. The seeming complexity, the continuities and discontinuities and ruptures are still following one fundamental pattern:

> *Men make their own history, but they do not make it as they please; they do not make it under self-selected circumstances, but under circumstances existing already, given and transmitted from the past. The tradition of all dead generations weighs like a nightmare on the brains of the living. And just as they seem to be occupied with revolutionizing themselves and things, creating something that did not exist before, precisely in such epochs of revolutionary crisis they anxiously conjure up the spirits of the past to their service, borrowing from them names, battle slogans, and costumes in order to present this new scene in world history in time-honoured disguise and borrowed language.*
>
> *(Marx, Karl: The Eighteenth Brumaire of Louis Bonaparte. 1852; http://www.marxists.org/archive/marx/works/1852/18th-brumaire/ch01.htm - 15/12/2008 11:21 am .)*

Isn't that in a way another expression of Tamino's poetic words I heard the evening before in the Opera House of Graz.

> *Dies Bildnis ist bezaubernd schön*
> *Wie noch kein Auge je geseh'n!*
> *Ich fühl' es, wie dies Götterbild*
> *Mein Herz mit neuer Regung füllt.*
> *Dies' etwas kann ich zwar nicht nennen,*
> *Doch fühl' ichs hier wie Feuer brennen.*
> *Soll die Empfindung Liebe sein?*
> *Ja, ja, die Liebe ist's allein.*
> *O, wenn ich sie nur finden könnte!*
> *O, wenn sie doch schon vor mir stände!*
> *Ich würde, würde, warm und rein,*
> *Was würde ich? Ich würde sie voll Entzücken*

– and if we look at that magic fight it had been as much a matter of individuals as any fight, any action is at the end am encounter of individuals in their social space.

The previous week had been for me very much a social event, a group experience: the work; the leisure time; even Aoiffe's visit to the doctor; and even the private conversation amongst friends: the evening I went with Sepp for dinner, the mornings with Joe at the breakfast table, the dinners we used as excuse to talk – or was it the other way round? All this has repercussions in its own way – experiences being now present by their absence. Now I am sitting here on my own though not alone, writing mails around the world and looking forward to meet privately with friends here in Graz. And it had been work, sure – and it had been a relaxing time, sure – who wants to and who can determine the borders? And it had been a time of heuristically lead, eclectic observation – and still, for me it had also been some kind of systematic research, referring to history, philosophy, sociology, economics, legal science and others. And I am asking again the question that guides me – Sepp said the one evening I would be generalist. And indeed, I am: a generalist and at the same time very specific, always looking at one fundamental question:

Which disciplines are the most important for social policy research and social policy-making? And how can we interpret their relations?

Saturday, December 6th, 2008: The plane with the students of the Higher Diploma Course in Social Policy touches ground: it is Vienna airport where they arrive with their lecturer while I have to admit that I do not even think of them, being caught in the world of Giuseppe Verdi's Don Carlo, sitting in the opera house, build by the architects August Sicard von Sicardsburg and Eduard van der Nüll in the style of Neo-Renaissance.

Are they really not in my mind? I arrived already on Wednesday, spending one business day, next day heading for a meeting in Spain and returning the same day late at night to enjoy the following day most pleasantly in the old imperial city with friends, and also watching out for nice and interesting spots to show the policy students on their first day of the study visit. Although I simply enjoyed the time, the visit in such a place is for me always a study visit, independent of the preparation of a programmed stay or a stroll through the main streets of imperial Vienna and the shoulder length alleys and courtyards of the old patriarchal governors and merchants, allowing in the somewhat fusty atmosphere of the coffee houses forgetting some of the worries, for many surely a welcome possibly to remember romances and dreaming of future ones. For me, walking through the rather unknown place, impressions from a previous short visit come back to my mind – no romance but impressions I have had during half a day I spent with Marco and Pietro, two colleagues and friends from Rome. On that occasion we went up to Grinzing, continuing to the Kahlenberg.

Irrespective of the miserable weather it is nice to return. What a spot, for me an amazing concentration of history in one place: if people see in other places a melting-pot of different groups and people, the Kahlenberg can probably be seen as pallet: the hinterland to the West a mountainous patchwork of dreamy valleys of which the openness of today is more the openness to tourism arriving from the different parts of the world rather than the openness of a player that is entirely drawn into a global economy; nor is it the openness of a citoyen du monde who left all claims to power behind.

All this has actually a long history – Frederick Engels already stated in his little piece on The Beginning of the End in Austria that

> *"[t]his chequered Austrian monarchy, scraped together by theft and by inheritance, this organised jumble of ten languages and nations, this planless mish-mash of contradictory customs and laws, is at last beginning to disintegrate.*
>
> *Honest German citizens have for years been fervent admirers of the director of this creaking state machine, the cowardly swindler and assassin — Metternich. Talleyrand, Louis Philippe and Metternich, three most mediocre minds and hence most suitable for our mediocre times, are regarded by German citizens as three gods who for thirty years have manipulated world history as if it were a puppet show. Going by his own daily experience, the honest citizen regards history as a kind of plot hatched in a tavern or as feminine gossip on a somewhat larger scale."*
>
> *(http://www.marxists.org/archive/marx/works/1848/01/27.htm - 16/12/2008 6:43 am.)*

Where does this leave us? Can we apply here, on the Kahlenberg, the view of the course methodology, spanning

- from methodology
- over theories of welfare state and social policy
- and moving to the analysis of the economy and law
- arriving at the project

– and always moving between the different steps and dimensions? Can we "see" the different methodological dimensions here on the Kahlenberg and on the following walk through the city of Vienna?

We are here in the "Eastern part of the Reich" – this is what the term Austria suggests. And the reference is not simply this "chequered Austrian monarchy, scraped together by theft and by inheritance" as we know it today but a much larger entity, by and large the *Sacrum Romanum Imperium Nationis Germanicæ*, commonly known as the *Holy Roman Empire of German Nations* and time and again changing: being invaded by the Turks, defended by the poles, occupying Hungary and founding the double-monarchy…

Seemingly all this is a matter of history – and trusting Frederick Engels' words from 1848

> *"The Hapsburg dynasty has ceased to reign."*

And is all this what we see, really just a matter of history and histories?

Already a little bit of imagination lets us see the winemaker just below the viewing balcony where we can still see the vineyards, framing from this side Vienna's cityscape, working on their small plots, carrying the ripe grapes in large baskets on their back into the small, somewhat shabby buildings. Although it is rainy and we get only a glimpse of the splendid view, it is easy to imagine the width of the territory of that empire: we can see the invisible borders to Slovakia, we can imagine Bohemia being just behind the nearby mountains and Budapest being somewhere further on the river Danube. And looking down on the river, we may hesitate to agree with Frederick Engels who stated in the quoted text which had been already quoted:

> *"Bourgeois civilisation followed the sea coasts and the course of the big rivers. The inland, especially the barren and impassable mountainous regions, remained the seat of barbarism and of feudalism. This barbarism was especially concentrated in the South German and South Slav inland areas. Protected by the Alps from Italian civilisation and by the mountains of Bohemia and Moravia from that of North Germany, these inland countries had the additional good fortune of being the basin of the only reactionary river in Europe. The Danube, far from linking them with civilisation, brought them into contact with a much more vigorous barbarism.*
>
> *When the great monarchies developed in Western Europe in the wake of bourgeois civilisation, the inland countries of the Upper Danube likewise had to unite in a great monarchy. This was required if only for the needs of defence. Here, in the centre of Europe, the barbarians of all tongues and of all nations associated under the sceptre of the House of Hapsburg. Here they found in Hungary a mainstay of solid barbarism.*

Here, however, we see the river, and we also see the mountains – the
contradiction between openness, the ajar door to the world and the
mountains as a bulwark that – during the long winter month – locks even the
light out of daily lives as if it would want to allow people to hide.

We see the mountains – from where we stand the eyes do not fondle the
Alps anymore, but we know the range stretches to the other side, Vienna
being the foot of the apophysis of the Alpine massive rocks, which are
covered by the conifers of the forests that belong even today to the nobility
and the green grass and colourful flowers of the unique alp-meadows. We
need only little fantasy to imagine that the hinterland of the imperial,
industrious and later even somewhat industrial area remained for a long time
coined by the small farms – the scarce soil of the beautiful mountainous
regions limiting the economic development and allowing the mountains as
well taking over the role of a border of thinking.

Supposedly Metternich claimed the necessary persistence of the patchwork-
structure of the country, saying something as: Leave the people with their
different languages, with their different interests and their different life
styles – it is this patchwork that allows the central power to stay in place.

– And as much as this is a practicable strategy to secure power over the vast
empire, it seems to match neatly the national pattern of governance: the
valleys and their economies as somewhat "independent" empires, a strict
feudal structure with the checks of patronising and patrimonial law of the
owner and the balances of mercy and charity. And we cannot overlook that it
is also the spiritual climate or Zeitgeist, as it may be called, providing a
seedbed for individualism – a few may serve as example: the aggressive
figure of Adolf Schicklgruber, later accepting his father's name: Hitler,
coming from the then Austrian-Hungarian Braunau to suppress the world in
the name of a supposed superior *Herrenrasse* (master race); the providers of
easy, mellifluous light heartedness for the saturated citoyenitee as Wolfgang
Amadeus Mozart or Johann Strauss in the ball-houses. It had been as well
the source of economic theories linked to Joseph Schumpeter,[84] Ludwig von
Mises, the soil for the development of the first and the second Viennese
school. As different as they had been, they were kept together by one idea:
the axiom underlying especially von Mises deliberations, namely the

---

[84]   Born in what had been Austria-Hungary at his time.

And it had been the country of great intellectuals, some of them for their time revolutionaries as Sigmund Freud; the, well, one may say boorish protesters as Gustav Klimt who aimed to turn the world around, though strictly remaining in their own little world of coffeehouses...

... and philosophers as Karl Raimund Popper and musicians as Arnold Schoenberg. – And one might think about the fact that amongst them many had been Jews; and many had to leave the country – as Jews or as intellectuals, who could not cope any longer with the narrow-mindedness of the mindset of indigenous empirealists[85] of the mountain people.

And those who stayed? Well, even not limiting themselves to coffee houses they could – with all the pros and cons – not shake off the chains of their history. Building on the contradictory structures of the old system allowed establishing a communitarian housing policy, making the city of Vienna actually the largest landlord.

It had been actually this reference to convention of the Austrian mindset that allowed the Austrian workers of the Karl-Marx-Hof to resist in an else unknown way the fascist attacks; and it had been the very same mindset that allowed clerico-fascist government and the crypto-protestantism.

And despite fighting fascism in the most severe form, the Austrian socialists also proposed the if-strategy, a strategy of opportunism and subordination. P. Berger, criticising this approach, presents it with an unreferenced quote:

> *"we are going to fight IF –*
>
> *If Parliament is dissolved,*
>
> *If the Social Democratic Party is dissolved,*
>
> *If the Trade Unions are illegalized,*
>
> *If the Social Democratic 'Defense Guards' (Schutzbund) is banned."*
>
> *(Berger, P.: Lessons of the 1934 Revolt in Austria. An Account of a
> Participant. Fourth International, July 1944;*

---

[85] Though the advocates of the empire had been surely as well imperialists, there had been another dimension which may well be captured by such a neologism.

http://marxists.architexturez.net/history/etol/newspape/fi/vol05/no07/berger
.htm - 18/12/2008 2:02 pm.)

The paradox is surely that the closeness depended entirely on the openness. Even today people say that the Rennweg in Vienna's east marks the beginning of the Balkan. And the fact that Austria had been always an interface of cultures means as well that there is a permanent confrontation, one may say the permanent challenge of a multicultural reflection, of course ranging from suppression over integration to acceptance and real togetherness.

So it is not astonishing to see the country as home of a strong right-wing movement and also as centre of UN and OECD.

– Power: Pouvoir, Posseremo, Possible ?!?!

– Can all this be better expressed than in the slogan I spot while I explore the advertisements at the airport the day I leave home? The poster[86] promotes "The Republic of Lauda as a state of mind" – thus linking the state of individual's mind to the "idea" of the state as governing power, creating the omnipotence of the hedonistic individual. Some will see it as example par excellence for postmodernism; I would see it as a renaissance of a pre-modern mindset, aiming on seizing people, leading them into the trap of a new form of feudalism.

In any case it is important to survey the mechanisms of control, a somewhat fine-tuned relationship which allows ruling in a sophisticated way of a glorified populism,

- stretching from paternalist and populist authoritarianism over charitable and communitarian nearness to intellectual palaver that wants to criticise and puts forwards dreams of flowery negation of power rather taking initiatives to consequently takeover responsibility and power;

- allowing the seemingly uncontrolled hedonism, though being in permanent exertion of pedagogical intervention.

And perhaps it is possible from here to rethink issues of social science – and as well from contemporary political debates. Much of the dispute around globalised free trade and restricted marketisation may well be seen as fight between

---

[86]   Advertisement for the airline owned by the former formula-1-champion Niki Lauda

- advocates of communities that are – really or seemingly – welded together by status-bound commodities, based on mutual control and restrictive and restricting meaning and

- advocates of societies that are based on contracts, based on restrictive and restricting law.

With all this, a question comes to my mind – an important question which will play a role throughout the study visit and beyond.

It asks to compare the accumulation regime and mode of regulation of Ireland and Austria. Being confronted with all these experiences. I am wondering what the meaning of history on the one hand and the process of EUropeanisation and globalisation on the other hand actually is about.

Monday, December 8th, 2008: The first point on the "official program" follows on Monday – a visit to the headquarters of the United Nations in Vienna – though it is actually an extraterritorial area.

Though it had not been the expected "special tour", it had been interesting enough, getting a glance of new approaches to the world government of which we learned the previous day. Though I know "these places", can occasionally go behind the glass walls and step through some of the glass ceilings, I feel occasionally simply as the small country-boy from Ireland: Listening to a presentation that suggests an open governance structure, that wants to appear as open for everybody and wondering about the naivety that is being carried on – presentations that refuse to acknowledged the reality, Cathy Byrne characterised by pointing on the "glass walls around democracy"
*(see http://www.ucc.ie/social_policy/democracy_behind_glass.htm -
19/12/2008 9:06 am.).*

It may be somewhat bizarre that at this moment the words by Dénes Katz from a travel report to Thailand/Bangkok gain a very specific meaning:

"The feeling of culture shock, simply mentioned in the guidebooks, really got to me only in the following days. Bangkok is a spicy mixture of traditional Asian culture of traditional Asian culture and the modern Western world."

(Dénes Katz: Global Explorer Jeggyel A Foeld Koeruel I; in: Horizon; ed.: Malév Hungarian Airlines; Budapest: Geoemedia: 2007 [11/2007]; 66-67; here 67)

What does this actually mean if we look at such statement in the perspective of general social science? What does it mean in a comparative perspective?

The complex buildings of United Nations, for which a couple of cent are paid as rent to the Austrian state which is formally the owner, may also cause a "culture shock" – though for the country boy in me it is a shock the other way round. As the building is quiet, we do not see the various dimensions that are usually dominating life in this UN-city: the pulse of various nations, the mix of languages, the different dresses, in many cases showing at least glimpses of their origins – Egypt, Africa, Northern America and South America... – seemingly just a colourful mix as the randomly order of the 192 flags: randomly because they could have decided as well to exhibit them in the alphabetical order of the capitals of the countries rather than the names of the countries. And there is one thing that may be less random: the names are listed in alphabetical order; but the language used for compiling the order is English – they could have used one of the other main languages; or they simply could have used the original language of all the countries.

And moreover, already on a quiet day as this Monday, a bank holiday in Austria, we can see an ongoing meaning: of divisions behind the suggested equality, the persisting closure behind the advocated openness: the "workers" with their black skin and the "white man" as the thinker; the network of relationships and intimate knowledge going hand in hand with bureaucratic rules and ordered power relationships. The calculability and accountability going hand in hand with the "right" of the financiers to determine the agenda and the actors, forcing Mary Robinson out of business, a fact that is quietly ignored by a general official notice *(http://www.unpo.org/content/view/118/81/; 15/12/2008 11:09 am.)* and equally forcing a national representative of human rights as Neill Crowley out of business *(see e.g. http://www.finfacts.com/irishfinancenews /article_1015513.shtml - 15/12/2008 10:49 am.; http://www.rte.ie/news/2008 /1212/equality.html - 15/12/2008 11:am..m.)* – the long arm of a new Machiavellian Prince, the residuals of a Leviathan within a system that claims equality and still hesitates to enforce equity. –Following from a look at language, there is a tiny incidence that may be considered as being interesting. The thesaurus suggests as one synonym for both one word: impartiality – reality, though, suggests impartiality for the first and strong devotion and a firm bias for the second.

And the visit of the Fundamental Rights Agency in the afternoon fits well into the picture. At stake are not simply a formal framework and its assessment. Rather, the question that remains obviously unanswered is the definition of topic, namely rights. The shortcoming of simple observation is clear by statistics presented by John. And of course, we face a paradox: didn't we see the day before the entire history of centuries literally unfolding in front of us? And now we face the question that even measuring something concrete as defined rights is actually impossible?

The paradox is, however, not a real one. At stake is that the studies presented lack in actual fact a common question and mutually agreed definitions and references. Though they use similar terms they use them without considering the historical and national embedding – we can say this in other words: they work without considering the people, the real life and life situation against which rights have to be assessed.

Talking about rights, exploring their meaning can actually not refer to abstract principles and it cannot rely on definitions given by any natural or possibly divine law. It has to look at the concrete circumstances of policy-making and the determinants that are established in order to define and implement rights. Or to put it differently, using the words Karl Marx wrote in 1857 in the Outline of the Critique of Political Economy (Grundrisse):

> *The economists of the seventeenth century, e.g., always begin with the living whole, with population, nation, state, several states, etc.; but they always conclude by discovering through analysis a small number of determinant, abstract, general relations such as division of labour, money, value, etc. As soon as these individual moments had been more or less firmly established and abstracted, there began the economic systems, which ascended from the simple relations, such as labour, division of labour, need, exchange value, to the level of the state, exchange between nations and the world market. The latter is obviously the scientifically correct method.* ***The concrete is concrete because it is the concentration of many determinations, hence unity of the diverse.*** *It appears in the process of thinking, therefore, as a process of concentration, as a result, not as a point of departure, even though it is the point of departure in reality and hence also the point of departure for observation [Anschauung] and conception. Along the first path the full conception was evaporated to yield an abstract determination; along the second, the abstract determinations lead towards a reproduction of the concrete by way of thought.*
>
> *(http://www.marxists.org/archive/marx/works/1857/grundrisse/cho1.htm - 18/12/2008 8:32 am.; emphasis P.H.)*

It then may be necessary to

concisely and critically comment on the terms as the following and look for and their meaning for instance in Irish social policy:

- Annual Budget

- Industrial Development

- Poor Law

- Partnership negotiations

- Community and Voluntary Sector

- Federalist principle

Tuesday, December 9th, 2008: It is time to move on, to look at the life behind the scenes, behind the glass walls – and as much as it is the life above the so-called glass-ceilings – the ceilings that do not allow us to reach the realms and rooms where decisions are actually taken, it is as well the life of which we are every day part – and which we often do not see as we are too much part of it; and the life which is often hidden under the carpets on which the rich walk.

The visits of local NGOs, representatives of local and regional government, the colleagues at the University in Graz. The week can be seen as well as some exercise of border crossing. We crossed a border by visiting Vienna and Graz; but all the people we meet are crossing borders with every single act and word.

They are representing their work and workplace and at the same time they are not, just being socio-individuals with their own opinion, ideas.... – and as much as we crosses borders we are kept in our own cocoon: the group, our personal socio-individuality, our dislikes and wishes – and as well by expectations and some simple mechanism of distraction. I mention the latter the other day, after the students and colleague left me. Being now on my own, being a little bit just "one of them" and still a "stranger" who is not entirely absorbed by everyday's business and routines the number of people who are begging seems to rocket. Did they only show now, after they didn't have to fear students looking for them? Or did my own integration into the group, the togetherness with the students and my colleague, the orientation on specific activities distract my alertness? And did the own and specific involvement distract as well from seeing some of the beauties – the row of houses along the Herrengasse, the 'roof-scape' which had been awarded by the UN as cultural heritage; from seeing many of the normalities as people doing their Christmas shopping, elderly people going into a coffee house for lunch – looking for nutrition for the body and mind.

– Growing together, growing apart.

Wednesday, December 17th, 2008 – the day of the flight home; somewhat bumpy at times, but without major incidence and as long as nobody checks if I fastened the seatbelt tightly of if I just have them open across the lap I don't bother – the narrowness of the seat is less convenient even there in the first row which offers plenty of legroom. Somewhat unusual the first part of the trip as the staff had been friendly, stimulated by celebrating the promotion of one of the colleagues. The announcements, formal and following strict rules had been interrupted by breaks, the speaker trying to concentrate, refrain from laughing. And adding some remarks – more private, still made public. Applauding passengers – and at the border control in London the introduction of a new system, for some at least.

A new EU-passport with a chip, making the procedure more smooth, more effective and... – and there is no reason for paranoia as they have the data anyway. If we accept to live in a global village we have apparently to accept that the traditional controls by our neighbours, their knowledge about things we are going to do before we actually do them is just transferred. Sure, there is a huge difference between the knowledge of the village priest, the control by a Machiavellian Prince, the stronghold by Hobbes' Leviathan and the information held by a systematically developed high-tech system of the so-called intelligence of the stupid white man?

But we have to look exactly what the essence of the difference is about. And at least one point may be of special relevance here: the need to look at details, asking

What are the key factors that evocate social intervention ('social policy issues')? Just try to think for example about at least 3 of them and consider the mechanisms of intervention and the reasoning behind it.

Saepe creat molles aspera spina rosas

(Publius Ovidius Naso)

A Day in Dublin – January 2009

I am not sure, why you alluded to that idea but in any case: Good is that I could resist possible temptations – so I am still single. And I thought I would know why you hesitated to say something exciting about our capital; well why you actually said that this is the most boring city, perhaps somewhat appalling and boring places if compared with the fancy places as Roma, Firenze, Berlin, Muenchen, Madrid or Praha and Budapest.

But good is that I am not only still single but as well that my visitor and I enjoyed a day of life in Dublin, talked a lot. So, perhaps unfortunately I didn't have time to write a new travel log: The day of a two friends in Dublin. But somebody else did something like it anyway long time ago, writing about man stranding in his own hometown, telling the story of Leopold Bloom and how he experienced the 16th of June 1904; and James definitely did have another sujet and he definitely did better job than I even could dream to do (though if I would write such a story it most likely would have something in common: my story would be as difficult to understand as his Ulysses).

The landing was as good as it could be – the fanfare letting us know that it was "just another Ryanair-flight on time…" – Ming-fang's thumb points up; her smile shows this bizarre expression, her age now being even less accessible. – Something I had been facing the last days during which – it is difficult to say… Well, perhaps I am only surprised because I know how old she is. And it is not a matter of age though she definitely looked younger than most Europeans of the same age. Bringing so many memories from my stay over in Taipei back to me – not only while we are talking about the corners of the little parks, the coffee shops in Wen-Zhou Street, meals in the restaurant in Xin-Sheng Road, the Da-an Forest park, the night markets of which she says "I never liked them but now, talking about them, I would like to go to one, diving into the vividness. Bringing memories back as well while we are talking about the colleagues and friends from the Taiwanese capital; and not only because we are chatting and laughing about ourselves and an easy life and the pleasures of 'dancing' – just playing with ideas and the differences of our own being, making not least language and writing to a dance, adding some ease to the difficulty of persistent estrangement of speaking a language that is foreign to both of us: simplified German. For her German is a language of which she says that she cannot fully express in it what she really means. And the way in which she uses the words and constructs the sentences, speaking occasionally in the third person of herself, makes it for me a language of which I am getting aware of the deep truth of some simplicity. During my shallow attempts in writing Chinese I frequently noticed that simplified Chinese is a move to abstraction, the signs losing the obvious link to concrete, 'imaginable' expressions as we find it in the classical sign for state whereas our simplified German is more concrete even when it comes to expressing seemingly abstract ideas and feelings. And this simplified German seems much friendlier – but this friendliness may have another reason, beyond language. But of course our conversation is as well a war dance: the dance of the daily fight of a people that is culturally not allowed to say no – and permanently is told no by the various international communities and the own national tradition of an Asian country; facing a people that is permanently saying no, complaining about everything – even about possibly not having anything to complain about. The quarrels about career making and the failures of subordination and resisting, the facing of arrogance and ignorance, the experience of dependence and independence in personal matters, the discrimination of suppression of various groups and nations...

Well, as I said, I am not going to write a little fairy tale about her – fascinating and irritating as she is, probably well worth writing a long story – but if that justifies already writing, I would have to write a story about nearly everybody I meet; and I will not really write about the day in Dublin, still being too irritated by the experiences and talks, too much caught by having been confronted over the last days with and having been living in five worlds of authoritarianism and control: Asia – which is always present since I collaborate with the young colleague or even since I had been over in Taiwan for the second time; Europe – as various as it is, it appears as own entity if seen from my regained Asian part-time identity; Asiaeurope – the world of an Asian woman who frequently states during these days: "In former times nationality never played a role for me; but since I live in Europe I think more and more about it; and I do so even more if I am required to get a visa and the like."; Eurasia – the perspective from Europe [or a European?] on Asia; and of course my own world, seemingly very personal, but definitely very individual world which I will probably never understand: a world of control by invariant, ingrained norms: experiences, routines, prejudices, morals...

Now, though I will not write about this 'first time Dublin-as-tourist experience', I cannot stop to tell you about the warm welcome in the hotel. The booking form states: If you arrive after 12 noon, you have to phone the hotel the same day, to confirm your arrival. Being not sure about our time of arrival, I call the Travelodge while waiting at Cork airport. Though I got a little bit the impression that the woman at the other end did not really know why I was doing this, I did what I was asked to do. And actually we arrive more or less on time, about 12:10 anyway. Check-in – the time for check-in is 15:00 – but we can check-in already, ten Euro extra charge. So I ask if we can just leave the luggage there in a luggage room. We are told that we can't.

Irrespective of the respect of my Buddhist companion's feelings – and this means to some extent: despite the personalised reminder of 'think-positive' – I burst out: "This is Ireland's..., this is skinning people coming along – welcome to Dublin." And I continue, leaning half across the counter "Listen, I know it is not your fault, but tell the manager...". A short word-quarrel...; I look towards my companion and it seems that Buddhist optimism and 'pacifism' and calmness left her, although she doesn't say a word. From talking about it later I see that she simply was not able even to believe that it was true what she understood – she thought she got something wrong. Doesn't it encourage arriving before 12, if the booking form requires to confirm arrival in case you arrive later than that? Well, we check-in, thus being able to leave the luggage in the hotel and go to Dublin, enjoying the day. We take the bus – have change ready as you will not get any money back – and drive through Ballymun. I talk a little bit about this area of the Irish capital – knowing about the problems here; and if I would not know about them, I could see at least some of them as they literally spring into the eyes: even after (part) refurbishment and even if I see the many changes since I had been here with a group of students that visited my institute, it is obviously not the 'first address' in town; and still I am somewhat hesitating – the buildings here look like bungalows if compared with many districts in our other capital: Taipei. Here the problems are still visible, whereas they seem to drown in an invisible mass between high raisers and in narrow streets in the other capital.

– "And what are we going to do? Did you look up on the Internet? Is there anything you want to see?" We are driving along the pretty red brick buildings nearer to the centre; some architecturally remarkable new buildings; the canal which provides some space for relaxation before arriving in the middle of the buzz of the city – and though all this is obviously part of the city, it recalls some specific part of Irishness: the British influence of the row-houses; the privatism of detached and semi-detached houses; the specific community sense, here still prevalent in a very similar way as it is depicted in J.B. Yeats' picture capturing the Liffey swimming.

As we both do not really have an idea, Ming-fang suggests going first to a tourist information – "We can get a map there and ask for museums and galleries." And she asks for apologies: "I am rather exhausted from the last weeks." She says this because she said before she even booked the flight that she would be a typical tourist: walking through the entire city, eager to see everything, and of course making photos of all the spots. "I am too tired to do this," she says. "Oh, you don't have to ask for apologies" I say. "Just lets do what you said. May be they have a proposal." And I continue, without showing my relieve: "We definitely do not need to do everything that a 'good tourist' would do." I am quite happy that I won't have to run through ten museums and galleries, it is not planned to do a little jogging exercise through Merrion Square, Stephen's green, Temple bar, passing Dublin Castle...

So we go into the office, just one next to the bus stop; I leave it to her – well, actually she takes responsibility anyway and asks for a city map. The women at the counter is really helpful, really explains everything (which leaves the burden of taking a decision to us) – and double checks the opening for the National Gallery of Ireland for which Ming-fang shows interest: "It is open until 5:30 pm."

We leave the counter: with a map and a little booklet, which explains all the places worthwhile to visit, where one can eat, shops, information... – Approaching the door, I briefly look back. The lady at the counter smiles, obviously amused by the stranger, or by us strangers: the one with the special accent and the bell-like voice; the other asking questions as if he actually already knows the place anyway. And the smile, as friendly it is, has a bit of, is somewhat..., hm, disagreeable, condescending.

Anyway, it seems that we have a plan: the visit to the National Gallery. So I turn left as we leave the tourist office, taking the direction to Trinity College. "We'll go there?" – While I had been convinced that this had been the guest's plan and I turn into the direction of the Liffey, I feel the hand on my arm: "Shall we go for a small lunch somewhere? We can research the documents and then we decide!?" – "Excellent! What does 'a small lunch' mean? Any idea?" And after a brief hesitation I propose: "We can go a little bit up the road. There is a tiny place, a local one. We usually go there when I am here for work; a place where people, who are working in one of the offices nearby, have their lunch. Little bit off the main street." – "Ok." And we go there, passing the fancy Gresham Hotel ("We can go here as well" – my joking proposal is rejected. "No, I do not like these places. They are..., hm, so clean, no: cold." And we talk about the experiences of five star hotels: "You know, when we Taiwanese go on holidays we always think we have to go to these hotels. It is a kind of tradition, the travel agencies organise this already..."), we move on passing the Gate Theatre at the corner of Parnell Street, the church at the corner of the Garden of Remembrance, turning right at Gardiner's Road, then North Great George's Street – finally we go up the few steps, enter the cosy place and are lucky: "For two?" and as we nod, we are directed towards a table. The waitress brings the menu but my companion is distracted: The open fire place, the festive decoration which is still left from Christmas and gives the room a nice, leisurely atmosphere... – and when we finally order I hear a question which is not related to the menu: "May I take a photograph?" The waitress, usually very hasty, business like and stressed is interrupted in her routines; is getting aware of another life beyond machine-like behaviour – "Of course, you can!" she smiles in a very kind, very natural way. – And of course, we do not research the documents and map, we do not make a plan but just chat about the world. About classical music – Western music, though I want to learn more about 'the other world'. "Actually I plaid the piano as child and I loved to play Western music. I do not know much about our traditional Chinese music…" – And so she talks about Chopin, Beethoven, Mozart and I present my little knowledge of erhu, guquin and the importance of melody and tone colour rather than rhythm and gaining a specific rhythm from – in the Western light – the lack of it.

And after chatting, after some photos are taken from the room and especially the fireplace, we glance quickly over the material we got and decide to go to the arts gallery. "Why did the lady in the tourist office say it is open until 5:30? Today is Thursday, isn't it?" Her small fingertip points on the line: Opening hours: 'Thursdays late opening.' She claps her hands, a thrilled "Hej" – the bliss is contagious. I really do mention the change, an awakening excitement. It seems that the fatigue of the last weeks is gone and the interest in other things comes to the fore, still a little bit overshadowed by the distraction of work related thoughts. "You say you are Buddhist." I look in her eyes. "Carpe diem. Just take the here and now. Allow Ming-fang to be good here, making use of the moment to complete herself, let her grow. The other things will develop as they are passing the way again. And you will always gain." Of course, it is only my understanding of what may be adequate – and it is as well my misunderstanding. Being of any religion does not mean that every act needs a thoroughly reflected decision – just the excitement is enough. As much as the presence of such cultural heritages is indeed permanent, something else is equally permanently present: the personal joy of exploring something new, and expanding the existing experience. Personally I developed this as a kind of skill, not going on holidays but, as Ashok would say, "watching at the flowers as they stand along the roadside." And it is not the idea of doing so, but the real distraction. Not a given date, but the real opportunity, coming along or actively looked for. "You are right!" – And I am near to say that I am of course right and there is no reason for even a hesitant doubt. And I am near to say that she didn't even once talked about Stephan – and I do hesitate not only because I do not want to remind her, but as well because I mention this second how deep he actually hurt me by his arrogance and ignorance. And I hesitate as well because I am getting aware, how much I hated to follow my spontaneous intuition when I was on the phone to him, answering such nonchalant character in the same blasé way: name dropping, challenging him and treating him somewhat as a child: "If you would have done your homework you should know..." – Necessary survival strategies that effect me to such an extent emotionally that it may be that they will actually be like nails closing one day my coffin.

Anyway, we are back on Connell Street, pass the Spire, now replacing the Nelson-statue – the landmark, pointing into a space which is after dethronement of good empty, replacing remembrance. Does the landmark want to say actually this: that a country that losing its history is in danger of losing its future? Is it a landmark of a cultural shock? I point on the GPO, telling a little bit about its meaning in history. I point on the old houses as for instance the one locating the department store Clerys – and the interruption of the house fronts by most ugly "modern" buildings as the one hosting Penneys. And all this is really more remarkable – for me and for her – than the other Asian, obviously Chinese people who are walking here as well; quite a lot, one could say, but still few if one considers that they are obviously 'the other'.

Ming-fang takes photos of the sites that are today probably more meaningful for the passer-by from other countries than for us: the GPO and of course O'Connell monument – "Just wait a while. I have to wait so that I capture people in front of the monument. People are part of a city." We cross the river: on the right the old Parliament which is today remarkably hosting one of the large banks; Trinity College on the left – surely deserving a quick explanation; and we decide to go to the monument of Molly Malone – one of the sites that had been mentioned in the booklet from the tourist office. Grafton Street, the shopping mall, is cramped; Stephen's Green is on the right and we are soon at the gallery, occasionally stopping to have a look at the memorial tiles, marking with quotes the way Leopold Bloom took in 1904. But just before we pass another building, the letters announcing Roinn an Taoisigh. I point on the building and it catches more attention than I expect. I pronounce the words in the best Irish that I am able to avail of and the young woman next to me repeats. "It is what in other countries they call prime minister, the Kanzler in German, or Hsing Cheng Yüan Chang as we say in Chinese." – "Oh, I see" she says, without being surprised. But she surprises me by her giggling. Seeing my puzzled face, she explains: "When I saw the word I thought it is a centre for Taoism." Though I join in the funny idea – not really in the giggling – another part in me hesitates, sees a very serious dimension. Is this not what state leadership should be about: the three jewels of Taoism – compassion, moderation and humility. But are such jewels something that can be achieved by wu wei, the principle of non-action?

We soon enter the huge building of the gallery – both being glad that we have plenty of time.

After I visited recently a special exhibition in Cork's Crawford gallery and enjoyed the unexpectedly interesting experience, I am at least open for another positive adventure. We enter, leave our jackets and her bag in the cloakroom, and look for the floor plan. I see a single one in Dutch language, and several flyers are in Gaelic and in French language. Another language is presented – I hand it over to Ming-fang: "That is for you. In Chinese and Japanese language." But she takes the German one. "It is easier as the Chinese/Japanese has only half of the information. So to say 'Two languages on the space of one'." So I decide for the French one, still looking in a searching way when we approach the information desk where more brochures are displayed. "You are looking for the English floor plan." I nod and the lady at the desk, very kind, takes one from the papers in front of her. "Here is one. But, please, can you recycle it on the way out?" Looking into my face and seeing my surprise she continues: "Well, you know, the cutbacks. We try to save as well in the small things." – "Every little helps" I say with a smile. "But it is only for the English?" – "We still have plenty of the others... ." So I stick to the French version and show it to her. "This is fine – language doesn't really matter. But today I am tourist, you know. Liking the little souvenir." We are ready now for an endless walk; I am really amazed by the variety of the exhibits – the permanent and the masterpieces of Hamilton and Turner. And though we speak with a low voice, we speak about some of the pictures. Share as well experiences of other galleries – she visited them on the expeditions through Europe: Florence, Madrid, Amsterdam, Paris...; I visited them on occasions of work related trips: the Prado, the large collection of Klimt and Schiele in Vienna, of Die Bruecke in Berlin, Dalí and of course Picasso... – some of them we both visited, though on different occasions, few we visited together and some of them only visited by one of us.

And we virtually look as well at and talk about the Asian arts, capturing nature and people in nature rather than focussing on gods, the depiction of the scripture and people as individuals. Is it the reflection of the orientation on self-perfection in nature versus perfection of the world and perfecting individuals to rule the world? And would we then be still allowed to speak of individualism as guiding only the one people, not the other as it is frequently suggested when we suggest a highly suppressive system given by Confucius, Mencius and Buddhist teaching?

– It had been several hours that we walked together through the museum: together, then separating, each of us having a closer look at some pictures or even sections, then meeting again. In a way thus reflecting the different cultures of our origin and the different points where we meet in history and in thinking and in feeling. We walked so to say along the last station – the J.B. Yeats museum. "Now we have to go here" – the finger points on the map: the museum shop. "May be I buy some postcards." – "Good that you say it – I always go as well to the museum shop." So we find ourselves in a short time at the shop near the back entrance. We look, we buy and after having already paid, going to the door of the shop, Ming-fang takes a calendar, looks at the back where all the pictures are displayed. She holds the calendar in her hand and moves towards the desk. I want to take the calendar, saying: "I will get it for you. As a present." She holds it tight. "No, Peter, I will pay." – "Just allow me... ." But she doesn't, looks into my face and then hesitates. "Ok, we make a game. If I win, I will pay and if you win you may pay." – "Ok then. What is the game? Tell me the rules, Ming-fang." Few moments later I know a new, rather long Chinese word, a new game and we are standing next to the door: first time parity, second time the same result, third time still no winner, not looser. "I have to concentrate now" – she briefly holds her fingertips against the temples, looks again at me with a smile. "Ready now" – and seeing it from the result she wanted to allow me the pleasure of giving her this small present.

As we stand outside the building, the fresh air blowing into the faces, I take a deep breath. Her voice asks: "You are tired?" – "Not really. No, but I am really positively surprised. I didn't expect this wealth of an exhibition in our capital." After looking at the street sign we bend the heads over the map. "You're Ok?" my partner can hardly understand a strong Dublin accent of the voice of an elderly man. "We're lookin' for Trinity. It's over there, isn't it?" I point to the left, over my shoulder. "Yeah, but cross the road h're 'n' turn to the left. It's the entrance th're." That is what we do and we soon arrive at the College's sports ground. "Do you mind? I would like to stand here for a while, watching them." – "Why should I mind? Actually I have a special relationship to this pitch." And I tell her the little story. I retired here some years back, during a conference, standing here with a colleague – he was at the time from Johns-Hopkins University, went later to LSE and had to move back to the States as his wife had not been able to find a job in Europe. But the somewhat funny part of the story was that we both came originally from Germany, thus struggling with using Helmut and Peter when we spoke English and Anheier and Herrmann, using the German language. And here, where some lads had been playing Rugby that day, we finally decided to use in any case the first name. "Sport as welding link?" she asks. "Well, perhaps. But that day we didn't really watch the moves on the pitch." We had been just standing here, talking about the jobs, the... – well, at that time we hadn't been German anymore, not really. But still, there had been the experience from the early times, being somewhat important." I stumble. "Or perhaps it had not really been the experience of the common past. Perhaps it had been something we have had in common, being different from what the others have and are!? Being strangers!?" It is this topic which is so frequent for me – and in my actual personal being of little real importance. But it is frequent because people expect the likes like me that it is important and has to be important and that the 'lost nationality' makes us special. We have to get visa, we sometimes have special passport checkpoints – and if we do not take the correct one, as I did this morning when I walked with Ming-fang through the non-EU-checkpoint, in this case thus jumping the much longer EU-queue, we are looked at with special suspicion and have to justify ourselves. And we ourselves mingle in often flippant ways nation, politics, character, ethnicity, establishing structures and status rather than seeing processes.

My speaking comes to a halt before I continue: "I say this because I remember a tiny thing from one of the last evenings, when we had been for a meal in Cork. We had been chatting about..., I am not sure what it exactly was about. Something from Taiwan; we had been chatting about it nobody who hadn't been there could understand. And indeed, there had been a couple sitting next to us, smiling with some bewilderment, infected by our cheeriness and at the same time not at all understanding our giggling. And perhaps even bewildered by seeing us giggling this way – seeing us and not just you doing it. We laugh, stretch out the hands towards each other, both at the same time... – and just this second I say "fifteen". – "Wrong"; the hands are back, stretched forward again – "five". – "Wrong again." And on the fourth or fifth occasion one of us predicts the right number. A silly game, still mutually bringing contagious, childish gaiety. We talk; and we continue strolling across the campus – the room with the Books of Kells is long closed – moving towards the old archway, leaving the college ground opposite of the building that previously hosted the parliament. Turning to the right we soon cross the Liffey – "Can you smell the water? It reminds me a little bit of Taipei. But here it is not as strong as it is at home." I hear some longing, though it is not named. "Once we went to the coast – when I had been a young student. The day before had been a typhoon and my parents didn't know that we were going there – they would have killed me. But it had been exciting. The waves..., you cannot imagine such high waves. I never saw such high waves again." And although I know the place, can imagine a group of young students standing there at the bewildering shore, I cannot really picture high waves. But this moment I imagine Tom, my neighbour. He once told me a story which has some similarity. He visited a relative of his, here in

Dublin. And they left into the countryside – running across the fields and retiring into the mountains. "Where there had been fields at that time you find today the city of Dublin, stretched out far to all sides. And the parents, used to the special security of the town, didn't know either where he was going. "Did you do similar things?" I am asked. Well, earlier; as youth. We went into the forests nearby and into the stone quarry, driving motorbikes and climbing in the tunnels. 'Easy rider', wild music, open-air festivals, drugs, and of course brand names for cars guitars and clothing – every village having a little 'Woodstock' festival and all tied together by Levi's and mini cooper and the sound of our music. And as much as it had been l'art pour l'art, it had been as well a time of closeness to nature. Did you read Goethe's 'Die Leiden des Jungen Werther'?"

– As we are standing at the traffic light, I look at the people around me; apparently we do not have anything in common. I look at my Taiwanese friend, standing next to me and we do not have much in common either. And I think of Tom – what is the connection between us. We are definitely all so different. Are we all so... – I am interrupted as we move on, crossing the road with all the others – tourists, shoppers, business people and people who look as if they would be on the way home after work. "Are you hungry?" Well, hungry enough to look for a restaurant. We walk through the docklands, a refurbished area struggling with times: first linking the countries 'developmental era' into what is called modernity; and now it will be struggling with maintaining a post-modern vision which never has have existed in reality with the reality of its crisis-stricken decline. We see the impressive building of the Department for the environment – I had been once there, impressed by the then minister, whom I assessed in the same way as I did assess the German President of that time: Being able to give a ling speech, saying nothing, and doing this rhetorically in an awkward way.

Finally we find a place where we spend the rest of the evening. A place where I hear that the tofu-specialities which I never really liked while I had been in Taipei but which they served as special treat, are actually something that is not typical for Chinese cuisine; rather it is for tourists and Europeans. We are sitting in a simple, comfortable location where we talk another time about arts, and the difference between European arts, depicting an outer world and Chinese arts, being much more linked to the realisation and perfection of the self in the present existence. I don't know the magic of coordination – chatting away, we suddenly stretch out the hands, one of us says "ten"; and all happens in a blink of an eye. Each of us had opened one of the hands, two open hands, and ten fingers. "Yeah..." – we look around us, now getting aware of the others. Yes, they had been looking, but friendly smiling and continuing their own chats. – Let them play...

We continue chatting and laughing about ourselves and an easy life and the pleasures of "dancing" – just playing with ideas and the differences of our own being, making not least thinking and language and writing a dance, adding some ease to the difficulty of persistent estrangement.

And I forget to think about the difference of what it means if I say "I am I" and if she says "I am I". One sentence and two entirely different dance steps.

A day with barely a quite minute. A day with many new impressions from Dublin and new insights into life – in general, but as well into the life of a young Taiwanese woman and a German-Irish man who actually may not be even that anymore. A day full of play and full of serious talks. A day which had been a kind of dance as well because of its language – the permanent translation. The translation not of words but of meanings. – We get the bill from the waiter – "We'll just share? Everybody paying 50 percent?" – "Yes" and with this word I push the exact amount towards her. She takes the money, puts it into her wallet and gets a larger bank note; holds it in both hands and gives it to the waiter, her eyes looking into his face, with a slight nod. – The translation not of words but of meanings. And the awareness of a permanent estrangement; the unending 'cultural shock' when crossing borders.

Later, when we say good night I ask her to pass on my regards to Shih-Jiun, Wan-I, Hsia-Hung... - "and please, my best regards as well to your husband. I hope he can join us next time!" I stroke Ming-Fang's arm and she does the same with my arm. We stand this way for a second or two – a holiday in Dublin.

The next morning. I am sitting alone at Dublin airport: gate C53; waiting for LH4985 to Frankfurt - or Bankfurt as Ming-fang taught me a new name for the German finance centre; sitting in the freezing cold of the barely heated hall where I am waiting for the vehicle bringing me to the aircraft. And I am thinking about hibernia. It may be that we are in Ireland on the way to justify the name – justify it in a new way.

I do not have to wait for a long time – I enter the B737, ready for the flight LH4985. It has a little bit of the previous day's Ryanair flight: The first four rows are 'reserved' – but here it is not to ease the weight for take off and landing. It is because a few seats are separated for the even less passengers who fly first class.

I sit down, get my free newspaper: The Irish Times. The headline dealing with what they call 'nationalisation' of the Anglo-Irish Bank; and I read the final confirmation: Ireland is another 51st state of the US; and Obama's real name is apparently – you said it once – O'Bama, his Irish ancestral home on the way of becoming heritage centre.

LH4985 – the German aircraft leaves with just less than one hour delay, still at a time when it is dark over Dublin and I can see the city, the fascinating flicker of the lights of the awakening Irish capital.

As well a developmental welfare state – over the last days I came again across so many similarities between the two island nations; and I asked myself again for many times why we always present the fact of development as problem rather than truly problematising the direction and way of development. Such question would really allow us to confront our thinking with the possible 'cultural shock' when crossing borders.

Only a few minutes later the aircraft pushes through the clouds – the sun appears on the horizon, a feeling of freedom, of hope for another enlightenment, shining through the frost pattern that covers the window.

May 8th – or from Jugendstil to Art Nouveau.

I am just returning from Brno and Prague, and today's date, the 8th of May, regains thus its meaning. In the words of the English wikipedia May 8th, 1945 is "Victory in Europe day – the unconditional surrender of the armed forces of Nazi Germany and end of Adolf Hitler Third Reich". The reason for mentioning it in connection with the Republic is that it had been as well the end of the Prague uprising of the Czech resistance against German occupation.

Sure, it is a "German thing". But having said this: after speaking on a conference organised by the Czech Presidency it gains some special dimension, going much beyond its German meaning: The European (business) fortress had been established at least as well on grounds of the wish for peace: "joining the pieces to make peace". Overcoming (some) national interests in order to create a – definitely biased – larger space (not least against the US and in particular against the then Soviet Union and the other socialist countries). It may be a paradox of history (or perhaps a "cunning of reason" as Hegel might have called such incidences?): it had been a EU-conference, organised by the EU's presidency - a country which is currently actually without own government. One could in some way say "A presidency's president is out of office."

The 8th of May 1945: About four years later, in 1949, the Federal Republic of Germany had been founded. While the later GDR, in consent with the leaders of the USSR, still wanted a unified, democratic (not socialist) Germany, the Western Adenauer, in consent with the allied governments of the US, France and Britain, insisted on splitting the country, the then Kanzler using words as "it is better to entire control half of Germany rather than having half of the control over the entire country." (I do not have the exact quote at hand.)

The 8th of May had been the "end of Adolf Hitler Third Reich". But how far did we really go on the way to end of fascism.

Some good news: After my presentation Michael Kocáb (I have had the honour and pleasure of giving the concluding speech, only followed by the organiser and Michael) to me, congratulating me to what I said: amongst others I made a clear statement that the current financial and economic crisis is a crisis of over accumulation, overproduction and over-commodification: producing negative social and environmental externalities for the sake of profit making rather than aiming on a society which acknowledges social relationships; that aims on fostering 'employment' rather than enhancing sound social relations and processes; attempting to transform everything into commodities and artificially taking it out of its generic context; I made clear that it is not a crisis of the lack of money but a crisis that has its causes in the appalling injustice of distribution, a crisis from which still too many people made their way out with undeserved wealth, blaming the poor for their supposed immoral and overstretched greed. To quote here as well the German poet, novelist and great writers:

"Erst kommt das Fressen, dann die Moral." ("Chow first, then moralizing")

Michael thanked me for my speech in which I criticised that the crisis apparently calls for order and overcoming the supposed greed but still allows the actual criminals: people whose pockets burst from the monetary profits they contain, their hands still dirty from the robbed goods, to sneak away.

I did not mention on the occasion of that speech that some committed suicide – after they saw themselves being caught in their bunker of a false economic system. Some, very few committed suicide only – too many could and did run away, at the same time unfortunately nevertheless being still amongst us.

May come back to the writer I quoted already? He once stated – a short time after 1945, a short time after 1949 – and we have to say it today for him:

> *Der Schoss ist fruchtbar noch*
>
> *Aus dem das kroch...*
>
> *(The womb is still fertile that gave birth to it...)*

May be it is blasphemy in a world in which wealth and profit is the new god - the new opium of the people, administered not by the theologians but by the marketenders of Wall Street and summit meetings. But then it seems that I could possibly apply in Czech Republic for asylum. But perhaps we awake before this is necessary.

And whatever it is that we are not able to say - one thing proofs again to be certain: history - and current policy is nothing else as "not yet concluded history", history in flux - does not follow a straight line. And each of us has to decide if s/he wants to follow the existing bends of the route, wants to help to bend the route where it needs bending and straighten it where it needs to be straightened.

And in which way ever we act, we will have to follow what Hannah Arendt calls "the self-evidence of the moral proposition". I started with writing "May 8th – or from Jugendstil to Art Nouveau". On the way to Prague, sitting in the train – EC 76 Gustav Klimt – I picked up the Travel Information which contained a little note on the famous pai.... No, he hadn't been a painter. He had been a personality of the Jugenstil – the youth style. And what Hannah wrote makes sense here: "The disadvantage of this complete adequacy of the alleged self-evidence or moral truth is that it must remain entirely negative. It has nothing whatsoever to do with action, it says no more than 'I'd rather suffer than do.' Politically speaking – that is from the viewpoint of the community or of the world we live in- it is irresponsible; its standard is the self and not the world, neither its improvement nor change. These people are neither heroes nor saints,... We might call them moral personalities, but we shall see later that this is almost a redundancy..."

And we see this complex mind set and interdependency in how Gustav, the 'moral personality', is now being defined. From the youth style to the new arts: the art nouveau. Just another "style" – allowing to say that Gustav "was a famous Austrian painter" and that he had been "in a very influential position among the [arts] of the monarchy and he was a popular portrait painter of Vienna society."

Just briefly I come back to Michael. At one stage of history we stood – so to say – against each other. Times change though – history changes – history change people and people change history. May be that we can go some way together now – even if we wear different shoes. It will not answer the question Niklas Luhmann frequently posed, asking how society would actually be possible. Perhaps it is not possible. There may be a good reason for the Czechs being famous for The Good Soldier Švejk, Pan Tau, Kaffka and string puppets. And I am sure to make society possible moral personalities are as important as those who want to be more than that. And asking the question Niklas asked is important – and even more so: it is only meaningful if we ask what society we want – a rather different question than the one frequently asked these days – the "economic question", the question on how to improve the economy. – However, there is seemingly a paradox: asking what society we want cannot succeed without fundamentally asking what kind of economic system we need - May, the 8th, one question still, or should we say: again?, requiring to be answered after 44 years, one question.

I hope you have some thoughtful moments at this remarkable date and send you best wishes,

Peter

Berlin – 5/19/09

Hallo, die Liebe vieler Besucher der Stadt Berlin und meine Eindrücke sind wohl ein wenig unterschiedlich – sicher ein Reflex der unterschiedlicher Vergangenheiten und damit verschiedener Gegenwarten. Hier nun etwas zur nunmehr wieder preußischen Hauptstadt – Du kennst ja mittlerweile meine versteckten Schreibambitionen.

Irgendwie finde ich es schon bemerkenswert: immer wieder wird dieses Ländle gepriesen, weil alles so sauber, zuverlässig und entwickelt ist. In Berlin habe ich jetzt die Vorbereitungen zur großen 60 Jahre Feier gesehen und irgendwie... - zumindest habe ich immer wieder hier im Ländle etwa Probleme, einen (free of charge) hotspot zu finden, Sauberkeit wird durch öffentliche Toiletten ermöglicht, soweit man denn bezahlt - mittlerweile selbst in Restaurants und zuverlässig sind manche Sachen durch schwachsinnigste Regulierungen. Ein wenig bekomme ich ja trotz alledem von der Krankheit etc. bei meinem Vater mit: Er hat wohl absolut abgebaut, wird durch (Morphium?)Pflaster schmerzfrei gehalten und halbwegs künstlich ernährt, aber geht nicht selbst zur Toilette - das aber ist Kriterium für Pflegestufe 1: "Scheiss Dich ein" - entschuldige die Worte, aber so scheint es wohl zu sein: solange man dies nicht tut, ist man kein Pflegefall. Damit ist jetzt eine seltsame Mauschelei am Gange, um ihn in ein Hospiz zu bringen.

Meinerseits war ich nun in Nordhausen und in Berlin, auf dem Wege nach Kassel. Berlin „begeistert" mich ja immer wieder: die Schaustellung von Macht, die sich freilich irgendwo mit dem großen kulturellen Erbe [Rätsel: berühmte Hochschule in Berlin, der Name fängt mit H an, setzt sich mit u fort und es folgt ein m – wie lautet der vollständige Name; Hinweis, der das Finden bestimmt einfacher macht: ich habe dort einmal einen Vortrag gehalten, und zwar meinen ersten öffentlichen ;-)] aber doch: das eigentlich bewundernswerte für das Volk ist - Brot und Spiele in Rom; Macht und Prunk für Berlin.

Freilich: Kultur gibt es immer noch und bedeutsame, aber persönlich habe ich immer den Eindruck, der Ort LEBT mehr von seiner Geschichte und BESTEHT durch eine gewisse Unnahbarkeit. Selbst in Brüssel, dem EU-Zentrum hat man den Eindruck von mehr „ganz normalem Leben" – in Berlin steht ein großer Block: der REICHStag, der den touristischen TAG reich macht.

Nun, es spielen sicherlich viele Dinge in eine solche Wahrnehmung – auch die Erfahrung des „gelernten DDR-Bürgers" in mir, der beim Blick auf die Pracht immer doch an das Wintermärchen des HH denken muss.

Viele Dinge, die auch dadurch nicht wirklich gelockert werden, dass ich dann gelegentlich gleichsam bei Ministers auf den Fluren bin (wenngleich es selten ist, denn selten bin ich dort im Orte).

Kultur im Land der Richter und Henker – sie ist trotz alledem; und sie hat nicht nur Grosse, sondern auch Grosses. Seltsame eben, dass dort Grosses oft im Hinterhof stattzufinden scheint – einen Schritt vom Hauptgeschehen und doch Welten entfernt. Natürlich fehlte die Kultur nicht, und schon längst gebucht hatte ich die Karten für den Studienbesuch einer jener Stätten für mein internationales Vergleichsprojekt: "Opern Europas". Orlando Paladino. Platz 14 in der ersten Reihe. Welch Freude. Hatte war ich kürzlich doch bei Daniel B., hatten sich unsere Blicke doch getroffen: Ein kurzer Blickaustausch mit diesem Genie der Musik vor einiger Zeit. Reihe 1/14 erlaubte mir zwar nicht den Blickaustausch mit dem Dirigenten (der hatte ja anderes zu tun und musste nach vorne und zur Seite, aber nicht nach hinten schauen), wohl aber den mit den anderen Mitgliedern des Orchesters – der Graben war kein Graben sondern gleichsam nur durch ein Geländer getrennt. Dies gibt so einem Opernbesuch eine neue Dimension. Man sieht: die freuen sich untereinander, lächeln sich immer an und da fühlte ich mich ein wenig provoziert. Versuch geglückt – und nun überlasse ich Dir, dies zu interpretieren: wir lächelten uns gegenseitig zu – dies wäre eine Erfolgsvariante; eine andere: wir lachten alle laut während der Vorstellung; Erfolgsvariante 3: wir lachten nicht lauthals los und retteten die Vorstellung. Alle anderen möglichen Erfolgsvarianten lägen wohl außerhalb des Opernhauses.

Nun, ich hatte von Freunden in Amsterdam die Empfehlung Berliner Ensemble: Dreigroschenoper bekommen (der gemeinsame Besuch bei meinem letzten Aufenthalt im schönen Amsterdam klappte nicht) und so hatte ich dann trotz der Karte, die ich schon für Sonntag hatte, auch noch Programm für Montag organisiert. Für mich irgendwie etwas sehr Persönliches – eben gleich um die Ecke. Kennst du das BE. Etwas schmuddelig, zuvor wollte ich noch etwas trinken - nahm aber angesichts der Preise eines Restaurants vor dem Gebäude des Ensembles davon Abstand. Und dann sah ich hinten etwas, ging weiter und... - einfach, etwas subversiv. Ich saß dort mit denen zusammen, die dann später auf der Bühne standen. Pechum, Mackie, Jenny.... Es hat etwas Persönliches, erinnerte es mich doch teils an eine Zeit, die längst der Vergangenheit zugehört und die doch noch Bedeutung hat – vielleicht auch Zukunft. Freilich: Mittelstand, Bildungsbürgertum... – und dann kamen am Schluss massiv die Verfremdungen neuer Art, durch die Inszenierung. Der Gang unverkennbar von Chaplin; die irgendwie aufkommende (geschickt gemachte) Verschränkung von Brecht'scher Harschheit und politischer Klarheit mit dem nahezu Kaffkaesk-

Chaplinschen Verfremdenden, der Absurdität zeigende Blick auf die *Modern Times*. Und dann die nach meinem Wissen auf Tucholsky weisenden Anleihen: Was schlimmer sei? eine Bank auszurauben oder eine zu gründen.... – und die Spannung: Applaus, oder weiter im Text, weiter in der Klarheit, die auch Erwartung zum Handeln in sich hat.

Es hat – für mich – immer noch den Flair von BB. Und trotz der so anderen Aufführung erinnerte ich mich an die Weigel, die Giese (welch fantastische..., nicht Schauspielerinnen: im Englischen sagen wir actor und das übersetzt sich eben in Schauspieler und ebenso in Akteur, Handelnder). Und ich erinnerte mich auch an eine andere Zeit in meinem Leben und das, was es damals bedeutete: die Feier des Sigi Jaehn, die Diskussionen und Vorträge an der Hochschule, Jürgen Kuczynski,... – Ich unterhielt mich am Ende der Vorstellung noch mit einem der Musiker, ging dann wieder in das ganz normale Berlin, doch nicht in das der Größe, der ausgestellten Macht der Neuzeit, sondern jenes Berlin eine anderen Größe: der großen Probleme, die auf den Hinterhof verdrängt sind – denke an die Kinder vom Bahnhof Zoo und an die Schule in Neukölln.

Und auch viele der „heimeligen Ecken": dort, wo gekämpft wurde, wo die bekannten Toten liegen und wo Menschen dem Tod, dem Wasser übergeben wurden – auch wenn manche Strassen ihren Namen dann etwas später noch für heute von ihnen gelernt haben, so waren es die Gegner, die Enkel ihrer Mörder, die die gegen sie die Strassen nahmen.

Es hatte mich an jenem Morgen schon nachdenklich gestimmt, als ich mich bei der von der Leyen im Familienministerium unterhielt. Ehrenamtlichkeit ist das Thema – dies sei nun unbedingt zum Schwerpunkt zu machen. Und eines der Probleme sei: es ist schwer, die Jugend einzubeziehen und dieses bürgerschaftliche Engagement ist eh alles eine Mittelschichtsveranstaltung – wie wahr: auch ein Mitglied der CDU findet mal ein Korn – das passiert ja selbst blinden Hühnern. Und dann ging es um dies und um das und um das Internet als neue Gemeinschaftsform und sonst was und irgendwann kam dann die Aussage: „So kriegen wir sie." – Tja, auch ein Körner-findenender Blindling bleibt ein dummes Huhn. Und auch wenn ein Kikeriki kommt, bleibt der Hühnerhof dreckig, wie ein Saustall.

Und obwohl ich Politik ein wenig „von Innen" kenne: von Frankreich, von EUropa, von Irland etwa; auch etwas die „inneren Höfe" von Taipei und Ankara, so ist es doch dort im Winterland immer etwas anderes – freilich vielleicht auch nur bedingt durch die „besonderen Zugangstüren", denn letztlich bin ich eben nur hier „einer von ihnen", auch wenn ich dagegen stehe. Es stellt sich dieser mir teils offene Apparat immer wieder mit einer wahnsinnigen Geschlossenheit dar: der Machtexhibitionismus einerseits und

Politiker und Amtsleute, mit denen ich zu tun habe: zugänglich – ich rief unter anderem einen dieser „Oberen" an, als ich wusste, dass ich noch ein wenig Zeit hatte und fragte, ob er Zeit für und Bock auf einen Kaffee hätte. Er hatte und wir trafen uns und wir plauderten locker und doch: alles, auch später das Gespräch mit einer Kollegin hatten unweigerlich etwas von jenem Apparat: Harte Arbeit hinter dem, was sich da zur Schau stellt. Kleinarbeit. Sicher oft auch ‚gute Arbeit', auch Politik, mit der ich übereinstimme. Und doch... – die ‚Apparatschicks' nannte man sie früher und ‚drüben', ohne sie auch nur zu kennen, denn die Grenze war ja für viele Westler geschlossen. Und der Blick auf die Mauer reichte, den eigenen eisernen Käfig als Gartenlaube mit goldenen Ziersäulen zu verklären. – Die Kuppel: sie suggeriert Offenheit, sie lässt den Blick sich weiten; doch sie erlaubt im Grunde nur den Blick nach Außen - den nach innen, den erlaubt sich nicht.

Man sieht sie oftmals nicht. – Zu leicht erliegt es sich dem Charme der Macht – der Illusion des Mit-Machen-Könnens. – Doch der Haifisch, der hat Zähne, und die hat er im Gesicht.

Ein Wintermärchen, fast mitten im Sommer.

Liebe Grüsse nun aus Kassel aus einem kleinen Fachwerkhaus, gleich am Stadtrand – nach einem wunderbaren Lauf durch die nahen Auen in der frischen Morgenluft,

Peter

Beherbergt also bin ich in einem kleinen Fachwerkhaus, gleich am Stadtrand – der Morgen lädt ein zu einem wunderbaren Lauf durch die nahen Auen in der frischen Morgenluft. Das Haus lädt ein zum Verweilen, überträgt eine Ruhe, der man sich kaum widersetzen... will.

Und doch, um 9:15 muss ich an der Hochschule sein – ein Gespräch über Zukunft. Und da ich weder den Weg zu dem Ort kenne noch den dann folgenden Weg zum Büro, breche ich relativ früh auf, auch um noch am nahen Bahnhof Wilhelmshöhe zu frühstücken – diese Art von Frühstück: ein schneller Espresso, ein schnelles Croissant und ein kurzes Gespräch – sind mir mittlerweile ein oftmals liebenswertes „Mitbringsel von meiner Italien-Reise". So packe ich meine Sachen und begebe mich auf den Weg – entspannt, denn obwohl die Verhandlungen letztlich über die Zukunft eines größeren Projekts entscheiden, hat es nichts Bedrückendes: es kommt, wie es kommen soll. Und das gibt eine gewisse Überlegenheit. Aus dem geplanten Frühstück wird allerdings in dieser Form nichts – vor dem Bahnhof sitzt Werner, schaut mich an, widmet sich wieder dem Kaffee, blickt wieder auf, will aber doch den Kaffee nehmen und stellt die Tasse gleich wieder ab. Unerwartete Gäste sind nicht unbedingt unwillkommen aber eben unerwartet und damit leicht unerkannt. Nach der Begrüßung besorge ich mir mein Frühstück und wir sitzen zusammen. Ich beruhige ihn: Nein, er hat sich nicht im Termin geirrt – denn unser Treffen ist erst am Freitag und er kann in Ruhe noch nach Berlin zu seiner Veranstaltung der AGJ fahren. Später, nach der Arbeit an der Uni und dem Treffen mit einem Kollegen, den ich mehr oder weniger flüchtig und doch irgendwie gut von früher kenne, schlendere ich ein wenig durch die Stadt, arbeite einige Zeit in einem Kaffee und ende im Touristenbüro mit der Frage nach dem *must*.

Ich entscheide mich für die Wasserspiele – der Sonnenschein verleitet und vielleicht ein wenig auch die Erinnerung an eine andere Gelegenheit, bei der ich durch dieses wunderschöne Gelände oberhalb des Schlosses spazierte, wenngleich ich seinerzeit nicht wirklich viel sah. Dichter Laubwald, wechselnd durchmischt mit bunten Blumen auf den dazwischen liegenden Wiesen, wenigen Nadelgehölzen und gelegentlichen Rhododendron-Sträuchern, derzeit in voller Blüte: die weißen, roten und pinkfarbenen Farben kräftig im Sonnenlicht scheinend als kleine Farbtupfer das grün auflockernd und zugleich doch seine Wirkung bestärkend. Die kleinen Seen und Bäche, die zum Verweilen einladend – zum Verweilen mit sich selbst. Die Ruhe – nicht gestört, sondern betont durch den Gesang der Vögel oder umgekehrt: den Canto der Tiere noch deutlicher zu Gehör bringend; die Verbindung, die man mit der Natur hier eingeht und bei der man zu sich selbst findet, haben etwas Doppeltes in sich: Entfernung von dem Alltagstrubel, von den Eindrücken des irgendwie unwichtig-werdenden: Machtkämpfe und Schaustellungen in der Grosstadt; Intrigen im Bildungsbereich... – was zählen diese Dinge, wenn es doch nur darum geht, sich selbst zu finden, zu verwirklichen als einzigartig. Welche Bedeutung haben solche Fragen, wenn man es doch letztlich selber ist, der nur einer, dafür aber permanenten Konfrontation ausgesetzt ist: der Gegenüberstellung mit sich selbst. Und je mehr ich mich von allem entferne, je mehr drängt sich mir ein Bild auf – ein Muster von Malereien, mit denen ich mich in der letzten Zeit verschiedentlich auseinandersetzte: chinesische Malereien, bei denen es eben auch darum geht, wie Menschen in die Berge streben um dort sich selbst zu finden: Sich selbst als einzigartige Wesen, die sich in der Einzigartigkeit und Eins-heit finden wollen: als Einheit mit der inneren und äußeren Natur. Und tatsächlich scheint es, dass jeder Schritt, mit dem ich mich entferne, zugleich ein Schritt der Näherung ist. Es hat nichts mit Religion zu tun, aber jeder Schritt der Entfernung lässt sich als Schritt zu Höherem empfinden. – Ich verstehe hier zu deutlich, worüber Pei-Shan, 劉淑瓊 und ich seinerzeit sprachen, als wir zu den heißen Quellen in den Bergen gingen; ich verstehe hier zu gut, was wirklich in jenen Malereien steckt, von denen mir Shih-Jiun erzählt hat. Und ich vergesse an das zu denken, an was ich mir zu denken vorgenommen hatte als ich von der Straßenbahnhaltestelle losging: die gedankliche Ausformulierung bestimmter Arbeiten für die unmittelbar bevorstehende Zukunft. Ich vergesse auch die Eindrücke der Macht, die ich in den letzten Tagen in Berlin...

... und stehe in gewisser Hinsicht unverhofft vor dem Monument: Herkules. Als Halbgott Zeichen der Größe. Als Gipfel des Barocken Parks nicht ein Überragen und Verkleinern der fürstlichen Macht, die ihm in des Wortes Sinn zu Füßen liegt, sondern zugleich eine Untermauerung genau dieser Macht. Sein Blick nach unten auf das Schloss gerichtet, scheint doch auch Schutz zu bieten – Schutz der Stärke über die Stärke, die über die endlos erscheinende Kasseler Allee wirkt und sich in das Land ausbreitet. Ein kleines Land war dieses Fürstentum einst wie all diese Fürstentümer und die Macht ließ sich nicht infrage stellen. Es herrschte Recht und Ordnung – und wo dieses Recht und Ordnung etwa den Flammen eines Kohlhaas hätte weichen müssen, ging es doch mit umso bedeutenderer Macht als Sieger hervor.

Was für mich auf meiner kleinen Wanderung zum Gipfel vielleicht ins Eins-Sein des befreienden Denkens hätte führen können, endete nicht im Blick nach oben, sondern nach unten: kulminierte wieder im Ausdruck der Macht, die selbst in der Stärke und Schönheit der Wasserspiele etwas Befremdliches hat. Wo selbst das Spielen des Wassers zum Wasserspiele erstarrt, und wo der Lauf des Wassers geplant sein muss, strikten Regeln unterworfen wird – nicht schlicht den Regeln der Natur selbst, sondern einer gebändigten Natur, die dem Menschen im Gut-Sein wie im Bösen Untertan sei. Es ist hier, wo das Individuum sich nicht als Persönlichkeit in seiner Rolle entwickelt sondern als Person, die sich erst im Verhältnis zu anderen gewinnt. Die sich personifiziert, wie sie ihre Götter personifiziert anstatt sie als Dämonen bestehen zu lassen und versucht, sich ihnen zu nähern.

War es nicht Jacob Grimm, der sich zu den künstlichen Brunnen und Strömen geäußert hat? Er meinte etwa, dass solche künstliche Spiele etwas Beeindruckendes hätten, doch nie das wirklich lustvolle und natürliche einer magischen Welt erfassen könnten.

Offenbar: das Volk der Dichter und Denker, ein Volk eben *dieses* Dichtens und Denkens, konnte wohl nur unter diesen Bedingungen entstehen. Selbst ein Garten wie derjenige, an dessen Beginn im 18ten Jahrhundert Landgraf Karl steht, ist geplant, ein Kunstwerk, welches so umfangreich in seiner Planung war, dass selbst die Realisierung etwa eines Drittel des Planes auch heute noch gigantisch wirkt. Ist es Zufall, dass das Bild des Plane beim Blick von oben dem Muster einer Pickelhaube entspricht? Oder ist es ein frühes Zeichen des später erfolgenden Eintritts dieses kleinen Landgrafentums in der preußische Reich? – Das Denken der Freiheit als Plan, als wohlgeordnete Entwicklung, wo selbst die Kritik an Herrschaft dazu neigt, diese Herrschaft erneut zu gestalten und vielleicht erneut gestalten muss um sie einst zu überwinden.

Aber *Vor dem Sturm* liegt ein weiter Weg, denn wie in jenem Fontane'schen Roman zu lesen ist: „Mit ihrer Brüderlichkeit wird es nicht viel werden, mit ihrer Freiheit auch nicht richtig; aber mit dem, was sie dazwischengestellt haben, hat es etwas auf sich." Mit der Gleichheit also, denn in jenem Roman sehen wir, dass ein bürgerlicher, gebildeter Konrektor ebenso heroisch zu sterben vermag, wie es einst nur die adligen Offiziere taten.

Als ich den Schlosspark verlasse, wieder nach Kassel gehe, denke ich an dieses Mammut-Projekt – and die Opfer, die bei dessen Bau erfolgten, an den Verkauf der Hessischen Männer, die zur Finanzierung dieses und anderer Machtprojekte an die Front der Amerikaner verkauft wurden. Leben, geopfert für die diesseitige Macht ihrer Herrscher. So ähnlich dieses Opfer wie dasjenige, bei dem Männer ihr Kleben verloren, um ihren Herrschern im Jenseits als Terrakotta-Soldaten zu dienen. So ähnlich wenn man den Tod bedenkt, und doch so unterschiedlich, wenn man an das Gesetz denkt – dort als endgültige Vereinigung mit der Natur gedacht: die Verwirklichung der Persönlichkeit; hier aber als Verwirklichung der Person als Individuum, welche nicht sich selbst folgt, sondern als Individuum sich isoliert und dessen

Einheit dort Vollendung findet, wo sie sich mit dem Gesetz verbindet – und
wo es sich letztlich doch nur selbst im Obrigkeits-Wunsch verliert: Dem
Wunsch, selbst Obrigkeit zu sein, oder dem Wunsch sich der Obrigkeit
unterzuordnen. Was bedeutet es da, wenn wir erkennen muessen

Es erben sich Gesetz' und Rechte

Wie eine ew'ge Krankheit fort,

Sie schleppen von Geschlecht sich zum Geschlechte,

Und rücken sacht von Ort zu Ort.

Vernunft wird Unsinn, Wohlthat Plage;

Weh dir, daß du ein Enkel bist!

Vom Rechte, das mit uns geboren ist,

Von dem ist leider! nie die Frage.

(Goethe: Faust: Mephisto)

On tour again.

– So I skipped doing the preparations of a lecture I have to give this new week and followed an invitation to the thermal bath in Hajdubösösmerny (don't ask me next time we meet how to pronounce this) and went as well to another concert – not being patient enough to wait 'til next week when I have to stay overnight in Budapest (don't worry, it is an obligation not being too hard on me). Still, I guess I can reconcile visiting the concert with my protestant work ethic and justify both by seeing it as cultural study. Actually the music is for me a new genre – at least as far as the life version is concerned. Here we call it 'afrodiszkó' – probably best translated with 'westernised afro-pop'.

What is amazing, indeed: although Debrecen is probably somewhat comparable with Cork (relatively large city in Hungary – as Budapest is extremely large in comparison – and the other places are villages [and have similarly un-pronounceable names as the Irish ones: is Aghabullogue, where I live really easier to pronounce than Gyongyossolymos where a friend of mine lives?]); but in terms of the culture there is a huge difference, here ranging from the odd folk-music to the most exciting top performances in any genre you want to see performed.

First things first – as said I followed the invitation to Hajdubösösmerny; and going to the bath was another thing altogether, showing me a specific privilege. Actually, going to this place was for me in a silly way exciting – guess similar to my first visit of a town the time I had been a child: when I went from the village in some province in Germany to the larger town nearby (a place with perhaps 100,000 people living there); similar to the first time I went in the tender age of [I guess] 35 to Barcelona – boy, seeing me the first time on an aircraft was so great. Clocked up enough air-miles in the meantime, I guess – and so I can get excited about meeting (I mean meeting, not any dating ambitions) a girl in a village in the far east of the EU. In the other part of my life I am discussing with a colleague about 'urban life' – he always says it is important to study urban life as most people live in cities. May be he is right (and I know he is). But I am frequently wondering in which way people are actually living – in cities, in villages, in the countryside. In other words, I am asking myself how arrogant are our scientific – usually well-meant – formulations: as soon as we try to translate one person's life into the words of another.

Isn't it usually the bright and clean bus we mention, talking about a trip with the holiday coach – and then acknowledging the fact that people are using their private car? Don't we forget too often that, wherever we go, we have the strange ability, seeing the exception of cleanness, of tidiness as rule –

and we usually ask for apologies if unforeseen visitors, who are not close friends, see the dust on the dashboard of our own car; if they enter our kitchen or living room as it is: somewhat untidy, the hair of the dog who enjoyed just before the warm place in front of the fire place still marking the carpet; the footprints of the cat – and even our own prints – in the entrance hall and the unwashed dishes on the table in the kitchen? Aren't we easily getting excited about the vast yellow and green brightness of the field with the sun-flowers during the summer, ignoring them at this time of the year – brown and: well, we may say their former blossoms hanging, like sad faces; considering the rain and mist as depressing rather than bringing the water we and the plants need (sure, sometimes drowning lives as well) and being a source for life; and even being sometimes an occasion we take to sit down to rest over a good cup of tee or coffee, an opportunity of getting acquainted while we are talking.

When Andrea and I walked after the hot springs and the Sauna and the swimming, back into the small town, she presented me again all the different buildings and monuments, we talked about the Hajdúk and their economic and social life, and how it shapes the town until today – not only by the reminiscent buildings, but as well by the footprints they left on social life: the wealth, the relation to the capital, the establishment of the social and educational system. The former, one could nearly say ancient influence of the Turks – here not as visible as in Budapest though from what I hear much more important: in the latter it seems to be somewhat omnipresent by the mention of the Turkish bath, or when one looks at many of the bazaar-like stands on the market but the actual presence in the capital is that of the Habsburgs, still silently residing, still coining both the secret unwanted power of the capital and equally the charm of the coffee-houses, the charity of the emperor, the love to culture...

After we sit down for lunch – not in one of the fancy tourist places but in a very local pub and restaurant with decent local food (and not even difficult for me though I am definitely amongst carnivorous people) we talked about the local market – and as I have as part of my dish fresh forest fruits, she mentions that nowadays some fruits cannot be bought anymore as they are not fulfilling certain EU-regulations. I remember the market of a town in West-Germany – and the 'special apples', we had been offered after getting somewhat acquainted with the farmer – a young women whom I remember as well for telling me the secret of the beautiful taste of green tomatoes. And I remember as well the one afternoon here in Hungary, visiting Dorottya, Tamás and my two little friends in Gyongyossolymos: We walked through the forest. After a while Abel saw a mushroom – and suddenly we all had been obsessed – not by higher education and getting more people into the third level system but by collecting mushrooms. With the old train we went back to the house – looking into the gardens along the rails: still some small, subsistence farming going on; occasionally we could literally pick apples from the trees which scratched along the roof of the wagons. – Tamás, an excellent chef, prepared a yummy meal with illegally collected ingredients. Similar to living on an island, located in a lake in the east of Finland: only one person around – WE, five people together.

Back to the Saturday, and Andrea's excitement, the pride telling the stranger about such simple things: the mushrooms, the apples; and the local and national monuments of histories long gone by; and the new government program: isolating the houses; and the ring-road around the medieval old city: a city which maintains its beauty through some 'untidiness', through its own specific structure which has to be explored in its own terms rather than being 'open' as the straight lines, dividing the quadrants of the new estates that had been build over the recent years outside of the old core – not only of Hajdubösösmerny: The capitalist united front against the socialist united front; the front which is based on speculation against the front which had been build on the debris of the war; the boring capitalist housing estate of pathologically displayed individualism against the not less boring 'sozialistische Platte'. – And if there are similarities, there is at least as well one fundamental difference: the latter meant housing for all, the first carries on what we learned from the Three-Penny-Opera: Those who are in the dark, cannot be seen – it is the shark that shows the teeth.

– 'We are the people', this phrase still sounds in my ears – and I see the crumbling of 'the wall', socialism had been building – rightly or wrongly – to protect itself against… 'We are the people' they say now – and the walls of Tesco, Aldi, Mango, Springfield, Dell, MAC, BMW and all the others make it difficult to hear the real voices of many who are just following their own way, now whispering for instance in the thermal bath of Hajdubösösmerny.

And how helpless are we then when it comes to the dark side of real life: hearing in the middle of all this about the death of the son of friend – and knowing that this is for him one death before his wife will soon follow, struck down from cancer – the doctors gave her a maximum of three years. Helpless when hearing just a day before about a good friend's operation – they detected cancer and though I know too well that it is not necessarily a reason to worry… – helpless as many of our recipes of socio-clinical treatment are, be it in medicine or social work or psychology where we may try hard to work but where we cannot replace a genuine touch, a smile and equally the genuine non-acceptance.

– When Andrea brings me back to the bus she wishes me save journey – and says that we would probably see next week when I have to teach the PhD-students of which she is one. And she says 'God bless'. I appreciate it, though I have to admit that the text-message, she sends later that day, offering me help if needed, is more reassuring than the dependence on the magic of an external power. And perhaps my actual appreciation is not the appreciation of the words, but the feeling of being allowed to enter into another world: the large world of a small village. The world I entered for many times and which can be found even in a small local coffee shop in a city as Taipei – with millions of people living, moving, being moved and then finding themselves between the bags with coffee beans, maintaining a world of genuine closeness – closed: difficult to enter, and difficult to leave without at least some scratches.

Well, coming nearer to the end of this little epistle, means as well coming back to the beginning - the concert: Mory Kanté. I see, better to say: I feel, it not least a voice against terror. For some time it allows to forget: to overlook those that are the actual concern of any such true fight against terror: the people I see on the way home, sleeping rough; to ignore thinking about the people who are too rich to walk home, just entering the limousine of which the door is opened by their chauffeur; to forget those who are not only sick, but who are on top of it punished by an increasingly privatised health system, being established in the name of freedom: the freedom of capital and the market. And it allows as well to forget the 'personal terror': bad luck, the worries about and of others, people that are near to us, people we call friends. It allows forgetting about it, as it creates in some strange, magic way a new person: one consisting of many, and many being one, moving in one, though varied rhythm. It is about movement: being moved and moving...

– On the way back I remember a visit to the Anne Frank house in Amsterdam - together with David and Yitzhak. At the time a moving experience for me. In a way the meeting of the three 'arch-enemies': a Jew, an Englishman and a German (though a German from Ireland - and looking back at the role of the Irish during WWII this doesn't make things any better), commemorating what happened, remembering the cruelty of fascism: perhaps each of us thinking in a different way: 'Der Schoss ist furchtbar noch... .' ('The lap is still fertile...' - from the Kriegsfibel, written by Brecht) After leaving the memorial house, at least I had been left speechless for a while – and I think the same holds true for my two friends. I remember a quote, which had been marking the end of the walk through the house. Not the words. But the meaning: 'Why do we worry about one child, Anne Frank, who went through this horror, through a human-made hell? There had been thousands and thousands going through the same and possibly even worse misery.' And it continued: 'If we would allow all these fates coming near to us we would break, we would be paralysed as we would not be able to cope with all of them. Already the one is difficult to bear.' Though being in 'the mercy of born after all this happened' (something like this had been said by the former German prime-minister Kohl), I still have to think of these words, of the visits with the two friends – and I mention something coming up in me against which I can only fight by fighting against terror: joining such rhythms from different parts of the world as they merge in such music as this afrodiszkó. Actually combining African, Caribbean, Islamist and 'Western' sounds and rhythms – merging them and sometimes changing between them much faster than the stupid white man is able even to think. And showing some limits of combination – limits of how far we can go in understanding each other, limitations of the depth we can reach when diving into another world ... it is about movement: being moved and moving...

–... and although it is not more than a concert, at the end probably rather ordinary, possibly happening in any other place in a very similar way, as commercial performance, performance of the commercial: it is latest the very specific rhythm of the clapping at the end that makes me aware of being here in this room of my home, the Hungarian chamber, joining another WE: the rhythm of the clapping which, I know, surprised many of you who visited the country.

And there is a tiny something in the entire story that makes me think about another question – or is it a question that is linked? I had been about four times here in Debrecen – and about three times I saw myself dancing. This time inspired by Mory Kanté; the other times by local people: gypsies, or you may call them Roma. – Well, when the time comes and I will be working again in Hungary during the coming two years, it will be in Budapest – the centre of the country, and closer as well to the centre of Europe. May be, I will be safer there, not so exposed to Anti-Terrorist movements like dancing – and well under control of those who have their own terror agenda – ops, did I forget an 'anti'. – Naughty boy, I am – of course, the fight against evil... – we all know about it, don't we? (though I have to admit, one day I had been nearly dancing there, in Budapest, as well – a most exciting concert in the Palace of Arts, two French musicians, two 'travellers' – and I leave it to you to find out if members of which travelling community: artists who usually travel anyway or academics, some of them a specific kind of traveller as well or ...

– Guess for my part I realise that I am in the wrong job. Andrea, talking about friends who are musicians, said that her impression is that they are not living in this world. And she talks as well about travelling – not to go away and stay away but to return with the idea of a better world, the idea to make it a better world here and then.

Sometimes I think social scientists may be a kind of musicians – and travellers. And may be that Shakespeare had been right, saying we are really all living on a stage – but he didn't name a space to escape...
... it is about movement: being moved and moving...

... and so I will return: to teaching, to research, to politics; so I will go back to teaching at Higher Diploma students in Cork and working with Taiwanese students on their PhD-thesis; and I will continue the old projects and will take up the new ones: new things to write, preparing teaching economics, and not least working on the new book series: not aiming on faked numbers and citation indices but on debates and finding ways that allow coming together. – Sometimes the rhythm is too fast to change – at least too fast for the stupid white man. But don't we have to try at least to overcome one day – setting new fire: not of reason but of reasoning.

But before getting back into this rhythm there is the rhythm of the Sunday – I meet a colleague whom I didn't know before: she invites me to her home for lunch: a nice home in the new estate near to the city, neat. After the nice meal, the boys leave the table and we talk about ordinary life: recent developments in the CAP (Common Agricultural Policy) and the likely changes of the budget and the expected impact on the development of rural life – all under the title of FP7 (7th European Research Framework Program) – as said, ordinary life.

When I return to Debrecen there is still time to go to the 'Modem' – the exhibition Szocreál. I go to the desk to by a ticket – opening the attempt of the conversation with my usual question: Sorry, you speak English? Entschuldigen Sie, sprechen Sie Deutsch? Pardon vous par - But I don't have luck and I am interrupted: She doesn't speak the supposed lingua franca; nor is she able to help in one of the languages of the former occupying force: the Habsburgian reign. 'Scusi, soltanto Italiano.' she proposes, asking and smiling? Ok then, unforeseen things happen – but isn't all this about real life? The entrance of an exhibition of socialist realism and the reception by an Italian speaking lady. Wasn't the claim of the time internationalism? What is bad about it? Alquanto,... si.... And I finally enter this world of realism, looking another time for the precise question.

– So, it is really a 'cultural study', isn't it? I always say that work is just fun – easy and simple, everything has a place – and if it doesn't have one, we find one, define a proper order. The really tough part of existence is life...

... its different sounds and rhythms – merging and sometimes changing between them much faster than the stupid white man is able even to think.

... it is about movement: being moved and moving...

Now, as I said, I skipped preparations; but still, I have to think about filling three hours of teaching...

You there, have a nice week!

Au revoir, Good bye, Ciao and of course:

Nagyon szépen köszönöm

Peter

Hi there,

survived this one: teaching English for foreigners (well, depending from where one sees it – at least 2/3 had been Germans which is not really foreign in Germany) and being adopted into this strange family setting.

Well, even if most of them are German my problem is to understand them – some of them speak this German: one word has to consist of at least 5 syllables, and a sentence is incomplete if it is not covering at least one page. Nice bunch, but really too German for a simple mind as me ;-)

And all this is happening in a town where one gets the feeling to be buried while still alive. Not sure, perhaps I got the first step wrong – some prejudice? – or I simply had been in the wrong area of this place? Or too many memories awaking from having been buried in a similar place during my childhood? Or another set of memories: seeing the 'members of my family' – once considered as being kin in thought, congenial - drifting into something they and I and we didn't agree with, seeing them now doing and living the same way, with an 'alternative touch' of youthfulness and free spirit, carrying outwardly the seal of a paw, though displaying the decision which marmalade/jam would this day be the nicest as the most difficult? Their freedom being the decision to start work late and stop early, admittedly doing some work then in the evening?

Strange – just sitting here I feel somewhat urged to listen to Milva's La Mia Età - translated as something like 'My age', 'My era'.

In any case I am frequently surprised about the difference between seemingly similar places: all having more or less the same number of inhabitants – this rotten town-village Siegen [say it to somebody who knows the place and you will hear: 'Poor Dear'], the – in comparison – vivid Cork (why does it come to my mind that you may be laughing now? It is the secret capital of Ireland, isn't it?) and Tours – a 'romantic', moony village, though even slightly larger than the other two (Reporting from here you will surely hear: 'Gosh, to Tours? That is lovely!'].

And in all cases, these are actually historically important places: The Krupps and Flicks in Siegen; the Kilmichael and the Crossbarry Ambush in Cork, Michael Collins in the Rebel County Cork; and Tours - with its varied and extremely history – a kind of bridge between the eras.

The varied history – and with all these variations in history, in shape and design, in - existing and lacking – amiability of the details of places and people I cannot help...

... going to meet the others for breakfast this morning, facing the difficult question of choosing marmalade or jam, talking about the all these important things: the importance of organising learning English as part of studying social science, the structure of courses and the nationally distinct approaches in 'social work', there is another thing springing to my mind – something very old, actually and perhaps something we should take into a consideration again. There are all these different crisis but there is one other: the general crisis of capitalism. When we talked about it: in the 60s and 70s, we had been pushed back, suspected communists and revolutionaries and representatives of 'sovietism'. Well, the radio news this day are again somewhat frightening: the crash of the finance market is not the crash of a market that is far away. And it is not a local crash. It is proof of a system that is going back – making huge steps, probably recovering; recovering for a new round of this famous game, loved by everybody: monopoly.

In the meantime the music in the background changed: Fine Settimana.

Be it as it is, tonight I am off to Ankara; not a nice place, but I like it – strange, isn't it? What makes us liking and disliking places? And of course: Why do we like some people and others not?

In any case, this next step of the journey will be an interesting one as well: seems that everything is perfectly disorganised – so I am just hoping that a kind and smiling Merhaba will get me through.

For now (dear me: even looking at it doesn't really help)

Allahaismarladik,

Peter

Hi again,

as I finally enter the aircraft for the delayed start I nod kindly towards the air hostess: Mehraba – and coming to the second welcoming person I say it even louder, nearly with a firm voice: Mehraba.

Didn't I say the last days to the students: one of the most important thing is to try, not to be afraid of making mistakes and taking as well the foreign language as something natural, something we just can use as we use the language we speak in our daily life. Still, my voice is hesitating when I arrive at my seat and the next air hostess is kindly asking me if she can help me, while I take off my jacket – a kind greeting is fine, but now I realise the 'danger' of entering a conversation that stops after the first word. 'Danke, es geht schon.' As I leave from the German FRAPORT I know that German language is most likely the language in which we can communicate.

Already at the check in desk I felt a very warm atmosphere: Is it because I am still a little bit euphoric from meeting a good friend – she is working near Frankfurt and we arranged to meet for lunch? – One of these odd meetings if one barely has the opportunity for doing so: Having lunch at the airport and dawdling a little bit through the terminal – landside (sure, a somewhat bizarre leisure time activity). Or is it because I felt relaxed again – seeing the vividness around me and being part of this alienated setting? Or is it just because I finally got two really nice mails from my colleagues with whom I will be working over the next days – and with whom, I am sure, will spend some nice and relaxing hours as well? – Be it as it is, I feel relaxed, playful. As I will arrive late at night and have to change terminals in Istanbul, I don't take my small suitcase on board. I have to ask the lady at the desk a question regarding my possible travel restrictions into the country but everything seems to be OK. And just being ready to leave the desk, I have to ask: 'And we will see in Ankara again?' She is a little bit disoriented… – I look at my tiny bag and she laughs, kindly nodding. It is not about flirting. It is more about what we frequently tried during the last week: learning language by playing with words, with precision and the lack of it – looking for meaning by looking at the context.

The flirt comes later, while sitting down for a coffee and a little girl actually begins to flirt with me. May be she is four, five years old – I am so unbelievably bad when it comes to guessing somebody's age. Anyway, the usual game we probably all know: our look meets, she turns around, but continually, somewhat cheekily and inconspicuously checks if I am still looking. And as soon as she recognises that I turn away she looks again, trying to catch my attention – but only to turn her own attention – seemingly at least – away. It is not an endless game but goes on for a while. And leaves some kind of mark behind – just playfulness and allowed openness.

Later I spot her again – when I move towards the gate, I see her actually walking to the same plane: really looking like a 'professional frequent flyer', her little suitcase rolling behind her, standing with the boarding card in front of the monitor and staring at the letters and figures.

And so it is no wonder that we are boarding the same plane – first I loose her out of sight and only after take-off I see her walking through the aisle. Now she starts to flirt with somebody sitting next to her own (and of course her parents) seat. I don't know if she talks German or Turkish with this person – though I do know that she is as fluent in one or the other as any child of this age is fluent in speaking any language that is called mother tongue. What ever she says, she is invited: the gentleman offers her his newspaper, a pen and points on a photo on the page. And now it is up to the little one to artistically beautify this person. Or is she writing something? She looks highly concentrated, draws the lines, following her own hand with the large eyes and pressing the lips together; and then… - of course she looks towards her new friend, indirectly asking for acknowledgement – and with the smile of her large, open eyes, the soother nearly falling out of her mouth while she smiles everybody has to acknowledge her.

Every special praise is answered with a little jump and laugh, the visibility of the nappies is a little bit distracting from the fact that she is already now a great artist.

Though we didn't reach cruising height and the aircraft did not yet level – the light of the seat-belt sign, well, let's say: is still a little bit glimmering – I take the opportunity to continue the proof reading of the book – gosh, I should have done this already but I allow distractions, perhaps need to allow them because of interim communication on the topic with colleagues who are working on similar issues. Silvia actually just sent her recent presentation in Durban, dealing with an interesting aspect and the dealing with the colleagues over in my previous 'summer camp' brings frequently new food for thought. And I am still waiting for a working paper from Barbara…

… and I have to interrupt the work again – one of these central questions of life. 'You ordered vegetarian meal?' The air hostess asks me kindly, and sets the meal in front of me on the tabletop. A really 'expensive dinner', I have to say – but it is nice, at least already a kind of preview on the next couple of days. And it is better to look forward to that rather than thinking about the really sharp metal cutlery that I find on the tray. I feel fortunate – stretching the legs, trying to do what I am told to do by the captain: 'Have a nice flight!'

Is it really setting something in scene? A matter of staging? Or a matter of self-representation? – The globetrotter. Working and living in the global village – frequently exchanging suitcase against wardrobe? Writing with the laptop wherever I can find a break. And seeing work actually not so much as burden but as well as an exciting experience, challenge and fulfilment. Seeing the variety of involvements not so much as permanent distraction but as diversity of tasks that belong together. Of course I have to think about this question – especially now, after reading a most stupid journal that was distributed at the gate: Vanity Fair – a journal that is presenting people on the stage. An interview-article with the son of the German political hoodlum Franz Josef Strauss, who damaged the country amongst others by spending huge amounts of money on the 'Lockheed F-104 star fighter' – a war plane which was not only expensive but as well obviously entirely useless. And his son, on the one side worrying about the loss of his father's party during the recent elections, celebrates on the other hand that the world is still well balanced. Being asked about the Oktoberfest he ascertains: 'It is nice to see how it develops every year further; to see that in the meantime actually many young people are going there. And actually they go there in Trachten (liveries, the traditional Bavarian dress) – you couldn't see this ten years ago. You see: despite the crisis of the CSU (the Bavarian Christian right wing party) – Bavaria is still very much alive.'

Another article on the IRA: the Irish question being presented as still ongoing conflict – not a political one (politics is barely mentioned, and only en passent) but as a matter of some paranoid individuals.

And most of the other articles on stars and glamour and gossip. Well, this is surely staging. And it is frightening: much of the current crisis of the financial markets is actually also staging, the consequence of basing 'markets' on virtual economic accumulation, without any material foundation. The material basis is pushed out of the way – and with the current crisis one thing is getting obvious: the remainder of the really productive sector is actually bursting like an air bubble. As it had not been the foundation of the previous development, it is now obvious that the productive sectors are now visibly not much more than an appendix of an entirely faked economic 'boom' over the recent years. And now globalisation shows a second face: rather than allowing externalisation of economic problems, it is now about synchronisation. And critics discuss if this is the end of capitalism, the re-emergence of socialised industries. They have never been really private – only the profits have been privatised. And rather then thinking about the possible consequences, the possible re-nationalisation, critics forget one thing: reality – production. Of course, we can only consume what we produce. And we only produce products, not air-bubbles on financial markets. And these critics forget another thing: we are far from re-nationalisation of institutions of the financial markets – it is more the other way round. Mind the note in the *Belgium Le Soir: Fortis est francais,* reporting on the Belgium bank being taken over by the French BNP Paribas.

Of course, my own life – or even our life as academics? – is following a similar pattern: there is no foundation of this work in any real productive force. But perhaps it is in my personal case just the other way round. This kind of life is not about following a faked economic glamour. Rather, it is about a movement, and even about maintaining resistance within a system of research and education that is cutting in its own throat. It is about going a sometimes lonely way. May well be that it is a wrong approach to life, but how can I actually worry primarily about a warm living room while people have (or claim to have) the power to set the world alight. And personally I am convinced that looking first for SSCIs, grants and money generating projects under the wider headline of 'beans-counting', looking for technical short term solutions which usually have the effect to create problems in another array is very much undermining striving for spaces of debate and dispute, developing relevant questions and working on them. At the end it is all about 'thesis eleven'.[87]

I am leaning back into the leather seat, my concentration moving between the text that needs to be corrected, the screen of the board TV and my little friend who is now standing in the aisle – still standing with the other passenger who offered her paper and pen. And this seems still to be much more attractive than the toy she got from the air hostess. And as she concentrates on her work she doesn't even hear the captain demanding a little bit hasty to return to the seat and fasten the seat belts. And she doesn't worry that the engine switches into a different mode, it nearly sounds as if the engines would be reduced to half of their power. Only seconds before the aircraft falls into the turbulence, she is taken by one of the parents and forced into the seat. And it is not at all clear if she cries because of this force or because the aircraft gets rather ruggedly back into the controlled and balanced cruising mode.

As far as I am concerned I am glad that I could just grab the laptop – I always think holding this supplement brain in my hands may be better than allowing it to follow the movement of the fall and 'bouncing against the air'. And the interruption is only short... . Nothing is lost – nearly. Of course, the calmness of some of the co-passengers is lost. And paradoxically this finds its

---

[87]   At least this may deserves explanation: it alludes to Karl Marx Theses on Feuerbach from 1845, the eleventh thesis reading: *The philosophers have only interpreted the world in various ways; the point is to change it.*

expression in a nearly frightening quietness: after the scream of one of the passengers ceases it is nearly frightening: nothing can be heard – just somebody sobbing somewhere, seemingly far away, seemingly coming from another world.

And it is soon that I am in another world – making another step into this one world of global capitalism.

Actually it had been one of the rather annoying things over the last couple of days in Germany to see this change of mind: people who claim to fight for social and human rights, being very much occupied by the situation of Turkish people living in Germany: 'no, not that we have prejudices' – and actually this is something they surely state during the academic debates and probably as well while teaching. But the then following description of the situation of people from that country is only concerned with problems of Muslims and social disadvantage. Of course, there are these issues, and they are problems, without doubt. But still my question is if we should speak so much of these problems rather than looking closely at the situation of the society in which we are living – here, well now I have to say there: societies that could maintain for substantial time their exclusives by... - exactly: by exclusion. The travelling community and the cigány and the Roma and Sinti and the asylum seekers: being marginalised and 'nichelised'. My suspicion and – admittedly personal – experience is that we fail to acknowledge the other not so much where we are afraid of the unknown. It is more where we face the known: our own unfulfilled wishes, that part of our own history. The part of our own reality and 'currency' – the part of the presence that we cannot understand and accept. – I am reminded of the talk with Zsuzsa: talking about Sinti and Roma... - all this is not least a matter of creating a middle class biased ideology. And as soon as they are taking not the position of the disadvantaged we want them to do we switch: not our ideology but our prejudices and lack of understanding can easily be turned again into progressiveness.

What I consider as highly problematic whenever I take part in many of these debates on religious fundamentalism, suppression and injustice is the lack of critique of 'our societies' on the same level. Western democracy and only some minor disrespects of existing principles? Rights of employees and only individual breaches? What is so specifically distinct when we look from the enlightened West at the rejection of women's rights in fundamentalist religious traditions? What is so problematic from a Western if we look at women, entirely covered by the hijab, only leaving the eyes barely visible? It is not about denying the possible problems. But at least one has to think as well about a superior who penalises an employee by rejecting an application for allowing her to take part in a special training? At least one has to think as well about not only young people who kill potentially themselves by the imams of 'haute couture', by the following the ideals of beauty: anorexia or obesity or bulimia or binge drinking or...

... or to take another question: Is it a problem of Indians, Cambodians and others who strive to look 'like the white man' – and like the white women, of course – or is it a problem of the failed enlightenment of those who force them to be like them to enter the ruling class to enter the circle of those who have (or claim to have) the power to set the world alight... ? – I dare to say another time again: Stupid White Man...

Especially as all this is surely not about individuals – not about individual bosses and individual presidents and individual enterprises. And it is not about a collective paranoia. It is about a very specific society: a society that pampers its middle classes, its foreigners and the exotic worlds of 1001-and-one-nights as long as it is useful as instrument of maintaining imbalances and its own appropriateness. They never beat the imams or the priests or the firebugs at the international financial markets – but when it comes to the first of Mai here or there, they are extremely fast; the police force is already waiting in the wings. And they will beat the imams if there is the danger that people stop to listen to their own priests and firebugs. But on stage we never see the questions, only the suggested answers of the one world, the real world which forced another real world into its knees.

At least one thought of the mentioned Vanity Fair, brought to paper by Rolf Koenig, shows that setting into scene actually takes place as means of hiding – and although he being concerned with homosexuality it can be seen as example for a huge variety of walks of life:

> *Religions make me angry anyway – and I doubt that this is stronger when it comes to topics of the Islam if compared with my anger with regard to other belief systems. In both cases it is enough that I am homosexual. How much sympathy should I have, experiencing this kind of sympathy from their side.*

And it is such a fine line between this sympathetic antipathy and the words of pastor Martin Niemoeller:

> *They came first for the Communists,*
> *and I didn't speak up because I wasn't a Communist*
> *Then they came for the Jews,*
> *and I didn't speak up because I wasn't a Jew*
> *Then they came for the trade unionists,*
> *and I didn't speak up because I wasn't a trade unionist*
> *Then they came for the Catholics,*
> *and I didn't speak up because I was a Protestant*

However, my next personal experience of hiding is an entirely different one. Time and location: about two o'clock at night, the guest house of METU. The door is locked, there is no bell, and knocking at the door doesn't show any effect. Still, I know from a previous visit that somebody is around. So I look for the phone number and ring. It takes some time – I hear are sleepy voice – and I understand as much as the person at the other end. Finally I hear the words 'I don't speak English' – and every other attempt has the same result... –... well, not quite as finally I hear a clicking noise and... - silence. 'Good god' says I – and you know too well that I didn't say this and you know too well that I definitely would think it even if it happens to say these words and finally you know as well that I cannot write down what I really meant. But the world isn't so bad, sometimes even I tend to believe that there is a gentle hand leading our way and occasionally even softens it. I hear steps, the door is opened; a kind though entirely helpless young man is standing there, inviting me to enter, looks at some documents and gives me a key. 'Tomorrow. 5 o'clock. Change.' Does that mean that I have to get up before five again? In other words that means: don't go to bed? Only god knows – and I know that I want to sleep! Now! Didn't do so since about 22 hours... - I open the door to the little apartment, then to the bedroom – it doesn't take long to find myself in bed, though it takes probably another two hours to finally fall asleep... - a nice name as insomnia sometimes doesn't rally make the fact as such easier.

Anyway, the next morning, after the usual routines, I sit down for breakfast: not luxurious but amiable in its simplicity, lovely the feta cheese and...., mmhh, I love this coffee: the smell, nearly drawing me into the kitchen as I don't see anybody around at this early hour, the strong flavour and still the somewhat mild character of the Turkish blend. Reading yesterday's Guardian which I still have from the aircraft says probably as much about the future as I would learn from next month' edition. And in a way (yes, I feel bad, the world in flames and my wee personal worry) I am keenly interested in another thing. Ipek told me yesterday that she checked again and everything is fine; the music in the background gives me some confidence as it has this notion of 1001 nights but there is this tiny question: what will happen to my accommodation for the nights from now on for the next week or so? – After a short while everything is fine – I am escorted to the next building, the young woman inserts the key.... - Hay Allah, Hay Allah. She tries everything, I try to help; she calls for somebody to come and finally I enter a nice apartment, definitely too large for the few days but a welcoming atmosphere, allowing me to forget for a while that I got less sleep than usual and allowing me not to think about several days with a rather tight agenda with teaching, research, discussion and writing though I don't know the details yet.

However, what I do know is that it is simply pleasant to have the first business meeting in the relaxed atmosphere on the large balcony of the Susam, the coffee shop on the Campus. It feels as if the still warm sun would softly fondle the face and neck and despite the documents on the table, despite looking at the students sitting at next tables – and despite as well the worry about a colleague in Cork whose job situation is not secured and a project application in France and lacking communication from a Hungarian partner and the sloppiness of a German colleague… -… of course… - perhaps the idea of staging the globetrotter; perhaps even occasionally suggesting the idea of an easy life. But I cannot change those things anyway – despite writing occasional reminders, occasionally making good for what failed beforehand. Occasional impressions of ease may well because of approaching things in a somewhat different way: analysing – thus joining the general chorus of the mourners about how difficult and hard and injustice life is; but then trying to do something…, well, trying to actually make changes, not so much in personal life perhaps, but in working on outsider-projects and living at least some of this other world that is possible. Not living it once every so often as social forum – in Porto Alegre, in London, in Hyderabad, in Paris, in Malmö, in Mumbai… – but (as well) in the less attractive places, and the less attractive positions. And doing as well something by refusing to join the main chorus; join those who do what Lemmini supposedly do (sure, at the end we all…). And of course there is the paradoxical fear: to be left aside of the way against which one decided to walk.

Did I just before say 'less attractive'? Again, the smell of the fresh pastry which the waiter brings to the next table, the taste of the coffee in the tiny cup with the engraved and painted colourful and golden ornaments is not at all without attraction, and looking at it here is attractive as it is sitting back home or somewhere else for a nice cuppa, for a relaxed talk and for intense and interesting work on 'thesis eleven'. Sure, the gentle atmosphere of young people, the pleasant *joie de vivre* of an international, i.e. open atmosphere of this campus and of course the sun are features that help. In a way as well the live altering decisions: tea (the tea is reeeally lovely here) or coffee (it is soooo tasty) and which kind of pastry – like others' daily choice of marmalade and jam. These decisions can't be underestimated – decisions that could change the whole feel of the day…God! may be, even the week! And still it is a question: do we go with these questions or do we allow them to go with us?

And as much as these are decisive issues, it is equally important: as much as it helps to know, as much it helps not to know too much; and not even to think about the minefield across which I actually move. The powder keg on which I am sitting – here in this state that lost its society, in a world that tries to build its wealth on air bubbles... and on a walk of life that is in permanent danger of being stopped.

Anyway, as much as we are all living in secular societies we expect these supports, the Good God, the Hay Allah... - and it seems that we claim to know more about the gods of others: the injustice, the lack of rationality, the ideological contortion of the religious system. And we appreciate only the one god, considering it as good and almighty, making good for the lack of our own might.

While enjoying another cuppa after I am left alone, I am continuing the proofreading of the text of the book:

In consequence, the two factors mentioned, i.e. equality and empowerment go hand in hand with two general 'instrumental' mechanisms, namely appropriateness and accountability. Important is to emphasise that the first is etymologically linked to property and the second has to be constructed around a principle of 'open balancing'. – And, of course, with such perspective the understanding of the meaning of property is historically different and thus depends on a concrete society, always being open for questioning.

Power – the lack of it, the lack of might... - no, it might not be overcome by providing instruments of formal sharing, co-decision and institutional coordination. It is a matter of everyday's life: appropriateness and accountability – Tu Lo Sientes?

I make some corrections and changes – typos and reformulations; editions, additions and deletions...; and I hear from the distance the Imams calling for the prayers; and I hear – in this location much louder – the students, walking somewhere across the campus. I do not know what the conflict is about. I do know: it is not part of the work packages suggested for the next project application. And it had not really been in one of the work packages on youth research, returning immigrants and economic prosperity – work packages have to give answers that allow avoiding asking any questions! And it is not like being buried alive in a society of saturated progressists or only discursive action.

Another day – though it is still rather dark and also a little bit nippy, it seems to be a promising day – 'summerish' though we are already well into October. Is it a reflection of the temperature, of the mist, of the sun that hesitatingly rises? Or is it an impression from the torrid soil and the seared plants? In any case, running up the mountain, through the forest, looking at the wide, hilly landscape presents a distinctive beauty, offers the experience of being a tiny element of the universe – so different to the isolation felt on overcrowded airports, during packed meetings and on conferences where one is at most an individual – perhaps even highly acknowledged as such but even more isolated – part of a work package, part of a lonely crowed.

From far away one can hear the wild dogs, barking, a little bit like the howling of wolves. A reminiscence of the emerging past – soon equally victims like the many of the people living still in shanty-towns and who may be lucky to live soon in the manifestations of urban renewal initiatives. Or who may not be lucky enough – if they are lucky then they may find a way into migration – a path into another country or a mode of inner migration.

Little later, after changing the direction and my jogging path brings me back to the guest house I see glistening light – not of the rising sun, but of Ankara, the huge city, awaking for a new day of business, a time of work packages and of imams calling for prayers and students – perhaps they were striving for their rights. The right to study? The right for work packages?

In any case, already this early hour I hear a helicopter, flying across the large array of the American-styled campus of the university.

Well, my dear friend,

Of course, the decision: which jam, marmalade, cheese…, of tea of coffee, which of the pastries is of crucial importance, provided we have a choice. And of course, this may mean different things: the availability of something; and perhaps sometimes as well the decision not to accept the routines.

And in the latter sense we have had a rich choice last Saturday, taking the opportunity to meet for a lovely brunch. 'We' means Kezban and myself. She said she would come at ten in the morning to the guest house – and already couple of minutes before the time I see her walking up the lane. I walk towards her – 'Mehraba, Kezban'; 'Mehraba, Efendi' she smilingly answers, kissing the cheek, our communication switches to English which is for me much easier to say the least.

It is only a short drive – though the traffic is not heavy it seems to be a trip over busy roads: extremely broad roads, no clear road markings, the flash lights frequently used and there are even less restrictions in making use of the horn.

We park the car in front of a place that is obviously the restaurant to which she invited me. A short walk across the car park – nothing can be seen anymore from the few drops of rain which sprinkled this morning the ground; I could have left the umbrella at home. We enter a very modern bakery and coffee shop – a variety of cakes and sweets and chocolates and…: Kezban sorts things out, is negotiating a nice place for us, where we can comfortably sit down. – After things are sorted, and she agrees to a very comfortable, spacious corner she says that brunch is now a very popular thing to do – and indeed: the place is crowded. I see couples, people having brunch-breakfast on their own, families – extended families I mean.

For somebody who never really stops to be and think as sociologist (or is it a private citizen, never being at work, always socialising with others?), the publicity of choice is something strikingly interesting. What a difference between the choice at home and the choice here in a public place? What difference? Some exposing themselves by the choosing the place of their house or flat (though 'my home is my castle' it is in this sense of course as well a public place); some showing their choice by talking and in an ostensive way showing it to others whom they allowed to come into the castle – the guests, for example, or even the 'public' choice within the family; and now the display – and self-display – of such choices: the brunch as private matter that is now made public, though not being public itself. Or is it a public matter? The socialising role of the family is at least getting clearer: the educating role and as well the role of making public, and the 'being part of the public'.

The variety of feta-cheese, the different yoghurts, the honey, the unusual pastry and tomatoes that taste like...: tomatoes – and as I have had coffee at home I prefer now to join Kezban in drinking tea. There is so much to eat – a variety that is too large to go beyond looking out for little bits, enough for getting the taste – but we have time and so we chat: 'little bits' as well. Her recent visit in Turin where she visited – I dare to say: our friend – Ümmuhan who is still working 'for Europe'. She is getting more and more critical about it – about the job, about being there on her own; about the EU, of which she gets to know more and more the details... - 'I know' – it may sound a little bit as if a sigh escapes my lips. 'I know' says I. 'It is somewhat funny. Some people arrive with a more or less positive approach – and loose definitely any enthusiasm or even, let us say: critical good-will as more as they are drawn into it. And others, being sceptical at the outset are developing a real enthusiasm by getting the opportunity to join the ballet on the stage of political exhibition and exhibitionism. The representative dinner being for one a chunk of food, getting stuck in the throat and causing suffocation, this chunk is a lure for the other. – Yes, I know. And I have to admit that it is sometimes both for one person. A f...,' no, I don't say it. But it is such a job: dangerous and perhaps this is the stress and actual burden of many of these jobs: not to slip. And of course there are not only the dinners. There are the various nice opportunities, the interesting discussions, the simply pleasant opportunities – as I, as we can experience now: would we be here for brunch without it? And would I meet without it next week friends in Cork? I probably would still not even have a cue where Cork is?

There are the visits to museums, concerts, exhibitions. 'Did you go to the Dalí exhibition?' I ask. I answer the enquiring look: 'I think it is now on in Istanbul. I saw a poster when I was getting to the gate.' Dalí... - what an artist, supposedly being mad; perhaps being one of the few who was reasonable in reflecting a mad world. And I talk report of my visit to the Museo Reina Sofia in Madrid, looking for this other brilliant, genius artist– it is a couple of years ago; and it is one of these unforgettable experiences: standing just on my own in front of this monumental painting, a kind of mural: Pablo Picasso's Guernica. An impression which was perhaps for me of special importance: undeniably German, undeniably being 'blessed by being born late' (as one of the former German prime ministers once said), and undeniably – unlike him – feeling the burden of history, feeling the burden of so many comrades whom I never new because they died during this period: in war, in concentrations camps, and feeling the heritage from the many I knew: those who escaped death in the concentrations camps, survivors who passed an obligation on to me:

(Attilio Folliero, Guernica, Madrid, Septiembre 1988 -
http://www.lapatriagrande.net/04_opiniones/attilio_folliero/guernica.htm)

Kezban just left: 'I am back in a minute'. While I am waiting for her to come back, I just stare straight into the direction where she was sitting before: a couple, caring for each other, passing treat to each other and looking at each other in this 'very special way', at the wall Klimt's picture 'The Kiss'. I once saw the original in the Austrian Gallery Belvedere in Vienna. The view through the window next to them showing the old, scruffy houses of the slum, many of them already replaced by the new houses: products of the urban renewal schemes, too expensive for the people who lived before in this area, and anyway not providing sufficient space for the stuff they would sell on their little, hand-drawn trailers while moving around.

– The time Kezban returns, I finally remember the name of the song which is played in the background: Natalie Imbruglia's soft voice – accompanied by the soft melody, sung by the choir and tightened by the beat of the drums and the sound of the electric guitar.

I'm all out of faith, this is how I feel

...

Illusion never changed into something real
I'm wide awake and I can see the perfect sky is torn
You're a little late, I'm already torn... torn.

Sure, Natalia is singing another song – but another song of the one concert: life. Isn't this life a dance – full of tensions, then followed by relaxation, possible only as solution of foregoing strain?

Sure, it is not long and I have to pay the price for the enjoyable time off: Arriving later at home, I finally see the documents which I had been expecting since a couple of weeks now: the files for the application about which I have to talk with the Turkish colleagues are finally arriving from the German colleague; the mail with the requirements for the Hungarian-Finish-Romanian-Russian-Irish project and the mail with the documents for the meeting on Monday. Small things are easily done: some communication on the planned study trip with the students from Cork; passing István's mail on to Paddy and trying to arrange a meeting for the Sunday after my return and... - well, the other things are little bit nerve wrecking, especially as I really dislike reading on-screen. What can I do? Nothing, but to read them on-screen. And at the end of the day I don't complain – it is interesting, some of it opens new perspectives – and some of the documents I actually include with some pleasure into the workload: commenting on a PhD-thesis linked to 'Asian section of my brain'. – And though the latter seems to be far away, it fosters as well my preparation for Monday: The title of the presentation I have to give during the workshop reads 'Clash of Civilisations, End of History, or Extended Hegemony?' One day of intensive work.

And this is a permanent topic, employing my thoughts while I am staying here. There is another way of putting the question – more down to earth, less academic: To which extent are we actually mystifying the other? This is in any case much easier: looking at the other, the contradictions, the dangers coming from there, the irrationalities… It is so easy to blame the other: the other person and the other system, allowing us to keep our own individual and systemic flaws low level. A society that is at the margin is not so much different of the centre as long as it strives to get closer, trying to be part of the centre itself. And such a position must cause contradictions: being here at METU, being able to look to the one side: the mountains a wide area of forest and wasteland; the other side the large buildings, knowing at least something about the life there: dense traffic, shops, decrepit estates and villas; apparent chaos and the well-ordered system of a nationalist system, controlled by a strong military force. A country of which the economy is marked by the Turkish tiger, by poverty-stricken agriculture, by surviving: serving tourists and by developing a mix of economies. Developing as well a mix of societies – a Muslim society in a Kemalist state. Being now for the third time here, I am getting more and more aware of the close link between the present nationalism and Islamist fundamentalism, the one fighting the other and at the very same time being a condition of each other.
Reality!

– And academic research is about that: Reality – not so much about books. Moreover, basically I can read books anywhere; but I can visit reality only in one place: in reality. So I briefly write to Hsiao-fang that I will send an answer to her request at a later stage; send a quick mail to confirm the time for an interview next week in Brussels, do the reading which I have to do now, but soon I walk to the nearby bus station – finally it is Sunday.

I know these minibuses especially from Moldova and Ukraine; and I know them from the last time I have been here. Still, here and now they changed a little bit –some are public, some private; some are fusty, clacking vehicles, others are modern minibuses and there is still one thing they have in common: the horn is the most important accessory, the drivers of all of them make extensive use – just in case. It takes a while to figure out how it works. Where they stop to pick up passengers, where it is possible to get off. I took the 'privileged seat', directly behind the driver: voluntary action – language course included. If somebody joins, the first thing is to sit down – and then the money is passed on to the driver, some sound accompanying the short trip of the money. I am the last who takes the money, hand it over to the driver – and try to match the sound which I heard before. People hand over the correct change, or I receive some coins to give it to the person behind me who gives it to the person behind… For me it is just a kind of game: I just pass on the sound; words, although I do not understand them. And I pass on the money – for me so often a foreign currency – not so much because it is Turkish Lira but because it is money, a currency which destroys so much of life, and so often it destroys many lives.

I leave at Ulus – Asuman proposed I could go there; and she said from there I should take a taxi for the short trip to the castle. A short trip? A taxi? I see already the red flag with the crescent moon and the star, marking the place to where I want to go, as Asuman recommended: visiting the Anatolian Civilisations Museum, going later for a coffee or for lunch. I don't really see the point in taking a taxi – and so I walk. First through the busy shopping mall which once had been the centre of the capital. Straight on – first along the main street. I look at the mosque, like another fortress between the shops. Something is now distracting my attention while I am walking nearer towards the building from red bricks – or is it the mosque itself that is distracting my thoughts? Is it the light of the glistening sun light? I am not sure until…: sure, it is this windmill-like advertisement right at the corner of the 'building of reverence to the creator': the four letter word Eros is written in read signs on the pink background.

I continue unmolested the walk, walk up the hill, leaving the main street and climbing the stairs – a long, park-like area, followed by an archway. I move towards the flag, go through the dark archway – drawn by the flag which is hammering with the harsh sound in the wind. A few steps only and…

…. the path is getting narrow, the way confusing. I walk along the old houses – some of the doors seem to be just for decoration, a formality without any real use: they would not protect against the cold – though the winters are harsh in this area. And they would not protect against burglars – but there is actually no need for this as it is obvious that nothing can be gained from the inside. Pokey lanes change with wide spaces. An old woman sits down in front of her house – before looking sceptical at me. I move on, pass the tiny corner shop, look for the entrance of the castle, want to go along the wall of the fortification. The smell of fire, a fence, barbed wire, blocks the way and I am forced to return. Perhaps I will find the way if I walk the other way round, if I look on the other side? I walk across the wide yard, the dispersed dust is finally caught in the corner, finding a rest only for a short moment – the wind causes soon sensation again. A boy walks along, mutters something that I don't understand. He is carrying a huge plastic can, bringing it to the old woman, who is still looking sceptical towards me. – Is she really looking at me? Or is it just my own feeling, the increasing awareness of being displaced – as much as she is displaced, not being really allowed to be part of the bustling life of the Ulus. Being excluded from the centre of the Ulus – the old centre of the city; being excluded from the Ulus – it is the Turkish word for nation.

Be it as it is, I only sense that as more as I loose the way, my steps are getting faster. I walk through another tiny gate – it is more a derelict door frame from a building that was once standing here, seemingly a long time ago. Now walking across a field, still following the fortifying wall, I have a strange feeling, I remember the film that I saw some time ago in Brussels: *On the Other Side* by Fatih Akin; I remember the last time when I had been here in Ankara – I talked with Kezban and Ümmuhan about exactly this film.

Am I now actor in a similar film? Or is it just the perception, the expectation, the idea which coins the reality – determines what is reality for me – determines my reality.

I cannot really follow this thought, I just want to get into the castle, and following this path must bring me there. Looking to the left I see the traffic – far away, and strangely enough the distance is getting larger as the distance to the abyss narrows. For many years I did not have the slightest feeling of acrophobia – but this here seems to be more dangerous than walking on the wing of an aircraft in cruising height. Some rocks – I have to climb down, walk on, though I look from time to time back, as I need to know if the boy is following me. He is not; a little bit further some kids are at play, skipping – next to a fire, next to the smell of burning car tires. Where is the entrance of the fortress – I am getting faster, though I am not yet running…

… and I stop. I look to the side, being somewhat paralysed – I cannot walk further, not here, the abyss too close to me; I try to walk through the grass – forward, but not so close … and after a few steps I turn around. No way of getting further forward – there the only one way forward and that would bring me in the middle of the squatter housing estate. I walk back; it is difficult to climb up the rocks which I came – not least as I have my laptop with me. Finally the idea was: visiting the museum, going for a nice lunch and quietly sitting somewhere for a coffee, perhaps even in the sun. However, I manage, I walk back, try to find the same way that brought me here. The noise of the traffic has something reassuring – and as nearer as it comes, as calmer I get. Back to the rugged way, through the large, dark archway.

Miau, miauuuu – a tiny cat, the white and beige fur a little it dirty or rough from a fight, is standing on the wall, looking at me. 'Hei, little one – are you lost, lost as I am?' the cute animal turns the head – surprised to hear somebody talking to her? Surprised about the foreign language? After she follows a few steps, I turn around, want to stoop down – but instead I say: 'But I cannot help you. I am lost myself – just a stranger – sometimes passing on a sound, even words although I do not understand them; sometimes paying in a currency which is as foreign to me, as a language is strange if one didn't thoroughly learn it.'

And I walk on; finally I see a taxi – it stopped where I wanted to go, and where I now arrive. This must be the feeling of somebody, who arrives on the top of a mountain after a dangerous tour, weary, carrying the heavy climbing gear – and seeing a group of tourists, with straw-hats and in their Kahala shirts. But what should I say: I survived another time – this time I did not feel threatened by over-familiarity but by the specific distance between the reality in which I usually move and the reality which I just escaped.

And definitely it is another world that I just entered: before the airiness of poverty, the submissiveness into a fate that apparently cannot be changed: not by Allah nor by the government. And here the buoyancy of tourism, the devotion to wealth. Still, it is one world – on the one side living the traces and consequences of this history: created poverty and powerlessness, the pressure of living a life here and now, the perspective barely reaching further than to the next day; on the other side the opportunity to visit the treasures of wealth, the richness of ancient rulers, the invention of culture that kept its appeal until today and will keep it beyond: beyond even the crisis of the financial markets which may result in less tourists walking around.

I enter the museum – and I am saluted. Amazingly the old man, who guided me through the museum when I had been here abut two years ago with Sibel and Kezban still remembers me. He wishes me an enjoyable visit – is obviously proud that I revisit the place, showing my continuing excitement and interest. What fascinates me while visiting these old cultures is the presence and dominance of goddesses; we find this huge respect towards women, the acknowledgement of women being the actual creators of life, in societies that are today possibly even disrespecting the right of women to live, at least her right to live her own life.

After the visit of the museum I walk the short way into the castle area – the impression of an old bazaar, the tiny shops and stands, offering everything the tourist wants: oil-lamps, carpets, traditional adornment – and of course: sesame bagels, nuts, dried apricots…, men carrying an ornate tray with tea.

I sit finally down in the little restaurant – another kind of museum, and it is such a stark contrast to see the displayed wealth in the middle of this quarter which is to a large extent characterised by extreme poverty. And it makes such a difference, indeed, to see the contradiction, seeing what so many countries and cities are able to hide, to deny without being able or even willing to overcome: the gap between rich and poor.

Despite the mouldy smack I enjoy the modest cheese and bagel lunch, relish the Ayran and the most beautiful view across this city. After working a little bit on the computer, I pay and leave; walk to the square in front of the castle, pass the various stands with dried and fresh fruit, maize, nuts of different kind. I walk to the other side, little stalls in a new building: arts-and-crafts shops. And although these are much smaller than the ones more towards the backyards, they look clean, modern and professional – and so are the prices. The tourists are here – and for them it is not too expensive. It had not been too expensive at least before they had been made aware that over-stretching budgets for an illusionary world comes sooner or later to an ungentle stop. Moving on, leads me through the real bazaar: locals trading everyday's stuff. Pots, pans, cleaning clothes… – and of course: clothes as jumpers, shirts suits… – sometimes the shop keeper looking very much like the dummy which is there for displaying the stuff; sometimes with wild gestures greeting passers by, not feeling too distracted by the cars that try to find their way through the narrow and busy lanes. – As before I feel permanently observed, knowing too well that I am actually the observer and the debris. I am one amongst many – and still, I am the only white man, the stupid whit man – well, perhaps not the only as a small group of Chinese tourists got here as well. In a way I am one of these people who returned as missionaries – this time not preaching the of word of god but this time suspected of preaching the word of modern market society.

I cross the main street of the Ullus where the bazaar continues. But here it is more a flea market. Books, sesame bagels, fruits, clothing,… I walk further as I saw the signposting to the Temple of Augustus and the Hacı Bayram Mosque. Before getting there I have to find my way further through the stream of people: it seems that anything can be sold here, and nothing catches really attention – at least none of the goods that is offered for sale. Perhaps the stall with diet-Kebab – not one of the stalls but a large shop along the street, following the trend of modern dietary; eye-catching perhaps the large orange-white ING ad – the sign of the bank I knew from Brussels and know more and more from any other place. Nothing eye-catching in this sense. Still, the process is different: the permanent bargaining; the people are different: the old women, covered in the hijab, looking full of interest at the young man how explains her the modern chain saw; the atmosphere is different: people walking with the tray full of tea glasses along – tea is important; men professionally polishing the shoes of others – effulgence is important; men, talking, negotiating and casually swinging the rosary – communicating is important, amongst ourselves and with others, and with the very other.

Again, sounds I do not understand, words; currencies that do not mean anything for me though I have to accept that they play a role as well in my life. And everywhere this plays a role: the headscarf – and still, 'a role' which can have thousands of meanings. And who talks about the beard of the prophet? It is, indeed, even for me obvious that now, near to the Hacı Bayram Mosque, the passers-by change: tourists, as far as I can judge: presumably many of them from other places in Turkey; but as well today's typical tourist population: from China, Japan... and of course West Europeans. – Here they allow the call of the Imams, admire it as exotic; here they see the old women with the hijab, standing in the ocean of pigeons as attraction for the photo shot; here thy walk along to visit the sites of pilgrim, buy in the small shops and stalls the traditional Schmuck, see it as beautiful as it is so habitual – they adore the symbols and forget to ask if they can have them without the symbolism.

– I walk into a shop, look around and stand rooted on the ground, looking at the TV screen with the advertisement. I am not good in guessing age. But what I see are children, in their very early teens perhaps – advertising clothes in a way as if they actually wouldn't need them at all, or as if they couldn't expect to get rid of them for displaying what is underneath. Obviously aiming on sexual attraction – without any idea of prudery in my mind I feel nauseated by the abuse of children for generating profit; and I feel perhaps even more disgusted by the fact that exactly these advertisers act up to moral guardians when it comes to Islam. Is this what they want instead: the provocation of paedophilia.

I leave the shop and walk on. I cannot see it – but a child is crying somewhere nearby. I am moving along, drawn into the busy stream of women and men and walking with them: women with head scarf or not, men having the beard shaped in the marked religious way or not, people dressed in modern clothes or the caftan as it is the typical traditional clothing. I remember, during the summer, while working in Munich, I saw as well women with head-scarf, barely leaving the eyes visible, walking across the Maxstrasse – one of the extremely rich shopping malls in that Bavarian place. Probably women from the United Arab Emirates, fleeing the unbearable heat of their home country and going for shopping in the Southern-German metropolis. The doors of the noble-shops being opened by 'their servants': Western men and women, who are glad to have a job.

Is actually today's problem the headscarf – be it in Munich, In Ankara or in Dubai? Is religious re-fundamentalisation the problem? Or is it the re-feudalisation of the economy? Individualised, idealised and virtually not based on capitalist production but on arbitrary patronage of players on the financial markets? The actors being the individuals who are looking for niches, depending on the subsistence economy on the one hand and the magnates, sheikhs, managers of the multinational cartels on the other hand? – A sufficient number of questions for a sociologist and economist passing by. A sufficient number of questions to get confused – not so much because it is so difficult to find an explanation but because it is so difficult to find a solution, a path-way of real development. I walk further, I am already on my way back, want to get something to drink – walking all the time and the heat made me thirsty. The area where I am now isn't as busy anymore as the spots I visited before. Taxis are parking at the main road, some of the drivers using the spare time to wash the yellow vehicle while they are waiting for the next customer; some of them leaning against the car, chatting, smoking...

... and I am just looking around for a place to sit down for a drink. 'Peter' – I hear my name being called. And after I hear it for the second time, I turn around. 'Irmak!?' – well the world is small, so Ankara cannot be much larger, can it? But the surprise is then even larger. 'Nasılsın?' – 'İyiyim, teşekkürler!' saying Hello, kissing cheeks – 'You are back again?' The surprise in her voice has a really welcoming undertone, though we barely know. I have to admit the pleasure is on my side – meeting her will allow me to look forward to some easygoing conversation. And we are entering one of these strange talks – starting where we left a couple of month ago. And though we only know from meeting on a few short occasions, there is enough to talk about: she doesn't go swimming anymore, changed to do some fitness training; she enjoys the teaching – though it is not really part of her work as assistant, she has occasionally the opportunity and likes to see now the other side: still being student, hoping to finish the MA early next year, the occasional teaching is a good experience, helping to understand, allowing to take a different perspective as well in debates, and also in writing. She ask me if I would know Manchester University – she considers to apply there for doing her PhD, and she is frightened when I talk about the possible financial conditions, but as well about the fuddy-duddy handling of financial issues by University and Department managements – a matter of which I heard in many universities, including my 'own' Irish one. The well-known feature:

wounded tigers are getting aggressive, loose control and forget the meaning of the term 'future'.

I hear about the ongoing conflict at our university here in Ankara: the conservative government of the city trying to put the left university government under pressure. Any harassment is welcome to stir the mood. And the conservatives should know: every stirring up carries the danger to be counterproductive. Not least as the students are not ready to bear this tyranny. Nor is many of the staff, especially the older colleagues are not accepting this kind of pressure. Irmak talks as well about the canteen – before the one main canteen had been a restaurant for all: good food for all, the same price for everybody and… a meeting place without borders. It had been also a place for open debates. But there is a change as well in our university itself: distancing, setting borders, defining spaces and defining difference. – At least with regard to the conflict between the external and the internal powers there may a visible sign: the helicopters, nearly always present, flying their circles over the campus; and the stands of different left groups, the posters and the sometimes boisterous disputing groups of students.

Irmak tells me about her recent reading. Many articles on the current economic crisis – looking for an answer on the question: What will it mean for the future development? She liked the headlines: The one asking 'Was Marx right?' – The others confirming: 'Of course he was!' – 'Of course, he was' I echo the latter. 'Didn't we know this in advance?' and we laugh. But I am immediately sombre again: 'These headlines are nice. But when I read that we would now turn to socialism I a getting seriously concerned, actually angry abut the misleading notion. It is not a simple matter of state intervention. It is a major and fundamental change of society. But you know yourself…' – 'But what do not understand: why does it happen now?' And I try to develop my understanding: the synchronisation of the international markets; the over-stretching of an economy that lost much of its productive basis; the lack of purchase power which is systematically inherent in the current accumulation regimes and underlying the mode of globalisation. We are already sitting on a sunny veranda, sipping the hot tea, and being looked at by the cat who is languorously lolling on the low wall, nearby, obviously enjoying the sun as much as we enjoy it – although it is nippy at nights it is now 26 degree.

And I try to explore with her the meaning of these processes – and their different interpretations. The writing of Umar Chapra and al-Ghazal; a theory trying to link economic thinking immediately to the Shari'a, seeing the Qur'an as basis for developing new econometric systems. – She looks at me: Where are you going now? And I tell her about my new job – or should I say the new jobs: Finland, Hungary; I say how pleased I am to be able to teach more economics. Of course I feel flattered when she says that I would surely be good in that. Still, I say: 'If you mean it, because I just explained some issues around the current crisis there is probably another reason for thinking my explanation would be interesting.' – 'The headline?' she says winking. 'The headline! Indeed.'

– And it is exactly 'the headline' that allows to develop a deeper understanding of these processes, not just on a superficial level, but also in a deeply historically guided understanding. And now I have somebody with whom I can explore the questions that came to my mind when strolling over the bazaar: Is religious re-fundamentalism the problem? Or is it the re-feudalisation of the economy? Individualised, idealised and virtually not based on capitalist production but on arbitrary patronage of players on the financial markets? The actors being the individuals who are looking for niches, depending on the subsistence economy on the one hand and the magnates, sheikhs, managers of the multinational cartels? What are the forces that allow in some areas the maintenance of feudal structures? And will it now be possible to foster a 'modern global feudalism'?

And with all this, another questions pops up. Where does production stop and where is it service and circulation? What is the role of morality? And where can we speak of 'proper economy' - production and trade – and where is the system prostituting itself and forcing people to prostitute themselves. Is the street-economy defined by the lack of a tax number? Is paedophilia in public, in a shop belonging to one of these chains for modern dresses, so different from the paedophilia by somebody who is brain-sick, looking at this kind of pictures on a private PC? Is the morality of the first really better than those whose hijacking equals hijab-ing? And is the one a faux-pas by individuals and only the latter systemic and systematic 'misconduct'?

After sitting there for quite a while, Irmak asks me if I want her to give me lift. 'I'm grand.' Though it would have been a good excuse to return in nice company, I prefer to use the public transport – though it actually may be privatised already. She brings me to the bus station. The difficult part is with me, the leaving person: Hoşça kalın. As she stays she says Güle güle. May be we see towards end of the week; then I will be back in the department. After a quick hug, I enter the mini bus. I have to stand as all seats are already occupied – fortunately a young man offers me his seat – after all the walking and the multitude of impressions I do not mind at all: Teşekkür ederim – my words are answered with a respectful bow.

It is quick drive – passing the many mosques, their towers not particularly high, the buildings not as impressing as those of the Christian churches – perhaps a sign for being grounded in everyday's life; passing the many shopping centres – protected by the military force, holding their heavy weapons to the fore; passing the gated communities, leaving just enough space on the wall for some sutlers who are offering their goods.

Now I really have to prepare the final bits of the meetings. A quick look at the mails – nothing really exciting, nothing that needs urgent reply – a quick note in the calendar: the room for next weeks meeting had been send to me.

A quick call – keeping in touch with my dear little daughter. Since some time she is so excited when she talks to me: her boy friend; studying sociology now (may god and allah forgive, I couldn't save her from doing this), and entering now a new, more independent stance. A little bit one of the old stories: one-parent-family, one child family and a notion of a specific shelter due to friendship and bad consciousness. Another consequence of precarisation – it is not a matter of jobs, but of forms of life that are still different from general life. It is not a matter of numbers; instead it is a matter of the structure of a society – sometimes allowing structures and functions contradicting each other.

Some reading, making notes of the contributions which I received much too late, making some notes as well on my possible contribution – part of it being very much the academic version of the present pages: *Clash of Civilisations, End of History, or Extended Hegemony?* A possible subtitle: *Why is it meaningless to teach people fishing when they are living in the desert and are vegetarians.*

The next day I go before the meeting to the Department – the first time during this visit we always met outside. My friend waves very friendly – the owner of the coffee shop. Our communication is limited – his English is as restricted as my Turkish is imperfect. Still, it is nice to be here welcomed, to have a little bit the feeling of being home – well, perhaps better to say: not to feel too lost.

Just before the meeting starts, I walk the few steps across the street, enter the other building for the workshop: a meeting, bringing some ten social scientists together who want to discuss *EUropean Social Policy in the Perspective of Turkey – the Meaning of the EU for Turkey and the Meaning of Turkey for the EU.*

The meeting room is much too large. Asuman and I begin to move the tables closer together, suggesting a working atmosphere rather than keeping the outlay of the room as it is: designed for presentations and large seminars –

but only few agree, being afraid that such change would limit the space for documents, for the laptop...

... but in actual fact there are not many documents on the tables. Instead, the microphone for the recording of every spoken word is permanently moved around to improve the quality of the footage. There is no tour de table – apparently it is expected that we know each other from reading. Or from the websites of LSE, MZES, Queens, ZES... . Or is it just my feeling – the others met two years ago, during a workshop on which the entire idea of this is planned publication is based whereas I am the only newcomer – having been invited for different reasons.

As mentioned, the meeting is about EUropean Social Policy in the Perspective of Turkey – the Meaning of the EU for Turkey and the Meaning of Turkey for the EU; and I hear the words institutionalism, path-dependency, peer-review, Routledge, functionalist and realist theories of integration, Sage publishers, Neo-Gramscianism, Edward&Elgar, marketing, citation index – and I am permanently asking myself how it is possible: again they accept the symbols and forget to ask if they can have it without the symbolism.

Of course, when I give my presentation at the beginning of the second day I cause some confusion – back to Salvador Dalí: *It is necessary to sow systematically bewilderment. By this creativity is set free.*

And such confusion is very much needed – especially here! – All this does by no means suggest that the discussion had not been interesting – but there is still some bitterer after-taste. Perhaps because I wear a dark suit? Perhaps because I am the only one who did not appear in a casual dress? Or perhaps because another foreign currency had been used? The currency of marketing scientific work – for me as foreign as money and sounds of a language which I do not speak?

– Salvador Dalí as well in terms of self-reflection.

Immediately after the meeting I leave the group for a while, before we meet again at the guest house from where we will leave into the city for the evening meal. They go by taxi from the Department building whereas I prefer to walk, humming a melody without exactly knowing why it comes up and resists to leave me – bella, ciao...

> *Una mattina mi son svegliato,*
> *oh bella, ciao! bella, ciao! bella, ciao, ciao, ciao!*
> *Una mattina mi son svegliato,*
> *e ho trovato l'invasor.*

And after a brief break for refreshment, the group meets. Asuman asks for apologies that she didn't make sure that there hadn't been some good choice of vegetarian food in the restaurant we visited yesterday. 'You know, when we organise such meetings, I am always responsible for these things: the needs of disabled people, of vegetarians...' – 'It hadn't been a problem at all. It really had been a lovely meal' – and I do not want to impose a dispute on 'social problems': disabled people, homosexuals, homeless, lone parents,... and vegetarians.

It is another lovely evening – and I mean it. In this relaxed atmosphere we have interesting and open talks. Alfio talks about his experience with people from LSE – 'they tend to be arrogant'; Karl is informing me about the developments in Bremen – the cooperation between private and public capital in the third level education and research; with Marcel talk about the new right in Austria... . And of course, being here and now in Turkey it is especially interesting to talk about the very recent developments: the PKK and the guerrilla tactics they employ in the south-east, the killing of some twenty soldiers just the day before and the bizarre socio-economic mix in that border region. The importance of the water question which makes it even difficult to find a solution like simply accepting an independent Kurdish state in Iraq. The social disadvantage of Kurds being one obvious thing; but as well the huge gap between the haves and have-nots; the feudal structures mixing with modern class conflicts and the political shifts within the PKK. It is frightening how political liberalism is interwoven with religious fundamentalism and it is even more frightening to see European and American democratic claims getting caught in the traps of formal democraticism where clear and rational partisanship is needed. And similarly: political reason is as well needed when it comes to Cyprus.

– In any case, so diplomatic everything appears to be here in daily life in Ankara, so present is at least for some a permanent threat – the threat that is standing behind the armed force at the shopping mall, the menace justifying to some extent his presence and the existence of x-ray tunnels at the entrance.

And all these rather global political uncertainties are mixed with questions – half jokingly, half seriously brought forward by one of the colleagues. Sure, prejudices – but it is the colleague from Italy who is wondering how to behave if he would see a girl, a nice girl and he would be tempted to look at her, and possibly feel tempted to talk to her... - and the following discussion – half jokingly, half seriously – showing the move between Italian and Turkish, between Western and Eastern prejudices and realities; mirroring the existence as being the reality of individuals and societies, of social individuals and individual's view and dealing with society. But here again: Perhaps it is just the perception, the expectation, the idea which coins the reality – determines what the reality is for each of us – our own reality.

Even here, in talks in a pub, names as Roy Bashkar, Margaret Archer find a place, side-by-side with casual jokes and the enjoyment of the music in the background and the occasional fear that is part of everyday's life in a state that lost its society, a society that is searching its future, and a hope, or better: different individual hopes that try to merge in some strange way past, presence and future.

– May be a clash of civilisations, surely not the end of history and hopefully not the extended hegemony by the little Neros: setting fire to the world, sitting on the mountain and enjoying from the distance of safe places the play of the flames.

A somewhat safe place are linked to the work of the few last days here at METU: preparation of an application for some research money and the hope, not to be squeezed by the 7th framework, a couple of hours teaching and certainly as well one or another cup of good Turkish coffee and some lovely Turkish vegetarian food – there is surely some delight in being in Turkey, Turkish delight.

I hope you will have some delight as well, wherever you are – just look for it, and if you cannot find it, you have to make possible to find it in the future. I have to go now – outside I hear the dogs barking, the helicopter turning its rounds. For me time to go jogging, before I meet the colleagues, before a last packed day of work and before I return to the other side – before I may return.

Hoşça kalın,

Peter

Merhaba, love; it is still morning – though already late for me. And the country is still somewhat occidental although borders are fluent. Taking the Ottoman Empire as reference, I dropped a brick the other day as I mentioned the Greek origin of our leader Atatürk. "Greek? GREEK? Did I hear GREEEEEK?"… "Well" I said conciliatory, "he was from Thessaloniki and if we look at from today's perspective one could say, well…, aham, Greece?!" – "Aeh, ja, ah, Selanik – well…"

Ömür and I walked on in peace – first together, then, later in the evening, apart – she had a get-together with friends. And although she invited me to join – "I really would feel honoured" she said quite convincingly, while looking straight into my eyes – I said it is probably better if I return to the guest house: "Otherwise you cannot talk with your friends – or I will not understand a single word."

It is really fascinating – the privilege to be allowed to learn normality, the privilege to get known of normal people. Though she is absolutely not normal, I mean: she is an exceptional young women – Ömür who joined me the one day for a walk and showed me a little bit around: some of the life in the Turkish capital.

We talked about "trivia" – politics, family and life, about music and religion; about sport: she says she loves gymnastics, volleyball and fencing – Ömür mentions this while we are standing in the bunch of people, looking at the weapons once carried by Kemal – she mentions it while she is throwing her head unruly up, smiling and adumbrating the movement of a combatant: stepping forward with the one leg, one arm stretched out, the other posed behind the back. She looks at me "I have a little epee as well, a very small one" and she takes a knife out of her handbag. From her words it is not clear if she sees it as weapon or just out of her appreciation of weapons.

We talk about identities and how to find them; about respect. "I do not accept borders, limits; I am open and do what I want – and I am able to do it; for instance strolling around with you." She links her arm with mine and sings a few beats "I see skies of blue, and clouds of white/The bright blessed day, the dark sacred night/And I think to myself, what a wonderful world…", she innocently laughs – But I accept borders as well: traditional borders but new borders as well.

Trivia, full of meaning: as we arrive on the site of the monument, she asks for apologies after I had to hand over my bag to the security personnel. They require that I leave it there – a linen bag with two books. I exchange I get a laminated card with a number – the voucher for later collection. However, she is allowed to keep her bag – despite the little knife, which passes without problem the x-ray belt.

Later – we are standing in front of the steps that lead to the actual building complex – she holds her handbag in front of me: "Please, hold for a second." And she pulls on her jacket: young, dressy, emphasising her feminine look, but covering her skin that had been hitherto exposed to the sun, showing to the eyes of people, and which I occasionally sensed when our arms had been close while we had been sitting side by side in one of the mini buses as I already know them from Dnjepropetrovsk, from Chişinău, from Lithuania...; or I sensed it while we had been walking across the markets and streets. – "It is not a rule"; she smiles somewhat abashed, but also confident from behind her dark hair. 'It is my personal decision. Sure, there are many things you can criticise when looking at Atatürk's politics. And I am not nationalist – but finally he is the founder of the Republic... – it is my country and I love this country. And it is my personal expression of respect." (and in a side remark it may be noted: I am from now on, while we re going across the courtyard of the monumental complex, the carrier of her bag – well, girls). Still, I can see some relief when she later takes off the jacket again, and our arms occasionally touch again: as we walk along the flower bed of the park around the monument, as she links her arms with mine while crossing the broad alleyways – in a city with 3,763,591 inhabitants on 2,516.00 square-km a dangerous way. As much as Taipei is a city dominated by scooters and Amsterdam by bikes, Ankara is the city of cars, seemingly without rules as the traffic in Paris around the l'Arc de Triomphe. And as pedestrian only those will triumph who do not hesitate, who stand together and walk together – a disrespectful touch?

... an exceptional young women, indeed – Ömür who joined me for a walk and showed me a little bit around.

First to the mausoleum, passing the government buildings, through the streets, later sitting on a bench in the park, eating "eriks" – a fruit that I never saw before [she said they would taste even better with salt and I jokingly offer to look for "a large M", pinching some salt – you see: ready for every sacrifice;-)]. Well, we enjoyed them without salt, threw the kernels just somewhere; we went to a pub: "Do you mind if I smoke? I usually don't smoke – but now, drinking a glass of wine"... And she flouted while I was drinking my juice: "You'll get drunk." "But you have the same as I have, technically speaking: juice." She looks puzzled, first; then she smiles. Later, in another place we enjoyed a Turkish coffee – I said, I would simply love it. "You really do? I love it too..." – and she told the waiter that I would be an Irishman, loving Turkish coffee: "Make sure you bring us a really good one." And she told me from real coffee and real tea. And her family: Her father always prepared the tea for breakfast – a fusion: first a little bit aromatic tea, then Arabic blend and finally Turkish. I could somewhat imagine the ceremony while listening to her – this tiny detail which probably shaped her love to the family as much as any rules can do. – And perhaps it was as well part of the little bit liberalism – or is it just as normal and abnormal as it is in our Irish families: as well in Turkish families the man may stand in the kitchen, helping with the preparation of the meals...

As pedestrian only those will triumph who do not hesitate, who stand together and walk together – a disrespectful touch? This is what I said with regard to crossing the busy road. But we talked as well about other dimensions of crossings: Here in Ankara it is not really a problem. "But in the place where I grew up (another large city of the country) I couldn't walk alone. Perhaps with my brother who is younger than me... – but not with you" Ömür smiles: friendly, serious – in a peculiar way sad and baffled "You are a foreigner, only attracting attention."

With the outwearing of the flamboyant lipstick her face gains something of a natural provocative look, frequently underlined when she takes her long hair in her hands, binding it to a kind of ponytail and hanging it over her shoulder. I ask where she comes from. "Tell me more. Something about your parents – if it is not too private." It is a little bit strange story – and in its strangeness it seems so typical for the country. Middle-class intellectuals; the father, after studying at METU working in a private business. Both parents availing of higher education by breaking to some extent with their families. Still, they are at the end conservative, not religious, not nationalists, but conservative – and accepting. "And if my father would not have studied here in Ankara, here at METU, I probably would not have been allowed to come here." I am wondering: Having the opportunity to go to the supposedly best university of the country but not being allowed. I will learn it later: education can still not be taken for granted; and for women this is even more true – it is the same, as I now it from elsewhere.

Ömür – rule braking as her family – with respect to small things as the little knife, rule braking when she tries to walk in the Atatürk museum against the pulse of the many visitors – and follows with a derisive smile the instruction of the guard.

And she knows well about the privilege she claims for her self: doing things that cannot be taken for granted and for which she studies, and for which she lives. For me it is the entire time while I had been here in Turkey, working in the Department of Sociology, remarkable that most of the students I met are extremely engaged, open – and not accepting anything as given just because it is said by any "authority". – An elite university!?

Is it by chance that she moves equally confident and jauntily on the bazaars of the narrow, busy side streets as she goes to the market stand? Taking one of the Eriks (a fruit I have never seen before) and starts to eat after kindly nodding towards the marketeer; then taking another fruit, cleaning it and giving it to me… "You like it?" After she sees me nodding she asks for a bag of the green fruits. And she moves equally easy across the modern shopping street, passing Starbucks, MANGO,… (Ba-)ZARA. And with the same ease she passes the beggars in the streets – many children who try selling small things, in particular little parcels with tissues.

Youth and experience, intoxicating joyfulness and 'adult' seriousness, light heartedness and ongoing reflection – just living now and living for the future – as if all this would be contradicting each other. Anyway, I had been lucky: the "somebody will collect you for a walk" did not end with a well-behaved and empty Wau-Wau nor with a sheepish-stupid Maeh of the wooden sheep as my Chinese Zodiac suggests. After the snooping in the beginning (meeting 'normal people' like Ömür is more exciting for me than the representation visit of her Excellency, the ambassador of Austria which is on the following day's program), it had been a nice and in different regard strange, estranging, end-stranging, friendly meeting for a day.

In a side remark it is worthwhile to mention that I have had similar encounters in Taipei, meeting young people – people who see not only their own development ahead but as well the development of a country which is in upheaval.

Entering the next day the breakfast room – Merhaba; Guten Morgen; Bon Jour, comment savez vous… ; Hei, hälsning; Shalom – in a way I love the flair of spaces of superficial multiculturalism, but I appreciate so much again the large privilege of the day before: not theatre, but learning what is really relevant: life. Not necessarily my life, not a life to which I would like to return – a life I would like; but a respectable life, a life combining a natural tension of consideration and emotion, of youthfulness in a traditional country.

At some stage – she talked about herself – she stated "You are a strange professor, not so distant, not so expecting and not just stating the rights and wrongs". For me praise – somewhat strange, and I perceive it also as nice. It reminds me of what a friend recently said, when I complained about so many disrespects of the institutional system when it comes to my position: "You may leave a different impression; you may leave some mental footprints behind which may be more important than the knowledge they can gain from textbooks." And what I really like is that some students: male and female alike, leave some footprints behind after they leave the courses, my universities. They allow me to make experiences with which they possibly influence my research more than the reading I have to do for my own writing…

I am still sitting at the breakfast table – it is Sunday and as I do not have any plans for the day I stay here, asking for another coffee, allowing the previous day to pass in my mind and as well making some notes on my computer. "You are ready?" I feel Kezban's hand on my shoulder – the colleague whom I first met in Berlin, later during a very brief visit here in Ankara and then, later again, in Vienna. A colleague and I suppose at this stage a friend who helped me here all the days to manage the "inwalkability" and imponderability of living in a rather unknown place.

– Obviously we misunderstood each other: I thought she would call me in case she would come along, but actually she meant she would come along anyway.

So I grab my computer and book, bring it into my room: "Just give me a minute." And really not later I am back, saying as well Hello to Ümmuhan, her friend: they know each other from childhood but she lives now in Italy, working for one of the EU-related institutions. We drive to Gölbaşı – a traditional town near the lake close to Ankara. A most beautiful morning – after a walk along the shore we sit down on the balcony of a café. And what else can one do in Turkey as talking about Italy; the work for an EU-related institution that deals with the "integration of the future states" – accession countries etc. While we are talking, a colleague Ümmuhan's calls. She is stuck on the airport while landing in Istanbul on a transit flight. The local officials do not recognise the special EU-passport that is issued for people working in that office. – A special ID which may suggest that the EU is as well something special, not there as institution or state-like body of and for the people?

We drive through the traditional town – though most of the buildings here are not traditional in their architecture. Even the mosques appear modern, new – though of course the old structure is reflected as well in their new architecture.

Later, while we are driving back to Ankara and pass the areas of urban renewal, I see that their towers are nearly invisible, hidden between the buildings, multi-storey buildings though not really high. And they are only visible as in this area we find a comparatively generous way of using space – mind, I say this, after having been in Taipei where the only limit in using space seems to be sky. "This is urban renewal" Kesban talks to Ümmuhan and me, only a recent project. "Housing here is extremely expensive. Those who lived here before, in the shanty towns cannot afford it anymore and had been moved to other places – they have accommodation now, better than what they have had before: but it is still not really up to possible standards." We move on; after a brief stop at the petrol station, after paying for the expensive fuel, we drive again on the broad road, without the road marking, without the considerate driving to which I am used and to which we are forced – and still: everything works fine with the apparent rule of permanent rule-breaking.

"Now we are really in Ankara" though it is actually a suburb, administratively part of Ankara, but obviously a different place. Kezban parks the car in the underground parking – "We just have to do some shopping – you know Carrefour?" – "Of course I do" and after a short pause I continue with a smile: "Yes, real Ankara!"

As we are going through the shop, I am usually one step behind the two women who are energetically making their way, knowing what they want, occasionally asking me: "This is OK with you?" As they know I am vegetarian, everything is OK.

Ümmuhan looks to Kezban, pointing on the fish: "The fish is cheap, isn't it?" I cannot stop myself: "Of course it is cheap – it is dead." Kezban, scoffing, nudges me.

A little later we are in the estate. A small garden in front of the terraced house; in the neighbouring garden three women are gathering, chatting and crocheting – and wearing the headscarf. Three generations. Merhaba – a short chat. Later I learn that the three had been nosy, eager to know something about the stupid white man: from where he is, why he is here and what they would offer him for the meal...

Before I enter the house, I take off my shoes "You are in a Turkish house, that is the rule" says Ümmuhan kindly and also determined – Kezban puts some slippers in front of me.

"Take a seat" – but I ask with a smile: "I am actually an excellent chef – what can I help?" Ümmuhan asks Kezban: "May he?" Kezban hesitates, nods and I begin to cut the onions, garlic, vegetables ("You are really an excellent assistant") and together we prepare a vegetable-pasta dish, salads (for me something special, something new: iceberg-leaves with spinach and mint – yummy). We are sitting outside on the veranda. The two other daughters arrived at the house next door: Now there are three women of one generation: one wearing the headscarf, the two others not; one of the others obviously bound to the house with the child, the other working in some kind of employed position.

The topics of the conversation around our table changed: the difference of palace and traditional folk music which I can barely detect; the film by Fatih Akin – for the young Turkish-Italian women the film seems to be rather interesting, though she says an Italian colleague who is specialised on Turkey issues had been rather upset about the wrong picture given, Kezban misses any statement, any focus, and I: well I saw the film several moth ago and I am not convinced either: may be because I saw the piece in Brussels: language, different languages at the same time, distracted by several subtitles...: there wasn't a focus – but perhaps all these interpretations had been as well a matter of different backgrounds. And again and again we talk about religion, Islam and its different streams. The symbols, the headscarf, the rites, the voice of the Imam, calling to the mosque – five times, but only the men as women are not expected to the same extent to go. Of course: the other topic is the national question, the relationship to the curds, human rights. These are always tempting topics; and at the same time I have the tendency to avoid talking about these topics, I approach them only carefully, keep away from frankly talking about it – in the beginning even a little bit here, while talking to friends. And I think to myself...: isn't it pretty much the same as it had been when I moved – way back – to Ireland. If we can believe statistics, we find even today more practicing Catholics there than we actually find practicing Muslims here in the country; there we find the holy water at so many doors, there we find many people going every day to church services – and there we find as well a... – well, lets put it this way: at the end somewhat unresolved national question. And isn't it pretty much the same as it is now in the country where I am originally from: the one half still feeling as "the better Germans", disguising poverty behind precarity; the other half, once having been declared by the then prime-minister Kohl as living in a space of blooming landscapes, having evolved as playing field for nationals, multinationals, transnationals – nationalists; and both together as country in which a job may still require membership in the church, in which affiliation to a specific political conviction may well mean some form of political prosecution.

Yes, we can recall the famous words, Karl Marx wrote 1943 in his Critique of Hegel's Philosophy of Right:

"Religion is, indeed, the self-consciousness and self-esteem of man who has either not yet won through to himself, or has already lost himself again. But man is no abstract being squatting outside the world. Man is the world of man—state, society. This state and this society produce religion, which is an inverted consciousness of the world, because they are an inverted world. Religion is the general theory of this world, its encyclopedic compendium, its logic in popular form, its spiritual point d'honneur, its enthusiasm, its moral sanction, its solemn complement, and its universal basis of consolation and justification. It is the fantastic realization of the human essence since the human essence has not acquired any true reality. The struggle against religion is, therefore, indirectly the struggle against that world whose spiritual aroma is religion.

Religious suffering is, at one and the same time, the expression of real suffering and a protest against real suffering. Religion is the sigh of the oppressed creature, the heart of a heartless world, and the soul of soulless conditions. It is the opium of the people."

Yes: the opium of the people; but as well it is something people do not understand, of which they take the rites, not the meaning. The Koran had not been written in Turkish, the translations are questionable – and it is especially the educationally disadvantaged who are controlled by a religion which is somewhat subordinate to the state. The head of the church here is not independent and responsible to god as Christianity would claim, is not impeccable as the pope but a ruler, himself ruled and still making his own rules. A blurring religion? Strong because it is exactly this: the nothing of the nothing?

In any case, also in those countries that are poor, there is the interest of some to rule 'their people'. – "And it is patriarchal" Kezban adds. And with this we arrive at discussing the history of religion... –

Later – we are now eating fresh strawberries and enjoying a cup of lovely, real tea – the one neighbour who is now left on her own in the garden of the next house, gets a cuppa as well though we do not share the conversation – the languages are too different.

We soon go back into the house – at least for here it is getting with twenty degree a little bit nippy. We changed the place, but not the topic while we are now sitting in the elastic chairs – modern rocking chairs.

History of religion. My modest contribution is by and large reduced on pointing out that, looking at the Christian religion the story with the apple has to be revisited: it may be true that she ate the apple; but she was not guilty as the worlds wants to tell us. He has to accept that he played a major part. If there had been anything at all: the eating of apple is not the entire story which lead to the fall of mankind.

Ümmuhan and Kezban did not know this and we continue talking about the long Process of Civilisation – as well a process of increasing suppression; of increasing alienation. Although gods may have moved away from the spheres of visibility but they are everywhere present; they may have different names but they are still the same and emphasise the holy family, respect – and they keep themselves in power by deviousness. We talk about the little excursion in the morning, the trip to Gölbaşı. A spot, traditional in another sense. The new recreation area had been visited not least by men with their mistresses: near to the city, but far enough to remain unknown. The problem, however, was: alcohol was forbidden. Subsequently the 'couples' stay away and now, the new visitors of the garden cafés are mostly the men, returning with their family – no alcohol needed.... .

Religion as such is the one thing – what is made out of it is something else. And how this is interlinked and how the reality is influenced by it, is again something else. If imam, priest, shaveling; if sultan, king, chancellor or president; if manager, stockholder or magnate: it is about power and power is the idea that reaches the masses; but it is only the idea that owns the material means.

Later we go to the car – I sit again in the back. Ümmuhan opposes: "You should be sitting in the front now. It is enough now with rule-braking of gender roles." With these words she smiles. But I am comfortable in the back seat – and so the involuntary paradox of history seems to be confirmed: the man, not allowing disagreement. With this thought my smile is freezing, helpless. Can't we change anything? Or do we have to see the change as matter not only of the context but as well how we relate to it?

It is already getting dark, the Imam calls but we are driving to the guest house. It had been a nice day with Kezban and Ümmuhan, a nice weekend with Kezban and Ümmuhan and Ömür.

Briefly we make the arrangements for the next day. We say Good-Bye, hug each other briefly. Take care... It is nice to sense the commonness; ephemeral the physical contact, but carrying something enduring.

...

It is dark since time now – the soccer fans, coming from an important match fill with their shouting the night.

I am sitting at the desk in my apartment, preparing the teaching for the next day. Challenging students, engaged and engaging; politically alert.... I really look forward teaching again, provoking, being provoked and looking together for something – for a better practice.

I lean back: Tradition? Modernity?

...

We frequently talk about one world, but probably we should speak as well about one time. One time from which emerges one future. There seems to be no tradition here and something as modernity there. If there is really one world there can be only one future, arising from one presence – actuality. Perhaps reason enough to re-read Bergson and look at his concept of durée.

...
I see trees of green, red roses too.
I see them bloom, for me and you.
And I think to myself... what a wonderful world.

... If they really bloom for all on this (w-)on(-d-)e(-r-)ful world
... We need to look for the coronations first, though.
I hope you will have nice day,
as-salaamu alaykum
Efendi Peter

Merhaba, maybe I can tell you more about my experiences – everyday's life again though slightly different this time. Normality of another kind.

And this time it starts more or less early.

Of course, early the morning I go for my jogging: though it is cold – the thermometer announces just two degree – it is most beautiful: the fresh air, the smell of the various trees, the birds singing and shouting. Something, something small is moving on the ground from behind a bush. I hesitate, see only the movement, but cannot identify it – a little hedgehog, seeing me, beginning to go in defence position. "No fight, don't be afraid" I murmur. There are other places to fight. I return after my usual round through the forest on the University ground. After having a shower and I have to write some e-mails: trying to comfort a friend who is suffering from the 'benefits' of the German system of subsidiarity that tells her: nobody is responsible – it is only you, the independent, mature, rational being. Then: congratulating 郭于禎 to her birthday; submitting a paper for a conference on "Boosting growth and productivity in an open Europe: The role of international flows of goods, services, capital and labour".

A person of whom I do not know even the name collects me from the guest house. We are dashing into the city centre – there are obviously symbols attached to some cars that allow to some degree braking rules – disrespecting speed limits, ignoring at least to some extent the red traffic light... – after a short time the driver stops the saloon car on the Atatürk Bulvari – the house is admittedly large, though between the high risers the only remarkable thing seems to be the bright yellow colour, the high fence and banners; else it is nearly low-key in its environment.

There is a long queue at the one gate, obviously Turkish people; but I take another entrance. I do not have to say my name, as I am expected: the man who opened the door only looks at the list, then checks the time and asks me to wait – "Please, here in the room – have a seat". I sit down on one of the Rococo-chairs and want to read a little bit, knowing that I am too early. I am currently again employed by Max Weber's studies on religious systems, reading the words from his 'Sociology of Religion':

"For example, there are frequently restrictions upon wife sitting at the same table with husband, and in some cases she is even prohibited from seeing him eat because she came from another kinship than husband's. Nor is table-community with others permitted to the king who is enclosed in by taboos, or to members of tabooistically privileged status groups such as castes, or tabooed religious communities. Furthermore highly privileged castes must be shielded from the glances of "unclean" strangers during cultic meals or even everyday meals. Conversely, the provision of table-community is frequently a method of producing religious fellowship, which may on occasion lead to political and ethnic alliances."

Before I can delve again deeper in what is written, the man enters the room again and says in German: "Please, you are expected." He opens the door, I cross the courtyard, and the door to the house is opened from inside. Already the short distance I am walking proof: it is a residence. Back to the women: Ayesha opens the door and guides me to the large parlour, passing the beautiful grand piano. I resist the temptation, sitting down, striking the keys. "Please, have a seat." – "Thank you", I adumbrate a bow towards Ayesha. Instead of sitting down, I prefer to look at the large picture while the woman leaves the room. Only a few seconds later the Ambassador – should I address her with Her Excellency? – enters the hall of the residency. "Good Morning." I stretch out my hand to great her, just say her name. Not the sweet nothings – but of course the nothings that open most of the talk amongst people who never met before. Similar to Kezban's neighbours: she is eager to know about the stupid white man: from where he is, why he is here and what...: "You would like a coffee? Or you prefer tea?" As I say that I would love a coffee, indeed, Ayesha is called and only little later she returns with freshly made coffee for me and a tea for the ambassador – the porcelain with the green ivy leaf against the white background..., I resist to look on the back of the saucer for the two resonate swords, crossed; but even without looking I am sure that it is the 'good old Meissen', the traditional flagship of this kind of niceties.

Actually, I am not sure at all about this meeting: yes, she is political scientist and my colleague from Austria suggested meeting her. Sure, why not? Though I don't think I should meet every political scientist in every place I am visiting... Anyway, I am sitting in the comfortable chair, diagonally of the charming and elegant women. I guess she is much younger than I am, wears a casual, though elegant dress – something that we tend to call timeless.

Although she is political scientist, she is now – as she says herself – political representative of the Alpine country here in Turkey. And although she is representative, I know too well that she does not have any power.

It flashes through my mind: gender: She, as women, ambassador – the men at the gate – the woman as servant of the woman (and of course, the visiting men) – the power-women in a powerless position. The real power-positions are still with men: the president of Austria, the prime-minister.... Is it the same in the University? I cannot argue in a sound way, only from a phenomenological insight: going through some of my 'life-stories', it seems that I am usually together with women: and indeed, predominantly these are the students I am working with; these are the colleagues: exceptions are those who are in decision making positions, those who are in the higher positions of this business. Men? Myself in a powerless position in this entire game of life, I meet them usually only cursory – a general rule of thumb, not more. And an impression only, there are probably studies on this; surely, there will be studies as well on the differences: nationally, with respect to different vocations – and perhaps even with regard of differences with respect of the right of following a vocation and 'having a job'. Surely, there are studies as well on the differences in time – the development of this one time in the one world. Still, it may be worthwhile not to forget to think as well about continuities – and as I mentioned the other day: the confirmation of involuntary paradoxes of history: the man, not allowing disaccord.

Not least: isn't it stunning that we sometimes trust more scientific studies, less the perception, the experience of our own life? Perhaps it is because we can store studies in bookshelves whereas we would have to deal with the practice and the contradictions.

And as well, the opening of education, meant to be democratic as process of an even closer, as more subtle tightening of strata.

> *Das Sein bestimmt das Bewusstsein*
> *Das Sein verstimmt das Bewusstsein*
> *Dass Sein vernimmt das Bewusstsein*
> *Das Bewusstsein verwirrt das Sein*
> *… wacht auf*
>
> *Existence determines consciousness*
> *Existence disgruntles consciousness*
> *Existence arraigns consciousness*
> *Consciousness baffles existence*
> *… wake up*

Be it is it is, at the end the good thing of this meeting that it is a business meeting without firm intention, without definite goal. One may say, rational but without any defined expectation. If it wouldn't be here, in Turkey, the array of another ruler, I would say we talk about God and the world. The relations between Austria and Turkey – the history and the slight distortion by current issues caused by the EU-integration processes: "But still, we try to avoid any serious disruption of the bilateral relationships." And she tells me about last visit of the minister for social affairs (I think), the visit later this week when my current place will be taken by the minister of education (may be it is another, but who cares) and an upcoming visit by the Austrian president.

Religion and the various cultural relations; as part of this the occasional contacts between the Embassy, Austria and for instance the Imams. I learn as well about the complexity again – it is here not different to what we experience at home – the major difference is probably that, caught in our own – golden or iron – cages usually do not recognise the bars nor the different little runways we have – everything seems to be known; everything is part of unconscious action. Social action as meaningful action as action in cages – the meaning is: we should not run our head against a brick wall. In the different context however, things become a different notion – while listening to the colleague, a famous allegory comes to my mind: Plato's cave parable.

I hear about the harshness of certain statements which play a role again: fundamentalist religious statements; and I hear as well about the different parties and a certain security which is generally assumed for the current power block. I hear about her 'studies', travelling to rural areas – "I travelled incognito, just leaving the car somewhere out of sight."

Issues that had been relevant in these areas, last year during the different election campaigns, did not lay any role in the public debates. The two most striking, or let's say remarkable issues are, however, not really concerned with Turkey, with the problems and challenges within the country. And they come up while we talk about the economic side: the development, the process of globalisation and the role that is left for Turkey – better: the role that is given to the country. "Look, the geopolitical role of the country is crucial as well." And we talk about the former Ottoman Empire – a positioning which is somewhat between orient and occident. The position that is – today – definitely coined by being located between the west and the east. "Let us leave the religious question in the strict sense aside. If you look at the situation and relations of the country today they are fundamentally changed." The elegant women talks about the visits. The various kings and sultans of the neighbouring countries are now frequently coming to the country – unimaginable up to some years ago; and it is only in this context that we can assess the relationships between the EU and Turkey. It is sometimes difficult to understand the low voice – does the political researcher want to say something that the politician is not allow to articulate? Is that – the two souls in my chest – the reason for her generally difficult to understand voice?

"When the current government party came into power it was not least the interest of America" she says. And she talks about the concern that Washington wanted to test the impact of having a Kemalist government in place, the opportunities developing from there, the meaning of a governmental change for gaining and stabilising power in the region.

The second remarkable issue is the European approach. "It is not about details – of overcoming Islam religion." I prick up my ears – of course it cannot be about that, can it? "But we have to aim in developing a value basis that is reasonable close to the European values." We talk about the possible, necessary, reasonable and impossible, unnecessary and unreasonable – we talk about – well again: power. At the end of the day we talk about 'the better capitalism, the better imperialism'.

The old story that is frightening not so much here, hearing it from a EUropean politician – it is more frightening as matter of the development of scientific work. The justification of different imperialisms by my colleagues Esping-Andersen, Inglehart and Albert, the suggested move from Manchester to Stockholm, the move from survival interests and self-expression interests, the move from the Potomac to the Rhine.

Well, there is something good about having 'good diplomatic relationships', I mean: having good relationships to the diplomatic corps. Getting the official confirmation of what one knows anyway – although it is, of course, not an official statement, not meant to be published (but then again, she didn't say that I should not publish anything).

When I leave we exchange business cards, I walk another time across the courtyard, knowing that I can easily leave, knowing that it is just two doors ahead and I will have left the court of the residence – but will I, well: will we ever be able to leave the Court Society?

...

I stay briefly in the city – after Saturday's walk with Ömür I gained a little bit the feeling for directions – just a stroll, relaxation, facetious wandering. I think back: walking here the other day. Gaudeamus igitur, iuvenes dum sumus. The youthful light-heartedness in which I had been caught by my young companion. And I recall as well the words I received in a mail by somebody of whom I hope that I may consider him as friend. He wrote: "I am old and grey and full of years' [or was it tears, or fears?]." I see myself in the reflecting glass of one of the shop windows, the grey hair; I remember the many tears in my own life: failing to stand up – or remaining firm on the ground; moments of fear return to my mind as standing firm meant in many cases that others had been arguing against it by seemingly pulling a string, not opening the ground on which I stood, but nevertheless making me fall in a kind of non-existence, victimised by ignorance, indicted by naming contradictions... – sometimes a price. Gaudeamus igitur, iuvenes dum sumus

– the experience was, however, that living as long as we are young does not at all mean avoiding conviction, determination and seriousness – on the contrary.

I turn my head away, again looking on the street now, seeing the people, imagine their lives: opportunism and resistance, former victims and their former hangmen... – I forget the grey hair, walk through the city – just a stroll, relaxation, facetious wandering...

... the national political centre, the international companions, the 'rich' shopping mall and some luxurious hotels – national and international 'trademarks'; somewhere here the huge mosque – later I will learn that it is a 'flagship' of the believers in Ankara. But even here, in the wealthy centre we find some peripheries, back roads, side ways that are part of the centre of wealth and also somewhat outside of the affluent centre. And it is beyond this centre that we find the less well-off – still having a reasonable income, but...; throw a stone into the water, and you will see: concentric circles, the waves lowering. Throw two stones – equally heavy, and with the same power – into the water, just chose a little distant places for their impulse – or try it with stones of different seize... But, after doing this, don't stay there in thinking the world is just a large ocean and we deal with people like with stones. Stones may be strong, people can act: and we can develop practice – sorry, the sociologist just gallops away. But at the end it is quite simple:

Das Sein bestimmt das Bewusstein
Das Sein verstimmt das Bewusstsein
Das Sein vernimmt das Bewusstsein
Das Bewusstsein verwirrt das Sein
... wacht auf

The Existence determines the consciousness
The Existence disgruntles the consciousness
The Existence arraigns the consciousness
The consciousness baffles the existence
... wake up

...

After briefly going back to my guest house, I trot from there the short way across the Campus to the seminar building: posters asking for recognising the first of May as holiday, as day of action for the working class: students walking to their seminars; people on the sports grounds; a poster inviting for a series of evening events: Flamenco performances; students standing, walking, kissing, chatting, laughing, men greeting each other and with this hugging each other, none of them with the headscarf. – I heard only the day before that in classes it is actually forbidden to wear the headscarf here in

METU – and as well there is a strict regulation on the campus. The Ambassador mentioned during our talk as well that the current president of the University would be a quite radical Kemalist.

I briefly talk to Helga, a colleague who emigrated way back from Germany to Turkey. Ideas of a new joined master program with some place in Germany, looking at language and migration....

... I go to the little bistro where I am already known. I listen to the words which I do not understand, of which I know however what they mean: "You want a coffee? A Turkish coffee without sugar?" – "Yes, hojam, splease." The older of the man gives a quick and nearly invisible sign to the younger one; he prepares the coffee and a woman takes the money. I soon hold the little cup in my hand, the flavour... – with this I sit down in front of the building – enjoying the pleasant sun. I still have to make some preparations for the class which will start in half an hour. Theory of science, ontology, epistemology and talking through the different projects the students are working on. It is not an easy task: doing some general course work on the topics mentioned, integrating the various topics of the research projects of the students who are doing there Master Degree or working on their PhD-thesis and at the same time trying to get the most out of it for individual projects. This is the formal framework; the informal part is: I do not know them, they have very different backgrounds and talking about open political issues has always its own dynamic – a challenge in a country of which I barely know the political constellation. And all this has to be accommodated in a short time – simple lectures are easy if compared with this; simple lectures are boring if compared with this.

And still, it is a kind of routine: reading texts while work is presented – making notes during the presentations and debates – sometimes being linked directly to the topic, sometimes going back on earlier remarks, sometimes trying to anticipate later debates – occasional notes as well for an entirely different context: some of the own writing, other lectures, political debates, trying to understand links, contexts: at the end it really is not about details... – still: it is a kind of routine.

I present myself – my interest, my unrest, my fortress: a fortress in the sense of willing to go my way of developing a 'social policy' that deserves its name, determined to work for the interest of people and not for the interest of countries; firm in looking for a way for one world in one time rather than favouring a many worlds, forcing them to go one way of so-called modernity and development.

After that the students present their work – I am positively surprised: although most of them are at the beginning of their work, they have rather clear ideas.

Mustafa – sure, not all men in Turkey have this name – but this is Mustafa: the only male student of those who are present (and as well in the previous lectures as in general: most of the students are female); working on his master thesis. "I do not believe in globalisation as process that overcomes national class and power structures..." He develops his point by making reference to some historical aspects of economic development but equally pointing on the development of mechanisms of global regulation... . Though, from what he says, economic theory would be a core moment of is entire approach – he sees globalisation largely in a constructivist perspective: being made by the media – he does not develop a media theory nor does he point on the need of analysing economic theories and he furthermore does not look at concepts of statehood, the meaning of power and power structures or for instance concepts of hegemony...

An exciting debate is evolving from here – the advantage of actually having such a mixed group. Economists, students who are interested more in issues of legal systems...

For instance Pinar stimulates debating some important points – important not least in regard to defining what we are actually doing as people working in the area of social policy research. Before joining the social policy masters she studied engineering, is keen to make her previous experience relevant for the new subject area – or is it the other way round? With her contributions we can easily come to debates on society, social and natural environment, social action and individual, social and societal practice.

And in between, sometimes while discussing complex issues of ontology, epistemology, seemingly out of the blue there is the question: "And what is in your country? Looking at the privatisation in Ireland (actually I didn't talk about this at all), who actually takes the state services over?" Well, the answers are never simple, the entire economy, the law, the development of social systems and the entire social fabric... . And as focussed as parts or the debates are we also find some moments that sound like being curiosities: The question, for instance, if one of these super-rich people can buy land, build houses, build a village with everything a village needs: shops... – and a church. And as confuse, arbitrary some of the issues seem to be: they open up insights in different systems; and they also provide points of departure for immediately relevant questions with respect to some of the research. For instance: the question of different legal systems: common law, Roman law, canon law; the meaning of different... – yes, we are of course back as well to studies of religion, back as well to Max Weber...

...

Another day, today I have only the usual work here in the university continuing with the workshops. It means as well that I can enjoy the breakfast in the guest house which is only served late: from 8:oo am. A weekday, somewhat different to the breakfast room at the weekend. The Merhaba; Guten Morgen; Bon Jour, comment savez vous... ; Hei, hälsning; Shalom was for the weekend – participants of workshops, conferences, really an international crowd. The ordinary weekday looks different, reduced: 'Marhaba' to the Turkish who are working here, most of them involved in running the guest house; 'Good Morning' to the guests: lecturers, project workers, missioners whose order is preaching 'Western rationality'. Actually to state it this way is somewhat wrong as English does not equal English – and what I actually hear at the neighbouring tables is the broad American pronunciation. Being somewhat alone here, without the observation of my friends and immediate colleagues, without my students, I try my best to apply the few Turkish words, saying Hello, asking for a coffee rather than a tea, saying Thank You. And I can only hope that it does not sound as ridiculous as it sounds from the American person at the next table. When he says 'kahve' to the waitress, one gets the impression that he wants to tell her how it is pronounced: kaah-vee, emphasising, overemphasising every syllable (and then he continues somewhat bossy: and bread). Knowing that I am in a similar danger, I have to smile (well: I would like to laugh and cry: The American, teaching Turkish to the Turks).

I know: you think I am racist, Anti-American – and sometimes I tend to admit. It is definitely not my favourite country and favourite people. But...

... but: The evening before I had been out with Umut and Sibel. Sibel, she was head of the department, a position that is in this country limited in time: one does it for few years and then pleasure, treasure and plague is handed over.

Umut returned only recently from the US where she worked on and finalised her PhD-thesis. Part of it was actually a field study in Mexico. And talking about her experiences, we talk of course as well about that country – and about my attitude. The fact that I would not be allowed to enter that part of the world, but as well the fact that nearly all experiences with people from there – admittedly experiences with a tiny, tiny number only – ended up in confirming my prejudices. The young woman is a little bit torn between what she knows and what she experienced: nice people, collegial, buddies. "They are naive" says Sibel and Umut agrees: "They are naive. The news they see on telly are the news from the neighbourhood." – "The news they make are of the world, news of proselytising the world" I add.

No, I am not Anti-American – it would be simplified. And I am not – and in several regards less and less Pro-EUropean. It is, it should not be about what I said when talking about the meeting with the Ambassador: 'The justification of different imperialisms by my colleagues Esping-Andersen, Inglehart and Albert, the suggested move from Manchester to Stockholm, the move from survival interests and self-expression interests, the move from the Potomac to the Rhine.' It is about human rights, about one world and one time. As I wrote:

'We frequently talk about one world, but probably we should speak as well about one time. One time from which emerges one future. There seems to be no tradition here and something as modernity there. If there is really one world there can be only one future, arising from one presence – actuality.' But it makes a difference who is defining this. It makes a difference which language we speak and who is actually allowed to speak – and I know that it makes a difference if we Westerners go to other places, teaching them how to pronounce coffee: in Turkish, in Chinese, in Vietnamese... or if we go there to find a common language.

And so I am getting a little bit placable when Umut talks about her supervisor over there, their stories from the world festival for the youth...

As much I think about the US, I think as well about the EU and other international bodies. My own experiences of getting collected at some airport. The car in which I stepped, marked by a sign... ; well, the car standing next was a car with a sign OECD-mission; another visible as mission of the World Bank, the UN – what is actually the difference when many EU-missions try to get away without openly making such 'mission statement'. My only personal comfort is: any of the missions on which I was, was a mission where I sang my own song – not necessarily promoting any career but for me the only way: Sic itur ad astra.

...

Another day – a normal day: getting up, the skin awaking under the rinse of the water, breathing the fresh air which enters the room through the window – first shift: writing mails to my students here and there, doing small things at the desk in the apartment; jogging, swimming,... – going for breakfast; little later I look up from the book, prick up my ears:

Ich kenne die Weise, doch ich kenne nicht den Text,

Ich kenn aber wohl den Herren Verfasser....

I know the melody, but I do not know the words

But too well I know the author....

(Of course, alluding to Heine's 'A Winter's Tale')

The North American asks for a coffee – it sounds a little bit depressed, some resignation in the voice, probably as he has to accept his failure of teaching the young Turkish woman how to properly pronounce 'kaah-vee'.

I walk to my Department – it promises to be a beautiful day, getting warmer again and already now, shortly after eight a pleasant temperature, foreshadowing indolent warmth for the day – the last day of April. It is as well the last day of the workshop-series, at least the workshop for the one group.

The girls have some snacks – ask me if I want a tea. They are really nice, it is nice being in this somewhat familiar atmosphere, in which a discussion develops that is informal and at the same time highly concentrated.

Hilal presents her PhD-project – "it such a great opportunity to present this to you", she begins and though it is of course a flattering remark for which I am grateful, I say that the main point really is to discuss the topic, trying to develop new ideas, trying to gain different perspectives and opening minds: Quality of Life – a comparative study, looking at Turkey, Bulgaria and Romania. The other students join, ask very specific questions – and at the end it is getting clear that the question of all these indicators and measurements is a highly political one, a matter of deciding what she is striving for. What seems to be a technical question of different measurement concepts is a political question of aims and challenges and... – power. We soon discuss what actually this European Union is about. Finally it is this what Hilal names as point of reference: Reaching the Quality of Life-standards in the context of EU-accession. Reaching the... I hold back: making the EU the most competitive and dynamic knowledge-driven economy...

After the long discussion in which I had to balance between the interests of the individual student and the group, I arrange another meeting with Hilal to talk through some specific point. "By then I will have time as well to read the document if you send it to me by e-mail" – I hand over my business card.

I meet Sibel, she arranged a meeting with Sencer, director of the social policy research here at METU. We walk across the Campus to the other building. Sibel takes one of the leaflets, preparations of manifestations: the first of May is not a recognised holiday. Though it does not mean that the challenges are not righteous. This is what the students state, preparing their activities of the next days, mobilising.

After briefly waiting in the antechamber, we enter the elegant office. We are welcomed. Sibel talks about how we met while working on the topic of precarity, the meetings in Vienna and Berlin, the support by the German Ministry of Employment and Social Affairs. I present my interest in broadening the research on social policy not least by adding a global perspective and Sencer immediately invites me to a conference, soon here in Ankara – though I have to decline due to another commitment. After the small talk, Sencer regrets: "As I understood you do not have much time today". Before I can say anything, Sibel nods: "Peter has to give another workshop the afternoon – we organised a pretty busy time for him." Looking at me, she smiles somewhat impish. "Well, then I propose we go for lunch here on the campus. Otherwise I would have suggested to go outside, but that will take too much of our time." Still, we have nearly two hours left – time enough for a decent lunch, indeed. We continue small talk, though it is slowly but surely getting larger, turning to more serious, mandatory issues. Talking with people in leading positions usually entails some specific seriousness. The students, the increase of numbers, the competition as there are more and more universities, not least so-called Foundation Universities: private institutions, the need of understanding the work as producing: highly qualified PhD-students, publications – and of course we talk about the criteria, the assessment procedures, the price... . Work in a third-level institution, training and research, speaking out and silence as business; wisdom, cognisance and truth calculated in their market price.

And then, after the main course, while Sibel and I begin to enjoy one of the sweet delights of the Turkish patisserie, full with nuts – it is a little bit as if Sencer would let the cat out of the bag. "I brought this with me" – he takes a document out of a plastic folder and emphasises that it is now official and so there would not be any problem talking about it. The new topic: the World Bank, the collaboration with the United Nations Development Programme: Part of it is the work on the Human and Social Development Index – "Well", he puts the paper in front of me, "actually it is now only the Human Development Index, they wanted to delete the explicit mention of the social." Sencer is not really concerned about this, as he sees an opportunity to still accommodate it in the existing version. "And they are looking for dialogue" – the man nearly gets excited, seeing now an opportunity not only for cooperation but as well for influencing the process. "We might be able to overcome the eclectic character of policy making. And the cooperation of World Bank and United Nations will definitely open new doors." A new development, not least starting from Ankara! – A new development, not least starting from Ankara?? I do not allow myself to openly ask this question. But I know that somebody else at the table has similar concerns.

...

Later the day, after my teaching, we briefly attend a presentation by Gillles Dorronsoro on 'The Question of Fields and Transformation of Resources'. The presentation is announced as first of a lecture series on Bourdieu. He talks about a study, some research. It is research in two places: Afghanistan and Turkey. The reference the speaker makes to Bourdieu is negative: starting from a brief presentation of the rather complex sociological concepts of field and habitus, he basically says: I could not apply them; the concepts are too complex to be translated into empirical research – and with this he fundamentally loosens the link and reduces the study on looking for a wide concept of resources: not only money but as well cultural capital, political capital... avoiding the difficulties of dealing with a complex reality by looking for an empiricist solution. – One does not have to agree with Bourdieu to fundamentally disagree with what Dorronsoro makes out of it. However, that is actually remarkable is that this kind of reductionsim is what can well be sold on the new market that comes along under the title academia.

– The sequencing of DNS seems to be trivial if compared with the complex task of reassembling it.

We have to leave before the end of the discussion, dashing to the Goethe-Institute – Sibel wants me to join as I still have a German passport – trying to gain some support for organising an event. It is a friendly atmosphere while talking with the head of the institute. She is very supportive – perhaps because she cannot do anything. The power is with the German government, the Ministry just withdrew some support for political and scientific work...; but as well the issues around controlling the Institute in the tensional field of working as a German Institute in Turkey: if two want to control rather than share resources problems are unavoidable. – Still, although there is no immediate success, all this is just a confirmation of what we are working on: precarity, and further precarisaiton. Though it may be nicely wrapped: as subsidiarity, as communitarism, as postmodernism that opens space for the development of individuals: it is a brute of a development that may be called refeudalisation. It is a confirmation of what I said here in my opening lecture at METU: As specific form of refeudalisation that undermines the process of socialisation: people being thrown into a whirling cauldron of social forces and left alone without any lifebuoy. It is as well a confirmation of the work of working on something else than the accumulation of indicators – the sequencing of the social DNS without considering it's reassembling.

In a way, it had been an interesting meeting, not least as it forced as well about linking the different dimensions of life: economic disintegration, political power, political control, political culture – and its sarcasms: the Turkish Prime Minister, in his speech on the eights of March, the International Women's Day, setting standards: every woman should have three children. Well, indeed, the EU discusses demographic change, worries about 'over-aging society'.

There is still a nice evening ahead: I visit Sibel's family – two children and Ali, the husband. While the dinner is prepared – the different typical Turkish dishes are put onto the table: white cheese, Hoşaf, vine leaves with nicely spiced rice, a pancake made of aubergines…; everything vegetarian and I begin to love this food more and more – I talk with Ali about his work. He is working as molecular biologist at another university, he tells me about the teaching, the development of the university and the international contacts – and the fast development of the subject as well. When I was going to school things hadn't been even known that the young people learn today at secondary school in biology. "Still," he says. "We may be good in analysing things. But it is another thing to put things together." Looking at the table I get the impression it is not really difficult. So many nice things, the variety, the traditional food and a very specific kind of concinnity, ease.

We talk about many different things – I try to get hold of the contradictions, try to understand a little bit of what is going on. For instance the need to pass a certain exam for entering one of the public services – it is not about a degree. It is about a test of general knowledge and only a pass with an outstanding result can bring you somewhere. For instance the need of a special certificate for entering the public service – again it is not about a degree. "Sure, a letter of the president is the best." – "Well, I can imagine that it helps." I have to smile. – A letter from a religious group helps as well; a letter singed by one of the Imams. "And then there is this Fethullah." I learn about schools, opening across the country, but especially in the east, spreading to the neighbouring countries. "These are seemingly secular schools." I hear and still they are not. They are under the control of Fethullah, they are financed by the bourgeoisie that hugely profits from the Anatolian tiger economy – "not the big bourgeoisie – they do not need religion, they do not have any faith" – and they are as well financed by the state. I learn about a sociological field research: the harmony it suggests in one of these tiger enterprises: the employer allowing staff to go five times per day for their prayers, the common band of faith, linking employer and employees, plastering any contradictions. – It is frightening: a disclosure of facts and developments and power. It is a frightening resemblance: Irish Catholicism comes to my mind. The suggested paradise of google-industries comes to my mind; and as well the naivety of so-called research on 'Wikinomics' – and idea brought forward by Taspcott and Williams, some 'Stupid White Men' which get answers by an somewhat innocent Anti-Shock-Doctrine. And I think also about the many other things I heard during the last days – seemingly matters of the past, and still very much amongst us:

The Taksim Square massacre;

the murder of people, the sudden disappearance of people – "the next day he simply didn't come to the University, and he didn't come for the next four years";

the burning of books – "I still had been a child and it had been so strange: it had been during the winter and my parents told me they would be burning the books because it had been so cold. So I walked into my room, looking through my books. I sorted some out, bringing them to my mum. When I said: 'Mum, you may have these as well', I tried not to cry – and today I know my mum tried very much the same."

...

The dot on the i however comes just when I think the topic is – for now – depleted: Fethullah lives now in the United States of America. I shake my head. The paradox of history – rather than the cunning of reason.

– The sequencing of DNS seems to be trivial if compared with the complex task of reassembling it.

...

I return late this evening, aft a day of talking to the VIPs – and I am surprised. It may be by chance, my room especially tidied up, some slippers are waiting for me, left there for me – a special treat, being able to stretch out the legs in a comfortable manner. I grab Barrington Moore's book: Social Origins of Dictatorship and Democracy. And my eyes catch the words on page 486:

"The assumption of inertia, that cultural and social continuity do not require explanation, obliterates the fact that both have to be recreated anew in each generation, often with great pain and suffering. To maintain and transmit a value system, human beings are punched, bullied, made into heroes, encouraged to read newspapers, stood up against a wall and shot, and sometimes even taught sociology. To speak of inertia is to overlook the concrete interests and privileges that are served by indoctrination, education, and the entire complicated process of transmitting culture from one generation to the next."

No, we are not allowed to get old and grey and full of years [or was it tears, or fears?]

Part of this had been the last day of April, the evening before the first of May.

And part of it reflects the experience of the first of May.

Listening to the news, it is not a spring of terrible hope, it sounds more than a spring of lost faith – tempus fugit.

But I hope, you: Ömür, Hilal, Mustafa, but as well you: 郭于禎, John, Wilhelm, Miriam, Sabine 丁允中, Natalja, Ирина, Grainne, Ipek... – I hope all of you will be able to look straight into the faces of your children: conscious and not being embarrassed for any reason.

Still, I listen with some worry, now in the evening, knowing how many people had been victimised in Istanbul. It may well be that the trade unions there employed a wrong strategy – we talked frequently about this during the day, the short breaks. But helicopters, as frequent as I can hear them this evening...

...

Das Sein bestimmt das Bewusstsein
Das Sein verstimmt das Bewusstsein
Dass Sein vernimmt das Bewusstsein
Das Bewusstsein verwirrt das Sein
... wacht auf

Existence determines consciousness
Existence disgruntles consciousness
Existence arraigns consciousness
Consciousness baffles existence
... wake up

Bon Jour; Dag, mijn vriend;

Well you see I am in Brussels now – do you actually remember what I wrote, closing the recent letter?

Existence determines consciousness

Existence disgruntles consciousness

Existence arraigns consciousness

Consciousness baffles existence

... wake up

I thought I would have written enough for a while. And indeed, writing more about my impressions from Turkey would be a major effort: writing about the reality of work there, the reality as well of going deeper into the country, into the field as we usually say. Urban development, the reality of shanty towns, of the old derelict cottage-like buildings side by side with the new edifices of the modern urban estates. It would take a long time to write about being together with the students, meeting many of them, joining Ömür now as student rather than as tourist guide.

The role religion, of Islamism and conservatism gains a different dimension here – a matter of linking religion and economic development, a matter of traditionalism in and outside of modernisation. And it would mean to go into detail about the differences: Sunni, Shi'a, the meaning of Sharia...

The last day, a nice breakfast: I begin to develop some admiration even for the US, as the Campus is so typically US-styled. And with this it is always full of life and thus always giving the opportunity for meeting people as it is the case as well the case on my last day; later meeting Sibel: there are so many things to talk about, as well things still to do: not least shopping, bringing some Turkish delight back to Ireland ("Sure, you can easily buy it at the airport but here we can buy some real stuff – the only problem is that there are only very few places where you can get it."). And not least to enjoy a real Turkish tea from the Samovar, hearing the humming of the water which is kept boiling by the charcoal. Later, the last dinner – at least for this time, looking back, talking about the conference in September, dealing with a new publication, to which Ipek wants me to contribute. Much later, I meet Kezban – she visited her hometown for a couple of days. It is, of course a special honour and pleasure for me that she returns just to say Good-Bye. Her flight is already coming late according schedule; but on top of it there is a delay and instead of arriving at just after 10 she arrives at after 11 at night. My flight is scheduled for 5 in the morning and I actually have to leave just after 3 – globalisation has something 'timeless', at least sleepless. Still, it is nice to see hear again before leaving. She has good news – at least some hope for a new, a better job she is striving for. At least for her the question which I read the other day seems not to exist anymore: "How shall our generation plan what cannot be planned?" I am glad for her. I am glad for her that she may be able to return as well to the place from where she comes, the place of which on the one hand says that it is much too warm to live there and which on the other hand is the place she still admires as home – I can feel it from how she talks about her parents, the nice surrounding – especially now, in spring... . We talk as well about Esping-Andersen, the possibility of model building in social policy analysis, the need of qualitative debates and of course, the future of academia – the clearance: warehouses have winter and summer sales; universities seem to have them now independent of time: getting rid of reason, or at least the shift to a reductionist version: instrumentalism.

We say Good-Bye, I bring her to the car; after briefly hugging and while she opens the door of her car, she asks me to write – "And I will write too" she adds – and I answer "Sure, but not immediately. First I have to keep fingers crossed, really hope that you do not have to ask this question anymore: How shall our generation plan what cannot be planned?"

Walking back to my room I think about the upcoming debate on the Social Policy Agenda. I would be really glad if he has luck; and I am so aware of how correct it is what I will hear in Brussels, namely that today "individual problems need collective solutions."

There is not much sleep for that night. And there is no sleep during the day: I cannot come to a rest – not on the plane, nor while driving this time by bus from the airport to the city, passing the complex of NATO buildings – a massive power block, similar to the military centres I saw in Ankara, the major difference being the various flags of the different NATO-member states rather than the one national flag; and I still cannot rest when arriving at the hotel, supposedly the crown of the place. Unfortunately I have to stay in the hotel rather being allowed to lodge in the cosy place where I am used to stay. Anyway, I prefer to go into the city, actually going to the museum. As the Magritte-exhibition is not yet opened in its new room I go to my other 'friend' in the Rue de la Régence, there looking at the paintings by Pieter Brueghel the Younger.

It is still early when I leave the museum and I go to sit a little bit in the park, enjoy the sun – and an ice cream and an espresso, paying probably three times as much as I paid the other day in Ankara. Sure, economics is not as simple as comparing the price of ice cream and coffee and moreover we have to keep in mind that an Americano, an espresso and a Turkish coffee are three different things anyway – and there are many other coffees…; and Islam is not Islam let alone that religion would be religion; that actors are actors…

Later again, while waiting in the hotel lounge for a friend, I listen for a while the briefing of a group of future managers. I look at the young people from different countries across the world: Asian, Indian, Africans, Europeans; I hear that it is a group from one country: the UK, actually from Cambridge, here in Brussels to visit various enterprises and to learn about the practice. Instructions are given: on the logistics, on behaviour when visiting the hosting enterprises, on the different topics and… : "If you talk to them mind that these are Europeans – they speak European English which is different from the English we speak." The instructor sees that I have to grin. He doesn't know that I do it with a grim notion: grim not least because I dislike this 'natural arrogance' of a better people he claims to represent. The better people of England? The better people of the business world? The better people of the instructors – trained and training in anthropology of international relations? The program seems to be exciting – the zoological study of managers, aiming on training managers: before you are caught for a life in the cage you should visitor of your future zoo. For the young men and women interpretative sociology, if it would exist at all, would mean: how do I interpret the view from my cage as experience of freedom? How do I use my power in a way that avoids hurting myself? – The luxurious hotel is surely part of the game: you know even if I use a slightly different wording: changing the length and weight of the golden chain they already forged for themselves, allowing a relaxation of their tension.

It is not too long that I have to wait. Besides my actually involuntary listening, I continue reading Barrington Moore's 'Social Origins of Dictatorship and Democracy', looking up again what he wrote on page 54 about the French maître valets:

"Some known as maître valets received a cottage, oxen, a few primitive tools, and an annual wage in grain and coin. The entire grain harvest went into the lord's storage bin. To the undiscriminating observer the maître valets with his cottage may have looked like a peasant as he worked his small farm with his family. Possibly he even felt like a peasant: Forster tells us that he had a certain prestige because often his family had worked the lord's far for generations. In strict economic terms nevertheless he was a wage laborer."

As said, it is not too long that I have to wait – looking up from my book I see Francesco coming into the hall of the hotel. I have to admit, I hesitate, very briefly only. We didn't see for considerable time but within a blink of an eye... : "Ciao Francesco." – "Ciao, Peter, come stai?" We hug each other, as 'real Italians' (well, he actually really is), kissing the cheeks. The lively welcome of friends after not seeing for a long time. And as well a somewhat... – estrangement? uncertainty? So many things happened after we met last time: He fell in love, is planning to move to Congo from where his girl friend is. Having worked in interesting though precarious jobs, the young man has plans for the future now: firm plans, though still open and flexible to do something that is interesting for himself but as well useful, meaningful for society, another society. We talk about our old friends – we worked together in a network when it still was a network rather than an organisation that strives to survive in the bog and swirl of the European Court of Power.

And about whatever we talk, whatever comes to my mind these days – while having been in Ankara, while being here in Brussels for conferences and while sitting and talking privately about politics and policies – is my very specific experience here from Brussels. Or should I say: 'our experience'? Well, it had been our experience in the sense of "me and the president" – not something to mention with pride, more with fear and a kind of abhorrence.

Being in Brussels, I lived at that time as usually close to the Rue Belliard – actually that time I had been in town for a couple of days for different meetings. I witnessed the subsequent build up of security over the various days: fences, roads being closed, helicopters scanning the city, especially around the nearby US-embassy. The one day I left for work, walking along the large four or five lane road, feeling bewildered. The usually busy street was like a place in a ghost town: no cars, only a few pedestrians walking along. Still, I was thinking about my own business – and only when I came to a side road it came to my mind: they blocked the road off, to make a secure space for GWB, the president, the emperor. And only a few seconds later "he" came: several (to say the least) motorbikes, a couple of cars including the presidents – wasn't it jokingly called "Road Force One" – and again a horde of motorbikes. Just a few minutes later, the street was free again – despite one of the four or five lane. And again a few minutes later I saw the little, comparatively modest escorts of some of the European heads of the state, moving to the same place for their 'common talk': The Council. How does this reconcile with the status of a guest? In which way is this going hand in hand with the understanding of democratic dialogue? What does this, though only symbolic, event say about the distribution of power? And does this shade anything on the relationship between governing bodies and the governed? – I remember that day: "we", "the president and me" are leaving the same day the country – not sure where he went; I had to go to Munich. My flight is one of the few flights that leaves the airport on time; another flight, actually being very much on time, is the 'Air Force One' – the aircraft of GWB. Most of the planes are delayed, many flights cancelled; there is chaos all over the place as the European airspace is for security reasons almost entirely closed.

– Well, Francesco and I left the restaurant; we now leave the place where we went for a coffee. "Va bene" – we shake hands – the same procedure as when we met: "Let me know when you around next time. Would be nice if we can meet again. I really like such talks." And our hands move around – still entangled but now pointing up. "Certamente" – it was really nice, nice to spend the evening with an intelligent young man, with somebody who actually didn't loose but gained enthusiasm over the last years.

It is good to know this, to remember it when I return from my jogging after the first working day here and now in Brussels. I had been jogging in the Parc du Cinquantenaire, thinking about the work of the last day: the presentations, the discussion; as well about the conversations in the evening during the dinner. All the important people from ministries, academia, civil society; working at the Council, the United Nations; having attended historical events... . I look into the cameras of the CCTV systems while returning to the hotel, jogging along the huge glass buildings in Brussels at the Rue de la Loi: buildings of the Commission, the Council, businesses – some coffee shops, bistros where during lunchtime everybody can be seen: people as you and me and also the Great Man (and the few Great Women who had been allowed to step forward) of History. People who shape world history – and it is sometimes difficult to decide who the real actors are, and who the supernumerary. At the end, perhaps we think too little – and in a wrong way – about those who are already working while I am still jogging, returning to the crown of the place – the hotel: those who are getting tools out of the cars, going to the building sites they are working on, those who are going to the mosque which I just past while running in the park. – Finally, history is not made by institutions; and the long chains of interdependence can easily break, especially there where the links are kept weak. What we easily forget is – as it is put into simple words in one of the contributions is "that Europe's reality cannot be found on the Place de Luxembourg" – the lively spot in front of the European Parliament.

As said, when I ended the last letter, I thought it would be it for a while – so I will keep it at least short for now – and I have to work anyway: the discussion of the future of Europe is going on, its social dimension. And I am trying not to get drawn into deep into pessimism. Sure, there is a little bit of a clan liability, perhaps simply based on the 'confirmed prejudice' while meeting Habsburg – but I cannot help to feel a little psychological indisposition looking at the participants, seeing the name van Oranje-Nassau – a repercussion, a resumption of court society, the palace now being one of the huge glass buildings in Brussels at the Rue de la Loi – in Dutch language the 'Wetstraat'. Rue de la Loi – Wetstraat. Rue de la Loi – Wetstraat – Loi – Roi? — Wet? – Wisdom, Science?

All the best – after having been robbed for paying for what they call excess baggage I am home, after going through multiple security checks at the airports, I have to make sure that nobody can steel my excess impressions, ideas, nobody can take away the excess spirit that goes through Europe and beyond, in the want for another world. All the best so from another living room of my home: the one on the little mountain in the part of the world which claims to be the rebel county. And also here, in the dozy province still awake, trying to find a balance between law and wisdom, between existence and consciousness.

Sideways:

October in the North

Dear All, finally I arrived home, sitting in the train - the beautiful Finnish landscape outside; and I am looking forward to a dip in the sauna and perhaps visiting granny, somewhere out in the countryside. Sure, home is something very relative and equally sure is that it is weird to say "Finally home" when you arrive in a place where people speak another language – and here people really speak still their own language. Also sure, visiting granny is for me here as much visiting granny as much I visit granny when Aghabullogue – just an adopted one, the one of the friends with whom I stay over the weekend before I move into the hotel which will then be "my flat" for some time. And not least visiting granny in the countryside is something that deserves qualification. Lapinlahti, the village where I stay, is itself a tiny place (the only remarkable the lake and a church build from timber, an amazing public library - amazing for such a small place and the little coffee-shop which is also a place for arts exhibition) – and "somewhere out in the countryside" is then something where it is more likely to meet bears and reindeers [yes, Joe, still some around, x-mas can go on in the old way ;-)] than people. And granny, residing there at the lake, residing already this time of the year in a place which is bright by the sparkle of the snow is always keen to have visitors like me: serving a meal for a huge family, heating the fire in the sauna and keeping the towels ready...

– her public. And actually it is this what amazes me. We do not speak much - sitting there for some time, saying nothing: "And this time you will give a presentation as well at Kelevi's University?" I adapt to local habits, don't answer immediately. Only later I say: "Yes, Hannele invited me to contribute to the MA." She nods – silence for a while; the sound of the TV from the neighbouring room is audible but not really present. "Well, it will be interesting. I think the students are nice." Kalevi says these words – and though this sounds as lively as a remark on how to fix a screw when fixing an electrical plug, I know that he says it with some emotional engagement.

Whenever I travel I amazed by meeting the different publics – market places of producing and exchanging and processing information.

Shortly before I left I had been on to Sibel from Ankara – with her and Kezban I am working on a book on Religion and Social Policy. Chatting to her on this, I asked then: "Actually, we are going for a study trip to Berlin. Any ideas on Neukoelln?" – "Leave it with me. When are you going?" Short clarifications and only little later I received a mail: Mustafa had been already in touch with Cengiz – I should give her a call. She lives in Berlin, works there in a kindergarden. She is Turkish but apparently already a long time in Germany – I concluded it from the way she speaks German: without the slightest accent and with more ease than I do at this stage: "Did you try the senates office?" – "No, I didn't. And actually I am more interested in hearing about the reality. These official representatives..." – "Right, I know. I could immediately talk about that one... . But lets stick to the point: organising your trip..."

The quietness of this place north of Helsinki; the modern train bringing me there: spacious even in the second class of the two-storey wagon, the special compartment for comforting toddlers and as well the 'kindergarden' from where I hear the laughs and noise of the playing kids (I cannot stop me to have a look: its a little bit a paradise – but isn't hat always the case if one looks at a lace where people can unfold their creativity, their joys?) and the 'restaurant carriag': the rye-bread with cheese and the smell of cinnamon finally making me weak: I enjoy the lovely taste of the warm pastry, I remember the words of a friend who once visited me in Aghabullogue on the day of Tom's cross-country event – though he lived already for some time in Ireland he said only then: "Well, finally I really arrived in Ireland!"); the coal quay market in Cork with its 'conservative-alternative flair': the stands of those people who had been doing there business there for decades and the stands of the 'alternative farmers', having one license for several people; the phone and mail network of my Turkish friend Sibel: perpetuating with modern means of technology a stunning network of traditional integrity, probably translating communitarian of the Islam into the world in which we both and most of our friends live: an anti-religious world – these worlds are so different – and still just dealing with one point: producing the social, giving space for activities: enforcing them and making them possible, places for exchange of information and more.

Niklas Luhmann meant that society is nothing else than communication - though he had been one of my academic mentors I dare to doubt. We frequently discussed this issue. But it is definitely right that society is nothing without communication and information.

It is nice to be home – here in Finland; and nice as well to know that Umut has now a fixed position in Ankara. Somewhat strange as I don't really know her – we only saw once for dinner; and little worrying to see Nollaig, my neighbour in Aghabullogue, being frequently tired; making me angry to see that some friends of my own party in the EP voted apparently recently for Jose Manuel; and looking with some hesitation at the work of the new food-coop in Graz about Brigitte mailed me the other day… and strange to see the different information and the different relevance in different places – though sometimes they seem to be the same: as on market places or as when they sing a birthday song as they do in the train, next to me. And though I cannot join in the refrain (at least not in their language) I can join in the clapping.

Information, networks, public spaces – the inclusion and exclusion and the most fundamental challenge of to where we can move from here.

Eväät myös mukaan – take away: you have to take it with you to be able to take it away, to overcome it. You have to fully understand these places to carry on with the inclusion, with building up social spaces and overcome exclusions and privatism (privacy would be the wrong term though it is a wrong privacy I am talking about).

May be strange idea to think about this while seeing mostly trees and laes outsides and while I should actually finish the preparation for the Social Policy Day of the Finnish Association of Social Policy. But perhaps it is not really strange - at least not for a stranger.

Take care,

Peter

Mosquitoes

Ever thought about these little animals and (social) policy?

At least I have to think about these beasts – though only by looking at the lake.

When I had been here in Finland some time back, I stayed for a while on a tiny island. And if I ever said that I had been there on my own, it is not quite true. Just on the shores there had been a seal, occasionally saying hello and there had been ants, busy in following their protestant work ethics and…., yes: these little and nasty animals, flying around in large groups, in seemingly unordered ways and sill showing at a closer look a well structured formation. Fortunately, they didn't like my blood which allowed developing some kind of peaceful coexistence. But later, when I visited briefly friends in Lapinlahti (before going to my workplace in Kuopio) they exhibited the limit of such coexistence. Canoeing across the lake and landing on the shore for a little walk, they proofed to be an utter nuisance. There had been spots, one nearly couldn't breath without inhaling a "full meal" of them, enough to serve as starter, main course and dessert.

Blood and light - they have the same effect on them as magnets on iron: providing a nutritious centre which makes their life.

Strange ideas here, halfway in the north of a country with its approximately 5 million inhabitants – a country which is located at the periphery of the European Union like Ireland. Finland, a country that exists in itself (roughly) of three parts: Helsinki and its immediate surrounding (well, yes: it is Finland as much as Dublin is Ireland); then the part north and east of Helsinki: scarcely populated, the larger towns and cities like "metropolitan Cork" - surely meaningful; and then the part north of the north: you can see bears and elks long time before arriving there, and even I met them (or at least there footprints – they are even less sociable than the ordinary Fin); but as further you go north, as more you find three things, extremes: ice, days, nights; and do not really wait for day and night, watch out for day or night. And as much as we like as tourists a visit to such capitals – be it Helsinki, Dublin, Berlin or Brussels – we love the remoteness of the countryside – be it really a countryside, or the shores of the open sea and lakes or the mountains and hills. And we are fascinated for instance by the remoteness of places like Lapland – a remoteness that means even distancing from what we know as nature: instead of the change of day and night we find there the "eternal light" during the summer and the "eternal darkness" with a fascinating twilight of the winter near to the Arctic. Remote from "nature as we know it".

Usually I do not have to talk about this. If I talk to friends and colleagues about working in Finland they think about Helsinki (as much as they think about Dublin when they hear Ireland). And though we all know that these capitals (heads, as the Latin origin "caput" suggests) are only part of the countries, they are the centre, pretty much the blood and light for humans. And they are attractive as little light bulbs: shiny enough to gather, and still being in a shadow of the larger lights: Paris and Berlin as centres of the economically strong countries, Brussels as the newly emerging political centre of the European Union; Luxembourg, Zurich but as well for instance Frankfurt as the centre of banking and financial services; Washington as the centre of world power, still much brighter if compared with world centres like New York, Geneva, Vienna as different places hosting the United Nations. In other perspectives still being in the shadow of the centres of an ancient world: Rome, Athens, Damascus, Istanbul – to name but a few and to limit myself (unjustifiably) more or less on the so-called Western world.

The problem with the light is: coming too near, you may burn the wings. And this means we find in many cases these complex relationships and socio-environmental links: centres, and the urban poverty. People moving towards the centre full of hope, still: remaining without perspective; the sub-centre orienting towards the centre: like Dublin or Helsinki, possibly asking questions like "Berlin or Boston".

In reality a rather complicated mixture, full of tensions, full of exclusions and inclusions: multicultural enrichment at times, blunt racisms and harsh competition at other times.

And as happy as I am for Oxana whom I could help to get a position at the United Nations, I am a little bit worried about her, seeing the attraction of power and the same time the danger of loosing it when absorbed by an uncontrollable machinery of regulations and uncontrollable long chains of interaction. Looking back at the long years of my struggles in the corridors of the European Institutions and the final decision at some stage: no way of staying, no point in remaining involved into a court society which equals the glamour and mendacity of the Court Society so nicely depicted by Norbert Elias.

If you ever travelled to and through Finland, the most stunning feature of the country is... – well, it is not really a "country"; it is more like a sea with islands; its many lakes, being kept together by some landmasses in between. The birch trees, in many areas another feature and little mountains: as low they are, they are rocky, often seamlessly linking into some of the many archipelagos. The beauty is about its emptiness, its remoteness which forces to cope with nature. And it is in these places of the beauty of remoteness, the confrontation with bare nature where we find actually a stunning openness and connectedness to the global world. A still high economic (GDP-based measurement) growth-rate; a highly-concentrated economy with many large firms starring; a highly concentrated industry as well in terms of the sectoral structure: electronics, namely Nokia [funnily enough Nokia produced rubber boots before blessing the world with mobile phones], playing a major role (though the overall picture is dominated by service industries); and finally a highly concentrated industry as well in terms of space: Helsinki (larger area), "the Finnish light bulb", making up for about a third of the GDP.

A highly concentrated industry – and while typing a typo slipped in, corrected now, but worth to look at: "concentraded" – concen-traded. And this economic success is indeed something that is traded across the country. I had been once sitting for a couple of weeks on "my own little island": remote, dealing only with nature (and writing a book on global social policy):

the excitement of the timber fire in the sauna, sweating in temperatures near to hundred degrees and then leaving for a dip in the cold water of the lake, just in front of the hut; swimming there every morning: a seal somewhere nearby, though rarely seen; during the afternoons picking the berries – and hoping that it is a beery and not by accident the nose of a bear who is hiding in the shrub; tasting the freshness of the fruits while sitting in the middle of nature, listening to the light wind, shaking the tall trees. And all this meant as well: dealing with my own nature – nobody else being around. You can imagine, how close we got: me and I (or I and me?), meeting everyday and not having anybody else to talk to. And nevertheless knowing that this "me and I" is just a part of the permanent involvement into relations and processes, only seemingly and temporarily taken out, put into another context. The only thing we could do: I talked to myself and myself had been talking to me who actually was I. Sounds weird and it had not been pathological, not really talking. But it had been an interesting experience for a couple of weeks (and so was the "re-entering into social culture"). An experience as well about how connected on is even here in this wild and lonely place. And it had been an interesting experience as well in other terms: as remote as this place had been, as well it had been connected to the weird wide world: the world wide web to which I had been magically linked via wireless.

And actually you find many such connections – surely not often on such islands (there it had been "only" electricity and Internet) but as standard in the small municipalities: free public libraries even in rather small municipalities - imagine a general public library, larger than the one in Cork, for a municipality of about 7,000 inhabitants; imagine perfect bus service making it possible for children to reach safely and comfortably the next school; imagine health centres in such municipalities, being free for everybody.

Sure, little light bulbs: education does not take place in the individual families as it had been the case a long, very long time ago in all our countries. Now education is "professionalised", taking place in schools; libraries replace the story teller at the indigenous fireplace; and the healer is replaced by the medical profession: GPs, specialists and a nursing team. Sure, all as well a matter of economies of scale. And so I am now brought into lecture theatres across Finland: "teaching" a course that can be visited in nine Universities of the country. I came from Ireland to stand in a lecture theatre in front of a camera - the result now magically located in a virtual world: the new VW: Volkswagen (it translates from the German into "People's Car" – right: the PC). – And all is in this way again about striving to the centre – though it may be even by a kind of imitation.

All this leaves this magic beauty of the country rather intact. And all this leaves the people as they are: if I can trust locals, we Finnish are little bit shy, not talkative and... – no, not stubborn. The term in the Finnish language is sisu. It cannot be translated, only being described. It is the hardness for instance of sitting in the sauna, sweating in extreme temperatures and staying there for really long times, throwing water on the hot stones to make it even hotter; and going after that in water which is just warm enough to not fall on you on form of little ice-cubes... – sisu: even after this you smile: you made it and it doesn't matter if nobody else knows that you made it – Sisu has something to do with just you. Finnish sociability is not about talking, anyway. – And all this does not by any means say that Finish people are not friendly, that they are stubborn, that they would be cold – look into the face of some of them and you will fall in love, being attracted by a warm and attractive smile (though there is always the danger that you are getting aware of this smile only after you already walked away).

Concen-traded. Of course you did it, at least as child. It is a little game of "arts". Do it again: Throw a stone gently into a lake – the water calm, unmoved. You will see the concentric circles, the power moving smoothly to the periphery, moving but also getting weaker. Throw two stones: and you will see how the concentric circles move into each other, smoothly perhaps or violently, building a new "power structure", building a picture with different colours changing and exchanging and merging and disturbing. Throw three equal stones and the same will happen – and now throw two stones again: different in seize, or different in the power (energy) you use in throwing them; or throw the second just with a tiny delay. – You see what happens? Try it. And if you don't like to play this way, just look at the mighty power of the United States of America and how they throw themselves into the global lake of negotiations: "peaceful negotiations" (for instance by cutting money or giving money to specific activities by the United Nations; for instance by bullying Mary Therese Winifred Robinson out of the office as UN High Commissioner for Human rights) or negotiations that are brute violence against other countries and against people.

It may be that we, as humans, could overcome at least to some extent many limitations, establishing long chains of interdependency as Norbert Elias used to say. And this means as well that we are able to transport ideas, products and wealth to the periphery like we transport electricity to the light bulb. With this we may allow the peripheries shining in bright lights. But still, it is the question to which extent we actually allow the regions to enhance their power as this usually remains in one place: the person and group that controls the power switch is usually much more in control of the situation than the person and group that may be able to control the bulb, that shines - but that cannot reach the switch.

There is much truth in what Norbert said about these chains - but there is equally much truth in what for instance Immanuel Wallerstein, Andre Gunder Frank or Giovanni Arrighi said: it is not so much about long chains but it about concentric circles: the centre-periphery structures, the concentration and centralisation of power and the establishment of dependencies. - Chains are as strong as the weakest link - but concentric circles are depending on and colonialised by the centre.

Still, there is one thing left to be said: Ever thought about paradoxes? The bulb is more likely in the centre. And a tiny experience here with my Finish fellow citizens (strange people, aren't they: http://dpoetz.intereduc.ch/blog/archive/2007/12/05/hard-to-digest-but-good-for-you.html) may be somewhat remarkable in this context: If you enter a sauna, one of these special places that are in this country in their own way public spaces, everybody being naked, so to say reduced on pure existence, you come across people who are actually talking quite a lot and who are not a little bit shy. Not near to the bulb but far away: where power relationships are of a different kind, not attributed by formal status nor going back to contracts.

So, it may be that the real centre actually develops sufficient strength to limit the power of the switch?

In the meantime, tomorrow morning, I will move on – not much, but little bit more to the centre: for a short time only back to Stockholm.

Take care – of yourself, and the world around you,

Peter

Familiarity

though the term is not really correct: finally it is the first time I am flying out of Kuopio airport.

But I should start at the beginning, not in the middle of the story. The flight is scheduled fro 6:15 am. and Juhani says he will collect me at 5:45 from the hotel. I gaze a little bit worried, this time not because he always turns up at least 5 minutes late. It is more that I think it may be a little bit late to catch the flight. "No, that is OK. It takes us only nine minutes to go there." – "Right, but..." – "No, it is OK. A domestic flight and there are definite rules...". A more or less long sermon and I am not sure if I am the worrier or if he is the worrier, knowing all these rules and sticking to them, making it in many cases impossible to stick to all the rules, for instance the rule of punctuality: if you have to complete so many forms, if you have to do so many things according to specified rules there is not much space and time left. Somewhat after 5 hrs. I collect my early breakfast – take-away: rye bread with cucumber, reflecting well our breakfast habits here in Finland. Too early for me, though I worked already a little bit after the long evening I spent with Juhani and Leena: I urgently had to send the stuff for the meeting in Poland though that will take place only in December.

Anyway, I sit down, having at least a coffee and leave at about 5:43:downstairs, opening the door and... – the car is already there: "Good morning." – "Good morning to you. Sorry for finally being responsible that you don't get your sleep." I put the suitcase into the boot, we drive and just before 6 we arrive at the airport. Only few people are around; I check in and we go together to the security check. "Don't forget to send me the document." – "No I won't. Will work on it today." – Well, thought I would have a day off but that spare time seems to be reduced. The security check goes smoothly, all this seems to be a little bit like a one man show – and actually it is: the two other people working here are women. I do not have a boarding card, I didn't get one though I checked in: "You just show your passport." Familiarity – one knows each other. So what is the point in all these documents, really?

No seat allocation either. So, another low fare airline? Couple of minutes later the door opens to the airfield, the few passengers show their passport and walk to the aircraft. Actually, as I am the last who arrives, I just walk through, and I am the second who walks through the glass door. Just this second I see a light being switched on: the light of the large garage, accommodating the fire brigade. So there it is a two men, two women show as there is a man in the garage whom I didn't see before.

I enter the aircraft, take the seat in the first row where I have a little bit more leg space.

The usual: "doors armed and cross-checked"; security announcements; "captain – crew. Take seats for departure." Language kind of criss-crossing: Finnish, Swedish – our two official languages; and English, the latter the official language of the world of flights, the world of the sky, heaven. So we may be lucky that, if we finally go to heaven, we are still able to communicate – and the really poor souls, down in hell, will be suffering by not having a common language, not being able to talk (but this is probably not true as I know a couple of English speakers whom I will meet down there when time is ripe for me to go).

The flight is too short to start something serious, so I take the board magazine. Here, in this part of the world: international air traffic, things change: not least as the Finnish board magazine, communicating globally, seems to be much more consume-oriented than the "real world" of Finland, a somewhat egalitarian country. At least my impression in Helsinki or Kuopio (and let alone Lapinlahti) is that the brands are present but really not central, don't matter. Different here: "Travel in Style" - and it means travelling stylish: well thought-through, well designed including the design of the brand name and asking to be well paid for.

I flip through the journal: I pause, looking at the headline An article on Chamonix, the Vallée Blanche....

... I don't really read the article, lean back and glance over the photos; my thoughts are turning back to my time in the snow. Little bit coaching and then, actually several years after leaving skiing behind, my first real tour experience. Barbara convinced me: "Sure, you can do it. It is one of the things you don't really unlearn." Yes, girl, I am still grateful that you convinced me with this ease, that you said "Sure, you can do it" in such a way that I didn't resist. – I can still remember my hesitation: a rather dull day. Preparing for the tour: "Fix this somehow to your chest." – "???" – "Don't look. It makes it easier to find you if you are buried under an avalanche." – "Oh, that is great. What a relief." – "Well, unlikely that we will be hit. It is more like the seat belt in the car. Do you worry about that every time you fasten it?" – "Sure I don't. And in any case, I trust you. Even if it would be only as I assume there is some self-interest in not being buried together." She smiles: "Good." A dull day that didn't stop us climbing uphill, the fur under the ski, making it easy – well somewhat easy. About 2 hours later, there are nearly no trees anymore, we finally reach the border: between "nearly no trees" and "really no trees" there seems to be a world: breaking this border, we break though another border: The sky is opening, the sun is blazing and three peaks are unfolding in front of us: unbelievable beauty, a stunning look at grandeur which impresses at least me: the untouched nature, the openness which invites one to stop and which also invites to move on, go for this endless walk to the – only seemingly – near peaks we are looking at. Only half an hour later we sit down. A little shelter, during the summer probably used by herdsmen. I do not follow Barbara's advice – and will pay for it by being heavily sunburned the next day. Exposing oneself to nature is one thing; lack of reason an entirely different one. After the "Jause", a special sort of snack, we move on. Another 4 hours walk uphill, only far away we see somebody else, already on the way downhill: A small dark, spot moving through the snow, and a white cloud of snow behind. Another 3 hours climbing – not used to it, I feel comfortable, acquiring the technique quite well – and... Another 3 hours climbing: yes, as stunning it is to go here, as enjoyable the way is: it is the goal, standing here, having achieved this, and looking around is simply "a life-time experience". Another 2 hours climbing: I look at my skiing partner - she knows, that she didn't promised too much. And she knows as well that such life-time experience still doesn't allow one to stop and one always longs to more of these experiences. Another hour left climbing: She knows that what is coming soon is not less exciting though it lacks a clear goal, this kind of goal. We arrive on the top, and the view seems to be endless, the world of mountains unfolding in front of the eyes, the feeling of being "on top": not on top of just this peak which looked so impressive as unique giant, bit on top of the world and still feeling to be in the middle of it. A rest – to rest this view, to settle, lock it in the memory. Still, it is soon about going down, sliding through the deep snow. Due to the speed we never dive deeper than to the hips. And actually, even if we are sliding through it, its lightness suggests that it is not really deep, lightness translating into buoyancy, hindering that we are definitely caught in the snow masses.

I awake from the daydream, from the memories of dealing with nature, checking out power. Pouvoir: abilities – pouvoir: strength and might. – And I experienced all this after three days seminar of a European "practice research project" on service provision and their marketisation – a project which finally turned into a power struggle with the European Commission, bringing me finally at one stage into the European Parliament for a presentation on failures of short-sighted attempts of standardisation. And paradoxically pushing me to demand a stronger European engagement rather than the simple rejection of Europeanisation.

At least I could win one struggle with power – an exciting one which I will never forget as long as there is some memory left. But it may well be that the loss of the other battle – if it actually is a final loss at all – caused so much distress that I will forget sooner than later.

I turn away from the daydream - turn the page over from Chamonix to an article on India and a clean water project. Another adventure with nature, though not as playful as the one I referred to before. An article on a UNICEF project: "determined to influence behaviour towards water usage and sanitation." It strikes my attention again to think about the difference between behaviour and acting – and the sometimes fluid, sometimes rigid borders.

Again, I am reading the article and recall at the same time what Sibel wrote the other day from Ankara, in the context of discussing a recent EU-report on the financial crisis and its impact on Turkey. She mentioned that the impact of the crisis is somewhat limited. There is still some fundamental issue: (a) the Turkish economy being a "real" one, having to cope with establishing a productive basis and being in this sense a "developing" rather than an "overdeveloped", turbo-capitalist system, (b) some marginal utilities from ongoing trade and (c) not least the coping strategies: people being permanently confronted with real and potential economic crisis, apparently better able to cope due to the preparedness. Well, something we discussed recently in Brussels, when I criticised Vladimir saying that the crisis came unforeseen. He agreed, one could have known, one could have prepared better – but he agreed by seeing it only as matter of mechanisms of regulatory mechanisms on high levels and he dismissed any reasoning that coping is a matter of a wider set of social quality: of bringing together economic, political and everyday's life under one heading. Sure and of course I agree: a strict regulative system would have helped to cope with some excesses. But that is the problem with any cancer treatment: a long as you fight the cancer cells by cutting them away it is hopeless battle and the fight can only be won by expunging the root.

Approaching 7 am., we are approaching Helsinki – a short stay, just enough time to look for a reindeer – but there is none left. Soon I am sitting again, ready for take off: leaving Helsinki at 8 hrs., arriving Stockholm at 8 hrs.. Apparently a rigid standstill, not moving by a single minute. And still, there are about four hundred kilometres between the two cities. And leaving Helsinki means changing the tune: Kiitos, Suomi. – Välkommen Stockholm – two smiles, three kisses. Every language is such tune in its own way, a special melody. And a Swede is sweet, the language like kisses and smiles: Välkommen Stockholm. I have to smile - not because I am "pronouncing a smiley" but because I remember a meeting with Henrik, Sven, Inga-Anna and Marcela, many years ago. Four Swedes – but only three of them native, the other a migrant from Macedonia. They towed me once away into a pub in Brussels. And talking about smiling sweet Swedes, I have to think now especially of Henrik. As said, we had been in a pub, Marcela standing with us, slightly but obviously moving with the rhythm of the music. Henrik looked at her, then at me, saying: "But mind, if you want to join us in this team for some time in Sweden, you have to be prepared. Look at her: she is lively, enjoying herself, adapts to what is going on around her. And than look at me: a kind of sad figure: a little bit chubby, a grey suit, a grey shirt, a grey tie. And looking like a shelf full of files." I laugh, Sven and Inga-Anna smile and Marcela laughs, takes Henrik and moves him around like a dancing bear until he has to laugh as well, hesitant, not able to resist – the rigidity of his social mask loosing its ground.

Anyway, this October day in 2009 there is still an hour to go to finally arrive in Sweden. Again I am privileged, have plenty of space, as actually there are only few passengers with me on board. "Armed and cross-checked. Captain

– crew, take seats..." – we depart in time, rigidly keeping rules and procedures which enable the system to work. Little later I see on the display that we reached 30,000 feet, I look at the announced speed on the screen. Bizarre - an unbelievable speed but looking out of the window it seems that we are standing. The clouds are getting darker and surround the aircraft. Although the light is switched on it is dark. It is a slightly bumpy flight but nothing to worry about until... – a scream somewhere in the back, the aircraft falls into a turbulence: a couple of feet, some yards or even more? I look out of the window, can see how the wing gives in, resilient, while the aircraft regains its stability. Reassuring flexibility – rigidity would have killed us, a wing, not being able to flexibly adapt would have broken away, leaving us without support. I feel sorry for the person who screamed, no sitting pale, inwardly sobbing. Still, I cannot do anything – and definitely not more than the board assistant who is there now, a little bit trembling himself - perhaps that is only because the aircraft regained stability but is still slightly "bumping over the clouds".

It may seem odd, but I am back to the skiing experience, the flexibility requested by moving, well: dancing through the snow. And I am back to the power struggle with, in and against the European institutions. And I am back to the long discussions we have had many, many years ago: classical theories on Marx: the relationship between basis and superstructure, Althusser and his proposal for structuralism and within these debates somewhere Antonio Gramsci and his considerations on political struggles: static warfare, supporting leg, kicking leg.

– Back to normality - the storm is over and we are back to daily life. "Ja, tack. Kan jag och ha mjölk också?" I answer the board assistant's question as she offers me more coffee. At least with the few phrases in Swedish I feel sufficiently safe; probably with mistakes, I am using one of the official languages of Finland - at least an attempt. Anyway, we are nearly there: in the country of smiles and kisses.

7:42 am., 237 mph., 3,000 feet 12 C ---- 7:46 am., I look through the window, we are through the clouds, I see[88] the airport in front of the aircraft, we approach the runway, opening in front of the aircraft like an artificial throat. It is only seconds later: I see the aircraft touching ground - elastically - a smooth landing after an at times turbulent flight. "Please keep your seat belt fastened during taxi. The mobile phones have to remain switched off..." 8 o'clock sharp I am already at the gate. I walk through the glass door which automatically opens in front of me. Välkomna i Sverige. I am captured by Silvia's smile who is there at the gate, Carl Gustav standing a little bit in the

---

[88]   life-video displayed on screen

background. – Indeed, it is not so easy to stay away from the politics and policies, from the political struggles and from the EU even if one wants. "Please, join." And I do not really have an excuse not to follow. It is long way out, it may be that it is actually not possible at all and we can only think about certain ways, remaining on the path, once chosen.

Anyway, I am now finding myself in one of the EU-capitals – one of the capitals, located at its periphery and nevertheless this weekend being the centre: the periphery hosting the centre; the centre: a major EU-summit meeting here in the periphery; the centre not staying rigidly in place, but showing at least on the surface its flexibility, encapsulating the periphery not by enforcing integration by power, i.e. might and force, but by offering some space for power, i.e. by allowing in some way the capability of the long chains and concentric circles. Flexibility allowing a firm grip.

But now it is already time to move on – after a weekend going to two kisses, one smile: Örebro, there being in the firm grip of a conference organiser. One of my last EU-activities in this position.

The first time I had been here in Sweden in this context had been probably in 2000, at the time having been invited to the honourable task of helping to prepare the Swedish presidency of 2001. It had been meetings in Belgium, but as well in Sweden. A relatively small working group; an exciting undertaking aiming on resembling two sides of pouvoir, an undertaking that is now institutionalised in processes of governance, caught in structures and barely allowing action.

The result not of that presidency in 2001 but of a long development: the institutional system opening: participatory democracy being offered in the Treaty, governance instead of a ruling government: a political runway, opening like an artificial throat in front of some political actors - or a catwalk?

Örebro -Two kisses, a smile - I hope they will never be poisoned for you.

Hälsningar och lycka

Peter

Tricky

At least in my opinion: we celebrate history and are celebrated by kind of indulging into history... and we loose history.

Ever thought about it? How many historical churches you visit while you are on holidays? How often do you look at parades and the royal houses and royal families? Do not say it would not be often as it may be simply due to the fact that there is no king or queen around. But then you go across the water, you will stand soon in front of one of this folks. – As said, Arlanda welcomed me with Silvia's smile and during the short time in Stockholm I had been more or less forced to attend two ceremonies in her favour. And now I arrived in Örebro – briefly going to the hotel, a first working meeting, scheduled for speakers and then the official welcome in Örebro – there had been two receptions, the one to which we as speakers had been invited to took place in Örebro Castle.

Oh no, of course I do not complain. This treatment is nice, without question. But nevertheless it is tricky. Distancing people by taking them out of life - rather than bringing these outer spaces into real life.

Sure, Rose-Marie – she can currently look at the castle as her official residence – definitely didn't come across as arrogant. Actually on the contrary: elegant and down to earth, open and in a positive talkative, socialising – I had been surprised when I learned later that she is Christian-Democrat. But then again: we are in Sweden. Though we didn't sit down in the kitchen – but then again: though there hadn't been too many of us we had been enough to fill casually the Reception Hall, having little snacks in the Banqueting Hall or chatting in the Yellow Room. Why stay put in a single place if there are so many rooms available: one for the small speech, one for the chat, another for the snacks and again one for the coffee. And as mixed as the crowd had been, as down to earth all this had been it is somewhat strange to be in such a place not like being in a museum, exhibiting the puppets of the past but to be there in the place where the past emerges as presence. Latest when I step by accident in the Royal Bed Chamber and see the alarm clock (looked a little bit like a special offer from IKEA) I have a strange feeling: is this still the centre – one of the centres that actually are ruling us, a present centre which is with all qualifications the mighty power, being build on our lack of capability to change our thinking and being? Is this what some people call postmodernity and that is actually caught in a seemingly iron cage of premodern limitations? – Kafkaesque.

The day before I talked with Eva about all this – well, we had been drawn to the topic when.... – well, yes, just at the palace. She had been cursing against the monarchy, expressing her unease especially against Silvia who seems to be particularly snobbish and demands to be recognised as Queen (bourgeois little girl as she had been when still living in Germany). Anyway, we talked about this bizarre stubbornness of political systems, Europe, claiming to be the most enlightened and secular region, having a catholic church being based in Rome, to be precise: in Vatican City, outside even of the Shengen area, the most fundamentalist Christian messages heralded by the pope, claiming caritas in veritate; Europe, accommodating... - well, have a quick look: though I cannot guarantee correctness, the following gives a reasonable overview, if linked to other EU-topics on the various agenda of these days, a possible title could be: EUrope – A futile soil for a new monarchy – EmporiUm.

Austria – monarchy until 1919

Belgium – monarchy

Bulgaria – monarchy until 1946

Cyprus – n/a

Czech Republic – monarchy until 1918 (as annex to Austria)

Denmark – monarchy

Estonia – n/a

Finland – presidential republic since 1919

France – monarchy until 1848 (though already before interrupted by the First French Republic)

Germany – monarchy until 1919

Greece – monarchy abolished in 1975

Hungary – monarchy until 1918/1946

Ireland – part gained independence in 1919

Italy – 1946

Latvia – n/a

Lithuania – n/a

Luxembourg – grand duchy

Malta – n/a/

Netherlands - monarchy

Poland – n/a

Portugal – monarchy until 1910

Romania – n/a

Slovakia – n/a

Slovenia – n/a

Spain – monarchy

Sweden – monarchy

United Kingdom – monarchy

So currently 7 out of 27

EUrope – A futile soil for a new monarchy – EmporiUm – a story to be written at the begin of the first century. I am frequently wondering about the strong and persisting meaning of all these glamorous scenes. To be honest, I cannot believe anymore that it is just a means of distracting people. It is our enlightened inability of truly thinking "the social". As I said in my presentation in Kuopio on occasion of the celebrations of the Social Policy Association in Finland, I see the values of the French revolution very much translated: "reinterpreting the liberty of rights into the freedom of contracts, the redefinition of equality on the basis of exchange and the understanding of fraternity in its capitalised form: as matter of social capital."

And even more, these values, as spelled out at the time, had been already the root for this interpretation: A revolution which established long chains of interaction, finding its roots already in the Renaissance: the invention of the telescope, an instrument for enhancing trade; the invention of the flight-machine: an instrument for "overcoming" the law of gravity (funnily enough, Leonardo worked on his machines before Issac explained that "Every point mass attracts every single other point mass by a force pointing along the line intersecting both points. The force is directly proportional to the product of the two masses and inversely proportional to the square of the distance between the point masses" (http://en.wikipedia.org/wiki/Universal_gravitation).

All this work by Leonardo and its later scientific consideration had been about looking far, reaching beyond the reachable and even in some ways – as I said in Cork: "humankind developing skills and the notion of replacing god and making and shaping the world".

And still, all had been about individuals and their performance, wealth being – seemingly – rooted in circulation (Fugger, Medici…) rather than in production.

Makes a bell ring? A (seemingly) financial in 2008 crisis; a global system, synchronised but not coordinated. Systems being build on Manchester morals, Casino behaviour and moving in turbo speeds.

And leaving those who cannot cope with this system outside: excluded, in poverty or precarity; self-excluding as intellectuals, not being able to cope with the flow of time, time flowing away in front of their eyes as Dalí's clocks which I could see the other day when visiting the exhibition in Stockholm.

Yes, as Jan hinted upon, it is "the dandy, first noted in his time of intellectual upheavals in England, later in France and Germany. Dandyism had been an expression of protest of an outdated nobility, loosing increasingly its leading societal role to the bourgeoisie and the industrial mass society. This surfaced by being distinguishably dressed and in pronouncedly elegant forms, and partly as well whims: So it is known that some walked, having tortoises on the lead, scornfully demonstrating to the bourgeoisie their exorbitant time (Karen Hoffmann: Der Dandy bei d'Aurevilly und Baudelaire ; http://www. hausarbeiten.de/faecher/vorschau/10047.html).

A capitalism based on circulation rather than production; a capitalism based on...

... – at least on some ways on derivations of the Machiavellian prince: Il Principe, with only one principle: the principle me, the pure individualism.

This makes governance so attractive: the principle me being asked to enter the stage, being challenged to compete there: gaining power as matter of capabilities for instance by attaining internet-literacy, making every document, even the president's e-mails, available only "one mouse-click" away. However, paradoxically squandering power comes along as as effective action. The increase of technicalities undermining the understanding of (its) meaning.

Isn't the reception in the castle, in this light, as well a little bit worrying? The poisoned smile, the gain of power as claimed in political calls for the self-responsible, self-maintaining individual, the denial of "such thing as society" (Thatcher) and...

... and the loss of the conditions which make it actually possible to live up to it.

The resurgence of the one-dimensional man. Not sufficient but futile for the Übermensch [overman] Zaratustra spoke about. A new dictator.

Too abstract? Too bleak? Sure, we didn't reach dictatorships again in "our" worlds. But yet, we face Berlusconi for a long time in his power-position: The patriarch, "father of his people". And most of us accept seamlessly Sarkozy, if we believe the Financial Times (24/25 October 2009: 6) he is "well positioned to be the dominant political figure, not just in his own country, but in western Europe. He has energy, charisma, intelligence an international profile and a strong political mandate at home." All these appearances reflecting the misled search for truth. Then, Caritas in Veritate translates well into – again quoting the Financial Times – "placing the veteran conservative at the centre of a new coalition government that will juggle a strained budget with delivering tax cuts", a person of which "Dirk

Schumacher, an economist at Goldman Sachs, said, Mr. Schaeuble was 'not a genuine fiscal expert but he has all you need to be a success [as finance minister]'."

Power replacing power - the charismatic leader rather than the expert. Not really better than the expert who masters in a perfect way instrumental reasoning without any sense of a subjective dimension.

Tricky, sure; the sequencing of DNS is a cinch if seen in the light of attempts to sequencing society; the latter stands just at the beginning again, requiring to dethrone machines and and charismatic leaders alike, making social space and social time in the same way available in the same way availed of time and space as physical entities.

You don't believe? – Lean back, look at the trees outside of the window while passing through the Sweden: the birch trees showing their colourful autumn clothes in endless forests, interrupted by the evergreen of the pines; the clearings with the bizarre forms of the stubs – surreal as the paintings by Dalí; the lakes, covered by the soft cloth of the fog of the still young day; the little islands, little peaks inviting for rests; farms that seem to be neglected at this time of the year: pretty but quite; the small houses, the timber painted in a warm red, promising at least to those who lived here the same warmth coming from the fire in the tiled stove. And look at the old man sitting opposite, the skin marked by physical work, the voice expressing experience and ambition at the same time – ambition to tell his story, and ambition to learn more. What is against all this excitement the traffic jam which that blocks the zebra-crossing and forces you to wait in the rain while you are going to the hotel or the annoyed receptionist in the hotel when you at your destination.

And it is here as well where the ugliness of the functional building gains attractiveness: the attractiveness of functioning for the people living there, offering space for people gathering, offering room for children to play, challenging the pure individualism to open.

You are not in Sweden? It doesn't really matter – Pippi Longstocking lived in Sweden; but really, she could have lived anywhere. But she had to do. As she knew that only then she would not be alone.

Just try it yourself - finally we may see the castles disappearing as we can all enter, together.

Just try...

Official Residence –

– Of course this sounds to be a matter of another world – and looking at Rose-Marie it surely is as weird as it is a different world when we step into Silvia's Carl Gustav's bedroom. The Ikea (like) alarm clock doesn't really make a difference, makes it perhaps even more surreal.

But is it sur-real or sub-real or counter-real? Or really simply Kafkaesque?

Actually it is not so devious as it actually seems – and it has history. I remember another visit in such residences though now I am taking about another times, when I still worked for the party, when I still lived in the West of Germany, when I still had been student and later, trying to enter working in the public services. The party had not been illegal but it had been a "black sheep", unwanted and though the party had been legal, members had been illegalised – the time after 1972. It had not been possible for us to work in any kind of public services. And though our newspaper had been legal it faced various forms of bullying. So we went out: Saturdays, selling the paper and talking to people about politics and policies. And living near to the (in those days) so-called Kohlenpott, the industrial area near to the Ruhr, characterised by coal and steel industry, we went frequently there, supporting the local group. Where we went? Well, where workers resided. Small houses, many of the originally built by Krupp, one of the industrial giants. Industrial patriarch in the heavy industry. And he actually built these houses – long rows with a very typical shape for the region, in some respect very much like the houses for instance in Barack Street in Cork: one story, small, long rows and in many cases with a tiny garden – for the workers: my home is my castle – and so, if I loose my job I loose my home: my castle and my reign. Finally, this imagine of "my house – my castle" had been very much as well about "my reign in the family". It had been an entire culture, encapsulated in the buildings: family reign and neighbourhood rules and the industrialism as supremacy. Princedoms, kingdoms and empires.

It is the experience I still gain occasionally, when visiting France – though the situation is different: when we go there from house to house, to people whom we know, selling the newspaper it is about keeping in touch, engaging in debates, listening…

– The governor's castle being in this light somewhat comparable now with the workers' home, isn't it?

And the workers' home surely with its own beauty: small rooms – yesterday, while being in the castle, I had been talking with Ariane, joking about the bedrooms, about the reception halls: offering enough space for a kindergarden, the kitchen, being large enough to host a restaurant kitchen…

And I told her about Sue Townsend's The Queen and I, the queen not being able to squeeze the large carpet from the palace into her "new home": social housing. The workers' home with the small rooms, the belling stag as the typical painting: expressing the longing for nature and strength. Everything tidy, over the top as tidiness had been demanded: punctuality and servility in the working place being passed on, "materialised" in the own home: my home is my castle. And the same kind of tidiness reflected in the servility of the character: half of the life is order: protestant order, protestant ethics... – the ethics of fulfilling demands of the system: subordination in this world as promise of freedom in the other world, thereafter.

And any attempt to break out of this world had been penalised: not performing in the job meant loosing work and home alike; and as well: not joining in the streamlined thinking meant disciplinary action – it had been the communists who had been taken first:

> "..., and I did not speak out—because I was not a communist;

> Then they came for the socialists, and I did not speak out—because I was not a socialist;

> Then they came for the trade unionists, and I did not speak out—because I was not a trade unionist;

> Then they came for the Jews, and I did not speak out—because I was not a Jew;

> Then they came for me—and there was no one left to speak out for me."

> (Martin Niemoeller)

– think about this when hearing next time about the trade-union free enterprise, part of the global economy, making child labour possible and even inviting to it.

But think as well about something else: all this had been as well about the other side, being kept away, being swept to places outside of the visible – the dandy, showing decadence in sur-realism had a counterpart, the urchin, the sub-real. A playful melody, presented by Franz Josef Degenhardt – it can be playful as it suggests in "Vaeterchen Franz's" protest song – the perspective of the at the time real, the dominant and well accepted: the establishment of the good bourgeois and also the good worker. And the playful melody carries the text:

Spiel nicht mit den Schmuddelkindern,

sing nicht ihre Lieder.

Geh doch in die Oberstadt,

mach's wie deine Brüder,

...

Don't play with the urchins,

Don't sing their songs

Go uptown,

Do it as your brothers did.

All this is not about wills and norms – it is very much about structures as well. The no-go areas of society: I remember times when in Cork the "good citizen" had not been allowed, or welcomed to go to the northern part of the town; I remember living for many years in Hamburg – only when returning to the city on my bike, it had been many years later, I saw an area which I never saw during the years I lived there: a kind of "slum", the ghettoised migrants in Harburg, being housed in protection buildings from the war, but now being used to protect society from the urchin. They had been simply invisible.

This is another danger of the museum-like cultures: we dive into history, visit the past and it makes us forgetting the present, the ongoing the injustices and exclusions around us, in the presence. The sur-realism of the castle – and its celebration, for many remaining a matter of glancing through the high-gloss pages of Hello-type – is very similar to the sub-realism which is exhibited in some galleries or museums: places that "blame history" without acknowledging that we are makers of history. Sure, we cannot be blamed for the historical past – but we surely have to be blamed if we do not learn from history.

And this means as well that we have to transcend history – have to transcend the closure of thinking.

As closed and closing as public and honourable receptions are, as closed and closing are some of the presentations these days: the political class looking more for how to sustain the borders and to sustain the mighty powers; the closure of thinking as well on the side of some academics: the closure of thoughts by the borders of slides of PowerPoint presentations. – Actually I feel some relief after my rather complex and philosophical presentation: Marilyn, academic as myself, from the West of England, and also Elsa from the local city council somewhere here in Sweden appreciate it, for instance the link I establish between participation and contribution – the question of the interlinking the dimensions of power.

Again: We cannot be blamed for the historical past – but we surely have to be blamed if we do not learn from history.

> *"Men make their own history, but they do not make it as they please; they do not make it under self-selected circumstances, but under circumstances existing already, given and transmitted from the past. The tradition of all dead generations weighs like a nightmare on the brains of the living. And just as they seem to be occupied with revolutionizing themselves and things, creating something that did not exist before, precisely in such epochs of revolutionary crisis they anxiously conjure up the spirits of the past to their service, borrowing from them names, battle slogans, and costumes in order to present this new scene in world history in time-honoured disguise and borrowed language."*

> *(Karl Marx, 1852: The Eighteenth Brumaire of Louis Bonaparte.)*

– Well, talk and think and… stop, just for enjoying yourself. After the debate we just have half an hour, briefly dropping the documents (and the laptop, of course) in the hotel room, then dinner in the convention centre. Everything in style – though one thing is somewhat distracting: the stage. The usual stuff: little speeches, honours and toasts and finally, after a lovely dinner, a final toast, more precise an announcement: Maria Johannson. A whole range of music: rock, jazz, blues – even the Piaf as tribute to the French friends. And it opens apparently doors. Next: Aretha Franklin, a Beatles/Hendrix merger, back to Aretha. Ludvig is the first on the dancing floor – well, the second, having been asked by somebody I don't know. It takes some time, but solely but surely… - I still resist, talk to Marilyn: academics… - she is the first, leaving with Victor the table. I remain stubborn, though my body imperceptibly swinging, though also trying in a strange way to hide. I see Ariane, waving, and I pretend not to see anything but she comes to my table, waves, undeniably at me: I cannot resist – I do not want to resist – a dancing bear, having been used to dance through the snow. I feel a little bit uncomfortable: the pin-striped three-piece suit and gaining security, self-esteem. Diane, Patrique, Conny, Anne… and many, many people I never saw before and probably will never see again. Only few "partner-dances", few "classical dances"; instead a movement striving for freedom – and what seemed to be a bizarre bunch from so many different ways of life, mixes now in an equally bizarre confidence.

> *"Oh freedom (freedom), freedom (freedom), freedom, yeah freedom*
> *Freedom (freedom), freedom (freedom), freedom, ooh freedom*
>
> *There ain't nothing you could ask I could answer you but I won't (I won't)*
> *I was gonna change, but I'm not, to keep doing things I don't*

Yes, it is a natural thing...

... just shake off the nightmares.

What thought to go finally to bed with, before a new working day will start soon.

Wednesday

the second and last conference day – half a day left in the town of two kisses and one smile: Oerebro. Supposedly the cradle of democracy though nobody said why.

I sit at the breakfast table – on my own and only few people are in the large room. I assume they are workers who are accommodated in this hotel for the time of working here on the specific job. Reading about Globalization... – do Elmar and Stephan really believe what they write?

> *"To bemoan the fate of democracy in globalization, or to cull for more democracy to control a seemingly unleashed economy, is to ignore an important point: the conditions that are currently described as globalization were created and advanced both in terms of their institutional foundations and their dynamic by parliamentary, democratically legitimated decisions. Globalization was and is subject to an ongoing plebiscite of consumers and voters and is shaped by this perpetual plebiscitum."*
>
> *(Rieger/Leibfried: Limits...: 31)*

– Gosh, and the world is flat and Hitler had been democratically elected or what.

I am frequently puzzled by the ongoing difficulties of my colleagues while walking on the ice – apparently moving between breaking the ice and slipping on the surface.

Well, I suppose they really believe what they write – at least Stephan is rather easy going in bending reality as long as he manages to look reasonably elegant. Having been recently in Bremen, meeting him, I really could not believe seeing him there, the usual behaviour – still the same arrogance as I remember it from the time from the time when we both had been working there: he left us in the department doing the teaching work while he "took time off", being on his own hobby horse: building up a kind of "public career". – And I am frequently puzzled by the blind acceptance of authorities not least in our so-called scientific community. Or shouldn't I be surprised at all? Finally it reflects much of the authoritarian character, bred by so many communities: Mutual control and lacks of borders going hand in hand with each other.

But I switch off, remember just the nice evening, have to smile – about what I simply enjoyed last night. Though I am definitely not a dancer (though sometimes a dreamer), I like it, especially if it is such an experience as the recent one: Different rules: from strict "classical dance" to the move of the body, hands and face in expression of the music; the overstepping of rules and living permanent change; individuals merging into a group – it is a fascinating process of merging beauty and movement; structure and process – the beauty through movement.

Well, I switch off this dream too: have to work a little bit before the conference resumes and I have to prepare the suitcase for the journey back to the centre later the day: Stockholm, from where I have to get the evening flight to the even larger centre: Brussels, the final meeting in the position in which I had been involved – always slightly changing, but having maintained it for about 20 years – actually for 24 years now.

On the way to my room I chat briefly with Thobias who replaced Helmut for the presentation, hear some news about the 'Centre for Social Innovation'. "And regards to Helmut." – "Yes, I will definitely pass them on. He will be glad to hear."

I nod towards Victor who had been sitting at my table during the evening before – seems to be that it would be extremely interesting to meet him again, then hopefully having more opportunity to talk.

Sitting in front of the computer, writing up some stuff I urgently have to send to Finland, I hear from outside the noise from the street: children, waiting in front of the school, just opposite of the hotel. They are back after a short break – excited, much they have to talk about when coming now back to there little centre.

Then, during the conference, a reasonably heated debate – though it is apparently easier to get close during dancing than during debates. Overstepping of rules and living permanent change. Here it is difficult again. Now, difference seems to be hindrance not least because we are looking again at a centre: the central conference document, being open for debate and coming to a vote; the moderators of the meeting, centring on the stage; and the policies, geared to the centre – in this case not least to Brussels: looking for the role of participatory democracy.

The way back is scheduled for the afternoon: I am lucky to have a reserved seat in the packed train. As there are a couple of us, we go on arrival at the airport together for dinner: even a candle and nice tableware would not make the airport restaurant a cosy place. Still, it is nice to sit together with Anne and Patrick: after working for many years in different ways together and against each other it is probably the first time that we talk more than five words privately. And of course, we speak as well about Hubert – friendships, not meaningful, not close and nevertheless still meaning a lot. Erdmute joins later, already at the gate – representing a new network, apparently one which may be interesting when it comes to the new project we are now approaching at the University of Eastern Finland.

It is some time left until I get my dessert and coffee on the plane. The kind of gingerbread reminds me: yes, probably difficult to avoid: again Christmas – this year as every year before. The only time I could avoid it had been when I had been over this period in Asia. Though even then it imposed on the passer by: money-makers that lost their centres and their meaning, reached out and as much as "they", Asian people begin to celebrate Christmas, we begin celebrating the year of the rat.

A long day, indeed – finally I arrive in Brussels, the newly emerging political centre of the European Union; or is it more to correct to say the centre of the newly emerging European Union. Are we here actually back to "state building". I take the key out of my pocket, open the heavy door to which I got so used over the many years, the door to the old house at the Rue de Pascale: a place which was getting a kind of home. I switch off the alarm system, go to my room. Everything is well ordered, tasteful. Everybody knows: the devil can be found in the details; but here we find also little angels. Still, though it had been a long day, and the environment invites more to relax it is nevertheless time to look at least after a couple of things: checking mails – good news: apparently small political action at UCC being awarded and students "getting the money back"; getting the agenda ready for the next day; writing a quick comment which I have to send when properly connected to the Internet again... – and having a shower.

Getting up again the morning – after some work and breakfast a chat with Nicole; ready for the meeting with Jacob, a colleague from the Commission with whom I discuss some publication; a quick stroll through town, getting some chocolate from friends – already a tradition; a surprise: I meet Susanna, a colleague from Finland – standing in a shop for a chat is as cosy as the airport dinner last evening; on the way back the confrontation with this extreme gap: extreme wealth and extreme poverty in the same spot, the grandesse of the global capitalist world and the limitation of not having sufficient means even for surviving in dignity – and nevertheless representing worlds apart...

Being here again I am wondering another time about the difference: an entirely political class again; but moreover, an entirely different life. Of course, the difference between centre and periphery or as well city and countryside: the peculiar cold and rigidity of the glass front of so may buildings here, compared with the smooth surface of the many lakes I pass the day before while sitting in the train from Oerebro to Bromma; the rather flashy sunlight, shining on the concrete and marble ground, compared with the warm light reflected in the colourful leaves of the autumn trees; the seemingly well-ordered moves on the streets in the Belgian and European capital compared with the vibrant moves of the birds that move from tree to tree; the window displays compared with the small timber houses on which I look, looking through the window of the train they appear as display of toys, inviting to wait for Pippi Langstocking and proposing that Lisa, Bosse, Lasse, Inga, Britta, Ole and little Kerstin would be somewhere around; still, the urban mildness compared with the cutting cold last morning when still jogging in Oerebro; the local market with its limited offers against the small market in the quarter, adding diversity of the offers of the global brands, the visible and open poverty and the visibility of huge gaps between the rich and the poor on the one hand and at least the image of an egalitarian setting on the other hand...

But it is as well the difference between powers: spaces of action that are manageable compared with the anonymity behind the European glass palaces: visibility, hiding the impossibility of reaching there; the variety of languages that welcome me at Brussels airport and in the streets of the city seen against the one melody of kisses and smiles – and the question what it actually mans to say we are speechless: Having lost the "own" language or being limited to only one language?; the extensive police security in Stockholm last weekend for the "Days of Development" and the low-key measures for today's meeting of the "heads" in Brussels; the new castles: NATO, Council, Berlaymont, Parliament and the old castle with walls as thick as rooms on the as two forms of Court societies...

Might dispersing towards the centre, abilities being covered, undermined in further and open development but as well fostered, finding a ground, fertilised for their specific development.

Nearly two weeks for me, but not yet the end of the journey. Ahead lies a full working day here in Brussels; an evening going out with Nicole – not yet knowing more; leaving early on Friday for a rather long working day with Laurent, trying to finalise the work on a book; in the evening visiting the Neapolis Ensemble & Ensemble le Nuove Musiche.

Another early morning raise to come: getting ready for the way home. Home then to a centre of life: first the remainder of the day in the office, catching up with some things, and hopefully as well being able to catch up with Franziska – and back in Ireland just in time for Tom's "hunter trial" on Sunday: cross-country horse race in Aghabullogue. But I will only take part by some kind of "administering", leaving the race to others.

– Occasionally needed: leaving the race to others. Surely exciting work and fields of experiences in several respects, though also surely demanding, requesting as well some kind of sacrifice. May be justified to say: "Well, if I wouldn't know it better, you one could be jealous."

But really, it is not about knowing and not about envying. It is just about acting. And it is about the difference between behaviour and acting – and the sometimes fluid, sometimes rigid borders. It is in any case about the words we will find when we stand in Berlin, Unter den Linden, at the stairs in the Humboldt University:

"Philosophers have hitherto only interpreted the world in various ways; the point is to change it."

But remind as well – I read this in yesterday's L'Echo (28/10/09: 15):

"L'economie, et notre société, n'est pas correctement définie par les modélisations standards d'équilibres compétitifs utilises par la majorité des économistes." And contradictions will never be eliminated by ignoring them.

So let us change…

Back, another time... – after teaching the recent week in Budapest at the Corvinus university, formerly Karl-Marx-University. Supposedly it is still one of the leading universities especially for economics – but having said this the same applies for every university now. Third level education, now increasingly a matter of passing on information, is not elitist anymore: it claims to be itself "the elite", centres of excellence, permanently stating innovation, the ability to adapt to change, the investment into the future, the orientation on performing on the international level, making us, who work there forget the permanent flops: the most recent pushing us to reduce phone costs, including: dial directly into the voice mail of students to leave messages (don't translate it into: "ask students to call you back – if they can pay fees they can pay as well part of the universities telephone bill.") including: use e-mail where possible (don't translate it into: "What cannot be said in an e-mail may not be worthwhile to be said.")

– Excellence – Excelling – Excel – the superiority of the spreadsheet: what does not fit into it is out as much as what is not in Wikipedia does not exist - and the open software is just an imitation of the closed business, the commons easily in danger to dig its own grave by establishing a counter-elite.

After teaching the last day until just after lunch, after a brief (well, about three hours isn't really brief, is it) visit in the research institute of the minister for social affairs and finally a visit in the Turkish bath, I spent the evening again in the office – Gyöngyi made it possible for me to keep the key. Later, I am one of the last people leaving the building – only a small group of students is still around, changing their clothes after some dance exercises.

I walk down the wide staircase, pass the table with the posters which I passed so frequently this week: when I walked from the office in the old building – the former customs house – into the new, purpose building of the university, everything utilised for modern third level education. The modern library for which I still have the library card, keeping it from visit to visit; the small corners where students can socialise..., well, they can, but the table has a huge sign, pointing out that it is for computer use; the class rooms... Going there I walk through the old large hall, tables, chairs, people chatting – it is a little bit scruffy – tables with posters... I read them, ignore them, being busy with other things: thinking a last time about the content of the next session of this intensive course on "International Macroeconomic Policies" here at the Department of World Economy. On the way to the seminar rooms it is this what employs my thinking; and on the way back it is the behaviour of the students: a few Hungarians, some Erasmus-students, and students who join in other ways on the "free global market of education":

from Greece, Catalonia, French, an American student, one from Namibia, from Syria, from China, from the Czech republic and some from Russia, Ukraine... – well, simply World Economy. Global use of computers, SMS... – why am I standing here. I am asking this myself as some of these students who do not listen (let alone showing any effort to answer questions simple questions on the dealing with two cows in different economic and political systems slightly complain that I do not provide written notes – well, yes, I comfort them: there are couple of books, notes I made on other occasions... Arrogant? Well, may be – but the reading time is over: the nice times, when I wrote books for children, reading them to my daughter. But even then I allowed myself to be carried away, explore new things together with Phanresia, together as well with Franziska who was not listening but joining in different ways, even if only by clinging to me, by letting me feel her feelings: her admiration, her fears, her interests... Reading notes instead of taking notes while listening; looking for information rather than working together for acquiring knowledge, understanding.

It is not really late when I leave - before I leave I finished the outline of a new publication project. A slow process...; shortly contacting Zsuzsa another time before I leave, so much energy still in her, a never ending story, even if she will leave us, she will surely remain being with us – and..., well I have to leave before they lock the doors; other things have to wait. Now I can walk downstairs, a last time, before returning in a couple of weeks. Not thinking about the next steps of teaching..., having some space top really perceive the posters: AIESEC, HP and the name of one of the few really global players of accounting...

Already on the way to the door to the East, I turn around, walk into the main hall, cannot stop myself looking up, looking into the eyes of the man sitting there: the statue of the former name giver, muttering the few words: Well, Karl... – it is a statement; and it is a question, an honest question to which I know no answer but only a vague, though itself concretising pathway along which I, along which we have to move in order to find it.

– Sure, "political and legal rights can exist only on an economic foundation. To be free citizens we must also be equal producers and consumers." Linebaugh: The Magna Carta...: 6). But isn't "free citizen" already a contradiction in terms: the city with its surrounding walls, limiting the space? The reference to production and consumption rather than productive consumption, their re-merger, the re-emergence of the genuine self in unity. It sounds so abstract – and I am simply looking forward to experience it in its simplicity...

I leave the building to the other side, nod towards the security staff: Köszönöm – és jó estét. It is quite; only few cars, few people are around. It is dark, the puddles making it awkward to walk the short way. But what is this little bit of awkwardness, compared with the long way that is laying in front?

But what is the length of a way if enough people join, walking it?

And there are, indeed, more again; not always visible, but walking – an entirely different sort of an invisible hand? Perhaps emerging to a fist one day. And perhaps a fist that touches us through its invisibility and smoothness, perhaps even tenderness.

Early next morning – though actually my usual time of getting up, I am getting to the train station. I am still not used to the limousine that brings me there. And I enter deeper into this world that is different for me: My luggage is taken, I show my ticket and I am brought to my seat: though a modern train it reminds me of an image I never saw in reality, a world I only know from books: Dostoyevsky, Tolstoy, Turgenjew; and also Kafka,... – A world with another pace, seen from hindsight, romanticised a pace it found by its own meaning, by its own right – from the hindsight... A pace that allows traveling – this is the image – long days, weeks across the country: trans Siberian. My "little transsib" experience of the day will take me in little more than 12 hours from Budapest to Berlin, being somewhat staled by the only two other people in the wagon: Americans, their broad, load voices going with me in the train, giving me the impression of a steamroller, a tank wiping out the rest of peace that is left. I try pushing it away – overhearing the loud voices, not smelling the alcohol, thinking these are just people, not a people, while looking out of the window: looking at the beautiful countryside that is still covered by snow: the forests and wide fields: old cottages, modern towns, the grape plants now standing bald, barely carrying a single leave villages, deserted industrial plants as well as those that are throwing out the CO_2 which may kill us one day – and of which we need the products today; churches, large faming estates, small plots and in the many gardens the even smaller plots allowing a kind of subsistence economy; the mountains passing, old castles – cloud-castles and maisons de plaisance... one huge, endless Jasnaja Poljana, one incessant scuffle of different ideas: contradicting, coming together, dissolving into something new and the direction giving by the people one may occasionally see, when the train slows down... I remember these people – at least some of them: from the time, when we had been driving part of this way in your car, talking about the experience of a long life here in this beautiful country – which country and driven with whom? What does it matter, just another beautiful country which I have had the privilege not only to visit but to live, to feel somewhat home, feeling this invisible hand of everyday's life – everyday's life with its "normality": its routines and contradictions being this place of a tender hand, a nearly inaudible breath... I nevertheless heard when we drove here where I go now by train: from Budapest to Sturovo, Beratislava, Breclav, Brno, Praha, Dresden and then finally Berlin, for me the end of the journey, the train moving on, if I could, I could have used the opportunity of visiting my daughter in Hamburg. Everywhere the presence of nothing, nothing else than pure being, existing in contradictions and mastering them! Solving them? It here where borders suddenly do not play a role anymore, where places are merging and coming much closer than they do when traveling by plane, a way of "traveling godlike, without people".

Still, the view on these beauties is frequently precipitously interrupted: the voices; and with it the memories of the American soldier who had been sitting next to me in the train – years ago, when traveling back from my studies at the Franz-Mehring Institute to the West. Memories of the stories older friends told me about the weirdly joint forces of the German and Allied tanks when it came to the end of WW II. Joint in killing friends – or trying to make their voices silent forever, even if they would still be able to speak. The joint forces that took me then as well under their observance – supervision – monitoring – mentoring...

Silenced by enclosures, by tightening rights, as well as widening their meaning: from the property of the lords – from the early rights of the simple landlord to the emperor; from the rights over goods and the propriety control over services and their delivery and now more and more as intellectual property rights - protection: "Die Gedanken sind frei" as a German song suggests, stating the freedom of mind; and the freedom now being perverted and strangulated by capturing thinking as matter of proprium rather than as appropriation in a collective process. Protection against private appropriation as we see it in the Magna Charta – and paradoxically establishing the stronghold of property by declaring existential rights as exception: estovers, chiminage to be paid by the poor..., in part the perpetuation of poverty and exclusion by granting rights, derived from the pure existence on the borders to non-existence. – Another border seems to be blurring – the border between a new crusade, now by (post)modern google-ing wikipedian commoners on the one hand and a new renaissance, striving for... – just (or just?) existence. – The train stops, Brno, the last time I had been here I had been congratulated by the Minister for Human Rights who took my words forward into later parliamentary meetings. A strange coincidence – writing this minute about justice?

The varied landscape while moving on is still covered by snow – evoking the pictures of simple lives, fighting for estoves, for exceptions, living on meagre means they get from subsistence economies – now some striving to maintain the street as common, aiming on keeping the steam roller out of the last resorts of the cities which are not yet marketised, commodified and enclosed; these poor who are, however, themselves already caught on the trap: their entire freedom, from means of production and security of existence allowing them to offer not even their work force but only the opportunity for the rich to feel guilty - these new commons as market ground for the sale of new kinds of letters of indulgence. New princes - new hopes of and for borderless spaces – Single markets? New commons?

I am nearing Praha – of course: Smetana's Ma vlast comes to my mind, I lean back, imagine the strong river, the free and untamable stream, growing out of the small spring.

And both: view on the present beauty, the past horrors and the ongoing distribution of licences to kill interrupted by simply looking forward...

... and the day after flying back... home. Home?

> if it is the home for you??...

Well, yes: if it is home for me... if you make it home for me; if you offer me this invisible hand to which I look forward to hold again, hearing the whiff of your breath, being surrounded by it without being able to say how it gets at me – just by the different pace, by allowing to feel the steps smoothly following each other without asking, without difficulties and only reassuring that the direction is maintained, the one direction with its permanent changes – the home of everyday's life – everyday's life with its "normality": its routines and contradictions being this place of a tender hand, a nearly inaudible breath... - the presence of nothing, nothing else than pure being. Taking me away from the ostentatious, and so obvious contradictory world of exceptions, of being caught in "importance".

From the visible and strangulating hands of permanent attention: every step to be justified, to be thought about "in the spirit of competitive world economy" and everyday's life. The visible hand of elegance and elitism - I know: it is an expectation which is even higher than expecting a life in a pipe dream. The world to be left behind – so strange and so easy to predict, despite the many prejudices involved. The journey by train, bringing me through Hungary, Romania, Czech Republic, Germany – the borders only being marked by slight changes: helló, salut, ahoj,... until the train stops in Bad Schandau, already announced by the train personnel as border city: While the train is waiting and I continue to read, I feel obliged to look up -

without really knowing why: border police standing in front of me and I suppress to mumbling "Good day, Winter Fairy" Tale *(http://socialpolicy. ucc.ie/heinrich_heine_Deutschland_A_Winter's_Tale.htm).* The train moves on – it is quite, the cleaning command, ops: cleaning team is silently taking the rubbish away: The subordinate warden disposing the rubbish, including the rubbish the world gendarmes left behind after their binge – they left the train already in Praha. – And the new passengers are welcomed – in German language, making us known of the train number, the destination and the stops – and letting us know: There is a restaurant between the first and the second class and the Hungarian team is expecting you there.

– Well, it implies not only the issue of nationality but also sets a good meal as division line between the classes.

Moving with us to the next station: Dresden. A flourish announcing the approach of the train like the Roman and other emperors probably announced their entry when coming to conquered areas and eras, entering through the arc of triumph. – The kind voice, announcing with frightening precision: The train will arrive 18:44 – well, admittedly 2 minutes before the scheduled time... – you will have connection to... – even the platforms for the connecting trains are announced, no hassle while traveling: "please, leave the train on the left side." – at least if one is able to understand the German announcement as the English translation is somewhat shortened: "Welcome at Dresden main station."

Later Berlin – the tine of arrival is not so loudly pronounced as it had been the case in Dresden – though it is a relatively small delay is is nothing to be proudly announced. The visible hand guides me further. As I can use my train ticket for the S-Bahn, getting to my accommodation, I have to buy a ticket for the next day – everything goes smoothly and only the remark of the some passengers on the train evokes suspicion: "Are they building again?" – "No, probably still because of the snow."... Well, the short walk from the S-Bahn station to the accommodation is worth than what I experienced during this winter in Cork: a visible sign of the visible hand to fail – as friendly it is on occasions, it shows its harshness here, asking here as well for own responsibility, for taking care of yourself, though the next seems to be pushed away – turning a winter fairy tale truly into a nightmare – the super-state of law and order leaving law and order now to independent gentlemen – the owners, if they are lucky, able to pay for somebody who cleans around them; less lucky if they are commoners, only allowed to move in the niches which are left open by the new lords. – What, then, is the difference between the Lords and the horse thieves?

Nothing wrong with order, with accountability, with reliability: the proverbial punctuality of the German rail has something beneficial, something admirable – as long as it works. And as long as we don't feel the permanently payment of this order, held up in society and community, in legislature and simple mutual control: observance – supervision – monitoring – peering – mentoring...

Airport Berlin-Schoenefeld – Sunday, about 9:30 am. – pass the security control: strong, visible the hand. "Is this your luggage" – the voice is not unfriendly, but firm. I nod, obedient after going so often through similar thorough special treatment, not causing any sorrow anymore, but still some annoyance. "Please, enter follow me..." – What can I do about it? Nothing about the rules – as little as they can do something about the rules they have to observe. Like the guys I saw earlier, when passing Moabit, the gaolers going to work. Sure, they have the key for the one door. And still they don't have and cannot have the key for the other door – and they don't need it because it is invisible for them: not perceived as contradiction, not requiring resistance.

Where and how can we find this presence of nothing, nothing else than pure being: our own acceptance of contradictions and the acceptance of resistance and lack of it, every day...

//P

Illustrations by Kerstin Walsh

Taipei

Dance Taiwan

National Gallery Dublin

Café

Visiting granny in Finland

Forest in Sweden

Örebrö

UCC

Budapest